Adult Attachment in Clinical Social Work

Essential Clinical Social Work Series

Series Editor: Carol Tosone

For other titles published in this series, go to
www.springer.com/series/8115

Susanne Bennett · Judith Kay Nelson
Editors

Adult Attachment in Clinical Social Work

Practice, Research, and Policy

 Springer

Editors
Susanne Bennett
National Catholic School of Social Service
The Catholic University of America
Washington, DC, USA
bennetts@cua.edu

Judith Kay Nelson
The Sanville Institute for
Clinical Social Work and Psychotherapy
Berkeley, CA, USA
jkaynelson@sbcglobal.net

ISBN 978-1-4419-6240-9 (hardcover)   ISBN 978-1-4419-6241-6 (eBook)
ISBN 978-1-4614-1455-1 (softcover)
DOI 10.1007/978-1-4419-6241-6
Springer New York Heidelberg Dordrecht London

Library of Congress Control Number: 2010935722

Springer is part of Springer Science+Business Media (www.springer.com)

With gratitude to:
Catherine "Cay" Hartley
$-$ *C. S. B.*

To the memory of:
Elise "Lise" Silverman Blumenfeld
$-$ *J. K. N.*

Acknowledgements

We would like to acknowledge Dr. Carol Tosone, the Editor of *Clinical Social Work Journal*, for her support, advice, and encouragement in the creation of this book. We also appreciate the contributors for their professionalism, cooperation, and careful attention to detail. They were delightful collaborators, and their hard work was much appreciated. Our editor at Springer, Jennifer Hadley, has also been a wonderful support to us through the publication process, for which we are most grateful.

We would like to thank the many colleagues who have been part of our journey in the realm of attachment theory and research, the students who have been so enthusiastic and interested, and the clients who are our best teachers. Our partners, adult children, and siblings at the center of our attachment circle are our primary supports with writing, in general, and with the production of this book, in particular. It is, however, our grandchildren Esther and Aurelia, just beginning to establish their "internal working models" of attachment, who have been our inspiration.

Contents

1 Introduction 1
Susanne Bennett and Judith Kay Nelson

Part I   Theory Development Regarding Adult Attachment

2 **The Origins of an Attachment Approach to Social Work**
   Practice with Adults 17
   Pat Sable

3 **Contemporary Theory and Research on Adult Attachment:**
   Where is the Field Today? 31
   Susanne Bennett and Judith Kay Nelson

4 **Clinical Social Work and Regulation Theory: Implications**
   of Neurobiological Models of Attachment 57
   Judith R. Schore and Allan N. Schore

Part II   Applications to Adult Clinical Practice

5 **Separation, Loss, and Grief in Adults:**
   An Attachment Perspective 79
   Judith Kay Nelson

6 **Listening Closely: The Significance of the Therapist's**
   Voice Intensity, Rhythm, and Tone 97
   Kristin Miscall Brown and Dorienne Sorter

7 **Using a Mentalization-Based Framework to Assist**
   Hard-to-Reach Clients in Individual Treatment 113
   Christine H. Fewell

**8   Attachment and Caregiving for Elders
     Within African-American Families** 127
     Susanne Bennett, Michael J. Sheridan, and Barbara Soniat

**9   Attachment in the Family Context: Insights
     from Development and Clinical Work** 147
     Janet Shapiro

**10 Applications of Attachment Theory to Group Interventions:
     A Secure Base in Adulthood** 173
     Timothy F. Page

Part III   Attachment Applications to Policy, Research, and Education

**11 Policy Implications of Attachment Processes in Adulthood:
     Caregiving and Family Preservation** 195
     Joyce E. Everett

12 Attachment Research: Contributions of Social Workers 217
     Joanna E. Bettmann and Rachael A. Jasperson

13 Implications of Attachment Theory for Social Work Education 253
     Susanne Bennett and Kathleen Holtz Deal

Index 267

Contributors

Susanne Bennett, MSW, PhD
National Catholic School of Social Service, The Catholic University of America, Washington, DC, USA

Joanna E. Bettmann, MSW, PhD
College of Social Work, University of Utah, Salt Lake City, UT, USA

Kathleen Holtz Deal, MSW, PhD
National Catholic School of Social Service, The Catholic University of America, Washington, DC, USA

Joyce E. Everett, MSW, PhD
Smith College School for Social Work, Northampton, MA, USA

Christine H. Fewell, MSW, PhD
Silver School of Social Work, New York University, New York, NY, USA
and
Institute for Psychoanalytic Training and Research, New York, NY, USA

Rachael A. Jasperson, MSW
College of Social Work, University of Utah, Salt Lake City, UT, USA

Kristin Miscall Brown, MSW
Psychoanalytic Psychotherapy Study Center, New York, NY, USA

Judith Kay Nelson, MSW, PhD
The Sanville Institute for Clinical Social Work and Psychotherapy, Berkeley, CA, USA

Timothy F. Page, MSW, PhD
School of Social Work, Louisiana State University, Baton Rouge, LA, USA

Pat Sable, MSW, PhD
School of Social Work, University of Southern California, Los Angeles, CA, USA

Allan N. Schore, PhD
UCLA David Geffen School of Medicine, CA, USA

Judith R. Schore, MSW, PhD
The Sanville Institute for Clinical Social Work and Psychotherapy,
Berkeley, CA, USA
and
Reiss-Davis Post Doctoral Program in Child Psychotherapy,
Los Angeles, CA, USA

Janet Shapiro, MSW, PhD
School of Social Work, Bryn Mawr College, Bryn Mawr, PA, USA

Michael J. Sheridan, MSW, PhD
National Catholic School of Social Service, The Catholic University of America,
Washington, DC, USA

Barbara Soniat, MSW, PhD
National Catholic School of Social Service, The Catholic University of America,
Washington, DC, USA

Dorienne Sorter, MSW, PhD
Institute for the Psychoanalytic Study of Subjectivity, New York, NY, USA

Editors

Susanne Bennett, MSW, PhD, is Associate Professor at National Catholic School of Social Service at The Catholic University of America, in Washington, DC. Her teaching in the MSW and PhD programs includes a course titled *Attachment and neurobiology: Implications for social work practice and policy.* She has published over a dozen articles on attachment processes, and her research focuses on the examination of attachment in caregiving relationships, particularly in social work supervision, elder care, and adoptive families. Dr. Bennett is a Distinguished Social Work Scholar in the National Academy of Practice and has maintained a psychotherapy practice for over 30 years.

Judith Kay Nelson, MSW, PhD, is on the faculty of The Sanville Institute for Clinical Social Work and Psychotherapy, a Ph.D. program in California, where she teaches attachment and the neurobiology of attachment. She has been in private practice for 35 years, specializing in long-term psychotherapy. She has spent many years studying, writing, teaching, and presenting throughout the United States and Europe on topics related to crying, laughter, and attachment. She is the author of *Seeing through tears: Crying and attachment,* published by Routledge in 2005, and numerous articles and chapters on crying, laughter, and attachment. She is currently working on a new book, *What made Freud laugh? An attachment perspective on laughter.* Dr. Nelson is a distinguished Social Work Practitioner in the National Academy of Practice.

Chapter 1
Introduction

Susanne Bennett and Judith Kay Nelson

Attachment theory and research were born out of John Bowlby's wish to understand the nature of the infant–mother attachment bond. In the seminal attachment literature, adults existed solely as parental caregivers to children. Attachment behaviors were seen as an innate part of the human evolutionary survival kit, designed to assure that the young would remain in close proximity to their parents so they too could survive and reproduce their own genes, becoming parents themselves. Bowlby (1969/1982) noted, almost in passing, that attachment behaviors continue throughout life, though they are less intense than in infancy. Later, he stated unequivocally that attachment bonds "are present and active throughout the life cycle" (Bowlby, 1980, p. 39). It was, however, his contribution of the idea of *internal working models* (Bowlby, 1973) of attachment figures and of self – the idea that early attachment/caregiving experiences form a script for attachment/caregiving experiences throughout life – that gave the biggest impetus to the expansion of theory and research about adult attachment.

Adult attachment research first began to appear in the early 1980s with the development of the Adult Attachment Interview (AAI) by psychologists George, Kaplan, and Main (1984), who were interested in the relationship between the attachment experiences of adults and the attachment classifications of young children in the Strange Situation (Ainsworth, Blehar, Waters, & Wall, 1978) research. A few years later, social psychologists Hazan and Shaver (1987) developed a self-report questionnaire to study adult romantic pair bonds. Early on, clinical social workers were in the vanguard of publishing articles in their journals (*Social Casework* and *The Clinical Social Work Journal*) about the clinical application of attachment concepts to the treatment of adults. Their realization that attachment-related issues were central to understanding clinical issues in adult psychotherapy led to publications on attachment and dependency (Sable, 1979), detachment (Sable, 1983), vacations (Webb, 1983), and termination (Webb, 1984). Sable (2000), who introduces the socio-historical context of adult attachment in Chap. 2 in this volume, went on to

S. Bennett (✉)
National Catholic School of Social Service, The Catholic University of America,
Washington, DC, USA
e-mail: bennetts@cua.edu

S. Bennett and J.K. Nelson (Eds.), *Adult Attachment in Clinical Social Work*,
Essential Clinical Social Work Series, DOI 10.1007/978-1-4419-6241-6_1,
© Springer Science+Business Media, LLC 2010

write one of the first books published on attachment theory applied to psychotherapy with adults. Social work clinicians, like the contributors to this book, seemed to recognize from the beginning that attachment theory is an ideal fit with social work's historic "person-in-environment" perspective and that it is applicable to practice with both children and adults.

Background of This Book

As authors of this chapter and editors of this book, we are both clinical social workers who have been teaching, researching, and writing about attachment for a number of years. We met while serving as adjunct faculty at the Smith College School for Social Work doctoral program in 2006, teaching attachment, object relations, and self psychology. At the beginning of our careers in the 1960s and 1970s, one of us (Bennett) became aware of Bowlby's ideas in her work with mothers and babies in neonatal intensive care units, while the other's (Nelson) connection with attachment theory was sparked by her curiosity about adult crying in psychotherapy. We each went on to use attachment theory as a basis for dissertation research for doctorates in clinical social work.

In the course of long conversations about our mutual interests in attachment concepts that summer at Smith, we found time to commiserate about the disparity between the widespread, creative use of attachment-derived concepts in social work practice and the small contribution social work clinicians, theoreticians, and researchers have made to the body of published literature on attachment concepts. As committed and strongly identified social workers, we chafed at this imbalance and thus felt compelled to respond to a call that summer for guest editors to produce a special edition of the *Clinical Social Work Journal*.

The idea we proposed to editor Carol Tosone was that we coedit a special issue of the Journal devoted to adult attachment and that the lead author on every article be a clinical social worker. We hoped in this way to grow the number of published social work contributions to the theory and research of attachment and to address the tendency within the social work field to think of attachment theory as being predominantly applicable to infants and children. In March 2008, that Journal, titled *Attachment-Based Clinical Social Work with Adults: New Directions, New Populations*, was published to an enthusiastic reception in the clinical social work community.

The articles in the special edition covered topics ranging from a neurobiological view of affect regulation (Schore & Schore, 2008) to an attachment perspective on laughter (Nelson, 2008). The section on clinical applications included treatment of individuals with eating disorders (Farber, 2008), military couples reunited after deployment to Iraq (Basham, 2008), and young adults in a wilderness program (Bettmann & Jasperson, 2008). Research articles exploring attachment processes among Orthodox Jewish women (Ringel, 2008) and in social work field supervision (Bennett, 2008) were also included. However, as is inevitable in a project on a topic as vast as attachment in adult clinical work, there were many gaps left unfilled.

To that end, we proposed a follow-up book to Springer, the publisher of the Journal, hoping to more fully address adult attachment and to further highlight social work authors and researchers.

We were interested in creating a book focused on the theory of attachment applied to clinical practice with a wide range of the adult populations familiar to social work. We designed the book to further address the theory's application to policies and academic issues of particular interest to social work clients and professionals. In order to create a common knowledge base and language, we planned to highlight the concepts, classifications, terminology, and research methods that have developed over the decades of work on attachment in general and adult attachment in particular. In brief, we are passionate about educating social workers regarding the research on attachment and moving social work into the mainstream discourse on attachment theory.

Attachment Concepts, Classifications, and Terminology

For clinicians new to attachment, differentiating attachment classifications is one of the challenging aspects of a theory that seems otherwise relatively simple to grasp. Understanding the dynamics of the *attachment behavioral system* and the distinctions between attachments in infancy and adulthood helps to clarify the confusion. Bowlby (1969/1982) originally proposed that the attachment behavioral system becomes *activated* in times of threat or danger, prompting a person to seek an *attachment figure* for support, comfort, or protection through *proximity-seeking behaviors*, such as smiling and crying, clinging and following, and the arms-up signal. Once the person gains a sense of *felt security*, the attachment system becomes far less active as he or she moves to explore the world beyond the realm of the attachment figure. Influenced by his studies of ethology, Bowlby came to see humans as inherently relationship-seeking and the attachment behavioral system as a hard-wired, normal part of human functioning, regardless of the individual's age. Infants by necessity are most likely to depend on the proximity of a parental caregiver as an attachment figure who provides a *safe haven* in times of stress and serves as a *secure base* for the infant's exploratory needs. As the child gradually loosens *attachment bonds* to parental attachment figures in the course of normal development, peers and romantic partners begin to serve as attachment figures in times of distress. A spouse, close friend, sibling, coworker, or perhaps an institutional leader or religious being (e.g., God) may serve as attachment figures for adults.

Adults have internalized their life-long relational experiences, which become mental representations of how to relate to others and how others relate to them. Bowlby called these internalized memories of attachment *working* models because they are dynamic and changing. Early in life, internal working models are shaped by attachment bonds to primary caregiver(s), usually parents, but they continue as a work in progress, open to change through ongoing relational experiences, and influenced by "a complex amalgam of historical and contemporary factors" (Mikulincer & Shaver, 2007, p. 46).

Just as it is essential to realize that internal working models can change, it is important to understand that attachment bonds have distinct characteristics. All close relationships are not attachment bonds, and all interactions with attachment figures are not attachment behaviors. According to the theory, an attachment bond in both childhood and adulthood has four characteristics, first defined as someone *wiser and stronger* who is a target for proximity-seeking (Bowlby, 1969/1982; Mikulincer & Shaver, 2007). Second, there is the existence of an *attachment interaction* (Weiss, 1998), with one individual using the other as a *safe haven* for protection or comfort. Third, the individual uses the attachment figure as a *secure base* for *exploration*, and finally, there is a feeling of loss or *separation distress* when an individual is separated from the attachment figure.

With these characteristics in mind, it becomes easier to see when a relationship actually constitutes an attachment bond. For example, two adults in early stages of romantic courtship may feel close and use each other as a base for exploration, yet turn to others in times of distress, especially when the distress is about the relationship. Similarly, a new employee may seek the proximity of a wiser supervisor and even use that person as a secure base, but the employee will not have separation distress if the supervisor is reassigned to another department. On the other hand, for two spouses who *have* developed mutual attachment bonds, their interactions are not always attachment interactions. The partners may at times, for example, relate with caregiving or sexual behaviors instead. Attachment behaviors are limited to those times of distress, when an individual needs to obtain comfort, support, and protection or when mutual delight is shared through play, positive affect, laughter, or at reunions.

Bowlby's closest collaborator, Mary Ainsworth (Ainsworth et al., 1978), observed in her early research that there are several distinctive patterns existing in the way individuals relate to their attachment figures. As discussed in more detail in Chaps. 2 and 3 of this volume, these childhood patterns suggest that individual attachment bonds can be either secure or insecure in a variety of ways: insecure avoidant, insecure resistant/ambivalent, or disorganized (Solomon & George, 2008). Though a child eventually develops a generalized internal working model of attachment, based on hundreds of internalized relational interactions, that model nonetheless has some flexibility, depending on particular individual relationships and life experiences impacting attachment.

Thus, the child moves into adulthood with a general interpersonal model or style of relating that may shift, based on the specific relational dynamics of the attachment figure and the moment. For example, if an adult feels secure and has a secure attachment style, he or she is able to cope with stress and confidently explore the world through solving problems, taking risks, and gaining assistance when needed. The secure adult is able to self-soothe and feel comfort, even when there is no literal proximity of an attachment figure. Yet if that secure adult moves into a relationship with another adult who is, perhaps, abusive, the secure person may begin to feel insecure, more mistrustful, and avoidant. Likewise, a person who has moved into adulthood with a generally insecure attachment style may develop a sense of felt security if he or she establishes a close relationship (such as a marriage or a psychotherapeutic relationship) with a partner who is secure.

In other words, attachment theory holds open the possibility of change. Though childhood attachment history is critical throughout development and serves to inform adult relational styles, attachment processes in adulthood remain dynamic. Indeed, psychologists Mikulincer and Shaver (2007) state that "...attachment theory is a prime example of the person x situation approach to understanding human behavior. It considers both general processes likely to occur in certain kinds of situations and individual differences in responses arising from a person's history of attachment interactions" (p. 80). We view this statement as confirmation of the fit between attachment theory and social work's person-in-environment approach to understanding human behavior.

Nevertheless, criticism exists that there is too much emphasis on categories in attachment theory, and confusion remains about the definitions of individual attachment classifications. Some of this confusion has emerged from misunderstandings about the empirical studies on adult attachment. Years after Ainsworth's initial studies of child attachment, the research on adults developed along two complementary, though different, trajectories. As we discuss in more depth in Chap. 3 of this volume, developmental and clinical psychologists primarily studied adult attachments using the AAI (George et al., 1984; George, Kaplan, & Main, 1996), which examines an adult's *state of mind* about attachments to early childhood caregivers. In a large body of research exploring the link between adult attachments in the AAI and child attachments observed through the Strange Situation procedure, these studies have been invaluable in understanding the *intergenerational transmission* of attachment and attachment across the lifespan. In a different line of research using self-report survey methods, social psychologists have investigated different questions related to the social-cognitive processes that affect both attachment behavior and attachment affect. This form of research has expanded knowledge of adult-to-adult relationships, such as romantic pair bonds. In addition to conceptual differences in these two lines of study, AAI and self-report, the research measures do not use the same terminology, though some of it overlaps thereby leading to confusion, particularly among clinicians as they interpret and apply the empirical findings.

Similar to many authors who write overviews of adult attachment, we too have been challenged by our desire to be clear and consistent in the language in this book, while being accurate in terms of the concepts discussed. We have asked the authors to use the terminology of the researchers they reviewed, and we ask readers to recognize that different terms indicate different measures of studying attachment processes. Table 1.1 represents a summary of some of the primary attachment measures discussed in this book and defines the categories used by the researchers and authors.

Table 1.1 Examples of attachment instruments: terminology and classifications

Research instrument	Research focus	Research method	Research categories	Definition of categories
Strange Situation Procedure (SSP) [Ainsworth, Blehar, Watson, and Wall (1978); Solomon and George (2008)]	Infant's attachment to adult	Observation of infant with adult and stranger (videotaped observation of child's reaction to separations and reunions)	Secure	Child explores room with interest; misses parent; often cries; greets parent upon return; prefers parent to stranger
			Avoidant	No crying at time of separation; avoids parent upon reunion; unemotional response to parent
			Ambivalent or resistant	Child possibly distressed prior to separation; ignores parent upon reunion; resistant to comforting
			Disorganized/ disoriented	Disorganized disoriented behaviors with no signs of strategy to manage behavior; unable to be comforted or to explore
Adult Attachment Interview (AAI) [George, Kaplan, and Main (1996); Hesse (2008)]	Adult's state of mind with respect to attachment and early childhood memories	Interview of adult (audiotaped in-person interview of standardized questions, open-ended answers; transcribed and coded)	Secure autonomous	Coherent, collaborative, valuing of attachment in interview; shows capacity for metacognitive processing
			Dismissing	Not coherent; derogatory and dismisses importance of attachment experiences; often idealizes primary attachment figure; lack of memory of childhood

		Preoccupied	Not coherent; preoccupied with past attachment relationships; may be passive and vague in discourse; involved with anger and fearful toward attachment figure; excessively blaming
		Unresolved/ disorganized	Incoherent; lapses in discourse or reasoning; may have prolonged silences in interview; unresolved regarding loss or abuse
Relationship Styles Questionnaire (RSQ) [Bartholomew and Shaver (1998)]	Adult to adult	Secure	Positive model of self and positive model of others; internalized sense of self-worth and comfort with intimacy
	Self-report survey (measured on a grid contrasting high to low degrees of intimacy, high to low values of self and other close relationships)	Dismissing	Positive model of self and negative model of others; avoids closeness with others because of negative expectations; maintains self-worth by defensively denying value of close relationships
		Preoccupied	Negative model of self and positive model of others; anxiously and persistently seeks closeness and validation from others, but finds close relationships frustrating and unsatisfactory

(continued)

Table 1.1 (continued)

Research instrument	Research focus	Research method	Research categories	Definition of categories
			Fearful	Negative model of self and negative model of others; highly dependent on acceptance and care from others but avoids closeness to prevent rejection or loss
Experiences in Close Relationships Scale (ECR) [Brennan, Clark, and Shaver (1998)]	Adult to adult	Self-report survey (measured on dimension of high to low levels of avoidance and anxiety)	Secure	Willing to rely on others; comfortable with dependency, closeness, and intimacy; generally high self-esteem (measured as combination of low avoidance and low anxiety)
			Avoidant	Unwilling to rely on others; uncomfortable with dependency, closeness, or intimacy (measured as high avoidance and low anxiety)
			Anxious	Fearful of rejection, separation, and abandonment (measured as low avoidance and high anxiety)

Organization of This Book

The three parts of this book are designed to be read sequentially. The social worker or other clinician new to attachment theory, or just beginning to think about adult attachment, will find it best to begin with Part I. These three chapters provide grounding in the theory of adult attachment and research, along with the more recently added insights of neurobiology and regulation theory. The six chapters in Part II that form the core of the book look at attachment-based clinical work with adults from varying populations, using different modalities, and addressing differing manifestations of attachment issues and attachment-related symptoms. The final section, Part III, moves attachment understanding to another level of discourse from a uniquely social work perspective: social policy, social work research, and social work education. A collection of study questions follows Chaps. 2–13, to deepen the critical thinking of clinicians and graduate students and increase understanding about these concepts.

Readers familiar with attachment theory and research and attachment-based clinical social work practice with adults will find much that is creative and new within the various chapters. People with this background may choose to approach the book by topic, either selected from the Table of Contents or the subject index. The following brief paragraph about each chapter serves as a guide to orient the reader to the book as a whole and to the content of each chapter.

Leading off Part I on the development of adult attachment theory is Chap. 2, "The Origins of an Attachment Approach to Social Work Practice with Adults," written by Pat Sable from the perspective of someone who has been on board with attachment since the early days of the theory's development. She was privileged to know John Bowlby personally and to have studied and consulted with him in Los Angeles, as well as The Tavistock Clinic in London. Although touching on the personal side of her connection with the history of attachment theory, Sable's primary focus is on the roots of attachment theory in general and the etiology of our current understanding of adult attachment in particular. Her introduction to the development of attachment theory and adult attachment provides valuable grounding for the reader approaching the remainder of the book.

Chapter 3, by Bennett and Nelson, is entitled "Contemporary Theory and Research on Adult Attachment: Where Is the Field Today?" Building on the historical perspective in Chap. 2, the reader is introduced to the current explosion of research into adult attachment. The chapter endeavors to summarize and sample the findings of contemporary research and the issues and controversies that have emerged between adherents and practitioners of the narrative and self-report methodologies for studying adult attachment. The highlights of the AAI research, a narrative methodology, include parent–child relationships, longitudinal studies, and attachment-based interventions and their usefulness. The self-report findings surveyed include an overview of the relationship between adult attachment and self-esteem, coping strategies, romantic partnerships, psychopathology, and psychotherapy.

Schore and Schore, who are in the forefront of applying the findings of neurobiological research to the understanding of attachment, are the coauthors of Chap. 4,

"Clinical Social Work and Regulation Theory: Implications of Neurobiological Models of Attachment." This chapter highlights the contributions of neurobiology to the biopsychosocial viewpoint that is basic to attachment and to clinical social work. Regulation theory, which sheds light on the regulation of affect, its development, personal and interpersonal aspects, and its centrality in clinical practice, is explained and applied clinically within the chapter. The section on right brain attachment communication looks at the nonverbal, noncognitive, often nonconscious aspects of clinical (as well as other) relationships and highlights the primacy of what is called *implicit communication* or *implicit relational knowing* and the ways in which social workers can benefit from understanding these phenomena.

In Chap. 5, which marks the beginning of Part II on clinical applications to adult practice, Nelson explores the topic "Separation, Loss, and Grief in Adults: An Attachment Perspective." The core of attachment theory includes the reactions that occur when attachment bonds are disrupted or broken, making it a foundation for understanding grief. Inspired by his questions about the traumatic separations he had so frequently observed in juvenile offenders, Bowlby (1960) took the opportunity to study infants separated from their parents when they were placed out of harm's way during World War II in England. The protest, despair, and ultimately life-threatening detachment he observed in the infants form the basis of grief reactions, not only in infancy and childhood, but throughout life (Bowlby, 1969/1982). The implications of this understanding as applied to adult grief, both individual and communal, are explored in this chapter.

In Chap. 6, titled "Listening Closely: The Significance of the Therapist's Voice Intensity, Rhythm, and Tone," Miscall Brown and Sorter use a clinical case of a traumatized adult in telephone therapy to illustrate the crucial importance of voice quality in the clinical exchanges. Beginning in infancy, much implicit communication takes place beyond the typically emphasized verbal modes. Miscall Brown and Sorter's chapter shows that increasing understanding and bringing a degree of consciousness to this predominantly nonconscious process enables the clinician to pinpoint difficulties, plan interventions, and heighten effectiveness. While this chapter highlights a particular patient's sensitivities and needs, the importance of voice intensity, rhythm, and tone is common to clinical relationships in general.

Mentalization, the ability to envision mental states in one's self and others, is a keystone of development and a key ingredient in what makes attachment relationships function effectively. Fewell, in Chap. 7, entitled "Using a Mentalization-Based Framework to Work with Hard-to-Reach Clients in Individual Treatment," explains the concept and its importance, beginning in childhood. She examines the ways in which mentalization-based treatment (MBT) helps expand the understanding of clients with addictions and other debilitating symptoms and those with histories of abuse or trauma. She then looks at the stages in the development of mentalization and how they may be manifest in adults encountered by clinical social workers. Fewell provides a detailed case illustration using MBT in work with one "hard-to-reach" client, a woman complaining of "self-hatred," weight issues, relationship struggles, and a drinking problem.

The final three chapters in Part II move from looking at attachment in work with individual adult clients to looking at work with families and groups. Chapter 8, "Attachment and Caregiving for Elders within African American Families," by Bennett, Sheridan, and Soniat, explores the caregiving side of the attachment relationship by looking at adult children and their elder parents within the African American community. The authors suggest that both the early attachment and caregiving relationships experienced within the family and the sociocultural surround, including the role of the church, religion, and spirituality, highlight particular strengths and issues in the families studied. Several case examples taken from interviews with adult caregivers of elder parents illustrate the relevance of an attachment framework for understanding and working with caregivers, as well as their attachment figures in later life, with particular focus on the African American family.

Shapiro, in Chap. 9, "Attachment in the Family Context: Insights from Development and Clinical Work," looks at the applicability of attachment theory and research to work with traditional, nontraditional, and at-risk families. Family based assessment, prevention, and intervention most often focus on the role of parents and their caregiving function relative to their infants and children. Romantic/sexual couple relationships, however, also involve attachments and are of the utmost relevance for understanding the parenting function and the potential resources available to the couple as parents. Shapiro illustrates the varieties and vicissitudes of attachment issues in work with families by focusing on adolescent mothers and their children, depressed mothers, substance-abusing parents, and post foster care adoption. She provides multiple case examples showing the practical applications of attachment theory in each of these family scenarios. The chapter concludes with a section looking at the family context of adolescent attachment and a clinical case illustrating the intergenerational transmission of attachment insecurity within a family.

Page, the author of Chap. 10, "Applications of Attachment Theory to Group Interventions," writes about the significance of attachment processes within clinical groups. In this first known overview on the use of attachment in groups, Page summarizes the research on attachment-based interventions for adult groups, which centers on three areas: psychiatric symptom relief, pair–bond relationships, and parenting, the most extensively studied group. Using the Circle of Security (Marvin, Cooper, Hoffman, & Powell, 2002) model as an example of group intervention with parents of young children, Page includes a case vignette highlighting the experience of one group member, a 23-year-old parent involved in the child welfare system because of child neglect. This particular attachment-based group model involves work between the group facilitator and an individual client in the presence of other group members who become a community of peers, providing group affiliations and attachments for each other, in addition to the relationship with the therapist facilitator.

Part III breaks new ground in the attachment literature, looking at the application of attachment to social policy pertaining to adults, research conducted by social workers, and research on social work education. Chapter 11, by Everett, is entitled "Policy Implications of Attachment Processes in Adulthood: Caregiving and Family Preservation." From the beginning when Bowlby's social work colleague John Robertson filmed the effects of prolonged separation on a hospitalized toddler and Bowlby studied children separated from their parents in residential treatment, attachment theory and research have impacted child welfare policies in regard to medical treatment and residential care. While these and other child-centered policies do impact adult parents, there has been much less direct application of attachment theory to policies impacting adults of all ages. Using case vignettes, Everett points to areas where current social policies are inextricably linked with adult attachment issues: child welfare, adoption, child custody, maternal incarceration, lesbian and gay parents, military service, and elder care. Everett concludes that many policy areas that impact adult attachments do not factor in the knowledge and findings from attachment theory and research, though doing so would benefit adults and families greatly.

Bettmann and Jasperson, in Chap. 12, "Contributions of Social Workers to Attachment Research," conducted an extensive survey of the social work and attachment literature looking for published attachment research performed by clinical social workers. While searching databases by profession is difficult and sometimes impossible, they were able to locate a large number of articles from the presumed thousands of studies in this area conducted at least in part by social work professionals. They then compiled the studies into five groups by the population studied (children, adolescents, young adults, adults, and families) and briefly summarized the methods and findings within those categories. Included in the chapter are five helpful tables referencing a sample of articles on attachment research studies by social workers, including measures used and a short summary of the empirical outcomes. It is hoped that this chapter will inspire pride and ownership of attachment competence within the social work profession and challenge more social workers to conduct, author, and publish the results of their attachment research.

Chapter 13, "The Implications of Attachment Theory for Social Work Education," by Bennett and Deal, explores the relevance of attachment theory to graduate education in general and social work education in particular. The authors examine each of the components of social work graduate education, including classroom learning, student cohorts, fieldwork internships, and supervisory relationships. Attachment styles, both general and relationship-specific, are important to understand in the educational context. Bennett and Deal look at the few research articles published on the topic of attachment and fieldwork supervision and share findings from their own experience with an attachment-based supervision training program for social work field instructors. Included in their study were student evaluations of their relationship-specific attachments to their supervisors. They also look at attachment as it impacts learning and critical thinking, as well as mentalization and empathy. Attachment theory, they conclude, offers a promising new perspective on social work education in all its aspects.

Conclusion

Attachment impacts almost every facet of adult life, from love relationships and families to work experiences, military life, educational processes, and social policies from the cradle to the grave. The 13 chapters in this book have enabled us to explore only a small portion of the attachment-related topics that impact clinical social work practice and education and the social policies and research that are of direct concern to social workers and their clients. While we had hoped to fill some gaps remaining after publication of the special edition on adult attachment in the *Journal of Clinical Social Work*, there remain many areas still to be explored. The list is long, but it seems important to highlight a few, particularly three chapters that regrettably had to be omitted from the original plan for this book: attachment-based couples treatment, attachment in gay and lesbian couples, and implications for attachment within a cultural context (with a specific focus on displacement trauma in the American Indian, Armenian, Latino, and Katrina victim populations). The list of additional topics is, of course, extensive since it relates to adult attachment and clinical practice in social work. There are endless case examples, for example, both from psychotherapy practice and from case management within agency settings, and focused on all ages, psychiatric diagnoses, and populations. In addition, there are attachment dynamics and behaviors that could be further explored clinically: anger, guilt, laughter, sex, violence, addictions, and body-image, to name but a few.

Limitations can be both frustrating and inspiring, and we are hoping for the latter result. Readers of this volume, we hope, will begin to think of their own areas of expertise and practice and ways in which they have applied, or would like to creatively apply, attachment theory. We further hope that researchers or clinicians with an interest in research will be inspired to design and implement attachment-related studies that interface with social work practice in all its many forms. Attachment is as an evidenced-based theory that serves as the underpinning for growing numbers of empirically validated treatment models. Thus, we believe that attachment theory holds promise for social work clinicians and researchers alike, especially given the current emphasis in our field on "evidence-based practice." Finally, we hope to raise consciousness about attachment-related issues among social work educators, social policy planners, and legislators who deal with attachment-related issues impacting millions of individuals and families, though they are rarely acknowledged in a direct way.

Social work is a vibrant, creative, and socially attuned profession. Our values firmly establish us as a profession committed to help prevent and/or relieve human suffering in all forms. Love and loss are at the center of attachment theory, as well as the center of social work practice. The consonance between the theory and the practice is clear. The challenge is ours to move forward with our work on attachment and to make a positive contribution to our clients, to the profession, and to society at large.

References

Ainsworth, M. D. S., Blehar, M., Waters, E., & Wall, S. (1978). *Patterns of attachment: Assessed in the Strange Situation and at home*. Hillsdale, NJ: Lawrence Erlbaum.

Bartholomew, K., & Shaver, P. (1998). Methods of assessing adult attachment. In J. Simpson & W. S. Rholes (Eds.), *Attachment theory and close relationships* (pp. 25–45). New York: Guilford Press.

Basham, K. (2008). Homecoming as safe haven or new front: Attachment and detachment in military couples. *Clinical Social Work Journal, 36*(1), 83–96.

Bennett, S. (2008). Attachment-informed supervision for social work field education. *Clinical Social Work Journal, 36*(1), 97–108.

Bettmann, J., & Jasperson, R. (2008). Adults in wilderness treatment: A unique application of attachment theory and research. *Clinical Social Work Journal, 36*(1), 51–62.

Bowlby, J. (1960). Grief and mourning in infancy and early childhood. *Psychoanalytic Study of the Child*, XV, 9–52.

Bowlby, J. (1969/1982). *Attachment and loss: Vol. 1. Attachment*. New York: Basic Books.

Bowlby, J. (1973). *Attachment and loss: Vol. 2. Separation*. New York: Basic Books.

Bowlby, J. (1980). *Attachment and loss: Vol. 3. Loss, sadness and depression*. New York: Basic Books.

Brennan, K., Clark, C., & Shaver, P. (1998). Self-report measurement of adult romantic attachment: An integrative overview. In J. A. Simpson & W. S. Rholes (Eds.), *Attachment theory and close relationships* (pp. 46–76). New York: Guilford Press.

Farber, S. (2008). Dissociation, traumatic attachments, and self-harm. Eating disorders and self-mutilation. *Clinical Social Work Journal, 36*(1), 63–73.

George, C., Kaplan, N., & Main, M. (1984). *Adult Attachment Interview protocol*. Berkeley: University of California. Unpublished manuscript.

George, C., Kaplan, N., & Main, M. (1996). *Adult Attachment Interview protocol* (3rd ed.). Berkeley: University of California. Unpublished manuscript.

Hazan, C., & Shaver, P. (1987). Romantic love conceptualized as an attachment process. *Journal of Personality and Social Psychology, 52*, 511–524.

Hesse, E. (2008). The Adult Attachment Interview: Protocol, method of analysis, and empirical studies. In J. Cassidy & P. Shaver (Eds.), *Handbook of attachment: Theory, research, and clinical applications* (2nd ed., pp. 552–598). New York: Guilford Press.

Marvin, R., Cooper, G., Hoffman, K., & Powell, B. (2002). The Circle of Security project: Attachment-based intervention with caregiver–pre-school child dyads. *Attachment & Human Development, 4*(1), 107–124.

Mikulincer, M., & Shaver, P. (2007). *Attachment in adulthood: Structure, dynamics, and change*. New York: Guilford Press.

Nelson, J. K. (2008). Laugh and the world laughs with you. *Clinical Social Work Journal, 36*(1), 41–50.

Ringel, S. (2008). Formative experiences of Orthodox Jewish women: Attachment patterns and spiritual development. *Clinical Social Work Journal, 36*(1), 73–83.

Sable, P. (1979). Differentiating between attachment and dependency in theory and practice. *Social Casework, 60*, 138–144.

Sable, P. (1983). Overcoming fears of attachment in an adult with a detached personality. *Psychotherapy: Research and Practice, 20*, 376–382.

Sable, P. (2000). *Attachment and adult psychotherapy*. Northvale, NJ: Jason Aaronson.

Schore, J., & Schore, A. (2008). Modern attachment theory: The central role of affect regulation in development and treatment. *Clinical Social Work Journal, 36*(1), 9–21.

Solomon, J., & George, C. (2008). The measurement of attachment security and related constructs in infancy and early childhood. In J. Cassidy & P. Shaver (Eds.), *The handbook of attachment: Theory, research, and clinical applications* (2nd ed., pp. 383–416). New York: Guilford Press.

Webb, N. B. (1983). Vacation-separations: Therapeutic implications and clinical management. *Clinical Social Work Journal, 11*(2), 126–138.

Webb, N. B. (1984). A crisis intervention perspective on the termination process. *Clinical Social Work Journal, 13*(4), 329–340.

Weiss, R. (1998). A taxonomy of relationships. *Journal of Social and Personal Relationships, 15*, 671–683.

Part I
Theory Development Regarding Adult Attachment

Chapter 2
The Origins of an Attachment Approach to Social Work Practice with Adults

Pat Sable

> *Intimate attachments to other human beings are the hub around which a person's life revolves, not only when he is an infant or a toddler or a schoolchild but throughout his adolescence and his years of maturity as well, and on into old age.*
>
> Bowlby (1980, p. 442)

Attachment theory is widely accepted and acclaimed as a major influence on psychological understanding and psychotherapy and has been gaining attention from social work researchers, educators, and clinicians. Its account of lifespan development has changed our thinking about the significance of certain close relationships, how they are made and maintained, and how they can be affected by disruptions such as separation or loss. An attachment approach offers a view of the emotional needs of children, emphasizing that the quality of early caregiving may have lasting effects on feelings of stability and security (Sroufe, Egeland, & Carlson, 2005). The development of these basic concepts of attachment is credited to the work of John Bowlby, a British psychoanalyst whose analytic training coincided with the development of object relations theory. Mary Ainsworth, a Canadian developmental psychologist, who was Bowlby's collaborator for many years, designed the research methodology that showed the concepts could be empirically tested, and she provided the impetus for the enormous amount of research that is continuing to expand the theory in the twenty-first century. This chapter provides a particular focus on historical aspects that are pertinent to adult attachment and traces the development of attachment theory from early in Bowlby's career when he began to formulate his ideas about affectional bonds. Though Bowlby conceived attachment as a phenomenon that operates throughout the life cycle, the field of adult attachment, including how the concepts are applied to psychotherapy with adults, has been less studied than his pioneering work on the mother–child bond.

P. Sable (✉)
School of Social Work, University of Southern California, Los Angeles, CA, USA
e-mail: esable@aya.yale.edu

S. Bennett and J.K. Nelson (Eds.), *Adult Attachment in Clinical Social Work*,
Essential Clinical Social Work Series, DOI 10.1007/978-1-4419-6241-6_2,
© Springer Science+Business Media, LLC 2010

This discussion begins with a look at the origins of Bowlby's ideas that have come to be called attachment theory, followed by a discussion of the contributions of colleagues who advanced his work.

John Bowlby and the Roots of Attachment Theory

Edward John Mostyn Bowlby was born in 1907, the son of a renowned surgeon to the King of England. The fourth child of three girls and three boys, he was sent to boarding school at eight, a common practice of many upper-class English families. He reportedly was unhappy, once telling his wife that he would not send a dog away to school at such an early age (Karen, 1994). According to his son, Sir Richard Bowlby, he experienced an even earlier rupture due to the sudden loss of his nanny when he was 4 years of age (personal communication). Karen (1994) suggests that the influence of this upbringing, and the culture that fostered it, are evident in much of Bowlby's theorizing about the affectional needs of children. In particular, his basic premise was that children should have continuous and reliable caregiving and that they could be emotionally harmed if the caregiver/child bond is broken, abusive, or inadequate. The story of attachment revolves around this conviction and the many implications it has spawned for theory, research, and psychotherapy.

Social work is also part of the attachment story. While in analytic training and after spending a year (1928–1929) in a small school for maladjusted children, where the histories of the children indicated they had been subjected to earlier adverse experiences, Bowlby was appointed to the London Child Guidance Clinic at Canonbury in 1936. He worked there until he left in 1940 to become an Army psychiatrist. It was at this clinic that Bowlby (1979) said he was "deeply influenced by the insights of two analytically oriented social workers" (p. 5) who introduced him to the idea that unresolved problems from a parent's childhood could be related to a current problem in their children. The social workers also introduced him to the idea of including family members in the therapeutic process with the child. Bowlby's appreciation of a social work perspective is still evident late in his career when he spoke to the Social Work Continuation Group in London. In a video of that presentation, he told the group that he "owed (social workers) a great deal of debt, gratitude" and that he "learned everything from social workers," such as their emphasis on "actual experiences" over fantasy (Bowlby, 1987).

Bowlby's interest in research can also be dated to his Canonbury years. As he spent time with the children and learned of their disrupted relationships, he felt traditional theory did not explain what he was seeing. He decided to collect data on some of the child and adolescent cases that resulted in his later groundbreaking articles on 44 juvenile thieves (Bowlby, 1944, 1946). This systematic research found that the young thieves had more prolonged separations or deprivations of care than a control group and also that it was more common for these children to be diagnosed as "affectionless," a term Bowlby described as those who exhibited "an extreme degree of the impaired capacity to make object-relationships" (p. 122). Therefore, even before the war, Bowlby knew he wanted to study how ruptured relationships could affect a child's personality development, and in 1945, when he became Director of the Department for Children and Parents at the Tavistock Clinic in London, he set up a research program to specifically study separation. He hired James Robertson, a social worker, who learned about observational research when employed at Anna Freud's Hampstead Nursery. Working with Bowlby, Robertson made a series of films documenting the distress of young children who were separated from their parents and cared for by strangers in unfamiliar settings. Bowlby then elucidated a sequence of responses – protest, despair, and detachment – to describe what he observed in the children following separation. He later hired Mary Ainsworth, whose analysis of Robertson's research data inspired her to undertake her own direct observation research.

At the same time, Bowlby was commissioned by the World Health Organization (WHO) to write a report on the mental health of homeless children. While gathering data in Europe and the USA, he communicated with numerous mental health professionals, including social workers. The monograph (Bowlby, 1951) is historical for its evidence regarding maternal deprivation, as well as its effect on social work, hospital practices, and prevention (Karen, 1994). The report was later published as a popular book, *Child Care and the Growth of Love* (Bowlby, 1953), and it turned out to be an international best-seller. Bowlby again credited social workers for implementing the ideas into work with children (Senn, 1977).

The WHO report brought Bowlby worldwide recognition, and his reputation was assured. However, he realized that an explanation of the processes that brought about the effects of maternal deprivation was missing. As with the data from Robertson's and Ainsworth's research, there was no theory to explain the observations. Bowlby wondered: If separation from caregivers had such distressing consequences, what could be the nature of the bond that would cause these ill effects?

Meanwhile, Bowlby was already dissatisfied with Freud's (1894) explanations of parent–child bonds in terms of psychic energy and drive theory, and he was searching for an alternative theory that would update psychoanalytic theory with the scientific foundation that he thought it needed. A friend mentioned the work of ethologists Lorenz (1952) and Tinbergen (1951) to him. As he read their literature, he saw they were investigating behavior in nonhuman species in a way that might be applied to research and theory with humans. In a break from traditional theory, Bowlby turned to animal studies in order to understand how enduring relationships form, first between infant and parents, and later between adult pairs, and he wondered what made these relationships sometimes go awry. Using ethological principles of the time, Bowlby (1969) hypothesized that it is biologically adaptive for human beings, like many animals, to maintain physical contact, and later, proximity, to their caregivers who become increasingly familiar and relied upon for care, safety, and protection. Bowlby also used an ethological perspective to describe a behavioral system of attachment that explained how the essential connection is maintained.

This shift from drive theory to ethology and control theory was a huge leap, proposing a conceptual framework that was controversial and sharply attacked by many of Bowlby's peers, among them Anna Freud and Donald Winnicott. Regardless, his confidence in the direction he was taking is apparent in an interview he gave in the mid-1970s: "We are now moving fast towards a unified paradigm. By the end of the century, we will get one… Now in my view, it is the ethologists who have the strongest paradigm of all, because the biological and evolutionary substrate they bring to the field, is immensely powerful" (as cited in Evans, 1977, p. 7).

The ethological–evolutionary perspective actually frames attachment theory with concepts that distinguish it from other object relations theories (for example, Kleinian theory and Fairbairn's object relations theory). Bowlby also drew on concepts from cognitive science and information processing to put forward a comprehensive theory that alleges there is a natural inclination to form lasting bonds – or attachments – with selective others and explains certain psychological problems as the internalization of adverse experiences diverting developmental pathways away from healthy functioning. From his earlier observations and his call for theory to be based on research, Bowlby emphasized events of separation, loss, or threat of separation as variables for study. Subsequent research such as Sroufe's (2005) has shown that a combination of factors is generally what increases the risk of disturbance. For example, studies of spousal bereavement find that childhood attachment experiences along with the circumstances of the loss, nature of the lost relationship, and social support affect adjustment (Bowlby, 1980; Parkes & Weiss, 1983; Sable, 1989, 1992). However, it was Bowlby's concepts, grounded in real life experiences, together with Ainsworth's research, that revolutionized child development theory and research and highlighted that experiences of attachment, separation, and loss have an impact on our emotional lives and physical well-being, not only in childhood but throughout adult years as well.

Consolidation of Attachment Concepts into a Theory

Bowlby's first paper suggesting the potential of ethology was published in 1953, while a paper coauthored with Ainsworth and colleagues (Bowlby, Ainsworth, Rosenbluth, & Boston, 1956) suggested a classification system with three relationship patterns in children reunited with their parents after prolonged separation. Three of Bowlby's papers which followed, built on ethology and developmental psychology, are considered the theoretical formulation of attachment theory: "The Nature of the Child's Tie to His Mother" (Bowlby, 1958), "Separation Anxiety" (Bowlby, 1960a), and "Grief and Mourning in Infancy and Early Childhood" (Bowlby, 1960b). These classic papers eventually expanded into three volumes: *Attachment* (1969), *Separation* (1973), and *Loss* (1980). In *Attachment*, Bowlby used ethology, an evolutionary point of view, and control theory to describe the nature of the mother–child bond. In *Separation*, Bowlby dealt primarily with separation anxiety and *internal working models* that are based on early attachment, separation, and caregiving experiences, thereby extending attachment theory to include an understanding of cognitive structures and processes. For example, he emphasized that for a sense of security it is crucial for the child to have experiences which develop an expectation that attachment figures will be emotionally available, sensitive, and responsive if called upon (Kobak, 1999). In the third and final volume, *Loss*, Bowlby dealt with grief and mourning as well as defensive processes and clinical implications. In its epilogue is a frequently quoted statement that is testimony to Bowlby's position on internal working models of adult attachment throughout life: "Intimate attachments to other human beings are the hub around which a person's life revolves, not only when he is an infant or a toddler or a schoolchild but throughout his adolescence and his years of maturity as well, and on into old age" (Bowlby, 1980, p. 442). Furthermore, in the earlier volume, *Separation*, Bowlby (1973) had also made it clear that attachment figures remain critical for fostering security and reducing fear throughout life: "Whether a child or adult is in a state of security, anxiety or distress is determined in large part by the accessibility and responsiveness of his principal attachment figure" (p. 23).

It is important to note, however, that during the initial efforts to study attachment, the focus was almost exclusively on infants and their relationships with their caregivers (Rholes & Simpson, 2004). It was also the period when Ainsworth made several contributions that were to become relevant to adult attachment, though her research was based on studying young children.

After completing work in London and then observational research of mother–child interaction in Uganda, Ainsworth returned to the USA where she began a second observational study of 1-year-olds, the landmark Strange Situation (Ainsworth, Blehar, Waters, & Wall, 1978). The Strange Situation is a 20-min structured laboratory procedure that focuses on the infant's response to separation from, and reunion with, the mother under conditions of increasing, though moderate, stress. Ainsworth based the experimental situation on her knowledge of Bowlby's ethological perspective which points out that there are a group of natural clues to danger, such as darkness, unfamiliar settings, isolation and separation from an attachment figure that elicit fear, and efforts by the child to attain proximity to a protective person or place. These clues signal an increase in the risk of danger and compel some type of action to keep a person in a safe and familiar environment surrounded by trusted companions – the attachment figures or caregivers. Moreover, if more than one of these clues is present, such as finding one's self alone with strangers, fear and alarm are intensified. The *Strange Situation* was also based on the ethological tradition of observing organisms in their natural environments: the videotaped and rated session in the laboratory came after extensive observations of mother–child dyads over the first year of life in their homes. Following the initial period of observation in the home, the infant and parent figure were observed as they react to the natural clues of an unfamiliar setting, the approach of a stranger, and two brief (3 min) separations and reunions.

Ainsworth's objective was to examine the balance between attachment and exploration by exposing the babies to several of the natural clues to danger. In addition to finding that separation could activate the *attachment system* and deactivate exploration, Ainsworth discovered individual differences in the infants' responses to separation and reunion, which she identified as *secure, insecure-avoidant, and insecure-resistant*. She also found that each pattern correlated to the mother's sensitivity to her baby's signals during the previous home observations, suggesting an important historical development of the theory – attachment patterns tend to persist over time. Infants classified as secure in the laboratory were found to have mothers who were sensitive to their baby's signals at home. Although they protested and curtailed play and exploration in the laboratory when mother was absent, on reunion they sought proximity to her, were more easily comforted and able to resume play than those classified as insecure. The infants had learned throughout their first year that they could rely on their caregiver to be available and responsive. In contrast, infants rated insecure in the laboratory were found to have less harmonious relationships at home. Those classified as insecure-resistant (sometimes called insecure ambivalent) were highly upset by their mother's departure, sought proximity and interaction upon reunion, but were not pacified. Exploration was inhibited, and they alternated between clinging and resisting contact. In other words, they were resistant to being calmed. Their over-activated, but ambivalent, attachment behavior was attributed to having a caregiver who was inconsistently responsive, coupled with a tendency to discourage exploration and self-reliance. On the other hand, infants classified as insecure-avoidant showed minimal distress at separation and ignored or appeared indifferent upon reunion. They had deactivated their attachment behavior due to insensitive, unreliable caregiving. Main (Main & Weston, 1982) explained avoidance as a "conditional or secondary strategy" (p. 49) to maintain some degree of proximity to unavailable caregivers, and she cited its occurrence in the behavior of birds and primates as well as young children. Sometime later, she also identified a fourth pattern, *insecure-disorganized*, which indicates the lack of an organized attachment pattern and an increased vulnerability to pathology and to dissociation (Main & Solomon, 1990). However, though a more maladaptive pattern of relating than the ambivalent and avoidant categories, none of the organized insecure patterns is in and of itself equated with emotional disturbance.

Another concept of Ainsworth's that has been adapted into attachment theory is that of an attachment figure as a *secure base* from which to move out and explore the world, and to which to return when feeling in danger or wanting refuge and comfort. This concept, together with that of *attachment patterns*, has been modified and extended to adult attachment, and therapists are finding the adult version of secure base to be a useful addition to their clinical understanding and practice interventions. For example, the therapist may be seen as offering a secure base for facilitating exploration into new experiences, both in revisiting the painful past as well as in venturing forth in the present. The concept of attachment patterns helps clarify how clients have internalized and organized their attachment experiences and how they are regulating their emotions and interactions with others (Slade, 1999).

In terms of attachment relationships between adults, the earliest research evidence came from studies of marital separation and adult bereavement carried out by Marris (1982), Parkes (1991), and Weiss (1975, 1982, 1991). From his work on divorce, Weiss (1974) conceptualized adult attachment as one of a variety of social provisions of relationships that adults require for well-being. The others are social affiliation, opportunity for nurturance, and obtaining help and guidance. Weiss also hypothesized that the rupture or loss of an adult pair-bond results in an "emotional loneliness," which is not the same as "social loneliness," defined as the loss of relationships in a group or social network. Weiss found that social networks ease the distress of loss but do not replace an exclusive relationship.

From their studies of bereaved spouses, Marris (1958) and Parkes (1965, 1969) described a grief process, which not only pointed out how painful the loss of attachment can be for adults, but has also become a yardstick for observing the experience of mourning. That process includes an initial numbness, which gives way to yearning and searching for the lost person, followed by disorganization and despair, and finally, some degree of reorganization (that is, adjustment). Parkes, joining with Weiss (Parkes & Weiss, 1983), also made one of the earliest attempts to identify the factors that might incline individuals to adjust poorly to bereavement. Problematic reactions were found to be associated with the type and security of attachment to the lost person and also with the quality of early attachment experiences with parents. The researchers theorized that an insecure attachment pattern established in childhood could create a vulnerability that later interacts with the stress of adult bereavement. Parkes (1973), who worked with bereaved adults, introduced the term "compulsive self-reliance" to describe the pattern of an adult who has deactivated attachment behavior and inhibits grief. He contrasted this with the over-activation of attachment behavior that occurs in a pattern of anxious attachment and chronic grief.

After this early period of research, which demonstrated that attachment behavior was a force across the life cycle that could inform the practice of psychotherapy with adults, interest in attachment theory began to accelerate. Bowlby's trilogy was completed by 1980. In the social work journal, *Social Casework*, Parad's (1981) review of the trilogy's third volume, *Loss*, stated that Bowlby's work was "imperative for social work educators, practitioners, administrators and researchers" (p. 356). Ainsworth's Strange Situation laboratory procedure was prompting research in developmental psychology such as Daniel Stern's (1985) infant observations and Sroufe's (Sroufe & Waters, 1977) longitudinal research with high-risk families, which began during an infant's first year and has continued over 30 years. Sroufe's research has found that early secure – or insecure – attachment is related to developing self-reliance, emotional regulation, and social competence, among other skills. The findings have furthered support for Bowlby's viewpoint about "continuity and change" (Sroufe, 2005, p. 349). That is, though patterns of adaption once formed tend to persist, they can be transformed by later experiences. The 1980s also produced two independent types of research on adult attachment that continue to be used: the Adult Attachment Interview (AAI) created by Main (George, Kaplan, & Main, 1996) and the brief self-report measure of adult attachment styles created by Hazan and Shaver (1987) (see Chap. 3 for further explanation of adult attachment measures).

As data on adult attachment has proliferated, subsequent theorists and researchers (see Chap. 3) such as Berman and Sperling (1994), Hazan and Zeifman (1999), and Holmes (1993) have all agreed that there is a behavioral system of attachment that remains active throughout the life cycle and plays a part in relationships that provide feelings of familiarity, companionship, and belonging. More recently, research on the neurobiology of attachment has linked the system to brain development by suggesting that attachment experiences early in life are processed and stored in implicit memory in the right hemisphere of the brain, and once encoded, these attachment experiences endure, providing a blueprint for what to expect and how to behave in later relationships (Schore, 1994). In other words, childhood experiences, carried forward in internal working models, color later relationships (Parkes, 2006). Schore (2003a, 2003b) has expanded this aspect of attachment theory by pointing out that early experiences also influence the later regulation of both positive and negative feelings and directly affect the body (see Chap. 4).

These links between attachment theory and insights from other scientific fields have produced a dynamic theoretical base that has implications for clinical practice. For example, Schore (2005) sees the context of psychotherapy shifting to a focus on "implicit nonverbal communications, bodily based affective states and interactive regulation" (p. 846). In other words, as we now understand it, the social work relationship is based on a panoply of nonverbal, right brain communications that both arouse and regulate affect. In terms of social work's person-in-environment tradition, attachment concepts taught in Human Behavior in the Social Environment fit well with the current focus on systems theory. For example, current attachment researchers such as Belsky (2005) and Sroufe (Sroufe et al., 2005) have shown that socio-cultural and ecological factors are part of a client's history that affect adaption and functioning.

Despite the large amount of research and literature on adult attachment, including the mounting evidence that key affectional bonds influence physical and emotional well-being, there is not yet a consensus of what actually constitutes an adult attachment relationship (Crowell et al., 1999; Hazan et al., 2004; Main, 1999; Sable, 2008). Pair-bonds have generally been the context for considering adult attachment (as well as the related caregiving and reproductive behavioral systems), but research, such as the Social Convoy diagram (Kahn & Antonucci, 1980), found that in addition to romantic pair attachments, adults also have a small number of relationships that are equivalent to attachment relationships (e.g., other family members, selective close friends, pets, or therapists). These are the ties that individuals rely on for emotional connection and protection in times of threat or difficulty and these are the ties apt to evoke grief and mourning upon loss (though pets do not fulfill the typical safety features assumed by the theory, the devotion some people feel toward their pets, especially dogs, suggests they provide elements of attachment and grief upon loss; Sable, 2007).

Another complication in delineating adult relationships of attachment is how to portray their functions and expression. The early literature focused on how a child targets attachment behavior to someone seen as older, stronger, and wiser, but this can be misleading when considering the reciprocal attachment behavior and sexual nature of relationships such as the pair-bond. Other issues concern what determines how and when an attachment is established and becomes a secure base. The theory envisions that it takes time, proximity, and familiarity for an attachment to form, but once formed an adult's attachment behavior is not as readily activated, and unless there is a traumatic event, the need for physical closeness is generally not as critical as it could be for a young child (Mayseless & Popper, 2007; Sable, 2008). Adults also have memory networks, which enable them to call upon mental representations of comforting experiences to soothe themselves or reflect on their situation and its possible consequences (Mikulincer & Shaver, 2007).

Current attachment theorists, for example, Schore and Schore (2008), agree with Bowlby and the earlier theorists of adult attachment that the attachment behavioral system remains active throughout the life cycle. Schore and Schore (2008) support ethological theorizing by noting that "attachment represents the evolutionary mechanism by which we are sociophysiologically connected to others" (p. 11), and they allege that the essential function of an attachment bond is "self and affect regulation" (p. 9). Their work is advancing the concept of adult attachment by elucidating how these regulatory processes provide the neurobiological underpinnings that sustain affectional bonds in adult years (see Chap. 4).

Closing Thoughts

For me, being involved in the study and development of attachment theory has been a great adventure. I first met John Bowlby in 1978 at a conference in Canada that was sponsored by the Clarke Institute of Psychiatry. That Bowlby was the keynote speaker at a conference titled "Current issues in child psychiatry" reflected the growing prominence of his new conceptualization of the mother–child bond. Held at a lodge on Lake Couchiching, the conference setting was conducive to the small informal groups that gathered around Bowlby, attempting to grasp what he meant by "attachment." I saw him listen attentively and respond patiently to questions and comments without ever letting on, for example, to a man who kept using the word "introject" that he disapproved of the term. Nor did he ever complain about the muggy weather like the rest of us did! He actually took early morning walks with his colleague Henry Hansburg, who developed one of the first research measures of attachment and separation, the Separation Anxiety test for adolescents (Hansburg, 1972).

At the time, there were only a few articles in the literature on attachment, especially of adults. I was quite excited that my first attachment publication on adult treatment was in press in the social work journal *Social Casework* (Sable, 1979). Bowlby graciously read the manuscript and was supportive and encouraging of my interest and effort to tackle attachment-based therapy for adults.

Another memorable exchange with Bowlby, which took place several years later, illustrates the core of his thinking about the relevance of real life experiences for development. While staying in my home in Los Angeles for a conference, Bowlby read the draft of my paper on "detachment" and attachment (Sable, 1983). He singled out and stressed the significance of a session where my client, Kelly, had asked me if I had been trying to help her understand that her fears and problems were the result of how she had been treated in her family. The realization of this, she stated, made her feel less hopeless and helpless about herself because now, as an adult, she could see her experiences in a new perspective, and therefore get better.

This message may not seem novel now since the role of actual experiences is no longer a charged subject (Holmes, 1993). At the time, however, Bowlby was sketching a new view of human relationships that not only emphasized the effects of the environment on psychological development, but dealt with our most profound feelings – our inherent, lifelong need to be securely attached to others, and the anguish and yearning we feel if these bonds are threatened or disrupted by separation or loss.

Productive into his final years, Bowlby (1991) continued the theme that separations and losses leave a lasting legacy. In his psychobiography of Charles Darwin, Bowlby speculated that Darwin's 30 years of mysterious chronic illness, anxiety, and depression in adulthood were the result of certain childhood experiences, most notably the death of his mother when he was eight that left him susceptible to breakdown when faced with stressful situations. In this last work, Bowlby (1991) easily could have been talking about himself when he wrote about Darwin, "What is striking is the courage with which he questioned the accepted doctrines and his determination to think things out for himself" (p. 212). Like Darwin, Bowlby was on a voyage of observation and discovery. In his courage and steadfast determination to chart his own course, to question and revise existing theory, he generated thoughts and ideas that over time would launch an eloquent, innovative theory centered around "the making and breaking of affectional bonds" (Bowlby, 1977).

In conclusion, the theory built on the foundation begun by Bowlby and Ainsworth seems to be remarkably enduring, offering therapists a knowledge base for understanding development and psychopathology, as well as informing psychotherapy (Eagle & Wolitzky, 2009; Shaver & Mikulincer, 2009). From roots in psychoanalysis and ethology, Bowlby (1969) put together a scientific framework that gives us a new and exceptionally creative account of why and how we form close affectional bonds with others. His contention that we are born "designed" by evolution to seek attachments carries through to adult years, to our enduring need to feel assured of caring and reliable relationships. Placing his concepts in an evolutionary perspective, Bowlby explained how protest, anxiety, and anger can accompany threat of separation from these figures or how sorrow and grief can accompany their loss, and that this has a bearing on how we understand and affirm our clients' basic feelings. John Bowlby once said to me that the true test of theory is whether it can be applied to alleviating the distress of our clients. As other chapter authors in this volume demonstrate, accumulating evidence that attachment concepts are relevant to adult psychotherapy suggests that the theory has indeed passed this test.

Study Questions

1. Explain how attachment theory is compatible with the social work focus on person and environment and fits with a social work understanding of culture.
2. Discuss Bowlby's early personal and career experiences and how they relate to his evolving ideas of attachment.
3. Identify the different theories and research that Bowlby included in formulating his framework of attachment.
4. Describe three basic assumptions of attachment theory and discuss their relevance to social work practice with adults.

5. Delineate and discuss the role of real life experiences in Bowlby's formulations for social work practice with adults.

References

Ainsworth, M. D. S., Blehar, M. C., Waters, E., & Wall, S. (1978). *Patterns of attachment: Assessed in the strange situation and at home*. Hillsdale, NJ: Lawrence Erlbaum.

Belsky, J. (2005). Attachment theory and research in ecological perspective: Insights from the Pennsylvania infant and family development project and the NICHD study of early child care. In K. E. Grossmann, K. Grossmann, & E. Waters (Eds.), *Attachment from infancy to childhood: The major longitudinal studies* (pp. 71–97). New York: Guilford.

Berman, W. H., & Sperling, M. B. (1994). The structure and function of adult attachment. In W. H. Berman & M. B. Sperling (Eds.), *Attachment in adults* (pp. 1–28). New York: Guilford.

Bowlby, J. (1944, 1946). Forty four juvenile thieves: Their character and home life. *International Journal of Psycho-Analysis, 25*, 19–53. 107–128.

Bowlby, J. (1951). *Maternal care and mental health*. Geneva: World Health Organization. Monograph Series No. 2.

Bowlby, J. (1953). Critical phases in the development of social responses in man and other animals. In M. Abercrombie (Ed.), *New biology* (pp. 25–32). New York: Penguin Books.

Bowlby, J. (1958). The nature of the child's tie to his mother. *International Journal of Psycho-Analysis, 39*, 350–373.

Bowlby, J. (1960a). Separation anxiety. *International Journal of Psycho-Analysis, 41*, 89–113.

Bowlby, J. (1960b). Grief and mourning in infancy and early childhood. *Psychoanalytic Study of the Child, 15*, 9–52.

Bowlby, J. (1969). *Attachment and loss* (Attachment, Vol. 1). New York: Basic Books.

Bowlby, J. (1973). *Attachment and loss* (Separation, Vol. 2). New York: Basic Books.

Bowlby, J. (1977). The making and breaking of affectional bonds. *British Journal of Psychiatry, 130*, 201–210. 421–431.

Bowlby, J. (1979). Psychoanalysis as art and science. *International Review of Psycho-Analysis, 6*, 3–14.

Bowlby, J. (1980). *Attachment and loss* (Loss, Vol. 3). New York: Basic Books.

Bowlby, J. (1987). Video of presentation at Tavistock Clinic, London.

Bowlby, J. (1991). *Charles Darwin*. New York: Norton.

Bowlby, J., Ainsworth, M., Rosenbluth, D., & Boston, M. (1956). The effects of mother-child separation: A follow-up study. *British Journal of Medical Psychology, 24*(3–4), 211–247.

Crowell, J. A., Fraley, R. C., & Shaver, P. R. (1999). Measure of individual differences in adolescent and adult attachment. In J. Cassidy & P. R. Shaver (Eds.), *Handbook of attachment: Theory, research, and clinical applications* (pp. 434–446). New York: Guilford.

Eagle, M., & Wolitzky, D. L. (2009). Adult psychotherapy from the perspectives of attachment theory and psychoanalysis. In J. H. Obegi & E. Berant (Eds.), *Attachment theory and research in clinical work with adults* (pp. 351–378). New York: Guilford.

Evans, P. (1977). A visit with John Bowlby. *APA Monitor*, 6–7.

Freud, S. (1894). *The neuro-psychoses of defence* (The standard edition of the complete psychological works of Sigmund Freud, Vol. 3, pp. 43–61). London: Hogarth. Translated from the German by J. Strachey, Ed., 1953.

George, C., Kaplan, N., & Main, M. (1996). *Adult attachment interview protocol* (3rd ed.). Unpublished manuscript, University of California, Berkeley.

Hansburg, H. G. (1972). *Adolescent separation anxiety: A method for the study of adolescent separation problems*. Springfield, IL: Charles C. Thomas.

Hazan, C., Gur-Yaish, N., & Campa, M. (2004). What does it mean to be attached? In W. S. Rholes & J. A. Simpson (Eds.), *Adult attachment: Theory, research and clinical applications* (pp. 55–85). New York: Guilford.

Hazan, C., & Shaver, P. R. (1987). Romantic love conceptualized as an attachment process. *Journal of Personality and Social Psychology, 52*, 511–524.

Hazan, C., & Zeifman, D. (1999). Pair bonds as attachments: Evaluating the evidence. In J. Cassidy & P. R. Shaver (Eds.), *Handbook of attachment: Theory, research and clinical applications* (pp. 336–354). New York: Guilford.

Holmes, J. (1993). *John Bowlby and attachment theory*. New York: Routledge.

Kahn, R. L., & Antonucci, T. C. (1980). Convoys over the life cycle course: Attachment roles and social support. In P. B. Baltes & O. Brim (Eds.), *Lifespan development and behavior* (Vol. 3, pp. 253–286). New York: Academic.

Karen, R. (1994). *Becoming attached*. New York: Warner.

Kobak, R. (1999). The emotional dynamics of disruptions in attachment relationships: Implications for theory, research, and clinical intervention. In J. Cassidy & P. R. Shaver (Eds.), *Handbook of attachment: Theory, research and clinical applications* (pp. 21–43). New York: Guilford.

Lorenz, K. (1952). *King Solomon's ring*. London: Methuen.

Main, M. (1999). Epilogue. Attachment theory: Eighteen points with suggestions for future studies. In J. Cassidy & P. R. Shaver (Eds.), *Handbook of attachment: Theory, research and clinical applications* (pp. 845–887). New York: Guilford.

Main, M., & Solomon, J. (1990). Procedures for identifying infants as disorganized/disoriented during the Ainsworth strange situation. In M. T. Greenberg, D. Cicchetti, & E. M. Cummings (Eds.), *Attachment in the preschool years: Theory, research and intervention* (pp. 121–160). Chicago: University of Chicago Press.

Main, M., & Weston, D. (1982). Avoidance of the attachment figure in infancy: Descriptions and interpretations. In C. M. Parkes & J. Stevenson-Hinde (Eds.), *The place of attachment in human behavior* (pp. 31–59). New York: Basic Books.

Marris, P. (1958). *Widows and their families*. London: Routledge and Kegan Paul.

Marris, P. (1982). Attachment and society. In C. M. Parkes & J. Stevenson-Hinde (Eds.), *The place of attachment in human behavior* (pp. 185–201). New York: Basic Books.

Mayseless, O., & Popper, M. (2007). Reliance on leaders and social institutions: An attachment perspective. *Attachment and Human Development, 4*, 73–93.

Mikulincer, M., & Shaver, P. R. (2007). *Attachment in adulthood: Structure, dynamics and change*. New York: Guilford.

Parad, H. (1981). Review of loss. *Social Work, 62*, 355–356.

Parkes, C. M. (1965). Bereavement and mental illness. *British Journal of Medical Psychology, 38*, 1–26.

Parkes, C. M. (1969). Separation anxiety: An aspect of the search for a lost object. In M. H. Lader (Ed.), *British Journal of Psychiatry Special Publication, No. 3: Studies of anxiety* (pp. 87–92). London: World Psychiatric Association and the Royal Medico-Psychological Association.

Parkes, C. M. (1973). Factors determining the persistence of phantom pain in the amputee. *Journal of Psychosomatic Research, 17*, 97–108.

Parkes, C. M. (1991). Attachment, bonding and psychiatric problems after bereavement in adult life. In C. M. Parkes, J. Stevenson-Hinde, & P. Marris (Eds.), *Attachment across the life cycle* (pp. 268–292). New York: Tavistock/Routledge.

Parkes, C. M. (2006). *Love and loss*. London: Routledge.

Parkes, C. M., & Weiss, R. S. (1983). *Recovery from bereavement*. New York: Basic Books.

Rholes, W. S., & Simpson, J. A. (2004). Attachment theory: Basic concepts and contemporary questions. In W. S. Rholes & J. A. Simpson (Eds.), *Adult attachment: Theory, research and clinical implications* (pp. 3–14). New York: Guilford.

Sable, P. (1979). Differentiating between attachment and dependency in theory and practice. *Social Casework, 60*, 138–144.

Sable, P. (1983). Overcoming fears of attachment in an adult with a detached personality. *Psychotherapy: Research and Practice, 20*, 376–382.

Sable, P. (1989). Attachment, anxiety and loss of husband. *American Journal of Orthopsychiatry, 59*, 550–556.

Sable, P. (1992). Attachment, loss of spouse, and disordered mourning. *Families in Society, 73*, 266–273.

Sable, P. (2007). Accentuating the positive in adult attachments. *Attachment and Human Development, 9*, 361–374.

Sable, P. (2008). What is adult attachment? *Clinical Social Work Journal, 36*, 21–30.

Schore, A. N. (1994). *Affect regulation and the origin of the self: The neurobiology of emotional development*. Hillsdale, NJ: Erlbaum.

Schore, A. N. (2003a). *Affect dysregulation and disorders of the self*. New York: Norton.

Schore, A. N. (2003b). *Affect regulation and the repair of the self*. New York: Norton.

Schore, A. N. (2005). A neuropsychoanalytic viewpoint: Commentary on paper by Steven H. Knoblauch. *Psychoanalytic Dialogues, 15*, 829–854.

Schore, J. R., & Schore, A. N. (2008). Modern attachment theory: The central role of affect regulation in development and treatment. *Clinical Social Work Journal, 36*, 9–20.

Senn, M. J. E. (1977). Interview with John Bowlby. In *Milton J.E. Senn oral history collection: History of medicine division*. Washington, D.C.: National Library of Medicine.

Shaver, P. R., & Mikulincer, M. (2009). An overview of attachment theory. In J. H. Obegi & E. Berant (Eds.), *Attachment theory and research in clinical work with adults* (pp. 17–45). New York: Guilford.

Slade, A. (1999). Attachment theory and research: Implications for the theory and practice of individual psychotherapy with adults. In J. Cassidy & P. R. Shaver (Eds.), *Handbook of attachment: Theory, research and clinical applications* (pp. 575–594). New York: Guilford.

Sroufe, L. A., Egeland, B., & Carlson, E. (2005). Placing early attachment experiences in developmental context: The Minnesota longitudinal study. In K. E. Grossman, K. Grossman, & E. Waters (Eds.), *Attachment from infancy to adulthood: The major longitudinal studies* (pp. 48–70). New York: Guilford.

Sroufe, L. A., & Waters, E. (1977). Attachment as an organizational construct. *Child Development, 48*, 1184–1199.

Sroufe, L.A. (December, 2005). *Attachment and Numon Development, 7*, 349–367.

Stern, D. N. (1985). *The interpersonal world of the infant*. New York: Basic Books.

Tinbergen, N. (1951). *The study of instinct*. Oxford, England: Clarendon.

Weiss, R. S. (1974). The provisions of social relationships. In Z. Rubin (Ed.), *Doing unto others* (pp. 17–26). Englewood Cliffs, NJ: Prentice Hall.

Weiss, R. S. (1975). *Marital separation*. New York: Basic Books.

Weiss, R. S. (1982). Attachment in adult life. In C. M. Parkes & J. Stevenson-Hinde (Eds.), *The place of attachment in human behavior* (pp. 171–184). New York: Basic Books.

Weiss, R. S. (1991). The attachment bond in childhood and adulthood. In C. M. Parkes, J. Stevenson-Hinde, & P. Marris (Eds.), *Attachment across the life cycle* (pp. 66–76). New York: Tavistock/Routledge.

Chapter 3
Contemporary Theory and Research on Adult Attachment: Where is the Field Today?

Susanne Bennett and Judith Kay Nelson

> *Much has been learned over the past 20-25 years about adult attachment, but it has become difficult for young scholars, or senior scholars in other disciplines...to dig into the mushrooming literature and understand the terminology, measures, and research methods they encounter.*
>
> Mikulincer and Shaver (2007, p. 486)

Attachment theory took a major leap forward in the mid-1980s with the expansion of research into the study of adult attachment. Ainsworth's (1967) early observations of mother–infant attachment patterns served as a foundation for others to conceptualize how adult attachments are formed and whether they are related to those observed in young children. Based on Bowlby's (1969/1982) assumption that internal working models of attachment exist throughout the lifespan, researchers explored whether adults are secure or insecure in their patterns of relating. This chapter summarizes contemporary adult attachment research and gives an overview of empirical measures. The Adult Attachment Interview (AAI) and several self-report measures are discussed in terms of their usefulness to understand adult attachment processes. The chapter also explores theoretical questions being answered by this growing body of research and the new directions being taken in the study of adult attachments in clinical relationships.

Many clinicians unfamiliar with attachment theory express confusion about the concepts, methods, and findings of adult attachment empirical research. We do not presume to discuss all the concepts or measures used in contemporary studies or to discuss all the research findings. Indeed, the body of attachment research literature is too vast and the measures too many for us to give an exhaustive overview. Instead, we examine the research methodologies that are being used today to explore attachment processes among adults. From almost the beginning of the empirical studies, the field has been divided into two camps of researchers who

S. Bennett (✉)
National Catholic School of Social Service, The Catholic University of America, Washington, DC, USA
e-mail: bennetts@cua.edu

S. Bennett and J.K. Nelson (Eds.), *Adult Attachment in Clinical Social Work*, Essential Clinical Social Work Series, DOI 10.1007/978-1-4419-6241-6_3, © Springer Science+Business Media, LLC 2010

conceptualize and, thus, operationalize the ideas of Ainsworth and Bowlby in different ways (Mikulincer & Shaver, 2007). To address this confusion, it is important to first understand the differences in these lines of adult attachment research.

In one line of research, social psychologists emphasize the dimensional or continuous nature of adult attachments in terms of *attachment styles*. Based on their observations that Ainsworth's original patterns of child attachment behavior in the Strange Situation procedure (Ainsworth, Blehar, Waters, & Wall, 1978) fell along a two-dimensional continuum of attachment avoidance and attachment anxiety, social psychologists proposed that infants primarily were avoidant in their behaviors (self-reliant and uncomfortable with dependency and closeness) or anxious (crying, with no exploration in mother's absence, but protesting upon her reunion) (Mikulincer & Shaver, 2007). Translating infant attachment behaviors into parallel adult terms, Hazan and Shaver (1987) created the first self-report survey that was used to measure adult romantic attachment styles along an avoidant-anxious continuum. Based on responses to this survey, adults were viewed as having one of three *attachment styles – secure, avoidant,* or *anxious –* and secure attachment was considered to exist in a person with low degrees of both avoidance and anxiety. Later researchers added a fourth category which they labeled *fearful* attachment, thus creating a four-box grid with high and low avoidance representing one continuum and high and low anxiety representing the other (Bartholomew, 1990; Bartholomew & Horowitz, 1991). The fearful category may be seen as a combination of avoidant/dismissive and anxious/preoccupied, thus appearing somewhat less organized than the other three categories.

In a second line of research, developmental psychologists conceptualize Ainsworth's patterns in terms of *attachment categories – autonomous-secure, dismissing, preoccupied,* and *unresolved-disorganized –* shaped by the early childhood attachment relationships of the adult. In 1985, Main and her students reported on the first study that used the newly created AAI (George, Kaplan, & Main, 1984), which questioned mothers about their "current state of mind with respect to attachment" and moved the conceptualization of attachment to "the level of representation" (Main, Kaplan, & Cassidy, 1985). While the Strange Situation focuses on attachment behaviors, the AAI focuses on how attachment processes are revealed through language and speech patterns. The premise is that narratives about early attachments disclose unconscious thoughts and emotions about internalized attachment processes (Hesse, 2008). Categories of attachment are determined through an assessment of how organized the speaker's state of mind is regarding past attachment relationships and how coherent the speaker's narrative is in conversation about this attachment history.

After the advent of the first self-report measures and the AAI, the study of adult attachment exploded. There is now a large body of empirical literature that is impressive in the significance of the findings and the variety of populations and problems studied (for a detailed review of this research, see Cassidy & Shaver, 2008, and Mikulincer & Shaver, 2007). However, debate continues about the overlap of dimensional versus categorical ways of thinking about attachment and self-report versus narrative lines of research. Mikulincer and Shaver note that "the two lines both derive from Bowlby's and Ainsworth's writings, and both deal with secure and insecure strategies of emotion regulation and behavior in close relationships" (p. 107). Yet it is generally agreed that these two lines of research evaluate different, though related, phenomenon and, as Mikulincer and Shaver point out, "sometimes relate similarly to outcome variables" (p. 600). Since self-report measures first emerged from social and personality psychology, they focus on the social and cognitive dynamics of adults. The AAI emerged from developmental and clinical psychology and focuses most on intergenerational and longitudinal patterns of attachment. There are significant differences in the techniques of gathering this data as well. Self-report measures inquire directly about conscious thoughts and behaviors, and these measures are easier to administer and code. In contrast, narrative measures are thought to tap into unconscious cognitive and emotional processes, the responses are more difficult to code, and investigators must undergo extensive specialized training to analyze the data for research purposes.

Emerging from the debate about measurement, empirical study has prompted important questions about adult attachment in general. For example, what are the roots of adult attachments, and how do life experiences influence them? Do childhood attachment patterns remain continuous throughout adulthood, or are these patterns malleable? In other words, do we have attachment prototypes (general internal working models of attachment) that remain relatively stable across the lifespan, or do our adult attachment styles change depending on the context of the specific relationship? Furthermore, is the organization of secure and insecure attachment patterns a culturally universal phenomenon? Empirical findings from self-report and narrative measures have converged to begin answering a number of these questions, and the findings both support and expand the original theories of Bowlby and Ainsworth (Mikulincer & Shaver, 2007).

Adult Attachment Interview

The AAI is one of several narrative measures of attachment, but it is the most well known and best regarded adult narrative instrument currently in use. The AAI (AAI protocol: George, Kaplan, & Main, 1996) is an hour-long semistructured interview that asks 20 questions about the speaker's memories of relational experiences with parents or primary caregivers in early childhood.[1] Other questions ask about parental separations, losses, illnesses, frightening experiences, and the speaker's perceptions of childhood influences on personality development. The interview design aims to "surprise the unconscious" (George et al.) of the speaker, due to the manner in which the speaker is asked to reflect on early childhood experiences. For example, near the beginning of the interview process, the speaker is asked to give five adjectives

---

[1]See Hesse (2008) for a modified list of the AAI questions that can be used by clinicians in practice.

or phrases to describe personal relationships with each parent as a young child. This response is followed by a request for memories of experiences that explain the rationale for each of the five descriptors. Throughout the process, speakers often free associate as they are asked to reflect on the link between early attachment relationships and adult functioning, and such responses give indications of the quality of their early attachment relationships.

Following the audiotaped interview, responses are transcribed verbatim, and the content and speech patterns of the speaker are classified into one of three organized categories, thought to describe the speaker's *state of mind* respective to attachment. These categories are *secure autonomous* (valuing of attachment relationships and experiences), *dismissing of attachment* (dismissing or devaluing of attachment relationships and experiences), or *preoccupied* (preoccupied with early attachment relationships and experiences) (George et al., 1996). Several years after creation of the initial AAI classification system, it was determined that speakers sometimes had lapses of coherence in their speech when discussing loss or abuse (Main & Hesse, 1990), and some interviews could not be classified clearly into a single organized category (Hesse, 1996). As a result of these findings, two more categories were added to the coding system: *unresolved/disorganized* and *unorganized/cannot classify* (Hesse, 2008).

Foundations of AAI Classification System

The AAI is based in part on premises about organization and flexibility in conversation. The creators of the instrument proposed that narratives about attachment reveal the manner in which cognitive and emotional processes are organized in the mind respective to childhood experiences with parents (Main et al., 2008). It was posited that *attentional flexibility* – how fluid and flexible a person is in conversation – gives clues to the speaker's state of mind regarding attachment experiences. Individuals who had secure and loving caregiver–infant experiences have the capacity to talk easily about their attachment history and move in a flexible, fluid manner in the conversation, without showing signs of defensiveness. They demonstrate attentional flexibility in contrast to dismissing adults, who move away from past experiences when they are asked about them, or preoccupied adults, who move toward discussion about these experiences. Although dismissing and preoccupied adults demonstrate *attentional inflexibility* in their conversations, their manners of conversing about attachment-related experiences are still considered to be organized (though *unresolved/disorganized* and *unorganized/cannot classify* are not) (Hesse, 2008). These ideas about flexibility in discourse parallel the movement and flexibility/inflexibility of infants. In the presence of their mothers, secure infants easily explore in the presence of their mothers, but cry for help when distressed or separated from them. Similarly, infants who are avoidant inflexibly move away from their mothers, while ambivalent/resistant infants inflexibly stay connected to their mothers and ignore their surroundings (Main et al., 2008).

In addition to the AAI's parallel with infant–caregiver attachment patterns, classification of the AAI has been influenced by the ideas of Grice (1975, 1989), a linguist who proposed maxims about logical, organized conversation (George et al., 1996). In the AAI, a transcribed text meets the classification of secure-autonomous if the speaker demonstrates Grice's four maxims for: (1) *quality* – "be truthful, and have evidence for what you say"; (2) *quantity* – "be succinct, and yet complete"; (3) *relation* – "be relevant to the topic as presented"; and (4) *manner* – "be clear and orderly" (Hesse, 2008, p. 557). Because the AAI is a semistructured interview, the speaker can free associate to the questions in his/her own conversational style, thereby revealing cognitive and emotional processes about attachment-related experiences. Adults are classified as secure-autonomous if they can discuss their histories in an organized, coherent manner – demonstrating Grice's four maxims, as well as attentional flexibility.

Other attachment classifications are determined, in part, by the manner and degree to which a speaker violates Grice's maxims when discussing attachment-related experiences (Main et al., 2008). Violation of the maxim of quality is evident when a speaker gives contradictory, inconsistent information, while violation of quantity is evidenced by a failure to recall any biographical information. Both of these violations are common among speakers who are dismissive of attachment. Speakers who are preoccupied with their attachment experiences, on the other hand, often speak with entangled, vague, jargon-filled language – a violation of the maxim of manner. Or they become tangential in their conversations and speak about present-day experiences when asked about the past – a violation of the maxim of relation. In other words, the less a person shows the capacity to discuss attachment-related experiences in an organized, coherent manner, the more the speaker demonstrates a state of mind that has attentional inflexibility and defensive organization in terms of attachment. At the extreme are speakers who violate Grice's maxims when asked about loss or trauma. These speakers show lapses in reasoning or in monitoring their conversations, such as when an individual speaks of a dead person as if that person were still alive. Speakers with these characteristics are classified as disorganized and unresolved with respect to trauma or loss (Hesse, 2008; George et al., 1996).

Overall, the main goal of the AAI analysis is to determine how coherent, collaborative, and reflective the speaker is, rather than to judge the actual details of the speaker's past (George et al., 1996). Individuals classified as secure-autonomous are speakers who are comfortable and at ease in their conversation about attachments, who speak with freshness and spontaneity, thoughtfulness and flexibility. They are able to monitor their thinking and revise their stories when new memories come to mind, but their narratives hold together in a logical manner. Without defensiveness, they give examples from childhood that make assessments of their life stories seem both honest and believable. This is in contrast to a transcript organized in an incoherent, contradictory manner, where the words used to describe parental relationships fail to match the experiences. For example, when a person says his mother was "loving" and "fun," yet he can recall no memories of experiences to support this idealized description, the transcript is more likely to be classified as dismissing of attachment, not secure-autonomous.

Highlights of AAI Research

Though there is growing appreciation of the value of the AAI as a clinical tool, it is foremost a research measure. Since the 1980s, rigorous psychometric tests have established the stability and discriminate validity of the AAI, and robust findings have been well replicated in dozens of studies in different population samples around the world (Hesse, 2008). This strong body of research has enabled a meta-analysis to delineate the distribution of AAI classifications across genders and populations. A 1993 meta-analysis by Bakermans-Kranenburg and van IJzendoorn found that 58% of the populations to date had been classified as autonomous-secure, 24% were dismissing, and 18% were preoccupied. Persons who received unresolved classifications on the AAI (19%) were given one of the other three major classifications. In this meta-analysis, 11% of the autonomous groups were classified as unresolved, while 26% of the dismissing groups and 40% of the preoccupied groups were unresolved as well. Significantly, there were no gender differences in the classifications of this study. Additional meta-analyses and individual studies using the AAI have produced noteworthy findings that have both supported and expanded the original theory of attachment. The following highlights some of the findings of particular interest to clinicians, and for a detailed summary of AAI research, see Cassidy and Shaver (2008) or Mikulincer and Shaver (2007).

Studies of Parent–Child Relationships

The original study using the AAI examined the association between parental responses on the AAI and the responses of the children of these parents on Ainsworth's Strange Situation five years previously. In this sample of 67 randomly selected dyads (32 mother–infants; 35 father–infants), findings suggested a "remarkable degree of overlap" (Main et al., 2008, p. 32) between parental responses and the infant attachment patterns. Parents who scored secure on the AAI typically had children who responded to that same parent in a secure manner in the brief separation and reunion portions of the procedure. Likewise, correspondence existed between insecure parents and insecure infants. There are numerous meta-analytic tests of studies based on this research design, such as van IJzendoorn's (1995) overview of 18 similar studies (854 parent–infant pairs in six countries), which found a two-way correspondence between secure parents and secure infants in 75% of the cases. Further studies have validated an association between unresolved/disorganized or cannot classify parental AAI interviews and disorganized/disoriented infant patterns on the Strange Situation (Main & Solomon, 1986). This vast and well-documented body of research underscores the important role of parental caregiving and supports the theory that children generally internalize the relational patterns of their primary caregivers, a basic tenet of Bowlby and Ainsworth. The findings serve to validate one of Bowlby's theories that attachments are generally transgenerational.

Longitudinal Studies

A number of longitudinal studies have been conducted in the USA, linking individual infant–adult attachment patterns, rather than infants and their parents. Some of these studies began with adults and compared their AAI scores with their Strange Situation scores obtained as infants (Hesse, 2008). Other studies have followed individuals prospectively from infancy into adulthood (see Grossmann, Grossmann, & Waters, 2005, for an overview of the major longitudinal studies on attachment). The Minnesota Study of Risk and Adaptation from Birth to Adulthood was the first prospective longitudinal study of attachment, beginning in 1975 and currently in its 33rd year (Institute of Child Development, 2009). In the third trimester of pregnancy, 267 first-time urban mothers were recruited for this study, and mothers and infants were tested before and after the child's birth, enabling an evaluation of the antecedents of attachment (Sroufe, 2005; Sroufe, Egeland, Carlson, & Collins, 2005). Based on a transactional model of development, the infants received a comprehensive assessment of their physical, cognitive, emotional, and social development, including the Strange Situation procedure at 12 and 18 months. The AAI was conducted when these individuals were 19 and 26, and at age 20, they received the Current Relationships Interview (CRI; Crowell & Owens, 1996), a measure that parallels the AAI, but asks about current relationships with partners. Significance existed between the Strange Situation at 18 months and the AAI at 26 years in terms of secure and insecure attachment ($p=0.012$), but there was not predictability to the specific organized categories (e.g., dismissing to avoidant or preoccupied to resistant). Of the secure infants, 53.2% were more likely to be autonomous at age 26, while only 35.1% of avoidant or resistant infants were likely to be autonomous 26-year olds. Disorganized infant attachments were strongly related to the AAI nonautonomous-unresolved attachments of the 26-year olds ($p<0.001$) (Sroufe et al., 2005, p. 298).

The salient findings of this exhaustive study shed light on questions about how adult attachment develops. The study supports Bowlby's view that early attachment relationships are "initiating conditions, launching individuals on pathways that are only probabilistically related to outcomes" (Sroufe, 2005, p. 362). Early attachments alone cannot account for adult development because development is nonlinear, complex, cumulative, and shaped by multiple influences other than early attachments. Yet these findings support Bowlby's theory that early development is not erased following change or distress, and individuals often return to their developmental trajectories. For example, early attachment security can establish a foundational structure that facilitates or mediates adjustment to life change and frustrations along the way. Sroufe concludes that early attachment is "an organizing core in development that is always integrated with later experience and never lost" (p. 365).

Studies Comparing Clinical and Nonclinical Populations

Reportedly, over 9,000 individuals have now participated in the AAI since it was created, thereby enabling more sophisticated meta-analyses and "a more grounded association between attachment representation and clinical disorders" (van IJzendoorn & Bakermans-Kranenburg, 2008, p. 70). To date, most AAI research has been conducted on nonclinical groups, and meta-analysis of studies of clinical groups provides insufficient evidence to document direct associations between specific clinical disorders and specific types of attachment. However, it is possible to say that there is "an overwhelming overrepresentation of insecure and unresolved attachments in clinical samples" (p. 70).

In their recent overview of clinical versus nonclinical studies, van IJzendoorn and Bakermans-Kranenburg (2008) covered data from 28 nonclinical samples, 61 clinical samples, and 16 adolescent samples, for a total of 4,200 participants who had completed the AAI. Their narrative review and quantitative meta-analysis of these samples suggested that people with internalizing clinical disorders, such as borderline personality disorder (BPD), were more likely to show preoccupied or unresolved attachments on the AAI, while those with externalizing disorders, such as antisocial personality disorder, were more likely to be dismissing or preoccupied. They noted that individual studies suggest that unresolved/disorganized attachments may play a role in the development of posttraumatic stress disorder or other dissociative disorders, and this category of attachment may place adults at risk for psychopathology in general. The van IJzendoorn and Bakermans-Kranenburg overview also revealed the existence of persons with secure attachment representations "even in the most psychiatrically disturbed groups of criminal offenders in maximum security hospitals" (p. 91). These researchers conclude that such "counterintuitive and intriguing cases" may point to "unexpected resilience or to unanticipated problems in the application of the AAI to (some) clinical populations" (p. 91). This overview cautions about overstating the association between specific disorders and specific attachment categories, and it emphasizes the need for additional attachment research on clinical groups.

Studies of Attachment-Based Interventions

The AAI is frequently used as a pre- and postmeasure to evaluate the outcome of attachment-based clinical intervention studies with adults, and it is incorporated into the treatment process of some treatment models (see Steele & Steele, 2008a, for expanded discussions of clinical interventions using the AAI). The following are brief summaries of three of the numerous intervention studies in which the AAI has been used:

1. Attachment and Biobehavioral Catch-up (ABC) program (Bick & Dozier, 2008) – an intervention program for 200 foster parents who were administered the AAI as a pretest; the measure then was used to guide the intervention process. Bick and Dozier conclude that "understanding of a foster mother's state of mind is a key to helping her provide nurturing, responsive care," and "the AAI is a necessary step in establishing rapport with the client" (p. 468).

2. Transference-focused psychotherapy for BPD (Diamond, Yeomans, Clarkin, Levy, & Kernberg, 2008; Levy et al., 2006) – a study of 90 patients diagnosed with BPD

in which three models of psychotherapy (transference-focused therapy, dialectical-behavioral therapy, and supportive therapy) were administered to separate groups to test the effectiveness of the interventions. The AAI was used as a pre- and post measure for all participants, and significant changes in the coherence of the transcripts were evident for those who experienced the transference-focused relational treatment. Diamond et al. (2008) state that knowledge of the AAI and the scoring system "may help the clinician in practice to listen for multiple, conflictual, and contradictory attachment states of mind, including fleeting secure states that may emerge from an exploration of the patient's history and from here-and-now interactions with the therapist" (p. 289).

3. Phase-based treatment for PTSD related to childhood abuse (Cloitre, Koenen, Cohen, & Han, 2002; Stovall-McClough, Cloitre, & McClough, 2008) – a sample of 150 women with childhood histories of physical, sexual, and emotional abuse who have been followed for 7 years and received phase-based treatment; patients were administered the AAI in pretreatment and 3-month posttreatment. Stovall-McClough et al. (2008) state that the AAI provided "valuable information regarding early family and abuse history that could not otherwise have been gathered during the evaluation" (p. 336), and the "AAI classifications helped clinicians to be better prepared for treatment" because they were able to understand "patients' strategies and deficits in emotional regulation and interpersonal relatedness" (p. 337).

Newer Empirical Studies

In addition to the studies mentioned above, the AAI has been applied to dozens of new populations over the past decade. Hesse (2008) reports that the measure has been used to understand attachment processes of adult holocaust survivors and their daughters, religious and spiritual groups, fraternal and identical twins, adoptive and foster parent–child dyads, daughters of parents with dementia, and blind or deaf individuals. In addition, the AAI is being used to examine the phenomenon of *earned security*, a classification of security given to individuals despite childhoods with unloving parents. Along with the self-report attachment measures, the AAI also is being used to study peer and couple relationships.

Usefulness of AAI in Clinical Work

Using the AAI for research purposes requires extensive specialized training and certification in administering the interview and coding the responses, and it is one of the most complex, time-consuming instruments used in developmental and clinical research. However, there is growing awareness of the interview's value as a clinical tool for assessing clients and understanding therapeutic and professional relationships. Clinicians not certified as AAI coders may still find that the questions enrich their work, particularly in the initial stages of therapy, and may use the instrument under supervision. Steele and Steele (2008b) recently proposed ten clinical uses of the AAI, suggesting how clinicians familiar with the interview questions and coding categories may incorporate this information into their work with clients. For example, such knowledge can facilitate the development of a therapeutic alliance because clinicians become attuned to the client's relational style, history of traumatic experiences and losses, and ways of defending against emotional wounds. The questions expose "the gravitational pull from early relationship patterns on an adult's mind and behavior" (Steele & Steele, p. 20) and help the therapist "identify the angel in the nursery" (p. 22). That is, the therapist may hear about how the client was rescued from an otherwise bleak early childhood, as well as the individuals who caused the client great distress.

Steele and Steele (2008b) further note that the AAI can provide a "reliable observation of reflective functioning" (p. 23) that can be useful to the clinician in setting the goals of therapy and gauging the treatment process. The AAI has long focused on how speakers monitor and then correct their speech in conversation – a process called *metacognitive monitoring* – and there is a *state-of-mind metacognition scale* used to analyze evidence of this process in the transcript (Hesse, 2008). Metacognitive monitoring, also known as *reflective functioning*, is considered central to coherent AAI narratives (Jacobvitz, 2008). Reflective functioning is the research terminology for *mentalization* – defined as the ability to imagine and reflect on the mental states of other people, as well as oneself, and a capacity to see how behavior and mental states mutually influence each other (Fonagy, Gergely, & Target, 2008). Awareness of the AAI assessments of reflective functioning may increase the clinician's attunement to the client's mentalization in the therapy process.

The concept of mentalization has drawn much clinical attention in recent years, particularly due to the work of Fonagy (Fonagy, Gergely, Jurist, & Target, 2002; Fonagy et al., 2008). Demonstrating his awareness of the clinical usefulness of the AAI, Fonagy eventually created a mentalization-based treatment model, developed out of his own AAI research on the reflective functioning of parents, and he has created a reflective-functioning scale. His treatment model, inspired by merging attachment research and psychoanalytic theory, is currently being used with diverse populations, especially in the treatment of persons with severe personality disorders (see Fewell, Chap. 7). Mentalization-based treatment also is being used with parents to increase their reflective functioning and awareness of their children's cognitive and emotional processes (Slade, 2008). Research suggests that as parents increase their mentalization, this "becomes a more powerful predictor of attachment security" in their children "than…global sensitivity" (Fonagy et al., 2008, p. 795).

Although social workers, increasingly, are receiving AAI training, incorporating the concepts into their work and asking their clients the AAI questions in psychotherapy, the tool has been used by few, if any, social work researchers to date. At this time, most attachment research with the AAI is taking place in affiliation with psychology labs of large research universities. The significant time involved in being trained to administer the AAI and then certified as a coder decreases the feasibility of using the instrument in nonfunded, time-limited research and dissertation studies. Self-report measures of attachment, on the other hand, are accessible to most researchers. The line of research based on self-report measures also offers a wealth of information about the social and cognitive processes of adult attachment.

Self-Report and Observational Measures of Adult Attachment

As mentioned above, self-report measures of adult attachment patterns were first developed to identify the impact of internal working models of attachment on adult romantic relationships. Over time, a number of additional self-report measures have been designed for looking at attachment-related issues in adults, but not focused on adult attachment style as such. In addition, adult attachment research also has expanded to include behavioral assessments based on videotaped laboratory observations of adults who are given stressful tasks or exposed to situations, pictures, films, or conversations designed to evoke attachment and caregiving behaviors. The videotaped sessions are then scored by trained observers who rate them for hyperactivation or deactivation of the attachment system and, in the case of couples, for caregiving responses to a partner's attachment behaviors.

Self-Report Measures for General Adult Attachment

The self-report attachment measures not aimed at classifying attachment styles and patterns in adults nonetheless look at dimensions of attachment that are related to attachment style, such as anxiety (hyperactivation of the attachment system) and avoidance (deactivation of the attachment system). They are designed to access all types of adult attachment relationships such as parent–child relationships (older children and adolescents), peer attachments, and other nonromantic primary adult attachments, which might be to a friend, a gang, a neighbor, adult sibling, teacher, mentor, parent, grandparent, or even a religious person such as a priest, pastor, or cult leader. Thus, these measures offer a means to assess attachment dynamics in adolescents or young adults who have not yet experienced close attachment to a romantic figure, or single adults who are not in a romantic pair-bond attachment. These instruments help raise awareness about the importance of internal working models operating in the circle of close adult relationships that may also qualify as attachments in the absence of, or in addition to, a romantic partner.

Examples of these more general attachment instruments are the Attachment History Questionnaire or AHQ, first copyrighted in 1982 by Pottharst and Kessler (see Pottharst, 1990), which measures adult memories of attachment experiences in childhood. The focus of this scale is on family history, including traumatic separations and losses, family support, and discipline. The 51 scaled items, plus a number of open-ended questions, yield four factors: *security and insecurity*, *parental discipline*, *threats of separation*, and *support from peers*. Mikulincer and Shaver (2007) believe that this promising scale has been underutilized and underdeveloped. Since attachment history is at the core of what is covered in typical psychosocial history-taking, and the attachment traumas, wounds, and issues are the usual focus of clinical treatment, the AHQ has direct clinical relevance as well as promise for further research.

A second self-report instrument, the Inventory of Parent and Peer Attachment or the IPPA (Armsden & Greenberg, 1987) aims to assess adolescent attachment to both parents and close friends. Crowell, Fraley, and Shaver (2008) point out that on the IPPA, "security with respect to parents and security with respect to peers correlate only about .30, indicating that adolescents relate differently to different kinds of close relationship partners…" (p. 612), including their peers. Armsden and Greenberg (1987) also used the IPPA to look at the relationship between secure peer and parental attachment ratings and self-esteem, life satisfaction, and coping strategies, finding security positively related to each of these variables. Holtzen, Kenny, and Mahalik (1995) used the IPPA to study a small group of young homosexual adults, finding that those who were secure in their relationship to their parents were more likely to have openly shared their sexual preference with their parents.

Behavioral Assessments

Rholes, Simpson, and Stevens (1998) are prominent among the researchers who have creatively used behavioral observation to measure the arousal and communication of attachment behaviors, as well as caregiving support in couples. In one study, for example, they looked at couples who had been dating for 18 months. Following the female's exposure to a threatened stressful stimulus, the couple was reunited and videotaped for 5 min before the threat was withdrawn. Trained observers rated the activation of the female partner's attachment system by her use of anxiety-related adjectives and the extent to which she expressed her feelings and reached out to her partner for support. The male member of the couple was rated for caregiving support based on his use of adjectives that point to reassurance and emotional support for his partner or for indications that he tried to avoid, downplay, or calm her anxiety. This behavioral assessment was then linked to previously administered self-report measures that focused on attachment styles and patterns, with avoidance being linked to less expression of anxiety by women and less supportive communication and behavior by males.

Crowell et al. (2002) also use behavioral assessment in couples' research, creating the Secure Base Scoring System (SBSS) for rating *secure-base use* by a stressed partner and *secure-base support* in the second partner. When a stressor or issue of concern is introduced, the secure-base use is scored from high to low quality on four subscales: clarity, maintenance, approach, and ability to be comforted. Secure-base support in the partner receiving the attachment signals is similarly rated high or low quality in terms of interest, recognition, interpretation, and responsiveness. As might be expected, the quality of the attachment arousal and the quality of the caregiving support are often highly correlated. The secure-base use and support subscales offer helpful ways of conceptualizing assessment and intervention in couple and family therapy and casework. For example, one intervention might be an educational approach used to point out to the couple similar low quality ways of asking for and offering support, or dissimilar low quality asking for support versus high quality offering of it.

Self-Report Measures of Attachment Style

Mikulincer and Shaver's (2007) book, *Attachment in Adulthood*, is an invaluable resource on self-report as well as narrative adult attachment research. Here the authors present meta-analyses of close to 1,800 studies arranged by theme, topic, and research instrument in order to demonstrate, compare, and contrast findings. For example, Table 10.6, "A summary of findings on attachment orientations and satisfaction in marital relationships" (p. 309), compares 57 studies going back to 1991, using a variety of instruments. Table 13.3, "A summary of findings on attachment orientations and depression in nonclinical samples" (pp. 380–381), compares 102 studies in subgroupings according to the type of attachment assessment used in the research. Though Mikulincer and Shaver are in the forefront of the use and development of self-report attachment research, their decision to include the AAI studies in the meta-analyses makes it possible to look for consistencies and inconsistencies in findings between studies using self-report or narrative instruments, as well as between different self-report instruments. They organize the meta-analyses into the following categories: mental representations of self and others, emotion regulation, self-regulation and personal growth, interpersonal regulation, caregiving, and sex. In addition, they also analyze the growing body of research linking attachment style and psychopathology, psychotherapy, and group and organizational functioning.

As noted earlier in the chapter, the majority of the self-report attachment style questionnaires, including the Adult Attachment Questionnaire or AAQ (Simpson, Rholes, & Phillips, 1996), the Relationship Style Questionnaire or RSQ (Griffin & Bartholomew, 1994), the Attachment Style Questionnaire or ASQ (Feeney, Noller, & Hanrahan, 1994), the Experiences in Close Relationships Scale or ECR (Brennan, Clark, & Shaver, 1998), and the Experiences in Close Relationships Scale, Revised (ECR-R; Fraley, Waller, & Brennan, 2000) were primarily developed for studying adult romantic relationships, which is reflected in the large number of studies that focus on dating couples and committed life-partners. However, as studies of child development and attachment have broadened to look at the impact of attachment style on all aspects of social, emotional, academic, and relationship functioning, interest has grown in doing the same with adults, including the impact of attachment style on a variety of other life experiences and levels of functioning. The ASQ, for example, deemphasizes romantic relationships, while with the ECR wording of individual items can be altered slightly to gear it to either one romantic partner, romantic relationships generally, or to various other kinds of close adult relationships.

At a recent Smith College School for Social Work Master's Thesis poster session, one of the authors (Nelson) noted that the ECR and ECR-R were used by a large number of students for looking at a wide variety of social and psychotherapeutic questions. Several of the students commented that the instrument worked well for their purposes because it is readily available and relatively easy to administer and score using a Web-based research program such as SurveyMonkey.com. These scales also have been translated into several languages.

The bodies of adult attachment research findings based on self-report instruments – and to some degree on the AAI as well – begin to fall into place logically once the principles of the attachment system and adult attachment styles are understood. These findings rest in particular on the distinctions between the primary attachment strategy of the securely attached and the secondary attachment strategies of the insecurely attached. The primary attachment strategy is to turn to available, reliable caregivers as a safe haven in times of distress and as a secure base for exploration, play, and pleasure when there is no distress. By contrast, the secondary or fall-back strategies of individuals who are preoccupied or anxious/ambivalent with respect to attachment are either to *hyperactivate* the attachment system (anxious/ambivalent or preoccupied) in an attempt to engage inconsistently available or overly aroused caregivers; or, in the case of those with dismissive or avoidant attachment patterns, to *deactivate* the attachment system in response to caregivers who are unavailable or unreliable. For a clinician, mastery of attachment style basics means that it becomes second nature to use them in hypothesizing about assessments, treatment interventions, and treatment plans. A short description of some of the findings from adult attachment research sampled below will illustrate their breadth as well as their theoretical and clinical usefulness.

Attachment Style and Self-Image

Self-esteem revolves around an individual's sense of being lovable, competent, and special. It makes sense that these qualities are established early in life in response to caregivers. Children who experience loving looks, soothing voices, caring ministrations, and playful interactions with their caregivers not only learn to respond in kind but also form an internal working model of themselves as worthy and capable in human relationships and in the world at large. As Mikulincer and Shaver (2007) write, people "treat themselves the way attachment figures treated them" (p. 153). They compiled more than 60 studies that examine the association between attachment style and self-esteem and found "without exception that attachment security is associated with higher self-esteem" (p. 155). Those with anxious/ambivalent or fearful attachments were found to suffer from lower self-esteem than those with secure attachment. For adults with dismissive, avoidant attachment, however, no specific self-esteem issues were detected in self-report measures, which fits with the avoidant-dismissive strategy of defending against vulnerability or distress, often layering it over with a narcissistic presentation and externalizing difficulties through projection. According to attachment theory, as well as other dynamic theories, dismissive or avoidant individuals do indeed suffer from low self-esteem, which may break through under certain kinds of attachment and other life stressors.

Attachment and Support-Seeking, Coping with Stress, and Affect Regulation

As neurobiological research has so convincingly demonstrated (see Schore & Schore, Chap. 4), affect regulation forms the core of the early attachment relationship between infant and caregiver. By the time adulthood is reached, the strategies of affect regulation internalized in the context of the earliest attachment experiences have coalesced into patterns that are reflected in attachment categories and styles. Securely attached people are able to soothe themselves effectively and, at times, comfortably turn to others for help with regulation. The metacognitive monitoring that is associated with secure autonomous states of mind in respect to attachment on the AAI provides one important manifestation of the means by which negative arousal or overstimulation can be observed, reframed, and coped with effectively. Individuals whose styles fit more with anxious or fearful patterns with their hyper-activated attachment systems and hypervigilance for distressing stimuli, would be expected to have a great deal of difficulty with self-soothing. Though they turn readily and willingly to others for help with negative arousal, their early experiences make such interactive soothing and regulation ineffective, inadequate, or difficult. People who have dismissing or avoidant styles, on the other hand, deactivate their attachment systems and are compulsively self-reliant, showing little inclination to turn to others for help in regulating their affect.

The above theoretical generalizations and clinical observations are well borne out in a large body of adult attachment research looking at support seeking, coping with stress, and management of emotional states by attachment style (Mikulincer & Shaver, 2007). For example, one study looked at affect-regulation strategies of former Israeli prisoners-of-war and found that securely attached, in contrast to insecurely attached, ex-POW's reported having drawn upon positive memories or imaginary positive encounters with loved ones as a way of regulating distress during their captivity (Solomon, Ginzburg, Mikulincer, Neria, & Ohry, 1998). Another study looking at coping strategies in relationship to attachment style found that those with dismissing or avoidant attachment coped with stressors by using denial, diverting attention, disengaging, or distracting themselves, strategies which have been labeled *distancing strategies* (Mikulincer & Shaver, 2007). In dealing with extremely stressful, chronic situations, however, distancing dismissive-avoidant strategies may fail, leading to high levels of negative arousal and distress. One example would be the reaction of some parents whose children have a life-threatening or chronic medical condition, such as a severe coronary heart defect (Berant, Mikulincer & Florian, 2001; Berant, Mikulincer, & Shaver, 2008.) In another study, diabetics scoring higher on avoidance used cognitive distancing and passive resignation to cope with their condition (Turan, Osar, Turan, Ilkova, & Damci, 2003). These coping strategies were associated with poor compliance with treatment plans.

Attachment and Romantic Partnerships

Intimacy, commitment, communication, conflict management, and satisfaction with the relationship are key elements in couple relationships that have been shown to be positively associated with secure attachment (Mikulincer & Shaver, 2007). For example, a classic couple issue, intimacy, focuses on the struggle to balance autonomy and closeness. In two studies, securely attached people made remarks in conversation that affirmed the importance of establishing this balance, while dismissive/ avoidant partners emphasized the need for independence and anxious/ambivalent partners stressed the need for closeness (Feeney, 1999b; Feeney & Noller, 1991). In looking at the difficulties couples have with managing their different desires for, and tolerance of, distance and closeness, there were more problems found in relationships when the male partner was dismissive/avoidant and the female partner was anxious/ambivalent.

Commitment to relationships is a key ingredient for couples, not only at the beginning, but throughout their history. The fact that adults must make a conscious and ongoing decision to stay together is a fact of adult romantic attachment that distinguishes it from parent–child attachment. As might be expected, securely attached people stand out in their willingness and ability to make and sustain commitments to a partner, whereas insecurely attached individuals demonstrate lower levels of commitment. This was found to be the case in almost all of the 20 studies analyzed by Mikulincer and Shaver (see Table 10.3), with the few outstanding exceptions occurring when the AAI, which focuses on parent–child attachment experiences rather than adult attachment exclusively, was used as one of the measures (Treboux, Crowell, & Waters, 2004).

Studies that distinguish between avoidant and anxious/ambivalent participants found that they differed significantly in their views and behavior relative to commitment. For example, anxious/ambivalent men obtained marriage licenses after 19 months of courtship, while for avoidant men, it was 46 months (Snechak & Leonard, 1992). Though both anxious/ambivalent and dismissive/avoidant partners report lower levels of commitment to relationships, differences in the source of commitment issues may stem from attachment style (Pistole, Clark, & Tubbs, 1995). The anxious/ambivalent partner's view that the relationship is unsatisfactory, inadequate, and disappointing likely may stem from their overwhelming need for an ultimately unattainable level of commitment and caregiving in an adult relationship. The lack of commitment associated with an avoidant person, on the other hand, comes more from a straightforward unwillingness or inability to commit for the long term.

Similarly, differences may be found in types of communication difficulties reported by couples with insecure attachment styles. Avoidant partners reported higher levels of emotional control (Feeney, 1995, 1999a) and, in a video-taped study, showed less affectionate nonverbal behaviors such as gaze, facial expression, tone of voice, interest, and attentiveness (Guerrero, 1996). Anxious/ambivalent partners were found in the Feeney (1999a) study to have a subjective sense of suppressing their emotional communication, based on disappointment with the lack of sufficient caregiving responses or perhaps in reaction to having been criticized.

Conflict management, while a challenge for every couple, is particularly difficult for insecure people in dating relationships, marriages, and long-term partnerships. The conflict management difficulties of the insecurely attached, as reported in a large number of studies using a variety of instruments (Mikulincer & Shaver, 2007, see Table 10.4), have to do with the their inability to express respect, caring, and empathy during the conflict, which securely attached couples are generally more able to do. One study of couples directly engaged in conflict, for example, found that less secure partners of both genders were more likely to display facial expressions conveying rejection (Kobak & Hazan, 1991). Conflict resolution is also impaired because of difficulties of the insecurely attached with compromise, and the increased incidence of destructive communication patterns such as withdrawal, coercion, verbal aggression, and expressions of rejection that have also been noted. In the studies of couple communication based on the AAI, similar relationships have been found between insecurity and destructive communication patterns in about ten studies, which Mikulincer and Shaver (2007) postulate may speak to the fact that the AAI is based on an interview, itself an interactive and communicative process. Of interest also is that the primary differences in findings relating to conflict management are based on the insecure-secure dimension alone rather than reflecting one particular type of insecure attachment. However, a study by Paley, Cox, Burchinal, and Payne (1999) noted that anxious/ambivalent women expressed less positive affect during conflict than secure women, whereas dismissive/avoidant women tended to withdraw.

While relationship satisfaction may be defined in a variety of ways, the general understanding is that it has to do with a sense of having one's needs met, which in attachment terms translates to having a reliable, available person to turn to in times of emotional distress (safe haven) and a person to provide effective support and encouragement for engagement with the outside world (secure base). Of the large number of studies (97 total in dating and marriage relationships) in their meta-analysis of research on this topic, Mikulincer and Shaver (2007; see Tables 10.5 and 10.6) found overwhelming evidence that relationship satisfaction in both heterosexual and homosexual couples is associated with secure attachment and dissatisfaction with insecure. However, five of the seven AAI-based studies showed exceptions to this general trend, which may be, as noted above, because the AAI focuses on parent–child attachment experiences rather than adult attachment exclusively.

Attachment, Group, and Organizational Functioning

The growing body of research on the relationship between individual attachment style and group or organizational functioning includes studies of group membership and leadership and the relationship between leaders and followers (see Page, Chap. 10). While clearly many group leaders are in a role analogous to the parent–child relationship with their soothing, guiding, and caregiving functions, groups themselves can also serve as symbolic attachment figures. Proximity to groups can be seen as providing a safe haven of soothing and security in times of distress, as well as a secure base for arousing and regulating positive affect and supporting exploration and growth. Based on this assumption, Smith, Murphy, and Coats (1999) constructed a self-report scale to look at attachment anxiety or avoidance with respect to groups. Closely modeled on the ECR items for adult anxiety and avoidance, anxiety with respect to group attachment is reflected in items such as "I often worry my group(s) will not always want me as a member," and avoidant group attachment is reflected in response to the item "Often my group(s) want me to be more open about my thoughts and feelings than I feel comfortable being" (as cited in Mikulincer & Shaver, 2007, p. 435). Higher scores on anxiety or avoidant attachment predicted lower engagement in group activities, more negative evaluations of social groups, and lower perceived support from groups. Higher attachment anxiety was also associated with stronger negative feelings toward the group, whereas higher avoidant attachment was associated with lower positive feelings about the group. In the case of membership in sororities and fraternities, more of the avoidant members reported thinking of dropping their membership.

Attachment and Psychopathology

While secure attachment may support a wide array of mental health, social, and occupational functioning, and affect regulation benefits, it is not necessarily indicative of the absence of psychiatric diagnoses or mental health issues, nor is insecure attachment equivalent to the presence of such a diagnosis. The more than 100 studies looking at the associations between adult attachment and depression and anxiety in nonclinical samples have consistently found, however, that secure attachment to parents or peers is related to lower levels of depression and anxiety (see Mikulincer & Shaver, 2007, Table 13.3). As might be predicted, anxious/ambivalent states of mind relative to attachment are positively associated with these symptoms. The findings relative to avoidant or dismissive attachment are less definitive, but about half of the studies found depression and anxiety higher in this group than in those with secure attachment (Mikulincer & Shaver). In clinical and high-risk samples, insecure attachment has also been associated with more severe symptoms of depression (Mikulincer & Shaver).

Two prominent symptoms of BPD are moderate to severe impairment in interpersonal relationships and the inability to regulate negative affect. Both of these features would seem to suggest a strong link to early attachment experiences and hence attachment style. In a number of self-report studies, anxious/ambivalent attachment was found in a significant number of patients diagnosed with personality disorders (van IJzendoorn & Bakermans-Kranenburg, 1997). Other studies have pointed to an association between anxiety and avoidance and personality disorders (Mikulincer & Shaver, 2007). As noted earlier in this chapter, however, findings from van IJzendoorn and Bakermans-Kranenburg's (2008) meta-analysis comparing clinical and nonclinical populations suggest the importance of not overstating a direct link between attachment categories or styles and mental disorders, despite the findings of individual studies.

Attachment and Psychotherapy

As clinical social workers and other psychotherapists become familiar with adult attachment theory and research, the question inevitably arises about the role attachment styles and states of mind play in the therapeutic relationship and the therapeutic process. While the clinical applications of attachment theory are relevant and accessible to psychotherapy, to date there has only been a smattering of research in this area. In terms of the question about the therapeutic attachment bond between patient and client, research has pointed to aspects of the therapeutic relationship that are consistent with an attachment bond. In terms of the provision of a safe haven, Geller and Farber (1993) found that clients turn to therapists in times of emotional distress, and Rosenzweig, Farber, and Geller (1996) found that such thoughts produce feelings of security or comfort. It is well-known clinically that separations from the therapist, even temporary ones, can be painful and lead to protest or despair. This observation has been established by Barchat (1989), independent of whether the clients were secure or anxious/ambivalent in their attachment patterns. In addition, Parish and Eagle (2003) found that the therapist was a secure base and that the tendency to experience the therapist as such was associated in a positive direction with both the duration and the frequency of the therapy.

General and Specific Attachment

Much of adult attachment research is based on the suggestions of Bowlby (1988) and Ainsworth (1989) that working models of attachment formed in childhood influence the quality of one's close relationships throughout the lifespan. Longitudinal developmental research on the quality and continuity of attachment now validates this basic tenet. Fraley (2002) concluded, based on a meta-analysis of longitudinal data from infancy to early adulthood, that "there is an enduring tendency for people to remain relatively close to their original roots" (p. 142), despite some variation over time in relation to specific attachment figures. Changes in attachment patterns have been assumed to be related to changes in the quality of parent–child interactions – for better or worse – with the possibility that similar changes could occur throughout the lifespan, as in couple relationships, mentoring relationships, or with psychotherapy.

Debate has, however, emerged as to whether adult attachments are best conceptualized in terms of a general attachment style (global interpersonal style) established early in life and pertaining to all of a person's close relationships throughout life, or in terms of specific styles that may vary across an adult's close relationships. Research suggests that there is value and relevance in both approaches and there is evidence that there is an association between the two. Klohnen, Weller, Luo, and Choe (2005) found that attachment to best friends and romantic partners made strong and independent contributions to prediction of general attachment style in adults. Fraley (2002) noted in his meta-analysis that "in adulthood, there is some degree of overlap between attachment security in the romantic and parental domains" (p. 141).

Bennett, Mohr, BrintzenhofeSzoc, and Saks (2008) adapted Fraley's (2005) Relationship Structures Questionnaire, a 10-item instrument designed to assess attachment patterns in relation to a specific person (e.g., parent, best friend, romantic partner), to look at the attachment features in the relationship between social work students and their field work supervisors. They found that the students' supervision-specific attachment styles may be associated with their general attachment styles, though, in some instances, supervision-specific attachment may be more influenced by factors unique to the particular supervisory relationship. This suggests that while a student may be secure in his or her general attachment style (i.e., generally comfortable with intimacy and closeness), he or she may develop an avoidant attachment style with regard to a particular fieldwork supervisor (see Bennett & Deal, Chap. 13).

Some research has suggested that *general attachment* style is most strongly related to dimensions of overall well being, whereas *relationship-specific attachment* is most strongly related to a particular relationship (Cozzarelli, Hoekstra, & Bylsma, 2000; Creasey & Ladd, 2005; Klohnen et al., 2005). Cozzarelli et al. suggest that relationship-specific measures of attachment, rather than general measures of attachment style, be used in instances where the focus is on a particular relationship, and Klohnen et al. found relationship-specific attachment representations to be substantially better predictors of relationship outcomes than general attachment models.

Conclusion

In comparing and contrasting the AAI narrative analysis of attachment categories with the various self-report instruments that measure for dimensions of attachment, a number of issues arise which require clarification. For example, the AAI is a highly refined interview process that requires much advanced training to administer. It is essentially a research tool that leads to distinguishing adult states of mind relative to attachment, based on early childhood relationships. In contrast, the self-report measures are easily administered and scored, making them more accessible for research when funding grants are not available to cover the cost of administering and coding the AAI. One difference that must be considered, however, is that the AAI does allow for the inclusion of unresolved/disorganized attachment, whereas the self-report measures on the four-sided grid do not have a category that captures this phenomenon in as reliable a manner. For social workers who are on the front lines of working with traumatized clients, this can be an important clinical and research distinction, as disorganization and its accompanying defense of dissociation may be highly represented in such populations. The AAI's discovery and inclusion of the earned secure category of adult attachment is also a concept that is important for clinicians and psychotherapists. To account for this phenomenon on the self-report measures, it is necessary to readminister the self-report instrument longitudinally to the same person in order to see if there has been a move from the insecure categories to the secure ones, a process that has been undertaken in recent research projects.

There also is controversy about what is gained and lost in conceptualizing attachment based on the AAI's categories of states of mind relative to attachment versus the self-report dimensions of attachment styles on the continuum measuring avoidance and anxiety. Seeing attachment styles on a continuum leaves room for appreciating individual differences within categories as well as the overlap that people may present clinically. AAI advocates, however, see more flexibility in detailed ratings by highly trained observers, who they assert are tuning in to the unconscious as well as the conscious aspects of working models of attachment. In their view, the AAI is the "gold standard" of attachment measures, while self-report measures only tap into conscious thinking about close adult relationships. The difference in findings between the two methodologies looking at similar research questions lends some support to this distinction.

For social workers, it is important to recognize that while there are large numbers of adult attachment studies that have been undertaken and reported to date, there are many gaps in the population groups that have been studied. As is so common with psychological research, much of the focus naturally lands on college student populations because of their ready accessibility for academic researchers. Because of that, the cross-cultural, high-risk, economically oppressed, and geriatric populations are underrepresented in the findings. Consequently, it is important for both researchers and clinicians to be clear about who has been measured, what is being measured, and how the instruments have been administered in order to meaningfully interpret and make use of the findings from the various studies. When preparing to do attachment research, much careful thought must go into the choice of appropriate instruments based on the hypotheses, age groups, goals, and variables in the research design. For clinicians who draw on methodologies and findings from both approaches in doing clinical assessments, planning treatment interventions, and understanding the attachment dynamics of clinical relationships with clients, the distinctions between instruments are less important than understanding the meaning of the theory behind them and how the findings relate to working models of adult attachment.

Study Questions

1. If you wanted to research the impact on older adults of losing friends, what type/types of instrument(s) might be most appropriate?
2. Think of a research question regarding adult attachment that is relevant to your current work or fieldwork setting and discuss the type/types of research instrument(s) that might be most appropriate.
3. List the three differences between the narrative (AAI) research instrument and self-report measures of adult attachment.
4. What are some clinically useful findings regarding adult romantic attachments?
5. List categories of adult attachment based on the AAI and describe each briefly. List the four attachment styles on the grid based on self-report studies and describe each briefly. Match the categories that overlap in the two classification systems.

References

Ainsworth, M. D. S. (1967). *Infancy in Uganda: Infant care and the growth of love*. Baltimore: Johns Hopkins University Press.

Ainsworth, M. D. S. (1989). Attachments beyond infancy. *American Psychologist, 44*, 709–716.

Ainsworth, M. D. S., Blehar, M., Waters, E., & Wall, S. (1978). *Patterns of attachment: Assessed in the Strange Situation and at home*. Hillsdale, NJ: Erlbaum.

Armsden, G. C., & Greenberg, M. T. (1987). The inventory of parent and peer attachment: Relationships to well-being in adolescence. *Journal of Youth and Adolescence, 16*, 427–454.

Bakermans-Kranenburg, M., & van IJzendoorn, M. (1993). A psychometric study of the Adult Attachment Interview: Reliability and discriminant validity. *Developmental Psychology, 29*, 1019–1040.

Barchat, D. (1989, June). *Representations and separations in therapy: The August phenomenon*. Paper presented at the meeting of the Society for Psychotherapy Research.

Bartholomew, K. (1990). Avoidance of intimacy: An attachment perspective. *Journal of Social and Personal Relationships, 7*, 147–178.

Bartholomew, K., & Horowitz, L. M. (1991). Attachment styles among young adults: A test of a four-category model. *Journal of Personality and Social Psychology, 61*, 226–244.

Bennett, S., Mohr, J., BrintzenhofeSzoc, K., & Saks, L. (2008). General and supervision-specific attachment styles: Relations to student perceptions of social work field supervisors. *Journal of Social Work Education, 42*(2), 75–94.

Berant, E., Mikulincer, M., & Florian, V. (2001). Attachment style and mental health: A 1-year follow-up study of mothers of infants with congenital heart disease. *Personality and Social Psychology Bulletin, 27*, 956–968.

Berant, E., Mikulincer, M., & Shaver, P. R. (2008). Mothers' attachment style, their mental health, and their children's emotional vulnerabilities: A 7-year study of children with congenital heart disease. *Journal of Personality, 76*(1), 31–66.

Bick, J., & Dozier, M. (2008). Helping foster parents change: The role of parental state of mind. In H. Steele & M. Steele (Eds.), *Clinical applications of the Adult Attachment Interview* (pp. 452–470). New York: Guilford.

Bowlby, J. (1969/1982). *Attachment and loss: Vol. 1. Attachment*. New York: Basic Books.

Bowlby, J. (1988). *A secure base*. New York: Basic Books.

Brennan, K. A., Clark, C. L., & Shaver, P. R. (1998). Self-report measurement of adult romantic attachment: An integrative overview. In J. A. Simpson & W. S. Rholes (Eds.), *Attachment theory and close relationships* (pp. 46–76). New York: Guilford.

Cassidy, J., & Shaver, P. (Eds.). (2008). *Handbook of attachment: Theory, research, and clinical applications* (2nd ed.). New York: Guilford.

Cloitre, M., Koenen, K., Cohen, L., & Han, H. (2002). Skills training in affective and interpersonal regulation followed by exposure: A phase-based treatment for PTSD related to childhood abuse. *Journal of Consulting and Clinical Psychology, 70*, 1067–1074.

Cozzarelli, C., Hoekstra, S., & Bylsma, W. (2000). General versus specific mental models of attachment: Are they associated with different outcomes? *Personality and Social Psychology Bulletin, 26*, 605–618.

Creasey, G., & Ladd, A. (2005). Generalized and specific attachment representations: Unique and interactive roles in predicting conflict behaviors in close relationships. *Personality and Social Psychology Bulletin, 31*, 1026–1038.

Crowell, J., Fraley, R. C., & Shaver, P. (2008). Measurement of individual differences in adolescent and adult attachment. In J. Cassidy & P. Shaver (Eds.), *Handbook of attachment: Theory, research, and clinical applications*. New York: Guilford.

Crowell, J., & Owens, G. (1996). *Current relationships interview*. Unpublished manuscript, State University of New York, Stony Brook.

Crowell, J., Reboux, D., Gao, Y., Fyffe, C., Pan, H., & Waters, E. (2002). Assessing secure base behavior in adulthood: Development of a measure, links to adult attachment representations, and relations to couples' communication and reports of relationships. *Developmental Psychology, 38*, 679–693.

Diamond, D., Yeomans, F., Clarkin, J., Levy, K., & Kernberg, O. (2008). The reciprocal impact of attachment and transference-focused psychotherapy with borderline patients. In H. Steele & M. Steele (Eds.), *Clinical applications of the Adult Attachment Interview* (pp. 270–294). New York: Guilford.

Feeney, J. A. (1995). Adult attachment and emotional control. *Personal Relationships, 2,* 143–159.

Feeney, J. A. (1999a). Adult attachment, emotional control, and marital satisfaction. *Personal Relationships, 6,* 169–185.

Feeney, J. A. (1999b). Issues of closeness and distance in dating relationships: Effects of sex and attachment style. *Journal of Social and Personal Relationships, 16,* 571–590.

Feeney, J. A., & Noller, P. (1991). Attachment style and verbal descriptions of romantic partners. *Journal of Social and Personal Relationships, 8,* 187–215.

Feeney, J. A., Noller, P., & Hanrahan, M. (1994). Assessing adult attachment. In M. B. Sperling & W. H. Berman (Eds.), *Attachment in adults: Clinical and developmental perspectives* (pp. 128–152). New York: Guilford.

Fonagy, P., Gergely, G., Jurist, E. L., & Target, M. (2002). *Affect regulation; mentalization; and the development of the self.* New York: Other Press.

Fonagy, P., Gergely, G., & Target, M. (2008). Psychoanalytic constructs and attachment theory and research. In J. Cassidy & P. Shaver (Eds.), *Handbook of attachment: Theory, research, and clinical applications* (2nd ed., pp. 783–810). New York: Guilford.

Fraley, C. (2005). Relationship Structures (RS) Questionnaire. Retrieved August 25, 2005 from *http://www.psych.uiuc.edu/~rcfraley/measures/relstructures.htm.*

Fraley, C. (2002). Attachment stability from infancy to adulthood: A meta-analysis and dynamic modeling of developmental mechanisms. *Personality and Social Psychology Review, 6,* 123–151.

Fraley, R. C., Waller, N. G., & Brennan, K. A. (2000). An item response theory analysis of self-report measures of adult attachment. *Journal of Personality and Social Psychology, 78,* 350–365.

Geller, J. D., & Farber, B. A. (1993). Factors influencing the process of internalization in psychotherapy. *Psychotherapy Research, 3,* 166–180.

George, C., Kaplan, N., & Main, M. (1984). *Adult Attachment Interview protocol.* Unpublished manuscript, University of California, Berkeley.

George, C., Kaplan, N., & Main, M. (1996). *Adult Attachment Interview protocol* (3rd ed.). Unpublished manuscript, University of California, Berkeley.

Grice, H. P. (1975). Logic and conversation. In P. Cole & J. L. Moran (Eds.), *Syntax and semantics: Vol. 3. Speech acts* (pp. 41–58). New York: Academic.

Grice, H. P. (1989). *Studies in the way of words.* Cambridge, MA: Harvard University Press.

Griffin, D. W., & Bartholomew, K. (1994). The metaphysics of measurement: The case of adult attachment. In K. Bartholomew & D. Perlman (Eds.), *Advances in personal relationships: Attachment processes in adulthood* (Vol. 5, pp. 17–52). London: Kingsley.

Grossmann, K. E., Grossmann, K., & Waters, E. (Eds.). (2005). *Attachment from infancy to adulthood: The major longitudinal studies.* New York: Guilford.

Guerrero, L. K. (1996). Attachment style differences in intimacy and involvement: A test of the four-category model. *Communication Monographs, 63,* 269–292.

Hazan, C., & Shaver, P. (1987). Romantic love conceptualized as an attachment process. *Journal of Personality and Social Psychology, 52,* 511–524.

Hesse, E. (1996). Discourse, memory, and the Adult Attachment Interview: A note with emphasis on the emerging cannot classify category. *Infant Mental Health Journal, 17,* 4–11.

Hesse, E. (2008). The Adult Attachment Interview: Protocol, method of analysis, and empirical studies. In J. Cassidy & P. Shaver (Eds.), *Handbook of attachment: Theory, research, and clinical applications* (2nd ed., pp. 552–598). New York: Guilford.

Holtzen, D. W., Kenny, M. E., & Mahalik, J. R. (1995). Contributions of parental attachment to gay or lesbian disclosure to parents and dysfunctional cognitive processes. *Journal of Counseling Psychology, 42,* 350–355.

Institute of Child Development (2009). *Minnesota longitudinal study of parents and children.* Retrieved July 2, 2010, from http://www.cehd.umn.edu/ICD/Parent-Child/default.html

Jacobvitz, D. (2008). Afterword: Reflections on clinical applications of the Adult Attachment Interview. In H. Steele & M. Steele (Eds.), *Clinical applications of the Adult Attachment Interview* (pp. 471–486). New York: Guilford.

Klohnen, E. C., Weller, J. A., Luo, S., & Choe, M. (2005). Organization and predictive power of general and relationship-specific attachment models: One for all, and all for one? *Personality and Social Psychology Bulletin, 31*, 1665–1682.

Kobak, R., & Hazan, C. (1991). Attachment in marriage: Effects of security and accuracy of working models. *Journal of Personality and Social Psychology, 60*, 861–869.

Levy, K., Meehan, K., Kelly, K., Reynoso, J., Weber, M., Clarkin, J., et al. (2006). Change in attachment patterns and reflective function in a randomized control trial of transference-focused psychotherapy for borderline personality disorder. *Journal of Consulting and Clinical Psychology, 74*, 1027–1040.

Main, M., & Hesse, E. (1990). Parents' unresolved traumatic experiences are related to infant disorganized attachment status: Is frightened and/or frightening parental behavior the linking mechanism? In M. T. Greenberg, D. Cicchetti, & E. M. Cummings (Eds.), *Attachment in the preschool years: Theory, research, and intervention* (pp. 161–182). Chicago: University of Chicago Press.

Main, M., Hesse, E., & Goldwyn, R. (2008). Studying differences in language usage in recounting attachment history: An introduction to the AAI. In H. Steele & M. Steele (Eds.), *Clinical applications of the Adult Attachment Interview* (pp. 31–68). New York: Guilford.

Main, M., Kaplan, N., & Cassidy, J. (1985). Security in infancy, childhood, and adulthood: A move to the level of representation. In I. Bretherton & E. Waters (Eds.), *Growing points of attachment theory and research: Monographs of the Society for Research in Child Development* (Vol. 50(1–2, Serial No. 209), pp. 66–104). Chicago: University of Chicago.

Main, M., & Solomon, J. (1986). Discovery of an insecure-disorganized attachment pattern. In T. B. Brazelton & M. W. Yogman (Eds.), *Affective development in infancy* (pp. 95–124). Norwood, NJ: Ablex.

Mikulincer, M., & Shaver, P. (2007). *Attachment in adulthood: Structure, dynamics, and change.* New York: Guilford.

Paley, B., Cox, M. J., Burchinal, M. R., & Payne, C. (1999). Attachment and marital functioning: Comparison of spouses with continuous-secure, earned-secure, dismissing, and preoccupied attachment stances. *Journal of Family Psychology, 13*, 580–597.

Parish, M., & Eagle, M. N. (2003). Attachment to the therapist. *Psychoanalytic Psychology, 20*, 271–286.

Pistole, M., Clark, E. M., & Tubbs, A. L. (1995). Love relationships: Attachment style and the investment model. *Journal of Mental Health Counseling, 17*, 199–209.

Pottharst, K. (Ed.). (1990). *Explanations in adult attachment.* New York: Peter Lang.

Rholes, W. S., Simpson, J. A., & Stevens, J. G. (1998). Attachment orientations, social support, and conflict resolution in close relationships. In J. A. Simpson & W. S. Rholes (Eds.), *Attachment theory and close relationships* (pp. 166–188). New York: Guilford.

Rosenzweig, D. L., Farber, B. A., & Geller, J. D. (1996). Clients' representations of their therapists over the course of psychotherapy. *Journal of Clinical Psychology, 52*, 197–207.

Senchak, M., & Leonard, K. E. (1992). Attachment styles and marital adjustment among newly-wed couples. *Journal of Social and Personal Relationships, 9*, 51–64.

Simpson, J. A., Rholes, S. W., & Phillips, D. (1996). Conflict in close relationships: An attachment perspective. *Journal of Personality and Social Psychology, 71*, 899–914.

Slade, A. (2008). The implications of attachment theory and research for adult psychotherapy: Research and clinical perspectives. In J. Cassidy & P. Shaver (Eds.), *Handbook of attachment: Theory, research, and clinical applications* (2nd ed., pp. 762–782). New York: Guilford.

Smith, E. R., Murphy, J., & Coats, S. (1999). Attachment to groups: Theory and management. *Journal of Personality and Social Psychology, 77*, 94–110.

Solomon, Z., Ginzburg, K., Mikulincer, M., Neria, Y., & Ohry, A. (1998). Coping with war captivity: The role of attachment style. *European Journal of Personality, 12*, 271–285.

Sroufe, A. (2005). Attachment and development: A prospective, longitudinal study from birth to adulthood. *Attachment & Human Development, 7*(4), 349–367.

Sroufe, A., Egeland, B., Carlson, E., & Collins, W. (2005). *The development of the person: The Minnesota study of risk and adaptation from birth to adulthood.* New York: Guilford.

Steele, H., & Steele, M. (Eds.). (2008a). *Clinical applications of the Adult Attachment Interview.* New York: Guilford.

Steele, H., & Steele, M. (2008b). Ten clinical uses of the AAI. In H. Steele & M. Steele (Eds.), *Clinical applications of the Adult Attachment Interview* (pp. 3–30). New York: Guilford.

Stovall-McClough, C., Cloitre, M., & McClough, J. (2008). Adult attachment and posttraumatic stress disorder in women with histories of childhood abuse. In H. Steele & M. Steele (Eds.), *Clinical applications of the Adult Attachment Interview* (pp. 320–340). New York: Guilford.

Treboux, D., Crowell, J. A., & Waters, E. (2004). When "new" meets "old": Configurations of adult attachment representations and their implications for marital functioning. *Developmental Psychology, 40*, 295–314.

Turan, B., Osar, Z., Turan, J. M., Ilkova, H., & Damci, T. (2003). Dismissing attachment and outcome in diabetes: The mediating role of coping. *Journal of Social and Clinical Psychology, 22*, 607–626.

van IJzendoorn, M. H. (1995). Adult attachment representation, parental responsiveness, and infant attachment: A meta-analysis on the predictive validity of the Adult Attachment Interview. *Psychological Bulletin, 117*, 387–403.

van IJzendoorn, M. H., & Bakermans-Kranenburg, J. J. (1997). Intergenerational transmission of attachment: A move to the contextual level. In L. Atkinson & J. K. Zucker (Eds.), *Attachment and psychopathology* (pp. 135–170). New York: Guilford.

van IJzendoorn, M. H., & Bakermans-Kranenburg, M. J. (2008). The distribution of adult attachment representations in clinical groups: A meta-analytic search for patterns of attachment in 105 AAI studies. In H. Steele & M. Steele (Eds.), *Clinical applications of the Adult Attachment Interview* (pp. 69–96). New York: Guilford.

Chapter 4
Clinical Social Work and Regulation Theory: Implications of Neurobiological Models of Attachment

Judith R. Schore and Allan N. Schore

> *By casting the right hemisphere in terms of self, we have a revolutionary way of thinking about the brain. A new model of the brain, therefore, must take into account the primary importance of the right hemisphere in establishing and maintaining our sense of awareness of ourselves and others.*

> (Keenan, Gallup, & Falk, 2003, p. 252).

Attachment theory, originally proposed by Bowlby (1969), has experienced a powerful resurgence over the last decade, not only in the mental health field but also in the biological sciences. Originating in an amalgam of psychoanalysis and behavioral biology, attachment theory is deceptively simple on the surface. It posits that the real relationships of the earliest stage of life indelibly shape us in basic ways, and, for the rest of the life span, attachment processes lie at the center of all human emotional and social functions. With the current incorporation of neurobiology into the theory, we now have a deeper understanding of how and why the early social environment influences all later adaptive functions. As a result of the recent integration of clinical data with developmental and neurobiological research, Bowlby's core ideas have been expanded into a therapeutically relevant model of human development: modern attachment/regulation theory. Indeed, in their recent overview of psychoanalytic developmental theories, Palombo, Bendicsen, and Koch (2009) conclude that current neuropsychological attachment theories are returning to the fundamental psychoanalytic questions posed by Freud's model of the human unconscious.

With its emphasis on human development, attachment theory shares with clinical social work a common biopsychosocial perspective. The field of social work has

J.R. Schore (✉)
The Sanville Institute for Clinical Social Work and Psychotherapy, Berkeley, CA, USA
and
Reiss-Davis Post Doctoral Program in Child Psychotherapy, Los Angeles, CA, USA
e-mail: jrschore@sbcglobal.net

S. Bennett and J.K. Nelson (Eds.), *Adult Attachment in Clinical Social Work*,
Essential Clinical Social Work Series, DOI 10.1007/978-1-4419-6241-6_4,
© Springer Science+Business Media, LLC 2010

traditionally focused on two core issues – person-in-environment and relationship. This theoretical orientation encompasses not only psychological relational dynamics beginning in infancy, but also individual biological and somatic factors and social/cultural influences that are both internalized and situational. This biopsychosocial perspective of social work is absolutely consonant with attachment theory's current explanation of the mechanisms that operate at the psychobiological core of the intersubjective context – the brain–mind–body-environment relational matrix out of which each individual emerges. We argue that individual development arises out of the relationship between the brain/mind/body of both infant and caregiver held within a culture and environment that either supports, inhibits, or even threatens it. One of the key elements of a "culturally competent" social worker is an awareness of the clients' pertinent relational beginnings held by their particular culture. These relational origins are forged and expressed in nonverbal attachment communications in the first year and influenced by the cultural surround. They indelibly shape the individual's way of experiencing the world.

In addition, the fundamental biopsychosocial perspective of clinical social work, like attachment theory, highlights the critical importance of unconscious[1] forces that drive all human emotion, cognition, and behavior within a sociocultural matrix. Thus, clinical social work also has incorporated Freud's fundamental conception of the central role of the unconscious in everyday life. From its beginnings, attachment theory, grounded in psychoanalysis and behavioral biology, has focused on how real experiences, especially in childhood, directly impact the unconscious system. This is a core principle of psychodynamically oriented clinical social work. The links between psychoanalytic social work and other psychoanalytic disciplines have recently been strengthened by social work's rapid incorporation of recent advances in relational psychoanalysis, self psychology, and neuropsychoanalysis. Indeed the last decade has seen a resurgence and expansion of Freud's model. In the broader psychological literature, Bargh and Morsella (2008) now conclude, "Freud's model of the unconscious as the primary guiding influence over every day life, even today, is more specific and detailed than any to be found in contemporary cognitive or social psychology" (p. 73).

Over this same time period classical attachment theory has also experienced a significant expansion. In 2000, A. Schore presented the Seventh Annual John Bowlby Memorial Lecture, and returning to Bowlby's methodology of integrating biology and psychoanalysis, offered recent findings from "the decade of the brain" to argue that modern attachment theory is essentially a regulation theory. That same year he published an article in *Attachment & Human Development* identifying Bowlby's (1969/1982) control system of attachment in the right brain. In an article in the 2001 issue of the *British Journal of Psychotherapy* he then extrapolated his neuropsychoanalytic model of attachment to the clinical encounter, including psychobiological models of attachment in the therapeutic alliance, and right brain-to-right brain communications in the transference–countertransference relationship (Schore, 2001a).

---

[1] In this chapter, we equate "unconscious" with "nonconscious," that is, implicit functions that occur beneath levels of awareness not because they are repressed but because they are too rapid to reach consciousness.

The current transformation of modern attachment theory, informed by neuroscience, even more deeply elucidates the early experience-dependent development of the human unconscious system, which remains active over the course of the life span. Regulation theory is derived from interdisciplinary sources, and it has fostered a dialogue not only within, but also among, various fields (e.g., psychoanalysis, neuroscience, psychiatry, traumatology, developmental psychology, pediatrics), including clinical social work. In an excellent volume, *Neurobiology for Clinical Social Work*, Applegate and Shapiro (2005) apply attachment neurobiology specifically to social work practice, and they too maintain that this theory is highly compatible with the biopsychosocial emphasis of social work practice.

Another major force that has propelled the transformation in attachment theory is the ongoing intense interest in emotion and emotion regulation. In fact, a number of clinical and scientific disciplines are now experiencing a paradigm shift from cognition to the primacy of affect, and this transition is expressed in a shift from cognitive to emotional theories of development. In a recent contribution on regulation theory, we argued that any theory of development and its corresponding theory of therapy must include psychobiological findings regarding precisely how early emotional transactions with the primary object impact the development of psychic structure; that is, how affective attachment communications facilitate the maturation of brain systems involved in affect arousal and in self-regulation (Schore & Schore, 2008). The rich intricacy of an integrative theory of neurobiology and attachment links brain–mind–body and encompasses the essential elements that allow us to comprehend and treat attachment-related disorders of self and affect regulation more effectively. There is currently both an experimental and clinical focus on how affective bodily based attachment processes are aroused, communicated, and regulated within the mother–infant[2] dyad. There is also an emphasis on how psychobiological attunement and relational stress impact, both positively and negatively, the experience-dependent maturation of early developing brain regulatory systems.

More than fifteen years ago, A. Schore outlined the essential role of attachment in the regulation of affect and emotional development. In his seminal 1994 volume, he integrated a large amount of existing interdisciplinary data and proposed that attachment transactions are critical to the development of structural right brain systems involved in the nonconscious processing of emotion, modulation of stress, self-regulation, and thereby the functional origins of the bodily based affective core of the implicit self that operates automatically and rapidly, beneath levels of awareness. The current shift of attachment theory from its earlier focus on behavior and cognition into affect and affect regulation reflects the broader trend in the psychological sciences. In a recent editorial of the journal *Motivation and Emotion*, Ryan (2007) asserts:

> After three decades of the dominance of cognitive approaches, motivational and emotional processes have roared back into the limelight. Both researchers and practitioners have come to appreciate the limits of exclusively cognitive approaches for understanding the initiation and regulation of human behavior. (p. 1)

---

[2] Throughout this chapter, we refer to "mother" interchangeably with "primary caregiver(s)." We are referring to the primary attachment figure, although we recognize that the infant's primary attachment figure may not be the mother.

This renewed emphasis on the emotional and social aspects of early development has allowed for a transformation of attachment theory into a pragmatic framework for models of both psychopathogenesis and the change process in psychotherapy. In our work, we have suggested that regulation theory can generate complex models of psychopathogenesis by linking early attachment stressors to the neurobiology of impaired emotional development, enduring deficits in affect dysregulation, and the genesis of personality disorders. The application of attachment principles to psychotherapy models also has been elucidated by focusing the treatment upon the affective dynamics of right brain internal working models encoding coping strategies of affect regulation that are activated within the therapeutic alliance (Schore, 1994, 2001b, 2002a, 2003a). In other words, the therapeutic relationship and the clinical social worker's use of self are central to interventions ranging from casework management, to foster home placement, adoption, and short and long-term psychotherapy.

Without the psychobiological component, earlier classical models of attachment did not directly address clinical phenomena that are essential to both developmental assessment and psychotherapy. A fundamental question of models of the change process of psychotherapy is how do relational experiences positively impact psychic structure? By integrating developmental and biological data, the fundamental links between attachment functions and their enduring effect on developing psychic structure throughout the life span are expressed in the developmental neuropsychology of, specifically, the early maturing right brain. This right lateralized emotional brain is deeply connected into the body and the autonomic nervous system (ANS), and it has a different anatomy, physiology, and biochemistry than the later forming left hemisphere. The right hemisphere processes not only emotion, but more precisely, unconscious emotion and is the locus of an implicit procedural memory system.

A central principle of our work thus dictates that attachment experiences shape the early organization of the right brain, the neurobiological core of the human unconscious (Schore, 2003b). Indeed, therapeutic interventions are rooted in these same implicit dynamic relational processes. In treatment, these right brain affectively charged attachment experiences are communicated and regulated within the therapeutic alliance. The co-creation of an attachment relationship between the empathic social worker and client has been seen as the sine-qua-non of clinical practice, and respect for the individual is, and always has been, paramount. The current expansion of neurobiologically supported attachment principles of interactive affect communication and regulation that occur beneath levels of awareness both explains and justifies this approach. The mechanisms of developmental change thus include modifications in both psychic function and structure, not only in the earliest but also in all subsequent stages of development. We argue that modern attachment/ regulation theory is consonant with the recent relational intersubjective trend in the psychodynamic literature, and it can be readily incorporated into the core of social work education, theory, research, and practice.

Toward that end, in this chapter we outline the general precepts of modern attachment theory and its relevance to the practice of clinical social work. We begin with an overview of the central role of unconscious interactive regulation in establishing attachment relationships and the lifelong impact this has on the development of the right brain and the implicit self. We then present the clinical applications of regulation theory in a section on interpersonal neurobiology of implicit nonverbal communications within the therapeutic alliance, followed by a discussion of affective bodily based transference–countertransference transactions. Finally, we offer some further thoughts on the implications of neurobiological models of attachment for clinical social work. In doing so, we assume some familiarity with the basic concepts of classical attachment theory (see Sable, Chap. 2 and Bennett & Nelson, Chap. 3, this volume), object-relations, self and relational psychology, and focus on integrating these models with their neurobiological underpinnings in order to offer an interpenetrating and overarching theory that is consonant with the bio-psychosocial foundations of clinical social work.

Psychobiological Core of Attachment Communications: Interactive Regulation and the Maturation of the Right Brain

The essential task of the first year of human life is the creation of a secure attachment bond of emotional communication between the infant and the primary caregiver (the mother in most instances). These affective attachment transactions are rapidly transmitted within the dyad in nonverbal visual/facial, auditory/prosodic, and tactile/gestural communications. In order to enter into this communication, the mother must be psychobiologically attuned to the dynamic shifts in the infant's bodily based internal states of central and autonomic arousal. During the affective communications embedded in mutual gaze episodes, the psychobiologically attuned, sensitive caregiver appraises nonverbal expressions of the infant's arousal and then regulates these affective states, both positive and negative. The attachment relationship mediates the dyadic regulation of bodily based emotion, so that the primary caregiver regulates the infant's postnatally developing central (CNS) and autonomic (ANS) nervous systems. In this dialogue, the "good enough" mother and infant participate in multiple cycles of attunement/misattunement/re-attunement interactions. Through these emotional transactions, an infant becomes a person, eventually achieving a "psychological birth" (Mahler, Pine & Bergmann, 1975). This preverbal psychobiological matrix forms the core of the emerging implicit self.

It is now established that emotion is initially regulated by others, but over the course of infancy it increasingly becomes self-regulated as a result of neurophysiological development and actual lived experience. These adaptive capacities are central to self-regulation, which can be defined as the ability to flexibly regulate an expanding array of positive and negative psychobiological states in various contexts, and thereby assimilate these emotional-motivational states into an integrated self-system. Optimal attachment experiences with the primary caregiver(s) facilitate both types of regulation: interactive regulation of emotions, while subjectively engaged with other humans in interconnected contexts, and autoregulation of emotions, while subjectively disengaged from other humans in autonomous contexts. Efficient self-functioning involves resilient switching between these two modes, depending upon the relational context. Both of these affect regulating strategies are not left brain, verbally cognitive, and explicit-conscious, but right brain psychobiological and implicit-unconscious processes. The fundamental role of these nonconscious attachment dynamics is therefore interactive psychobiological regulation.

At the most essential level, attachment represents the evolutionary mechanism by which we are sociophysiologically connected to others in order to co-regulate our internal homeostatic affect states. At all points of the life span, interactive psychobiological regulation supports the right brain survival functions of the human self-system (Schore, 2003a, b). This principle is echoed in current developmental brain research, where Ovtscharoff and Braun (2001) report that "The dyadic interaction between the newborn and the mother...serves as a regulator of the developing individual's internal homeostasis" (p. 33). Notice the similarity to Kohut's (1971) proposal that the infant's regulatory transactions with the maternal self-object allow for maintenance of his homeostatic equilibrium. In addition, we now know that dyadic attachment regulatory transactions impact the development of psychic structure; that is, they generate brain development (Schore, 1994).

Even more specifically, the regulatory function of mother–infant social–emotional interactions acts as an essential promoter of the development and maintenance of synaptic connections during the establishment of functional circuits of the right brain in critical periods of infancy (Schore, 1994; Siegel, 1999; Cozolino, 2002). Confirming this, in a recent near-infrared spectroscopy study of infant–mother attachment at 12 months, the researchers conclude: "Our results are in agreement with that of Schore (2000) who addressed the importance of the right hemisphere in the attachment system" (Minagawa-Kawai et al., 2009, p. 289). Neuroscientists studying the human social brain now contend that throughout the lifespan, "The neural substrates of the perception of voices, faces, gestures, smells and pheromones, as evidenced by modern neuroimaging techniques, are characterized by a general pattern of right-hemispheric functional asymmetry" (Brancucci, Lucci, Mazzatenta, & Tommasi, 2009, p. 895).

Furthermore, A. Schore (1994, 2003a) has elucidated how the maturation of the emotion processing limbic circuits of the infant's developing right brain is influenced by implicit intersubjective affective transactions embedded in the attachment relationship with the primary caregiver(s). Implicit processing underlies the quick and automatic handling of nonverbal affective cues in infancy, and it is "repetitive, automatic, provides quick categorization and decision-making, and operates outside the realm of focal attention and verbalized experience" (Lyons-Ruth, 1999, p. 576). The dyadic implicit processing of these nonverbal attachment communications are the product of the operations of the infant's right hemisphere interacting with the mother's right hemisphere. Attachment experiences are thus imprinted in implicit memory in an internal working model that encodes strategies of affect regulation and acts at implicit nonconscious levels.

Attachment experiences thus shape the experience-dependent maturation of the right brain, and in this manner they impact later personality development and functions. From infancy throughout all later stages of the lifespan, this right lateralized system is centrally involved in implicit affective processes and in the control of vital functions supporting survival and enabling the organism to cope with stresses and challenges. The implicit self-system of the right brain that evolves in preverbal stages of development thus represents the biological substrate of Freud's dynamic unconscious (Schore, 2002b). A growing body of studies report that unconscious emotional memories are stored in the right hemisphere (Gainotti, 2006), that this hemisphere is centrally involved in "maintaining a coherent, continuous and unified sense of self " (Devinsky, 2000, p. 69), and that a right frontal lobe process, one that connects "the individual to emotionally salient experiences and memories underlying self-schemas, is the glue holding together a sense of self" (Miller et al., 2001, p. 821).

Right Brain Nonverbal Attachment Communication: Implicit Communications Within the Therapeutic Alliance

It is important to note that early nonverbal experiences may be either regulated or dysregulated, imprinting either secure or insecure attachments (see Sable, Chap. 2 and Bennett & Nelson, Chap. 3, this volume). In marked contrast to an optimal attachment scenario, in a relational growth-inhibiting early environment of abuse and/or neglect, the primary caregiver of an insecure disorganized–disoriented infant induces traumatic states of enduring negative affect in the child. This caregiver is inaccessible and reacts to her infant's expressions of emotions and stress inappropriately and/or with rejection, and therefore shows minimal or unpredictable participation in the various types of arousal regulating processes. Instead of modulating she induces extreme levels of stressful stimulation and arousal, very high in abuse and/or very low in neglect. And because she provides no interactive repair, the infant's intense negative affective states last for long periods of time.

Watt (2003) observes, "If children grow up with dominant experiences of separation, distress, fear and rage, then they will go down a bad pathogenic developmental pathway, and it's not just a bad psychological pathway but a bad neurological pathway" (p. 109). This is due to the fact that during early critical periods, organized and disorganized insecure attachment histories are "affectively burnt in" the infant's rapidly developing right brain (Schore, 2001b, 2003a, 2009a). Less than optimal early relational experiences are imprinted into the right brain, and these insecure internal working models of attachment that encode inefficient strategies of affect regulation are nonconsciously accessed at later points of interpersonal emotional stress. Modern attachment theory suggests that these right lateralized insecure working models are a central focus of affectively focused psychotherapy of early forming self pathologies and personality disorders. These right brain relational deficits are described by Feinberg and Keenan (2005):

> The right hemisphere, particularly the right frontal region, under normal circumstances plays a crucial role in establishing the appropriate relationship between the self and the world…dysfunction results in a two-way disturbance of personal relatedness between the self and the environment that can lead to disorders of both under and over relatedness between the self and the world. (p. 15)

All forms of therapy currently view affect dysregulation and relational deficits as a fundamental condition of psychiatric disorders, including personality disorders, and therefore share a common goal of improving the effectiveness of emotional self-regulatory processes (Schore, 2009b).

Bowlby (1988) asserted that the reassessment of nonconscious internalized attachment models that encode strategies of affect regulation is the essential task of psychotherapy. Indeed, current relationally oriented therapeutic contexts that optimize right brain intersubjective communication and interactive regulation attempt to explore and alter insecure internal working models of the self and the world in the context of the therapeutic relationship. Decety and Chaminade's (2003) character-ization of higher right brain functions is directly applicable to the psychotherapy of disorders of the self: "Mental states that are in essence private to the self may be shared between individuals...self-awareness, empathy, identification with others, and more generally intersubjective processes, are largely dependent upon...right hemisphere resources, which are the first to develop" (p. 591). These particular implicit right brain operations are essential for adaptive interpersonal functioning, and are specifically activated in the therapeutic alliance. Indeed, right brain expansions of "implicit relational knowledge," stored in the nonverbal domain, lie at the core of the psychotherapeutic change process.

As the right hemisphere is dominant for the broader aspects of communication and for subjective emotional experiences, the implicit communication of affective states between the right brains of the members of both the infant–mother and patient–therapist dyads is thus best described as "intersubjectivity." The neurobio-logical correlate of this intersubjectivity principle is expressed in the dictum, "the self-organization of the developing brain occurs in the context of a relationship with another self, another brain" (Schore, 1996, p. 60). This is true in both the developmental and therapeutic growth-facilitating contexts. The interpersonal neurobiology of modern attachment theory has thus been a rich source of information about the essential role of intersubjective, nonconscious, nonverbal right brain communications in the psychotherapy relationship (see Miscall & Sorter, Chap. 6, this volume). On this matter Stern (2005) suggests:

> Without the nonverbal it would be hard to achieve the empathic, participatory, and resonating aspects of intersubjectivity. One would only be left with a kind of pared down, neutral 'understanding' of the other's subjective experience. One reason that this distinction is drawn is that in many cases the analyst is consciously aware of the content or speech while processing the nonverbal aspects out of awareness. With an intersubjectivist perspective, a more conscious processing by the analyst of the nonverbal is necessary. (p. 80)

It has been found that 60% of all human communication is transmitted nonverbally (Burgoon, 1985); attachment transactions are also transmitted within the therapeutic alliance in similar nonverbal expectations and attitudes. Clinical social workers access this affective relational dialogue not only in therapy but in clinical encounters of any kind, including case management and family counseling. These clinical dialogues convey more than left brain information. Rather, right brain interactions beneath the words nonverbally communicate essential nonconscious affective relational informa-tion about the inner world of the client (and therapist). We suggest that clinical social workers are experts in these intersubjective processes, and that understanding more about how the process works may enhance therapeutic effectiveness.

Modern attachment theory offers a deeper understanding of the psychobiological mechanisms that underlie the clinical encounter. It is now accepted that the "nonverbal, pre-rational stream of expression that binds the infant to its parent continues throughout life to be a primary medium of intuitively felt affective-relational communication between persons" (Orlinksy & Howard, 1986, p. 343). Right brain transactions thus mediate the relational unconscious as it is dyadically expressed in adult attachments as well as in the psychotherapeutic encounter. Lyons-Ruth (2000) characterizes the affective exchanges that communicate implicit relational knowledge within the therapeutic alliance. She observes that most relational transactions rely on a substrate of affective cues that give an evaluative valence or direction to each relational communication. These occur at an implicit level of rapid cueing and response that occurs too rapidly for verbal transaction and conscious reflection.

Scaer (2005) also describes essential implicit communications embedded within the therapist–client relationship:

> Many features of social interaction are nonverbal, consisting of subtle variations of facial expression that set the tone for the content of the interaction. Body postures and movement patterns of the therapist…also may reflect emotions such as disapproval, support, humor, and fear. Tone and volume of voice, patterns and speed of verbal communication, and eye contact also contain elements of subliminal communication and contribute to the unconscious establishment of a safe, healing environment. (pp. 167–168)

Such right brain communications, more so than conscious verbalizations, reveal the personality of the therapist as well as the client.

Due to the commonality of implicit intersubjective right brain-to-right brain emotion transacting and regulating mechanisms in the caregiver–infant relationship and the social worker–client relationship, developmental attachment studies have direct relevance to the therapeutic process. Schore (2003b), delineating the nature of implicit and explicit processes in the psychotherapeutic context, writes that during treatment, the empathic therapist is consciously, explicitly attending to the patient's verbalizations in order to objectively diagnose and rationalize the patient's dysregulating symptomatology. However, the therapist is also listening and interacting at another level, an experience-near subjective level, one that implicitly processes moment-to-moment socioemotional information at levels beneath awareness.

A fundamental question of any treatment encounter is how we work with what is being communicated but not symbolized with words. How we understand and relate to an unexpressed unconscious emotion depends on our capacity to receive and express nonverbal communications. In discussing presymbolic processing, Bucci (2002) observes, "We recognize changes in emotional states of others based on perception of subtle shifts in their facial expression or posture, and recognize changes in our own states based on somatic or kinesthetic experience" (p. 194). These implicit communications are expressed within the therapeutic alliance between the client and therapist's right brain systems. Neuroscientists now contend:

Human beings rely extensively on nonverbal channels of communication in their day-to-day emotional as well as interpersonal exchanges. The verbal channel, language, is a relatively poor medium for expressing the quality, intensity and nuancing of emotion and affect in different social situations...the face is thought to have primacy in signaling affective information. (Mandal & Ambady, 2004, p. 23)

As in the developmental attachment context, implicit right brain-to-right brain communications are an essential vehicle within the therapeutic relationship. The right hemisphere is important in the processing of the "music" behind our words (see Miscall Brown & Sorter, Chap. 7, this volume). When listening to speech, we rely upon a range of cues upon which to base our inference as to the communicative intent of others. To interpret the meaning of speech, how something is said is as important as what is actually said. Prosody (the emotional tone of the voice) conveys different shades of meaning by means of variations in stress and pitch, irrespective of the words and grammatical construction. These data support suggestions that the preverbal elements of language – intonation, tone, force, and rhythm – stir up reactions derived from the early mother-child relationships, the internal working models of attachment. In recent writings Andrade (2005) concludes, "It is the affective content of the analyst's voice – and not the semantic content – that has an impact on the patient's store of implicit memories" (p. 683).

During heightened affective moments these right brain dialogues between the relational unconscious of both the client and therapist (like the attachment communications of the infant and mother) are examples of "primary process communication." According to Dorpat (2001), "The primary process system analyzes, regulates, and communicates an individual's relations with the environment" (p. 449). He observes, "Affective and object-relational information is transmitted predominantly by primary process communication. Nonverbal communication includes body movements (kinesics), posture, gesture, facial expression, voice inflection, and the sequence, rhythm, and pitch of the spoken words" (p. 451). In addition to psychoanalytic authors who have implicated the right brain in primary process functions (see Schore, 1994), neuroscience researchers now contend, "the right hemisphere operates in a more free-associative, primary process manner, typically observed in states such as dreaming or reverie" (Grabner, Fink, & Neubauer, 2007, p. 228).

It is important to stress that all these implicit nonconscious right brain/mind/ body nonverbal communications are bidirectional and thereby intersubjective (see Schore, 2003b for a right hemisphere-to-right hemisphere model of projective identification, a fundamental process of implicit communication within the therapeutic alliance). As Meares (2005) describes:

Not only is the therapist being unconsciously influenced by a series of slight and, in some cases, subliminal signals, so also is the patient. Details of the therapist's posture, gaze, tone of voice, even respiration, are recorded and processed. A sophisticated therapist may use this processing in a beneficial way, potentiating a change in the patient's state without, or in addition to, the use of words. (p. 124)

Implicit right brain-to-right brain intersubjective transactions mediate what Sander (1992) calls "moments of meeting" between patient and therapist. Current neurobiological data suggests, "While the left hemisphere mediates most linguistic behaviors, the right hemisphere is important for broader aspects of communication" (van Lancker & Cummings, 1999, p. 95). A. Schore (2003b) proposes that just as the left brain communicates its states to other left brains via conscious linguistic behaviors, so the right nonverbally communicates its unconscious states to other right brains that are tuned to receive these communications. Regulation theory thus describes how beneath the exchanges of language, the implicit affects of the client are communicated to, and regulated by, implicit systems of the therapist. In other words, intersubjective relational psychotherapy is not the "talking" but the "communicating" cure.

Intersubjectivity is therefore more than a match or communication of explicit cognitions. Regulated and dysregulated bodily based affects are communicated within the intersubjective field co-constructed by two individuals, so this field includes not just two minds but two bodies (Schore, 1994, 2003a, 2003b). At the psychobiological core of the co-constructed intersubjective field is the attachment bond of emotional communication and interactive regulation. Implicit intersubjective communications are thus interactively regulated and dysregulated psychobiological somatic processes that mediate shared conscious and unconscious emotional states, not just mental contents. The essential biological function of attachment communications in all human interactions, including those embedded in the psychobiological core of the therapeutic alliance is the regulation of right brain/mind/body states. These ideas resonate with Shaw's (2004) conclusion:

> Psychotherapy is an inherently embodied process. If psychotherapy is an investigation into the intersubjective space between client and therapist, then as a profession we need to take our bodily reactions much more seriously than we have so far because…the body is "the very basis of human subjectivity." (p. 271)

Transference–Countertransference and Affect Regulation: Right Brain Mechanisms of Therapeutic Change

Regulation theory's right brain perspective of the treatment process allows for a deeper understanding of the critical intersubjective factors that operate at implicit levels of the therapeutic alliance, beneath the exchanges of language and explicit cognitions. One such essential mechanism is the transference–countertransference relationship. There is now a growing consensus that despite the existence of a number of distinct theoretical perspectives in clinical work, the concepts of transference and countertransference represent a common ground. Our neuropsychoanalytic perspective of regulation theory describes the central role of implicit right brain-to-right brain nonverbal communications (facial expression, prosody – or tone of voice, gesture), in unconscious transference–countertransference affective transactions, an essential element of treatment of severe psychopathologies and a common mechanism of all forms of psychotherapy. This interpersonal process occurs whether one is working primarily with cognitive material or at depth. Clinical social workers have always paid close attention to this essential nonverbal mechanism of the therapeutic process.

Recent psychoanalytic models of transference now contend that "no appreciation of transference can do without emotion" (Pincus, Freeman, & Modell, 2007, p. 634), and that "transference is distinctive in that it depends on early patterns of emotional attachment with caregivers" (p. 636). Clinical theoreticians describe transference as "an established pattern of relating and emotional responding that is cued by something in the present, but oftentimes calls up both an affective state and thoughts that may have more to do with past experience than present ones" (Maroda, 2005, p. 134). This conception is echoed in neuroscience, where Shuren and Grafman (2002) assert:

> The right hemisphere holds representations of the emotional states associated with events experienced by the individual. When that individual encounters a familiar scenario, representations of past emotional experiences are retrieved by the right hemisphere and are incorporated into the reasoning process. (p. 918)

Other researchers report that the right hemisphere is fundamentally involved in the unconscious processing of emotional stimuli (Mlot, 1998) and in autobiographical memory (Markowitsch, Reinkemeier, Kessler, Koyuncu, & Heiss, 2000).

According to Gainotti (2006), "the right hemisphere may be crucially involved in those emotional memories which must be reactivated and reworked during the psychoanalytical treatment" (p. 167). In discussing the role of the right hemisphere as "the seat of implicit memory," Mancia (2006) notes: "The discovery of the implicit memory has extended the concept of the unconscious and supports the hypothesis that this is where the emotional and affective – sometimes traumatic – presymbolic and preverbal experiences of the primary mother–infant relations are stored" (p. 83). These implicit procedural memories are expressed in transferential right brain-to-right brain nonverbal communications of fast acting, automatic, regulated, and especially dysregulated bodily based stressful emotional states. Transference has been described as "an expression of the patient's implicit perceptions and implicit memories" (Bornstein, 1999, p. 170).

Transference–countertransference transactions thus represent nonconscious, nonverbal right brain–mind–body communications, and they are outputs of both the CNS (central nervous system) and ANS (autonomic nervous system). Facial indicators of transference are expressed in visual and auditory affective cues quickly appraised from the therapist's face. Countertransference is similarly defined in nonverbal implicit terms as the therapist's "autonomic responses that are reactions on an unconscious level to nonverbal messages" (Jacobs, 1994, p. 749). In monitoring somatic countertransferential responses, the empathic clinician's psychobiologically attuned right brain tracks at a preconscious level, not only the arousal rhythms and flows of the patient's affective states, but also her own somatic countertransferential, interoceptive, bodily based affective responses to the patient's implicit facial, prosodic, and gestural communications. In this manner, "The right hemisphere, in fact, truly interprets the mental state not only of its own brain, but the brains (and minds) of others" (Keenan, Rubio, Racioppi, Johnson, & Barnacz, 2005, p. 702).

In this intersubjective dialogue, the psychobiologically attuned, intuitive clinician is learning the nonverbal moment-to-moment rhythmic structures of the client's internal states from the first point of contact and is flexibly and fluidly modifying his/her own behavior to synchronize with that structure, thereby co-creating with the client a growth-facilitating context for the organization of the therapeutic alliance. The attachment between therapist and client is established over time, allowing for the expression of socioemotional experiences that resonate with the original infant–mother attachment history. Over the ensuing stages of the treatment, the sensitive, empathic clinician's monitoring of unconscious psychobiological process, rather than conscious verbal content, calls for right brain attention in order to match the patient's implicit affective-arousal states. The empathic therapist also resonates with the client's simultaneous implicit expressions of engagement and disengagement within the co-constructed intersubjective field.

In turn, these collaborations of the therapist's and client's subjectivities allow for right brain communications and interactive regulations of dysregulated affective states. The importance of this connection is stressed by Whitehead (2006):

> Every time we make therapeutic contact with our patients we are engaging profound processes that tap into essential life forces in ourselves and in those we work with... Emotions are deepened in intensity and sustained in time when they are intersubjectively shared. This occurs at moments of deep contact. (p. 624)

These heightened affective moments also afford an opportunity for interactive affect regulation, the core of the attachment process. Ogden, Pain, Minton, and Fisher (2005) conclude:

> Interactive psychobiological regulation... provides the relational context under which the client can safely contact, describe and eventually regulate inner experience...It is the patient's experience of empowering action in the context of safety provided by a back-ground of the empathic clinician's psychobiologically attuned interactive affect regulation that helps effect...change. (p. 22)

These clinical principles especially apply to working in enactments with patients with a history of relational attachment trauma and pathological dissociation (Ginot, 2009; Schore, 2007, 2009a). Such work implies a profound commitment by both participants in the therapeutic dyad and a deep emotional involvement on the part of the therapist (Tutte, 2004). Indeed, research now indicates that psychotherapy is superior to pharmacotherapy in patients with a history of early childhood trauma (Nemeroff et al., 2003) and that long-term psychodynamic therapy is effective in treating personality disorders and chronic mental disorders (Leichsenring & Rabung, 2008). Ultimately, effective psychotherapeutic treatment of early evolving self pathologies (such as severe personality disorders) can facilitate changes in the right brain, including alterations of the internal working model and more effective coping strategies for affect regulation. This interpersonal neurobiological mechanism allows optimal treatment to potentially transform "insecure" into "earned secure" attachments.

It is certainly true that the clinician's left brain conscious mind is an important contributor to the treatment process. But perhaps more than other treatment modalities, psychodynamic psychotherapeutic models are now intensively focusing upon the critical functions of the therapist's "unconscious right mind." The right hemisphere plays a dominant role in the processing of self-relevant information, affective theory of mind (Schore, 2003b), empathy (Schore, 1994; Shamay-Tsoory, Tomer, Berger, & Aharon-Peretz, 2003), as well as in mentalizing (Ohnishi et al., 2004), all aspects of the treatment process. A body of studies now indicates that psychotherapy induces changes in the brain. Glass (2008) summarizes these findings: "Recent research in brain imaging, molecular biology, and neurogenetics has shown that psychotherapy changes brain function and structure. Such studies have shown that psycho-therapy effects regional cerebral blood flow, neurotransmitter metabolism, gene expression, and persistent modifications in synaptic plasticity" (p. 1,589).

The field of clinical social work has always highlighted concepts such as clinical sensitivity, empathy, and creating a sense of safety for the client, as well as the disciplined use of self in forming a therapeutic alliance. In cases of early self pathologies, deep emotional contact and interactive affect regulation can be made in both case management and counseling, as well as short or long-term psycho-therapy, if the neurobiological principles of working with conscious and unconscious affect are held in the clinician's mind *and* body. In this challenging work, more so than cognitive understanding, relational factors lie at the core of the change mechanism. To be optimally effective with these disorders of affect regulation, the expert clinical social worker must access not only the explicit, but even more importantly the implicit, bodily based self formed in the clinician's own attachment history. Regulation theory thus dictates that at the most essential level, the intersubjective work of psychotherapy is not defined by what the therapist says to the patient, or does for the patient (left brain focus). Rather, the key mechanism is how to *be with* the patient, especially during affectively stressful moments when the patient's subjec-tivity is disintegrating in real time (right brain focus).

Further Implications of Neurobiological Models of Attachment for Clinical Social Work

A recent explosion of developmental and neurobiological research has added substan-tially to Freud's (1895/1966) clinical model, first proposed in his *Project for a Scientific Psychology* (Schore, 1997). Bowlby (1969/1982) returned to this psycho-biological perspective in his creation of attachment theory. As psychoanalysis pro-gressed in the second half of the last century, it evolved drive, ego, object-relations, self, and relational psychology. But over this time period, attachment theory, perhaps more than any other psychoanalytically based model, focused the sensibilities of psychodynamic clinicians onto an awareness of real life experience – a hallmark of social work theory and practice – and a keen focus on early development as the root of all. Then, beginning in the 1990s, a renewed interest in emotional processes and dramatic advances in neuroscience re-emphasized the biological component of the biopsychosocial frame, thereby providing a remarkable underpinning and expan-sion of all the pertinent developmental psychoanalytic theoretical concepts that came before. Using this knowledge on a daily basis, finding new understandings in clinical assessments, shaping therapeutic interventions from relevant theory, and providing a unique awareness of the adaptive nonconscious functions of the implicit self are some of the profound results of this theoretical integration.

Bowlby (1969/1982) originally stated that attachment behavior was based on the need for safety and a secure base. A psychobiological update of his seminal conceptualizations indicates that the evolutionary mechanism of attachment is much more than this. By focusing on emotional and social development, neurobiological research demonstrates that attachment dynamics represent the essential matrix for creating a right brain self that can regulate its own internal states and external relationships. There is now consensus that psychobiological attachment experiences allow psychic structure to be built and shaped into a unique human being. Our task as social workers and as therapists is to understand and facilitate this developmental process with our clients of all ages.

The developmental understanding that arises from this updating of Bowlby's important work informs more complex models of treatment of the early forming attachment pathologies that lie at the core of severe personality disorders. Regulation theory explicates the enduring untoward effects of attachment stressors on the implicit self-system, from mild and "ordinary" peculiarities that create and shape individuality, to severe trauma and neglect that interfere with and derail normal development and that require long-term therapeutic involvement to get back on track (Schore, 1994, 2002a, 2002c, 2003b, 2005, 2009a). This profoundly developmental clinical perspective is rooted in the clinician's explicit and implicit awareness of early attachment regulation/dysregulation, a thorough knowledge of right hemispheric emotional development, and a deep understanding of the dynamics of implicit procedural memory. Familiarity with the rapid right brain mechanisms that underlie bodily based, nonverbal affective communication is essential in this approach. A keen apperception of one's own somatic countertransference is a key element of the intersubjective field co-created between therapist and client.

As cited above, a substantial amount of scientific and clinical research now strongly supports the fact that the therapeutic relationship can repair damage and create new structure that is more able to cope with the demands of life. Modern attachment/regulation theory explains how the therapist's participation in "external" affect regulation supports the emergence of more complex "internal" regulatory capacities in the patient. The psychotherapeutic process is based on the same developmental psychobiological attachment mechanism. In this manner the therapeutic alliance acts as a growth-facilitating social environment that can promote the development of not only an "earned secure" attachment (Phelkos, Belsky, & Crnic, 1998), but an expansion of the patient's right brain, the biological substrate of the human unconscious.

In both the change process of early development and psychotherapy, a central tenet of regulation theory dictates that any individual's personal trajectory of emotional growth, including the development of his/her unconscious, will be facilitated or inhibited by the context of his/her family and culture. Attachment outcomes are thus the product of the interactions of both nature and nurture, the strengths and weaknesses of the individual's genetically encoded biological predispositions (temperament) *and* the early dyadic relationships with caregivers embedded within a particular social environment (culture).

A regulation model of attachment deepens the bio-psycho-social-cultural perspective of clinical social work. Furthermore, the developmental model of modern attachment theory has implications not only for the social work profession's involvement in the psychotherapeutic treatment of individuals, but also for the culture, an area of prime interest to social work. Tucker (1992) observes, "the baby brain must begin participating effectively in the process of social information transmission that offers entry into the culture" (p. 79). He asserts that social interaction that promotes brain differentiation is the mechanism for teaching "the epigenetic patterns of culture" (p. 122), and that successful social development requires a high degree of skill in negotiating emotional communication, "much of which is nonverbal" (p. 80). Tucker concludes that such emotional information engages "specialized neural networks in humans, within the right hemisphere" (p. 80). This conceptualization clearly suggests an important and unique role for clinical social work in infant mental health and optimal right brain development.

In particular, attachment programs aimed at prevention and early intervention. This chapter outlines and highlights a large and important body of knowledge that requires careful study. It is outside our usual social work "comfort zone," and thus often omitted in current masters and doctoral education. We cannot afford to continue overlooking the valuable insights available by applying neuroscientific knowledge to social work and psychotherapeutic principles. The expanding knowledge of these disciplines needs to be incorporated in our professional curriculum to promote not only a more profound understanding of the impact of diversity, but more effective relational and therapeutic skills.

Study Questions

1. How is attachment theory transformed by neurobiology?
2. What is the importance of the right hemisphere in development and psychotherapy?
3. What is interactive regulation?
4. What is the importance of transference and countertransference for clinical social work?
5. What neurobiological attachment principles did you learn in this chapter that will inform your work with adults?

Acknowledgment This work was supported by a grant from the FHL Foundation.

References

Andrade, V. M. (2005). Affect and the therapeutic action in psychoanalysis. *International Journal of Psychoanalysis, 86*, 677–697.

Applegate, J. S., & Shapiro, J. R. (2005). *Neurobiology for clinical social work: Theory and practice*. New York: W. W. Norton.

Bargh, J. A., & Morsella, E. (2008). The unconscious mind. *Perspectives on Psychological Science, 3*, 73–79.

Bornstein, R. F. (1999). Source amnesia, misattribution, and the power of unconscious perceptions and memories. *Psychoanalytic Psychology, 16*, 155–178.

Bowlby, J. (1969/1982). *Attachment and loss. Vol. 1: Attachment.* New York: Basic Books.

Bowlby, J. (1988). *A secure base* (2nd ed.). New York: Basic Books.

Brancucci, A., Lucci, G., Mazzatenta, A., & Tommasi, L. (2009). Asymmetries of the human social brain in the visual, auditory and chemical modalities. *Philosophical Transactions of the Royal Society of London Biological Sciences, 364*, 895–914.

Bucci, W. (2002). The referential process, consciousness, and the sense of self. *Psychoanalytic Inquiry, 5*, 766–793.

Burgoon, J. K. (1985). Nonverbal signals. In M. L. Knapp & C. R. Miller (Eds.), *Handbook of interpersonal communication* (pp. 344–390). Beverly Hills, CA: Sager Publications.

Cozolino, L. (2002). *The neuroscience of psychotherapy.* New York: W. W. Norton.

Decety, J., & Chaminade, T. (2003). When the self represents the other: A new cognitive neuroscience view on psychological identification. *Consciousness and Cognition, 12*, 577–596.

Devinsky, O. (2000). Right cerebral hemispheric dominance for a sense of corporeal and emotional self. *Epilepsy & Behavior, 1*, 60–73.

Dorpat, T. L. (2001). Primary process communication. *Psychoanalytic Inquiry, 3*, 448–463.

Feinberg, T. E., & Keenan, J. P. (2005). Where in the brain is the self? *Consciousness and Cognition, 14*, 661–678.

Freud, S. (1895/1966). Project for a scientific psychology. In J. Strachey (Ed. & Trans.), *Standard edition of the complete psychological works of Sigmund Freud* (Vol. 1, pp. 295–397). London: Hogarth Press (Original work published 1895).

Gainotti, G. (2006). Unconscious emotional memories and the right hemisphere. In M. Mancia (Ed.), *Psychoanalysis and neuroscience* (pp. 151–173). Milan: Springer Milan.

Ginot, E. (2009). The empathic power of enactments. The link between neuropsychological processes and an expanded definition of empathy. *Psychoanalytic Psychology, 26*, 290–309.

Glass, R. M. (2008). Psychodynamic psychotherapy and research evidence. Bambi survives Godzilla? *Journal of the American Medical Association, 300*, 1587–1589.

Grabner, R. H., Fink, A., & Neubauer, A. C. (2007). Brain correlates of self-related originality of ideas: Evidence from event-related power and phase-locking changes in the EEG. *Behavioral Neuroscience, 121*, 224–230.

Jacobs, T. J. (1994). Nonverbal communications: some reflections on their role in the psychoanalytic process and psychoanalytic education. *Journal of the American Psychoanalytic Association, 42*, 741–762.

Keenan, J. P., Gallup, G. G., & Falk, D. (2003). *The face in the mirror: The search for the origins of consciousness.* New York: Harper Collins.

Keenan, J. P., Rubio, J., Racioppi, C., Johnson, A., & Barnacz, A. (2005). The right hemisphere and the dark side of consciousness. *Cortex, 41*, 695–704.

Kohut, H. (1971). *The analysis of the self.* New York: International University Press.

Leichsenring, F., & Rabung, S. (2008). Effectiveness of long-term psychodynamic psychotherapy. A meta-analysis. *Journal of the American Medical Association, 300*, 1551–1565.

Lyons-Ruth, K. (1999). The two-person unconscious: Intersubjective dialogue, enactive relational representation, and the emergence of new forms of relational organization. *Psychoanalytic Inquiry, 19*, 576–617.

Lyons-Ruth, K. (2000). "I sense that you sense that I sense...": Sander's recognition process and the specificity of relational moves in the psychotherapeutic setting. *Infant Mental Health Journal, 21*, 85–98.

Mahler, M., Pine, F., & Bergman, A. (1975). *The psychological birth of the human infant.* New York: Basic Books.

Mancia, M. (2006). Implicit memory and early unrepressed unconscious: Their role in the therapeutic process (How the neurosciences can contribute to psychoanalysis). *International Journal of Psychoanalysis, 87*, 83–103.

Mandal, M. K., & Ambady, N. (2004). Laterality of facial expressions of emotion: Universal and culture-specific influences. *Behavioral Neurology, 15*, 23–34.

Markowitsch, H. J., Reinkemeier, A., Kessler, J., Koyuncu, A., & Heiss, W. D. (2000). Right amygdalar and temperofrontal activation during autobiographical, but not fictitious memory retrieval. *Behavioral Neurology, 12*, 181–190.

Maroda, K. J. (2005). Show some emotion: completing the cycle of affective communication. In L. Aron & A. Harris (Eds.), *Revolutionary connections. Relational psychoanalysis. Vol. II. Innovation and expansion* (pp. 121–142). Hillsdale, NJ: Analytic Press.

Meares, R. (2005). *The metaphor of play: Origin and breakdown of personal being* (3rd ed.). London: Routledge.

Miller, B. L., Seeley, W. W., Mychack, P., Rosen, H. J., Mena, I., & Boone, K. (2001). Neuroanatomy of the self: Evidence from patients with frontotemporal dementia. *Neurology, 57*, 817–821.

Minagawa-Kawai, Y., Matsuoka, S., Dan, I., Naoi, N., Nakamura, K., & Kojima, S. (2009). Prefrontal activation associated with social attachment: facial-emotion recognition in mothers and infants. *Cerebral Cortex, 19*, 284–292.

Mlot, C. (1998). Probing the biology of emotion. *Science, 280*, 1005–1007.

Nemeroff, C. B., Heim, C. M., Thase, M. E., Klein, D. N., Rush, A. J., Schatzberg, A. F., et al. (2003). Differential responses to psychotherapy versus pharmacotherapy in patients with chronic forms of major depression and childhood trauma. *Proceedings of the National Academy of Sciences of the United States of America, 100*, 14293–14296.

Ogden, P., Pain, C., Minton, K., & Fisher, J. (2005). Including the body in mainstream psychotherapy for traumatized individuals. *Psychologist-Psychoanalyst, 25*(4), 19–24.

Ohnishi, T., Moriguchi, Y., Matsuda, H., Mori, T., Hirakata, M., Imabayashi, E., et al. (2004). The neural network for the mirror system and mentalizing in normally developed children: An fMRI study. *NeuroReport, 15*, 1483–1487.

Orlinsky, D. E., & Howard, K. I. (1986). Process and outcome in psychotherapy. In S. L. Garfield & A. E. Bergin (Eds.), *Handbook of psychotherapy and behavior change* (3rd ed.). New York: Wiley.

Ovtscharoff, W., & Braun, K. (2001). Maternal separation and social isolation modulate the postnatal development of synaptic composition in the infralimbic cortex of octodon degus. *Neuroscience, 104*, 33–40.

Palombo, J., Bendicsen, H. K., & Koch, B. J. (2009). *Guide to psychoanalytic developmental theories*. New York: Springer.

Phelkos, J. L., Belsky, J., & Crnic, K. (1998). Earned security, daily stress, and parenting: A comparison of five alternative models. *Development and Psychopathology, 10*, 21–38.

Pincus, D., Freeman, W., & Modell, A. (2007). A neurobiological model of perception: Considerations for transference. *Psychoanalytic Psychology, 24*, 623–640.

Ryan, R. M. (2007). Motivation and emotion: A new look and approach for two reemerging fields. *Motivation and Emotion, 31*, 1–3.

Sander, L. (1992). Letter to the Editor. *International Journal of Psychoanalysis, 73*, 582–584.

Scaer, R. (2005). *The trauma spectrum: hidden wounds and human resiliency*. New York: W. W. Norton.

Schore, A. N. (1994). *Affect regulation and the origin of the self*. Mahweh, NJ: Erlbaum.

Schore, A. N. (1996). The experience-dependent maturation of a regulatory system in the orbital prefrontal cortex and the origin of developmental psychopathology. *Development and Psychopathology, 8*, 59–87.

Schore, A. N. (1997). A century after Freud's Project: Is a rapprochement between psychoanalysis and neurobiology at hand? *Journal of the American Psychoanalytic Association, 45*, 841–867.

Schore, A. N. (2000). Attachment and the regulation of the right brain. *Attachment and Human Development, 2*, 23–47.

Schore, A. N. (2001a). Minds in the making: Attachment, the self-organizing brain, and developmentally-oriented psychoanalytic psychotherapy. *British Journal of Psychotherapy, 17*, 299–328.

Schore, A. N. (2001b). The effects of a secure attachment relationship on right brain development, affect regulation, and infant mental health. *Infant Mental Health Journal, 22*, 7–66.

Schore, A. N. (2002a). Advances in neuropsychoanalysis, attachment theory, and trauma research: Implications for self psychology. *Psychoanalytic Inquiry, 22*, 433–484.

Schore, A. N. (2002b). The right brain as the neurobiological substratum of Freud's dynamic unconscious. In D. Scharff (Ed.), *The psychoanalytic century: Freud's legacy for the future* (pp. 61–88). New York: Other Press.

Schore, A. N. (2002c). Dysregulation of the right brain: a fundamental mechanism of traumatic attachment and the psychopathogenesis of posttraumatic stress disorder. *Australian and New Zealand Journal of Psychiatry, 36*, 9–30.

Schore, A. N. (2003a). *Affect dysregulation and disorders of the self.* New York: W. W. Norton.

Schore, A. N. (2003b). *Affect regulation and the repair of the self.* New York: W. W. Norton.

Schore, A. N. (2005). A neuropsychoanalytic viewpoint. Commentary on a paper by Stephen H. Knoblauch. *Psychoanalytic Dialogues, 15*, 829–854.

Schore, A. N. (2007). Review of Philip Bromberg's 'Awakening the Dreamer: Clinical Journeys'. *Psychoanalytic Dialogues, 17*, 753–767.

Schore, A. N. (2009a). Relational trauma and the developing right brain. *Annals of the New York Academy of Sciences, 1159*, 189–203.

Schore, A. N. (2009b). Right brain affect regulation: An essential mechanism of development, trauma, dissociation, and psychotherapy. In D. Fosha, D. Siegel, & M. Solomon (Eds.), *The healing power of emotion: Affective neuroscience, development, & clinical practice* (pp. 112–144). New York: W. W. Norton.

Schore, J., & Schore, A. (2008). Modern attachment theory: The central role of affect regulation in development and treatment. *Clinical Social Work Journal, 36*, 9–20.

Shamay-Tsoory, S. G., Tomer, R., Berger, B. D., & Aharon-Peretz, J. (2003). Characterization of empathy deficits following prefrontal brain damage: The role of the right ventromedial prefrontal cortex. *Journal of Cognitive Neuroscience, 15*, 324–337.

Shaw, R. (2004). The embodied psychotherapist: An exploration of the therapists' somatic phenomena within the therapeutic encounter. *Psychotherapy Research, 14*, 271–288.

Shuren, J. E., & Grafman, J. (2002). The neurology of reasoning. *Archives of Neurology, 59*, 916–919.

Siegel, D. J. (1999). *Developing mind: Toward a neurobiology of interpersonal experience.* New York: W. W. Norton.

Stern, D. N. (2005). Intersubjectivity. In E. S. Person, A. M. Cooper, & G. O. Gabbard (Eds.), *Textbook of psychoanalysis* (pp. 77–92). Washington, DC: American Psychiatric Publishing.

Tucker, D. M. (1992). Developing emotions and cortical networks. In M. R. Gunnar & C. A. Nelson (Eds.), *Minnesota symposium on child psychology. Vol. 24. Developmental behavioral neuroscience* (pp. 75–128). Hillsdale, NJ: Erlbaum.

Tutte, J. C. (2004). The concept of psychical trauma: A bridge in interdisciplinary space. *International Journal of Psychoanalysis, 85*, 897–921.

van Lancker, D., & Cummings, J. L. (1999). Expletives: Neurolinguistic and neurobehavioral perspectives on swearing. *Brain Research Reviews, 31*, 83–104.

Watt, D. F. (2003). Psychotherapy in an age of neuroscience: bridges to affective neuroscience. In J. Corrigal & H. Wilkinson (Eds.), *Revolutionary connections: Psychotherapy and neuroscience* (pp. 79–115). Karnac: London.

Whitehead, C. C. (2006). Neo-psychoanalysis: A paradigm for the 21st century. *Journal of the Academy of Psychoanalysis and Dynamic Psychiatry, 34*, 603–627.

Part II
Applications to Adult Clinical Practice

Chapter 5
Separation, Loss, and Grief in Adults:
An Attachment Perspective

Judith Kay Nelson

> *But, you see, a traumatized child as I was once, long ago, and one who recovers, as I did, has a wall between him and pain and despair, between himself and grief...*

Brodkey (1994, p. 71)

Grief and loss are at the core of attachment theory and at the core of clinical social work practice. When teaching *Loss,* Bowlby's (1980) third volume, I ask students to inventory their clients, past and present, looking for issues of separation, loss, and grief. As they think through the question, their list quickly grows to include not only losses by death but also divorce, relocation, immigration, empty nest, retirement, infertility, and job loss, to name a few. It quickly becomes clear that loss and grief are central to the presenting problems or underlying issues of essentially every client. The following chapter explores how an attachment perspective informs clinical understandings of grief and the kinds of interventions that grow out of that understanding.

Theoretical Underpinnings for an Attachment View of Adult Grief

Attachment and separation are two sides of a coin. Attachment is necessary for survival, and painful reactions to separations from the attachment figure serve as a powerful motivation to maintain proximity and thus protect and preserve the attachment bond (Bowlby, 1969/1982). Bowlby's early work with juvenile offenders alerted him to the fact that, as a group, they had suffered a tremendous number of traumatic early separations from, and losses of, primary caregivers. Bowlby realized that he needed to understand the nature of the attachment bond in order to make

J.K. Nelson (✉)
The Sanville Institute for Clinical Social Work and Psychotherapy, Berkeley, CA, USA
e-mail: jkaynelson@sbcglobal.net

S. Bennett and J.K. Nelson (Eds.), *Adult Attachment in Clinical Social Work*,
Essential Clinical Social Work Series, DOI 10.1007/978-1-4419-6241-6_5,
© Springer Science+Business Media, LLC 2010

sense of the reactions when those bonds were threatened or severed, leading him ultimately to the development of attachment theory.

During World War II, British infants and young children were moved to group homes in the countryside to keep them out of harm's way, giving Bowlby the opportunity to observe first hand their reactions to separation from their caregivers. In his early article on grief and mourning in infancy, Bowlby (1960) noted that the infants' reactions changed over time. When his/her parent first left, a child over the age of 6 months would, "cry loudly, shake his cot, throw himself about, and look eagerly towards any sight or sound which might prove to be his missing mother" (p. 15). This highly urgent distress behavior, which Bowlby labeled *protest*, was clearly meant to alert and disturb the caregiver and bring about an immediate end to the separation. If there was no reunion within hours or days, the infants would sink into a quiet despair, appearing to give up hope that their caregiver would hear them and return, a response that Bowlby designated as *despair*. Finally, if the separation continued and no relationship was established with a consistent substitute caregiver, then the infants would become silent and enter a final life-threatening stage Bowlby called *detachment*.

Bowlby noted that over the course of a lifetime, most separations are temporary, with the permanent loss of an attachment figure being a rare event. Hence, the loud, urgent crying of the protest phase is designed to bring an end to the separation as quickly as possible. It is only when the separation is prolonged and hope of a reunion fades that the infant sinks into despair and the cry is no longer loud, urgent, or frequent. If there is no reunion and no substitute attachment figure, detachment does indeed threaten survival, and the infant may die.

When Bowlby (1961) later studied the reactions of older children and adults to the loss of a close loved one, he observed the same three reactions: protest, despair, and in some instances of prolonged and unresolved grief, detached depression. He wrote, "When he weeps, the bereaved adult is responding to loss as a child does to the temporary absence of his mother" (p. 333). The one significant difference is that older children and adults are able, through caregiving from living and/or internalized attachment figures, to work through their grief to a stage that Bowlby called *reorganization*.

Caregiving and Grief

Attachment cannot take place in a vacuum. A response from a caregiver is necessary for the establishment, maintenance, and repair of an attachment bond. The *attachment system* at all ages relies on the *caregiving system* of an attachment figure, and it is through the caregiving responses that separations are ended, separation distress soothed, and permanent losses grieved and reorganized, or healed. The two systems – attachment and caregiving – are interconnected so that the activation of one creates a reciprocal, contingent response in the other, forming the basis for what we clinically refer to as intersubjectivity. For example, attachment behaviors such as crying, the arms up signal, or distress screams and calls are effective means, not only of alerting caregivers, but also of arousing their distress, thus encouraging them to respond with behaviors such as touch, soothing sounds, words, and gaze to regulate and relieve the distress – the infant's distress and ultimately their own as well.

The nervous systems of infant and caregiver are intertwined in such a way that negative arousal, such as separation distress in the infant, creates negative arousal in the parent/caregiver – and to a certain extent to anyone within earshot (Schore, 2003). Parents wired to test heart rate, blood pressure, and skin responses showed increased diastolic blood pressure and heart rate, as well as skin conductance measures consistent with attention, tension, and autonomic arousal – all pointing to a strong urge to take action (Boukydis, 1985; Boukydis & Burgess, 1982; Donovan & Balling, 1978; Donovan & Leavitt, 1985). Brain imaging studies of breastfeeding mothers listening to infant cries found that there was increased activity in areas of the mothers' brains, such as the right orbitofrontal cortex, known to be related to maternal activity in other animals (Lorberbaum et al., 2002).

Adults' distress signals are also attachment behaviors that alert others to their alarm about separation. It is clear that if an adult is crying in the corner of a room, everyone present will be alert to the message and most people will feel an urge to respond, though they may decide against doing so given the circumstances (Nelson, 2005). Neurological imaging studies of adults listening to other adults cry (some of which are in the planning stages) may also provide additional clues about the physiology of our caregiving systems.

Separation, Loss, and Grief Defined

Separations between attachment figures are painful in order to encourage proximity between infants and their caregivers, as well as adults and their mates and close loved ones. During infancy, all separations, even short ones, are potentially life-threatening and hence produce great distress. However, with maturity, increased attachment security, and cognitive development, brief and sometimes even prolonged separations may be tolerated. Though such separations are uncommon in the tribal societies closer to our environment of evolutionary adaptedness (Bowlby, 1980), they are a constant reality for most western families and their children.

Permanent separations, however, are another matter. Attachment bonds are not made to be broken. They are made to endure. When an attachment bond is lost or severed, even if it is planned, expected, or developmental, it results in the activation of attachment distress and the prolonged state of negative arousal known as grief. Grief is the attachment system's response to dealing with permanent loss of the attachment figure.

Research has shown that attachment-figure loss provokes intense negative arousal that has been compared both poetically and scientifically to physical pain. Even social rejection and exclusion by strangers in one fMRI study – minor losses relative to permanent separation from an attachment figure – were found to activate the brain regions associated with physical pain (Eisenberger, Lieberman, & Williams, 2003). Intense painful affect also accompanies the severing of attachment ties when love relationships end through breakups, separations, and divorces (Mikulincer & Shaver, 2007).

If separation from the caregiver is the prototype of infant grief, death of a close loved one is the prototype of adult grief (Nelson, 2005). Permanent loss of an adult attachment figure feels like the same threat to survival that separation from the parent evokes in an infant and triggers the same attachment behaviors, especially crying, and grief reactions: protest, despair, and detachment. The occurrence of crying – a universal attachment/separation behavior at the death of a close loved one, as it is at separation from a caregiver in infancy – occurs throughout history and in every culture in the world, even when crying is forbidden or believed dangerous to the life of survivors or to the passage of the soul in the next life (Habenstein & Lamers, 1963; Kracke, 1981, 1988).

Other less intense separations and losses, acting like "miniature deaths," may also trigger grief reactions. These losses may be large or small, present or past, literal or symbolic, threatened or imagined (Nelson, 2005; Simos, 1979). Any loss involves severing a bond with someone or something to which one is attached, whether it be a loved one or a country, a home, health, money, possessions, a community, a language, a job, a lifestyle, or self-esteem, security, identity, reputation, respect, or freedom -of-choice, to name a range of examples. The loss may also be of an ideal or a wished-for but unrealized attachment, such as bearing a child, earning a degree, having a nurturing relationship with a parent, or finding a marriage partner.

In preparing this chapter, I recorded the losses brought up by my adult clients in one day of my psychotherapy practice. They included in the six people I saw that day: the premature death of a parent, the deaths of several close friends while in high school, terminal illness of an aging parent who had been abusive, retirement, a cross-country move and the loss of home and friends, the abrupt end of a 10-year affair, a sibling with a life-threatening cancer diagnosis, a threatened job loss, a threatened demotion, exclusion from a gathering of siblings, the lack of a life partner, denigration of competence from a parent and a boss, miscarriages, and infertility. Losses such as these, experienced by human beings of every age and in every culture, losses from the obvious to the subtle, the present or the past, may trigger a grief reaction manifest as protest or despair and resulting in either detachment or reorganization.

The Stages of Grief

Each stage of grief presents with a different set of behaviors, affects, and attitudes and represents a different goal or aim relative to the loss (Bowlby, 1980; Nelson, 2005). Each stage also triggers differing responses in potential caregivers. The clinician is assessing and responding to these distinct differences "intuitively," which is to say the distress or negative arousal of the client triggers a companion response in the caregiver/caseworker/therapist and often serves as a nonconscious guide to these responses. Grief in the client is a two-person, intersubjective experience impacting the therapist, who is guided by his/her own internal experience of the client's grief, colored by the therapist's own grief about personal losses.

What clinicians refer to as "intuitive" responses to client's attachment affects, including grief, are what is called *implicit relational knowing* (Lyons-Ruth, 1998), which is nonconscious knowledge based on the attachment/caregiving experiences and affect regulation patterns established early in life. To the extent that implicit relational knowing can be conceptualized consciously, it can guide the clinician in understanding affect arousal as shared by client and clinician, with affect attunement to the client and with affect regulation – both that of the client and the clinician (Nelson, 2005, 2007). An attachment perspective on grief helps to make the therapist's nonconscious, implicit knowledge more explicit, thus guiding the therapist in better understanding and weathering the grief of the client.

Protest

Protest throughout life, as in infancy, is an urgent signal of distress designed to avoid or undo a loss and bring about a reunion. From an evolutionary standpoint, it is designed to be an effective emergency signal serving to bring about a reunion after a traumatic and potentially life-threatening separation. It is the front-line defense against a painful separation, most of which, as Bowlby (1969/1982) pointed out, end in reunions. Even when the reality of a permanent loss is immediately apparent, the default response is protest. A taxi driver described picking up a man who had just received news of his mother's death. The bereaved sat with his arms "folded in an X across his chest, fingers spread wide, clutching his shoulders as though to keep his quaking body from flying apart. 'I want my mother back!' he bawled" (Newsham, 2000, p. D8). In the film *The Messenger* (Moverman, 2009), about an army next-of-kin notification team, protest is in evidence in scene after scene. When family members are told about their loved ones' death in Iraq or Afghanistan, their protest responses range from screaming "no" or vomiting, to slapping, spitting, swearing at, or threatening the informants.

The protest phase of grief in response to the sudden death of a close loved one is understandable, and in most instances engenders a deep sense of sympathy and empathy. Most people can identify with what it might feel like to lose a mother, father, child, or spouse, and the wish to resist truly taking in the news that the loss is permanent. However, protest grief also occurs in response to other less apparently significant losses when it may strike a much different chord in potential caregivers.

Starting in childhood, it makes sense that a toddler screams in protest because her mother is leaving for work, but not if the toddler is similarly screaming in protest for being denied a sugary treat or asked to put on her shoes. Caregivers who sympathize with the use of a high urgency attachment behavior to avoid a separation from the mother have a much harder time when a child protests to avoid the loss of a cookie or the end of playtime. Similarly, when an adult spouse tearfully protests a partner's threats to cancel a birthday dinner in favor of a fishing trip, the urgent demand to "undo" the loss is clear to the partner, but it comes across as angry and accusatory, and typically engenders more resistance and guilt than empathy.

Protest represents an angry refusal to surrender to a loss. All the grief energy goes into reestablishing the threatened connection and fighting any indication that the loss is irrevocable or permanent. The internal state that accompanies protest grief ranges from anger and rage to hurt feelings, frustration, denial, and disbelief. Adults in the protest phase of grief feel the pain of their anger and resistance to the loss deeply, and they want potential caregivers to respond immediately to relieve or undo the precipitant. Unfortunately, their efforts often backfire and cause interpersonal distance and resentment instead of the desired caregiving action to rectify the situation.

A woman in her late 60s, for example, entered therapy at the insistence of her adult children because she was so "angry" about her late-life divorce 3 years prior. Even though her husband had remarried, she was intent on getting him to see his mistake and come back. She could talk of little else with her children or her friends, who found it impossible to soothe her in any way. They often expressed impatience with her and would insist that she "get past it" and make a new life. Even when sympathy is felt and offered, those protesting their losses are not usually responsive. They want action, not comfort. In other words, protest grief blocks the griever's ability to reorganize, leaving her or him stuck instead in chronic grief. This client's aggressive demand for restoration of the marriage relationship, for example, was a way of symbolically and defensively maintaining a connection to her lost attachment figure, preventing her from surrendering to the loss and moving on to work through her grief and reorganize her attachment ties to other close people in her life.

Protest grief over personal and societal losses may also be seen with people disenfranchised through oppression, occupation, dislocation, or war. At the communal level, such protest can be a viable, healthy, and productive way to mobilize and avoid further traumatization. The AIDS activist group "ACT UP," for example, was known for their "in-your-face" political action tactics. They organized noisy, highly visible protests taking on drug companies, insurance companies, the medical establishment, and government bureaucracies. Their motto was "Silence equal death." Because they did not want to face death or see others do so, they protested in highly visible ways and, in the end, succeeded in bringing about much needed social change and the release of experimental drugs that transformed HIV/AIDS into a chronic illness, rather than a terminal one. The outcome of the protest confirmed that it was indeed a successful means of avoiding the loss of so many lives.

Protest on a communal level can, however, become problematic when it is expressed as armed aggression, terrorism, torture, threats, blame, and hostile epithets – violent "protests" of all kinds. It is particularly problematic in terms of reorganization when undoing or averting the losses of one group takes place at the expense of another's losses, as when possession of certain territories is in dispute, or where one group's religious practices exclude the practices of another group. Chronic, ongoing protest, including hostile aggression, precludes reorganization for either group, as we see, for example, with on-going protests between pro-choice and pro-life groups or with deeply entrenched partisan politics.

Despair

When infants protest a separation but there is no reunion, they eventually sink into a desolate state of despair, their only sound an occasional low wail. Despair occurs when hope of reunion with the lost attachment figure has faded. Similarly, adults who have lost a close loved one or who are facing losses of other kinds enter the stage of despair when they acknowledge there will be no happy ending, reunion, or reconciliation. Time cannot be turned backward; the lost object will not reappear. With despair there is surrender to the loss, taking in the reality rather than pushing it away.

The pain of despair is intense, but paradoxically, it is this stage of grief that, unlike protest, enables the mourner to move back to connection and attachment. Despair is the means by which loss and grief are reorganized into something new, realigning existing attachments or forging new ones, while maintaining a symbolic or internalized connection with the lost object. Caregiving received from internalized attachment figures or through direct aid and comfort from others is, as in infancy, a necessary part of the process of moving from despair to reorganization, from loss back to love.

Despair accompanied by vulnerability that is raw and heartfelt stirs potential caregivers to feel sympathy and evokes a desire to reach out with compassion and comfort. Despair draws caregivers closer, thus enabling the person in grief to replace despair about "survival" with a life-affirming sense of hope. A client in her late 80s returned to therapy when her beloved cat died. She reported that she had been crying several hours a day since losing her. I offered sympathy and comfort as she described the cat's adorable behaviors, how he was like a family member, a caregiver who responded to any hint of distress, "attuning" to her affect by jumping into her lap, purring, and offering her soothing through warm physical contact. As a notoriously cantankerous older woman who evoked strong reactions in others, she was pleased by the total acceptance and unconditional love of the cat. As the weeks in therapy wore on, she began, with my support, to work actively at distracting herself through various activities, and the crying in despair began to dissipate. Eventually she overcame her resistance to getting a new cat, and soon was deeply attached to him, transforming her grief from despair to reorganization. She maintained her affectionate internal connection with the former cat, whose picture remained on her desk, while at the same time she was able to establish an attachment to the new one.

While despair is a necessary stage in moving through grief, it can also result in immobilizing sadness characterized by helplessness and hopelessness. Individuals and social groups faced with insurmountable losses may feel so stunned or numbed by loss that their energies are drained, creativity sidelined, and hope overwhelmed. People who experience cumulative or repetitive trauma may also find it difficult to recover from despair. For example, Katrina victims who may have lost a loved one, a home, a community, a job and financial security, and who relocate to a hostile or detached environment with people and customs foreign to them, may find themselves in a permanent cycle of despair. They lack potential caregivers and sufficient hope or energy to accept overtures from those who may appear.

Reorganization

Bowlby (1980) defined reorganization as the bereaved coming to recognize that the loss is permanent and that their life must be reshaped around the new attachment reality. If all goes well, and soothing caregivers are available, despair may begin to alternate with examining the new situation and considering ways of meeting it. This is a process, he wrote, of "reshaping internal representational models so as to align them with the changes that have occurred in the bereaved's life situation" (p. 94).

For individuals experiencing the loss of an attachment figure, the reorganization may involve being able to attach to someone new, as with the older woman described above, who decided after a period of grief that she did want to get a new cat. The divorced woman who had been so vehemently protesting her lost marriage for 3 years eventually felt she had nothing to lose in experimenting with internet dating and began to reorganize internally as she opened herself to possible new relationships. A man who was immobilized by grief and despair after he was fired from a long-term job, suffered for a year in an isolated, detached depression. At the insistence of family members, he joined a group of other professionals struggling with job losses, and after a time was able to reorganize. He began to network with former associates and make inquiries about finding a new position.

We are also familiar with personal losses that have been transformed into humanitarian organizations such as MADD (Mothers Against Drunk Drivers), or into legislative changes such as Amber's Law that mandate public notification of child abductions immediately, or Ryan's Law that requires insurance companies to offer coverage for individuals diagnosed with Autism Spectrum Disorder, Asperger's, or Pervasive Developmental Disorder. There are also countless families who have established memorial funds in honor of lost ones or to prevent other families and individuals from suffering similar traumatic losses, or to support those who do suffer them. Valentino Achak Deng, one of the Lost Boys of the Sudan, who survived unbearable trauma, desolation, bereavement, and loss in that country's devastating war, told his life story in the book *What is the What,* in collaboration with writer Dave Eggers (2006). Not only does the story itself memorialize the children who died and the families who suffered, but proceeds from the book also help raise funds to help Deng's surviving family and community, thus transforming and reorganizing his loss into new attachments for him as well as other survivors.

Attachment Styles and Patterns of Grief

Normal grief is set in motion by the inability to gain proximity to an attachment figure. As in childhood when an attachment figure is chronically unavailable, bereaved adults are forced to turn to the secondary attachment strategies of hyperactivation and/or deactivation of the attachment system. Mikulincer and Shaver (2007) suggest that these secondary strategies temporarily set in motion during grief may aid in the reorganization process and that both strategies contribute to reorganization.

> Without a degree and at least some periods of attachment-system hyperactivation, a mourner is not fully capable of understanding the depth and meaning of the loss. But without a degree of deactivation, the mourner may remain stuck in grief, unable to transfer attachment functions to new figures. (p. 75)

Securely attached adults, it would appear, are best able to balance and make use of these temporary secondary strategies in their healing process. Hyperactivation, the attachment strategy typical of the anxious/preoccupied individual, includes negative arousal in the form of distress and crying, a needy longing for the attachment figure, and difficulty with being soothed – qualities consonant with the protest stage of grief. Deactivation, the attachment strategy typical of the avoidant/dismissive individual, includes the use of distraction, trying to suppress thinking about the loss, and "downregulating the intrusion of painful thoughts and feelings" (Mikulincer & Shaver, 2007, p. 75). The older woman mentioned above who was grieving her lost cat, for example, used both of these strategies on her way to reorganization. When she first came in, she described crying up to several hours a day with longing for and missing the cat. After a few weeks, she began to consciously use deactivating strategies, particularly distraction, to help regulate the overwhelming hyperactivation. She was able to reorganize and eventually reattach to a new cat utilizing both strategies.

Grief in Securely Attached Adults

Fraley, Fazzari, Bonanno, and Dekel (2006) studied people exposed to the 2001 World Trade Center attack 7 and 18 months afterward, looking at attachment style dimensions and depression. Friends and relatives of these victims were also asked about their adjustment before and since the attacks. People with secure attachments were found to suffer fewer symptoms of PTSD and depression and were seen by friends and relatives to have had good adjustment both before and after the attacks. Securely attached people who had lost a spouse were studied by Fraley and Bonanno (2004) at two time periods – 4 and 19 months postbereavement – and were found to experience relatively lower levels of grief, depression, anxiety, and posttraumatic stress.

Securely attached people also are more inclined to seek help and emotional support in the face of a loss than are the insecurely attached. In other words, as would be expected, those whose pattern of attachment is based on early and subsequent experiences with reliable and available affect-regulating attachment figures are most inclined to look to attachment figures when there is a serious loss. As Mikulincer and Shaver (2007) write, "Overall, research indicates that attachment security fosters support seeking, generally in constructive and effective ways..." (p. 199).

The entire picture relating to grief is much more complicated for insecurely attached adults. Bowlby (1980), among others, pointed to two types of unresolved grief reactions: chronic mourning (hyperactivation) and absence of conscious grieving (deactivation). Individuals whose general attachment style is an insecure one, relying on one of these two opposing strategies, may find it difficult to temporarily incorporate the unfamiliar, less comfortable strategy enough to reach a stage of reorganization.

Grief in Anxious/Preoccupied Adults

Anxious/preoccupied individuals typically intensify or hyperactivate their negative affects. Thus, when grieving they present with high vulnerability and emphasize their need for attention and care, though seldom do they feel it is sufficiently forthcoming. Along with this presentation, they have hypervigilance, with somatic changes, heightened recall, and ruminative thoughts, and a tendency to make catastrophic appraisals of events that amplify the threatening aspects of both major and minor losses (Mikulincer & Shaver, 2007).

Even though anxious/preoccupied people are not hesitant to communicate their attachment affect, they are not able to ask for and receive help in ways that help them to heal. Mikulincer and Shaver (2007) speculate, based on research, that worries about rejection and abandonment prevalent in those with anxious/preoccupied attachment seem to "... disorganize their efforts to seek support. These worries, coupled with doubts about others' supportiveness, can sometimes inhibit direct requests for help and channel support-seeking efforts toward nonverbal expressions of helplessness and distress" (p. 199).

Grief in Avoidant/Dismissing Adults

For those with an avoidant/dismissing style, deactivation of the attachment system is the hallmark. When grieving, these individuals suppress the attachment affects and behaviors, such as crying, and suppress thoughts of their lost loved one. The traditional wisdom about absent grieving suggests that deactivating affects, attachment behaviors, and distracting oneself mentally are defenses expected to lead to later symptoms and suffering (Bowlby, 1969/1982). However, an individual whose avoidant/dismissing style is pervasive may have been so distant and detached from a "close" loved one prior to the death that he or she may be able to move forward without obvious signs of mourning and with no apparent ill-effects over time (Shaver & Fraley, 2008). Other research (Mikulincer, Dolev, & Shaver, 2004), however, dovetails with clinical observation (Nelson, 2005) in noting that certain avoidant/dismissing individuals are sometimes deeply impacted by significant losses. Their deactivation defenses, effective in everyday situations, are ineffective (Birnbau, Orr, Mikulincer, & Florian, 1997). Devastating losses such as the breakup of a relationship, the loss of a spouse, or the death of a child arouse unfamiliar and deeply uncomfortable attachment affects. In one study over 7 years, avoidant mothers of children with a congenital heart defect showed greater mental health impact and marital dysfunction than other attachment style groups on measures administered at three time periods (Berant, Mikulincer, & Shaver, 2008).

Grief in Disorganized/Disoriented Adults

People with disorganized/disoriented attachment patterns are perhaps at the greatest risk to have unresolved grief due to the loss of a close loved one, as well as other less significant losses (Lyons-Ruth, 2003). Their propensity toward dissociation in the face of painful attachment affect is based on histories that include physical or emotional abuse, severe neglect, or psychotic, fearful parents (see the Brodkey quotation just below the title of this chapter about his inability to react when told he was dying). Lyons-Ruth's (2003) longitudinal study of attachment identified a number of caregiving patterns that may lead to dissociation: "withdrawing responses," "negative-intrusive responses," "role-confused responses," "disoriented responses," and "affective communication errors," such as contradictory cues, non- or inappropriate responses, physical distance or withdrawal, and sexualization (p. 890). On the AAI, parents whose infants were disorganized "often contain indicators of unintegrated areas of thinking related to loss or trauma, such as uninvited intrusions of the topic into the interview or contradictory references to the topic across the interview" (Lyons-Ruth, 2003, p. 894). In other words, disorganized parents may also dissociate with attachment stress and may be ineffective regulators of their children's affect, meaning that propensities toward dissociation with grief may be transmitted intergenerationally.

In the clinical situation, the disorganized/disoriented individual may describe feeling "numb" or "dead" in response to a loss, or there may be a blank dissociative denial of any feelings. In describing the etiology of this extreme method of defending against attachment affect, including grief, Lyons-Ruth (2003) notes that "dissociated events are neither consciously experienced nor lost, but rather are unthinkable..." (p. 900). In the case of abuse, distressing affect early in life may have been created and/or escalated by the caregivers, rather than regulated. Dissociation is a last-ditch defense against unthinkable rejection and overwhelming negative arousal, such as that faced when there is a loss.

Alternatively, with grief and loss, dissociated individuals may hyper-react, becoming suicidal, or alternately cling to, berate, and reject caregivers. These responses are reminiscent of disorganized infants in the strange situation who react to separations from their primary caregivers with behaviors such as freezing, head banging, throwing toys, running away from the caregiver upon reunion or hiding in a corner (Solomon & George, 2008).

Attachment-Informed Treatment of Grieving Clients

Clinicians work with clients in all stages of grief. The losses triggering that grief range along a continuum of severity from developmental losses such as empty-nest or retirement, to planned losses such as immigration, long-distance moves or military deployment, to unexpected personal losses such as terminal illnesses or job terminations, or relationship losses. Traumatic losses such as war, rape, forced immigration, and deaths due to combat, murder, natural disasters, or violent accidents are also highly represented in client populations in a variety of settings. In addition, there are subtle, less visible losses that trigger grief reactions, even years after the fact, such as the loss of hopes and dreams, symbolic possessions, animal companions, a happy childhood, health, and youth.

Even losses experienced by previous generations may trigger grief reactions in children, grandchildren, even great-children, and beyond. The literature on children and grandchildren of holocaust survivors struggling with their families' profound losses supports this fact (Bar-on, 1995). Rita Ledesma (personal communication, December 18, 2009), in her study of grief and attachment in American Indian communities, noted that living side-by-side with battlefields and burial sites where trauma occurred keeps the pain of grief alive. Survivors deal with their grief through "healing/honoring behaviors such as praying at a site, leaving medicine bundles, burning sage." In the book *Jane: A murder,* author Maggie Nelson (2005), niece of murder victim Jane Mixer, describes growing up with a deep sense of grief and death in her fantasy life – to the point of insisting to her friend that she had a younger sister who had disappeared, even though she was never told of her mother's sister nor the circumstances of her death as a college student.

Facing such a multiplicity of losses challenges the clinician who must stay fully present, attune to the grief, and help to regulate it. Dealing with so much grief and intensity is stressful for clinicians and requires awareness of one's own grief reactions, past and present, the degree to which those losses are acute and the grief activated. In addition, the clinician must be aware of his/her own typical attachment affect patterns and style, and whether there is a tendency to deactivate or hyperactivate the attachment system and, by extension, the caregiving system. Furthermore, having a supportive caregiving network is essential for the clinician, including consultants, supervisors, friends, and partners.

The following example of grief in a securely attached client illustrates how an attachment perspective can help with all aspects of the clinical process from assessment to intervention. An attachment perspective also provides a context for handling the difficult, though necessary, countertransference reactions that mediate attunement to and regulation of the painful, distressing attachment affect present in grief. While this case represents a grief in response to the death of a close loved one, the process is similar to other losses.

Loss of an Adult Son in a Securely Attached Woman

Maxine, a woman in her early 50s, had been in therapy for about 2 years, dealing with grief over the end of her long-term marriage brought about by her husband's addiction to prescription medications. By the time she made the decision to end the marriage and enter therapy, much of her protest grief over the divorce had subsided. Her despair, however, was manifest in weeping, anxiety and depressed mood, especially when she would face a new challenge, such as buying a house on her own.

Maxine was able to make immediate and appropriate use of the therapist's support and guidance, in the manner of a securely attached person. She was able to use support in regulating her affect, and I had the feeling of being an effective therapist. Within a year, reorganization was beginning, manifest in two ways: her diligence in making sure that her former husband was medically and financially all right (in the divorce settlement) and dating a healthy, supportive man. Her reorganization included a connection with her former spouse through their remaining child, while also moving to establish a new attachment with her boyfriend.

Near the end of the second year of treatment, I received an urgent call from Maxine informing me that her oldest son had been killed in a motorcycle accident. During the early weeks after the loss, Maxine's protest took the form of tearful anger at her son for insisting on riding his motorcycle on the freeway in spite of the dangers and her pleas. Gradually, within a few months, she began to be more despairing, weeping, and mourning the loss of his humor, his warmth, and the promise of his future as a writer. At this point, she would "oscillate" between despair (hyperactivation of the attachment system) and distraction (deactivation of the attachment system). About 6 months after her son's death, she joined a group of bereaved parents, and with the support of the group, her new boyfriend, her surviving daughter, and the therapist, she began to manifest signs of reorganization. The reparative part of the reorganization – the way of staying connected to her lost son – was through closeness with his former girlfriend and some of his motorcycle buddies. She also began collecting and editing his unpublished stories and poems and planned to publish them as a memorial to her son.

While the countertransference arousal of grief was noticeable during the divorce phase of the mourning, the loss of her son made it acute. As a parent of adult children, I was all too easily able to identify with her loss. Her raw protest and despair aroused excruciating distress in me as well. At times I struggled to contain my tears, fearing that if I cried she would feel she had to restrain her grief to protect me – that my attachment behavior would thrust her into the caregiving role. On the other hand, sharing her sadness was no doubt obvious to her in my body language and facial expression, thus making it clear that I was in the experience with her, while still enabling me to serve as a safe haven and secure base.

Grief in the Insecurely Attached

It is important to note, as described above, that people whose attachment strategies and styles typically involve hyperactivation or deactivation of the attachment system are less likely to be able to comfortably use the attuned, regulating presence of the clinician. They will, in the case of the anxious/preoccupied grievers, be needy and clingy but very difficult to soothe, and prone to stay stuck in the protest phase. The avoidant/dismissing adults, on the other hand, to the extent that grief reactions are deactivated will be unlikely to voluntarily seek therapeutic help. Only if the deactivating defense is unsuccessful and attachment distress overwhelms them will they suffer and seek help. Couples dealing with a common loss who have different attachment/grieving styles are at great risk for separation themselves because of their inability to attune to and regulate each other's grief. One example is the well-known phenomenon of relationship difficulties that may develop between parents after the death of their child.

A thorough familiarity with the affect arousal patterns associated with each of the insecure attachment styles provides the clinician with guidance in understanding and responding to the different ways of grieving. Differing countertransference responses also provide information relevant to the grieving process relative to each attachment style. Finally, the client's attachment history and reports of current close relationships also provide valuable clues about internal working models of attachment.

The clinician's goal in work with grieving individuals is to attune to their grief and help them work toward reorganization in the context of the therapeutic attachment/caregiving relationship. Thinking about grief from the standpoint of attachment and caregiving helps to guide the clinician by making regulating responses more conscious and, when difficult, more bearable. The types of attunement and regulation, for example, differ depending on the attachment style of the griever.

Empathic affect attunement can be a form of regulation in itself. However, it is most effective with the securely attached. People who are insecurely attached typically are unable to be soothed by attunement alone. The anxious/preoccupied person has difficulty making effective use of the therapeutic relationship because it stirs up anxiety and fear of rejection based on an internal working model of unreliable, unpredictable, and over stimulating caregiving. The clinician's role in working with an anxious/preoccupied client is to maintain a calm, reliable presence while helping him to contain and deintensify grief-related affect. It is often a long, slow process, as with the older woman protesting her divorce mentioned above. The clinician must strive to remain calm and soothing in the face of repeated devaluation and rejection, which can easily lead to countertransference irritation, judgment, or apathy. Understanding the grieving process and the attachment wounds beneath the constant protest and devaluation can help to soothe the clinician during this often trying process.

The avoidant/dismissing person, on the other hand, tends toward compulsive self-reliance and deactivation of the attachment system. In situations where the loss has broken through their deactivating defenses, the clinician may need to help the client temporarily deintensify the arousal. Over time, however, as the therapeutic attachment/caregiving relationship is solidified and begins to feel safe, helping the grieving person slowly move toward intensifying the attachment affect is the goal. A woman I saw right after her diagnosis with terminal cancer, for example, presented with a plea for help in stopping her tears. I tried in vain to reassure her that her grief was expectable and appropriate, but the unaccustomed attachment affect made her far too anxious and upset. She needed time to regroup and form a therapeutic relationship before she could tolerate the appropriate grief. To that end, I suggested some ideas to deintensify the grief and crying so that she felt safe enough to continue in the relationship. Pushing for attachment affect too soon is counterproductive, meaning that the clinician must be accepting and patient until the person feels safe, often a slow process.

Perhaps the most challenging clients are those whose early caregiving experiences were so traumatic that they are at times disorganized/disoriented in their attachment style. Helping to regulate their intense affect, which may include rage and hostility, along with suicidal despair alternating with detachment and dissociation, challenges the equanimity of even the most grounded clinician. Maintaining a steady, soothing, regulating presence through all of it is of primary importance.

When there are periods of relative calm, the therapist may work with the client to link the strong or dissociated affects in the present grief to early experiences with caregivers, thus helping to provide much-needed "scaffolding" (internal structure).

Grief in the Countertransference

Although we do not normally think of countertransference affect arousal in response to writing a case, I found myself with a severe stomachache after writing about Maxine, even though she is a highly disguised composite of two clients who lost adult children. My first ever experience of psychosomatic stomach symptoms occurred when I was in my early 40s and was hired to do a grief group for parents of newly diagnosed developmentally disabled infants. My symptoms began to occur immediately following those groups. My efforts to attune to and help regulate the pain of these young parents struggling to let go of their dreams and fantasies about their new infants and to reorganize around the reality of their severe physical and mental handicaps seemed to trigger my symptoms. When I returned home after the group, I found my attachment needs heightened as I sought extra hugs from my children and partner. After completing the case description, above, I stopped and wrote e-mails to both of my daughters, thereby touching in with my own secure base.

In doing research about crying by the therapist (Nelson, 2005), I found many examples of therapists overcome by the grief of their clients, sometimes in empathic identification as with my situation above, and sometimes because it coincided with their own losses – either in content or in time. For example, one therapist cried when her client was talking of her struggles with infertility, recalling her own. Another was crying as she was caught up in the acute grief of a young college girl whose sister had been killed in a crosswalk, when the therapist's sister died suddenly. Another therapist described crying with a young man who was grieving for his father, reminding her of her own son's grief for his recently deceased father, her husband.

Some grief reactions encountered in the course of therapeutic work can trigger such a strong personal reaction that the therapist feels unable to be fully present in the work. Because of this, clinicians must be frank with themselves about their limitations to work with certain people or certain types of losses that may coincide too much in timing or type to their own. If their grief becomes obvious to the patient, it may be necessary to briefly disclose the personal loss that is interfering. It may also require, as several therapists in my research stated, that they return to therapy, seek consultation, or even at times refer the patient.

Conclusion

As Bowlby pointed out, the loss of an attachment figure hurts for a very good survival reason – to keep us from straying from our attachment figures so that we can be safe, secure, and, at least in infancy, survive. The countless number of songs and poems linking lost love with "sighing," "crying," and "dying," shows how the threat to survival is felt by adults suffering an attachment loss, even if adults are not literally threatened with death, as are infants.

As professional caregivers, it is necessary to recognize, grieve, and struggle with our attachment and caregiving issues. It is important because these are the raw material of our intuitive and implicit procedural responses, the signals we use to attune to and help regulate our client's attachment distress and our own. The subjective experiences of the client are interwoven with the subjective experiences of the therapist, thereby creating feelings, conflicts, attunements, misattunements, and enactments in the context of the therapeutic relationship. We grieve with our clients; mutually regulate our affect; and when all goes well, we eventually reorganize right along with them. The more we understand and rely upon the knowledge available in attachment-based separation/grief theory and research, the more the intuitive and implicit relational knowing is conscious and available to help guide us in the often overwhelming and uncertain arena of the clinical and casework relationship.

Study Questions

1. What are the phases of grief and what is the meaning of each phase?
2. What are typical caregiving responses to each phase of grief?
3. How does the grief of securely attached people differ from that of (a) anxious/preoccupied, (b) avoidant/dismissing, and (c) disorganized/disoriented individuals?
4. Give examples of your caregiving/countertransference reactions to the grief of a client (or someone close to you).
5. Give examples that show how different people have reorganized after a significant loss.

References

Bar-on, D. (1995). *Fear and hope: Three generations of the holocaust.* Cambridge: Harvard University Press.

Berant, E., Mikulincer, M., & Shaver, P. (2008). Mothers' attachment style, their mental health, and their children's emotional vulnerabilities: A 7-year study of mothers of children with congenital heart disease. *Journal of Personality, 76,* 31–65.

Birnbau, G. E., Orr, I., Mikulincer, M., & Florian, V. (1997). When marriage breaks up: Does attachment style contribute to coping and mental health? *Journal of Social and Personal Relationships, 14,* 643–654.

Boukydis, C. F. Z. (1985). Perception of infant crying as an interpersonal event. In B. M. Lester & C. F. Z. Boukydis (Eds.), *Infant crying: Theoretical and research perspectives* (pp. 187–215). New York: Plenum Press.

Boukydis, C. F. Z., & Burgess, R. L. (1982). Adult physiological response to infant cries: Effects of temperament of infant, parental status and gender. *Child Development, 53,* 1291–1298.

Bowlby, J. (1960). *Grief and mourning in infancy and early childhood* (pp. 9–52). XV: Psychoanalytic Study of the Child.

Bowlby, J. (1961). Processes of mourning. *The International Journal of Psychoanalysis, 42*(4–5), 317–339.

Bowlby, J. (1969/1982). *Attachment and Loss: Attachment* (Vol. I). New York: Basic Books.

Bowlby, J. (1980). *Loss: Sadness and depression* (Vol. III). New York: Basic Books.

Brodkey, H. (1994, February 2). Dying: An update. *The New Yorker, LXIX,* 70–84

Donovan, W. L., & Balling, J. D. (1978). Maternal physiological response to infant signals. *Psychophysiology, 15*(1), 68–74.

Donovan, W. L., & Leavitt, L. A. (1985). Physiology and behavior: Parents' response to the infant cry. In B. M. Lester & C. F. Z. Boukydis (Eds.), *Infant crying: Theoretical and research perspectives* (pp. 241–259). New York: Plenum Press.

Eggers, D. (2006). *What is the what: The autobiography of Valentino Achak Deng: A Novel.* San Francisco: McSweeneys.

Eisenberger, N. I., Lieberman, M. D., & Williams, K. D. (2003). Does rejection hurt? An fMRI study of social exclusion. *Science, 302,* 290–292.

Fraley, R. C., & Bonanno, G. A. (2004). Attachment and loss: A test of three competing models on the association between attachment-related avoidance and adaptation to bereavement. *Personality and Social Psychology Bulletin, 30,* 878–890.

Fraley, R. C., Fazzari, D. A., Bonanno, G. A., & Dekel, S. (2006). Attachment and psychological adaptation in high exposure survivors of the September 11th attack on the World Trade C enter. *Personality and Social Psychology Bulletin, 32,* 538–551.

Habenstein, R., & Lamers, W. (1963). *Funeral customs the world over.* Milwaukee: Bulfin Printers, Inc.

Kracke, W. (1981). Kagwahiv mourning. *Ethos, 9*(4), 258–275.

Kracke, W. (1988). Kagwahiv mourning II. *Ethos, 16*(2), 202–222.

Lorberbaum, J., Newman, J., Horwitz, A., Dubno, J., Lydiard, R. B., Hamner, M., et al. (2002). A potential role for thalamocingulate circuitry in human maternal behavior. *Biological Psychiatry, 51,* 431–445.

Lyons-Ruth, K. (1998). Implicit relational knowing: Its role in development and psychoanalytic treatment. *Infant Mental Health Journal, 19*(3), 282–289.

Lyons-Ruth, K. (2003). Dissociation and the parent–infant dialogue: A longitudinal perspective from attachment research. *Journal of the American Psychoanalytic Association, 51*(3), 883–911.

Mikulincer, M., Dolev, T., & Shaver, P. (2004). Attachment-related strategies during thought-suppression: Ironic rebounds and vulnerable self-representations. *Journal of Personality and Social Psychology, 87,* 940–956.

Mikulincer, M., & Shaver, P. (2007). *Attachment in adulthood: Structure, dynamics and change.* New York: Guilford Press.

Moverman, O. (Writer) (2009). *The messenger.* In M. Gordon (Producer). USA: Oscilloscope Laboratories.

Nelson, J. (2005). *Seeing through tears: Crying and attachment.* New York: Routledge.

Nelson, J. (2007). Crying is a two person behaviour: A relational perspective based on attachment theory. *Attachment: New Directions in Psychotherapy and Relational Psychoanalysis, 1*(3), 280–293.

Nelson, M. (2005). *Jane: A Murder.* New York: Soft Skull Press.

Newsham, B. (2000, May 22). Somebody's Mother. *San Francisco Chronicle,* D8.

Schore, A. N. (2003). *Affect dysregulation and disorders of the self.* New York: W. W. Norton.

Shaver, P. R., & Fraley, R. C. (2008). Attachment, loss, and grief: Bowlby's views and current controversies. In J. Cassidy & P. Shaver (Eds.), *Handbook of attachment: Theory, research, and clinical applications* (2nd ed., pp. 48–77). New York: Guilford Press.

Simos, B. (1979). *A time to grieve: Loss as a universal human experience.* New York: Family Service Association of America.

Solomon, J., & George, C. (2008). The measurement of attachment security and related constructs in infancy and early childhood. In J. Cassidy & P. Shaver (Eds.), *The handbook of attachment: Theory, research, and clinical applications* (2nd ed., pp. 383–416). New York: Guildford Press.

Chapter 6
Listening Closely: The Significance of the Therapist's Voice Intensity, Rhythm, and Tone

Kristin Miscall Brown and Dorienne Sorter

> *The music of life shows its melody and harmony in our false*
> *note, according to the scale of our ideal. The tone of one*
> *personality is hard like a horn; while the tone of another is*
> *soft like the high notes of a flute.*

Khan (1996, p. 166)

Though the case of "Anna" discussed in the following chapter occurred in a private practice setting, the theories, concepts, and interventions apply broadly to the field of clinical social work as a whole. Perhaps the most direct application has to do with the impact and importance of close listening. Increasingly, research suggests that words spoken are merely one part of the emotional communication of an individual's narrative. We all engage with rapid-fire speed in a variety of unconscious processes, and a vast majority of these processes are interpersonal, that is, they occur between individuals. Listening closely therefore entails a multiply layered, simultaneous observation of words, vocal rhythms, and body language within self and other. This presents a greater challenge when contact with clients occurs on the telephone, which is often the case when engaging hard-to-reach clients or those with a history of depression (Ludman, Simon, Tutty, & Von Korff, 2007). By expanding our outreach to clients to engagement via the telephone, we provide yet one more medium through which clients may access services.

Often times in social service agencies, practitioners work with clients without the benefit of a comprehensive longitudinal picture of their individual histories. But the social worker may be able to learn about an individual's early life experience by paying close attention to the manner in which s/he relates to others in her/his current circumstances, thus contributing valuable information to the important social work tool, the biopsychosocial assessment. If, for example, agency clinical

K. Miscall Brown (✉)
Psychoanalytic Psychotherapy Study Center, New York, NY, USA
e-mail: kristinmb@verizon.net

S. Bennett and J.K. Nelson (Eds.), *Adult Attachment in Clinical Social Work*,
Essential Clinical Social Work Series, DOI 10.1007/978-1-4419-6241-6_6,
© Springer Science+Business Media, LLC 2010

team members were able to discuss their experiences with their clients and their observations about their clients' interactions with other clients in a community setting, those observations could become an important part of formulating a deeper understanding of clients and contribute to better treatment.

Far from being the sole domain of the private practice therapist, attachment theory and its related fields provide clinical social workers with innovative prevention strategies, particularly in the field of Early Intervention. Moreover, the theorists discussed in this chapter clearly emphasize the need to understand the many contexts through which trauma is repeated intergenerationally, thus providing an urgent plea to raise awareness about violence prevention and comprehensive family intervention when possible. Social work has traditionally been at the forefront of systemic social change rooted in the understanding of the individual within the society and cultures at large. Attachment theory and the expanding field of neurobiology stand in the foreground of rooting the practice of clinical social work in bi-directional, co-constructed experiences. This framework represents an important departure from some of the older models of clinical work that have historically emphasized the internal workings of the psyche at the exclusion of the variety of interpersonal environments of one's real world interactions.

Treatment Beginning: The Case of Anna

Anna says to me during our in-person intake interview, looking right at me, "There is something I have to tell you." She holds my gaze as if to see whether I flinch or betray some measure of worry about what she needs to tell me.[1] "Say whatever you are able," I respond. We sit quietly for a few moments. She takes in a shallow breath, "I don't know that it really means much, but I guess the fact that I have never told anyone means something… don't know what but…" She shifts slightly, her foot nervously bouncing. "My parents divorced when I was only three so my mom, brother, and I were alone for most of my childhood. My mom's room was down the hall from me, and I remember that starting when I was ten, I used to wake up at about 5:00 in the morning… every morning…" she paused. We are quiet. "Did something wake you?" I inquire gently.

"Yeah, you could say that," she smiles anxiously. "It was my mother. She woke me up. Well *she* didn't, but the sound of her voice did. I first remember it when I was in fifth grade. I thought that something was happening to her when I would hear her screaming. It frightened me. I actually remember that I thought she was having a baby or something. One afternoon when I got home from school, I heard her screaming like she did in the morning. I followed the sound and found myself at her bedroom door. I was scared; she sounded like she was in pain. I opened her door and walked in… when I saw her, I walked right out. I thought I was going to

---

[1] Kristin Miscall Brown is the treating therapist. Dorienne Sorter is the supervisor.

throw up, but I just went to my room and turned on my music. From that day on, I slept with a Walkman by my bed. Every morning, my alarm would go off just before 5:00; I would put my headphones on so that I did not have to hear her. I did this every day until I left for boarding school in the eighth grade."

The sounds Anna heard were those of her mother masturbating. This early relentless and pervasive perturbation of Anna's aural field served as a model scene of invasion and affect dysregulation that characterized her relationship with her mother. In this chapter, we will explore the impact of this particular form of impingement and how it affected her attachment to her mother and also, many years later, her attachment to her toddler-aged daughter, Chloe, and to her therapist. Our interest is in the many ways that voice patterns, tone, and rhythm have played a particularly significant role in 4 years of a treatment that has taken place over the telephone as a result of her move out of New York City following the disaster of 9/11. Telephone sessions were a potentially challenging medium for a woman who had to fend off, mediate, tune out, and attempt to regulate an intrusion born of sound. When treatment sessions moved to the telephone, the client/therapist bond was solid. Her clear desire to continue the work via telephone despite a long history replete with traumatic early experience with her care givers, emotional unrest, and mistrust of closeness indicated to me that I should follow her lead and continue the treatment via telephone. Through close attention to voice and a careful coordination of verbal matching and state sharing, the client and I have been able to establish more robust and reliable interactional patterns than those she had grown accustomed to throughout her childhood. An additional benefit of Anna's enhanced affect range has been that it has enabled her to do what her mother could not: acknowledge and ask for help with the overwhelming states of anxiety and agitation she experiences as a parent.

Attachment Theory, Neurobiology, and Adult Treatment

Stern (1985) focused on the infant/mother dyad in his seminal book, *The Interpersonal World of the Infant*, illustrating in detail the multilayered nature of mutual influence in the dyad. Many of Anna's interpersonal challenges throughout life stemmed from the early, poorly regulated, and misattuned attachment styles of her mother. Anna could not consistently rely on her mother to tune to her affective state, nor could she count on her mother's ability to self-regulate so that she could be available to Anna for soothing and/or affect regulating.

The ideas of mutual influence and forms of relational meaning in both mother/infant and therapist/client dyads contain elements of both conscious and nonconscious forms of communication. Clinicians in the Boston Change Process Study Group (2008) divide these two domains of communication into the *reflective-verbal* and *implicit*. They define a key concept of *implicit relational knowing* as the knowledge about how to be with each other that "typically [operates] outside focal attention and conscious experience, without translation into language… it is part of our nonconscious processing… that never has been put into words, has never had to be, or never could be" (pp. 128–129). The reflective-verbal domain, they propose, grows out of the implicit in several ways, but we will emphasize here the significance of the "sloppiness" (p. 137) of spontaneous speech. They propose that because spontaneous speech contains the layer of paralinguistic communication (rhythm, tone, melody of the words themselves), the verbal utterance contains within it sloppiness in pursuit of the "right" words. This sloppiness is "dynamic, unpredictable, very messy, and widely distributed through the body" (p. 137), conveying an aliveness to our words that is, in fact, what distinguishes them from those of a robot or automaton. They state: "This body/mind dialogue of implicit experiencing and reflective-verbal processing makes it possible for a psychoanalyst and a patient on the couch, not seeing each other, to know so much of the implicit and to share an intersubjective space" (p. 138). We would extend this to include the situation of the therapist/client pair working on the telephone where the visual cues are similarly absent but the implicit and reflective-verbal very much present.

Beebe and Lachmann (2002) suggest that dyadic interactions are made up of face-to-face exchanges, verbalizations, synchrony of responses, and mutuality of interchanges. Timing, vocal pauses, and vocal rhythms are matched and influence one another in a bi-directional pattern in communication between infants and adults as well as adult-to-adult. This process in which adults unconsciously match one another's vocal patterns – also known as *vocal congruence* – is a further example of implicit relational knowing (Beebe & Lachmann, 1992).

In a bi-directional system, each person's behavior is predictable from (and not caused by) that of the other. We are influencing, and being influenced by, our partner's words and actions. Particularly at the nonverbal level, mother and infant, as well as therapist and client, participate in a moment-by-moment coordination of the rhythms of behavior. This is the fundamental nature of social behavior. Each partner has continuous rhythms of behavior, for example, sound and silence, movement and hold. Even the moments of verbal or gestural silence are communicative. The rhythms of behavior of two partners are always coordinated in some way, usually outside of awareness (Beebe & Lachmann, 2002). In a telephone therapy, face-to-face exchanges are absent except through memory of facial expressions or fantasies of the expressions on each other's faces. When expression by voice is the only modality, nonverbal components of communication are only conveyed auditorily.

For Anna, the silence of nighttime became a haunting precursor to her mother's loud and relentless verbal intrusion. When Anna needed her mother's presence, her mother was often subsumed by distance and dissociation as a result of her own history that was replete with multiple layers of trauma. Unpredictability was the operating principle in Anna's relationship with her mother. What was outside awareness in her relationship with her mother was not only the "rhythms of behavior" but also the notion of awareness itself. To know more was to feel more, as we discovered in our work together, and to feel more in her mother's presence was potentially a recipe for collapse. Anna remembers yelling at her mother about something when she was a teenager and her mother's response was to put her fingers in her ears and cry, "Stop! Stop! You're hurting me!" As Anna shut out her mother's voice, her mother shut out Anna's voice. Both Anna and her mother were overwhelmed by voice and became cocooned in their own worlds.

Allan Schore has been at the forefront of the convergence of attachment theory and neuroscience and their implications for psychotherapeutic treatment of adults. One of his most significant contributions has been in the exploration of right brain-to-right brain communication between parent and child and therapist and client and its significance in attachment outcomes. The right brain is responsible for the more intuitive, implicit, nonlinear forms of communication. Schore (2005) cites Decety and Chaminade (2003): "Mental states that are in essence private to the self may be shared between individuals… Self-awareness, empathy, identification with others, and more generally intersubjective processes, are largely dependent upon… [r]ight hemisphere resources, which are the first to develop" (p. 591). Schore (2001a, 2001b) notes that the mother's right brain is largely responsible for "comforting functions," of the caregiver, while the infant's right brain is geared toward attachment. He emphasizes that the growth of the right brain continues throughout the lifespan but that its maturation is experience-dependent. One might speculate, therefore, that if the early development of an individual's right brain was compromised because of caregiver misattunement, abuse, or neglect, significant change would still be possible within the therapeutic experience in psychotherapy as the therapist's right brain engages the client's in a right brain, spontaneous, implicit, and explicit meeting of minds. As Rotenberg (1995) states: "The emotional relationships in the process of psychotherapy are covering the deficiency caused by the lack of emotional relations in early childhood" (cited in Schore, 2002, p. 469).

It would seem that Anna's mother was unable to engage in any kind of empathic perception of Anna's emotional states, which left Anna in a vacuum, unable to experience comfort as coming from the aid of another. Thus she was at a complete loss when her daughter Chloe needed to "use" her for her own growing self-regulatory processes. Throughout the course of the developing relationship between Anna and her therapist, new bi-directional ways of "being with" began to take hold in the course of the nonconscious, mutually influenced mode of communication. The fact that the bulk of the treatment of this case occurred on the telephone presented a challenge, because it necessitated that the therapist be that much more tuned to the subtle shifts and changes in the quality of the verbal exchanges (voice patterns, tones, and rhythms) to attend to and titrate her verbal utterances to best meet the emotional needs of the client at each moment.

Client History

Anna began treatment about a year after she married. She was living with her husband in New York City but spending most of the day alone, as she had not found a job that she enjoyed or could commit to. She was driving down the road one day and thought to herself, "You know, things would be much easier for everyone, myself included, if I just ran my car into a tree…" This level of despair frightened her deeply, and though she remembers wanting to "just move on with [her] life," she realized that in order to have any semblance of one, she needed to talk. She desperately wanted to have a family of her own but felt a deep sense of emptiness that not only concerned her but also mystified her. "I feel like I should be really happy. But I'm not and I don't know why." She called and made her first appointment.

Anna's father left her mother when Anna was three and was never again consistently involved with Anna or her sibling. Anna recalled feeling regularly like she was a burden to her mother. The slightest upset would send her mother into a rage or into a mass of tears on the floor, crying that her children didn't understand her. Anna remembered many occasions when she would find her mother chattering to herself in a manner that frightened Anna. She also remembered many occasions when she would visit with her father for a summer vacation and tell him that she did not want to go back home to her mother. "Instead of asking me why, he just looked at me blankly and said everything was fine… but he married her; he lived with her. He knew she wasn't fine." She was similarly ignored by her grandmothers, the only real parent figures she had as a child. Though they tended to her by ensuring she was well clothed, taking her out to lunch, and grooming her to become a proper upper class lady, they, too, did not tune into her desperate pleas to be rescued from her mother. Some of those pleas included refusal to do any work for school, difficulties with peers, and clear signs of anxiety and trauma such as head banging. "The best thing my grandmothers did for me was to decide that I needed the discipline of a boarding school. Sounded good to me; it got me away from my mother." But because the unacknowledged burden of her mother's instability and her father's abandonment were never spoken about, Anna turned inward and moved onward, resigned to the belief that no one genuinely wanted to hear what she truly felt or thought. Thus she hid behind her stunning beauty, simultaneously hoping and dreading that someone would ask her what was really going on underneath the veneer she so carefully protected.

In face-to-face work, I came to understand that Anna obscured affect behind an engaging smile. I felt thrown off in the beginning when she would report an event that seemed to be quite disturbing as I listened to her words, but her smile belied the words. I came to discover that she was not aware that her affect and words did not match. Additionally, as a result of a tacit lack of attention on the part of most adults in her life as a child, Anna had no words for her emotions. This resulted in a terrible internal terrain of loneliness and wordlessness about her own experience. She had been so accustomed to accommodating her mother that her own world of emotions was a far off universe, unknown, untraveled, and replete with fear. I had to tune in on a microlevel of communication, paying attention to minute details of facial expression, body language, and tone of voice to begin to reach her, to recognize her. Once our treatment moved to the telephone, this challenge became even more crucial as we strove to secure a strong attachment through which Anna might safely begin to navigate with me the foreign terrain of her internal world.

When Anna announced that she could no longer live in the city after the events of 9/11 and that her move out of town was imminent, I was initially worried. I thought about her history of isolation as a primary coping mechanism and was concerned that she might just disappear into that old, safe way of protecting herself. However, because I also knew that we were well into a deepening treatment, I agreed to continue our work by phone. It was only as the move came closer that I realized that part of my resistance to phone treatment involved my own difficulty with the fact that I would miss seeing her. Interestingly, as I imagined how much I would miss our face-to-face sessions, I became curious about Anna's potential uncon-scious need for a certain kind of regulation of our closeness and connection. For Anna, this was a movement toward safety. For me, it symbolized a loss. Gaze and physical proximity were crucial elements I had come to rely on as staples of my therapeutic listening that were no longer present. I also noted another fascinating element – a kind of parallelism. In her childhood, Anna gained control over her mother's aural intrusion by putting on earphones at 5:00 every morning. Now she could again be in control by holding the telephone for our sessions. This time, however, she controlled tuning in, rather than tuning out. I knew it was far too early to make an interpretation of this kind. So I chose to listen and to yield to her uncon-scious communication of a need to contain our contact in sound alone.

Because Anna and I no longer had eye contact, body language, or a simple smile of acknowledgment, I began to listen very closely to how we spoke to one another. The move disrupted the nonverbal components of our vis-a-vis relationship, thus making it imperative for us to reestablish through voice alone what had come so naturally to us when we met in person. At first, I had no idea what I was listening for, but I began by closing my eyes as she spoke. It is said that when someone loses her hearing, her eyesight and acute awareness of vibration sharpens and when someone can no longer see, the ability to hear and sense movement is magnified. By encouraging the sensory deprivation of eyesight, I sought to increase the sensi-tivity of my hearing. I intentionally allowed myself to be blind. It was very hard at first. I was agitated and jittery. I wanted to ask Anna what she was doing or how she was sitting. I could not find a comfortable position in my own chair. But when I asked Anna how the transition to phone was going for her, she remarked that it worked really well because it allowed her to go about her day but then take a purposeful break to focus on our session no matter where she was. Sometimes she would call from the park in her car. Sometimes she would sit outside on her patio in the sun while we spoke. Anna had found ways to be in control of vocal sounds. What once was an intrusion became something that she now welcomed. She seemed to be adjusting better than I. But after a handful of sessions, I settled into my blindness and began to listen.

Telephone Therapy Literature

With the swell of fast-moving technological advances over the last decade, therapists are challenged to meet the changing needs for communication that our clients often present. Greater global communication has brought more frequent travel around the world, which often leads to clients traveling several times per year.

With dramatically improved telecommunications born of fiber optic phone lines, inexpensive phone cards charging less than three cents per minute for an international call, satellite services such as Blackberry, and free Internet phone services such as Skype, staying in contact with our clients is easier than it has ever been. No longer must there be a mandatory interruption of the treatment when our clients are not able to be present in the office setting. This ease of the technical aspects of communication, however, can present a dilemma for therapists. It forces us to study our own resistance to anything other than face-to-face communication. We have to understand the specific reasons we would choose not to continue treatment when circumstances require that in order for the client to remain in treatment with us, we must consider the option of telephone therapy.

Manosevitz (2004) states, "For this generation, sessions or a significant part of an analysis on the telephone may not be as strange to [clients] as it is to their analysts. In keeping analysis current with the social milieu, we need to change" (p. 39). Addressing issues of regulating a relational distance, Bennett (2004) notes that telephone therapy "can be used as a means of negotiating closeness or distance for patients struggling with transitional space" (p. 240). Coen (2005) posits that the therapist must first focus on establishing safety with those clients who struggle with fears of intrusion or impingement. He suggests that the option of telephone therapy is a way to promote slow growth of closeness with the therapist. Brisch (2000) explores the treatment of adults with early attachment insecurity and has noted some important factors when treating those with patterns of avoidant attachment styles:

> For those patients with a highly avoidant attachment representation... the telephone is an opportunity to remain in contact without breaking off therapy... Most of these patients had traumatizing experiences with close care giving figures during their infant development. Such experiences cause them to have a highly ambivalent or even extremely avoidant attitude toward attachment figures altogether as they fear that their relationship with their new attachment in the person of the therapist can become as frightening and traumatizing as have been their caregivers. (p. 386)

How the therapist and client utilize the telephone will partly determine its success. Moldawasky (2004) and his study group identified three factors related to the successful use of telephone treatment: "(1) both patient and analyst have a strong desire to continue the work, (2) there was an existing in-person relationship established during office sessions, and (3) there had been successful progress on transference–countertransference issues during face-to-face sessions" (p. 5).

Pattern, Tone, and Rhythm

When we turn our attention to communication shared within the therapeutic dyad of client and therapist, dialogue takes on a rich, multiply layered form. Knoblauch (2000) noted the importance of micropatterning of repetitive rhythms and its variations for the regulation of affect and sense of self with other as "ordered, relatively safe, and predictable or disordered, dangerous and chaotic" (p. 19). The early morning awakenings Anna endured serve as a poignant example of a sense of self with other that is "disordered, dangerous, and chaotic" (p. 19).

The loneliness and isolation Anna experienced each morning as she ensconced herself behind her wall of music was emblematic of being with a mother who was, in fact, quite disordered, certainly chaotic, and likely dangerous. Anna learned to expect erratic, crazy, inappropriate behavior from her mother. "It always felt like we were a burden to her, like she never really wanted to be a mother." When I asked Anna about her earliest memory of her mother, she recalled a photograph she found later on as an adult. "My mother is sitting on the couch with my brother, David. He's grinning at the camera as he sits beside her on her left. I am propped up on a pillow on the other side of her... she is holding a bottle, feeding me. It's the look in her eyes that still stands out for me... she is just staring off into space away from David and away from me. Her left elbow is on the back of the couch propping up her head. Her other hand is attempting to feed me, but she's looking away from me, staring off into space. She couldn't be more disinterested or disconnected." Thus Anna felt both distant from her mother and terribly overwhelmed by her, a paradox that would likely have made her attachment to her mother disorganized and patterned by instability.

Vocal rhythms (Beebe, Jaffe, Lachmann, Feldstein, Crown, & Jasnow, 2002; Beebe, Knoblauch, Rustin, & Sorter, 2005) become particularly important in the absence of the other forms of face-to-face interactions. Some basic definitions of sound (Merriam-Webster, 2007) provide the necessary foundation for attending to the dynamics of voice:

- Tone: vocal or musical sound of a specific quality. <spoke in low *tones*> <masculine *tones*>
- Rhythm: (1) the aspect of music comprising all the elements (as accent, meter, and tempo) that relate to forward movement; (2) movement, fluctuation, or variation marked by the regular recurrence or natural flow of related elements.
- Pattern: a natural or chance configuration.

Taking into consideration all three dimensions of tone, rhythm, and pattern, I realized that treating Anna via telephone would require a bit of intuitive improvisation. I would have to match her rhythms in order to determine whether or not I encouraged or discouraged progressive communication. I would need to harmonize with the tone that felt most organic and then listen for the quality of Anna's response. I would also have to work to notice if there were any particular patterns or manners of speaking on either of our parts that enlivened flat effect, deadened alive affect, or simply encouraged Anna to say more.

As our work continued over the years, Anna's relationship to her daughter, Chloe, came to the fore. Prior to having children, Anna said she absolutely wanted to parent differently than she had been parented. Once she had a child, however, she found it difficult to carry out that intention. Anna described Chloe as a hyper-vigilant baby who remained so as she developed, consistent with an insecure ambivalent-resistant attachment style. Chloe was easily excitable, difficult to soothe, and attached to Anna, much like Anna was attached to her own mother. Beebe and Lachmann discuss the insecure-resistant child: "Insecure-resistant toddlers both seek the mother and resist the contact, failing to be comforted" (Beebe & Lachmann, 2002, p. 154). Anna related that Chloe whined incessantly when they were together. Nothing Anna tried in her efforts to meet her daughter's needs ever seemed right. Given Anna's anxious response to tone, rhythm, and vocal patterns, Chloe's vocalizations drove her to distraction and frustration. What was worse for Anna was her knowledge that Chloe appeared to be nearly angelic when with anyone else – such as her babysitter or father. Depending on the day (and I would suggest depending on her dominant affect or mood), Anna's response to Chloe's shrill, whining voice vacillated from "well, I just try to limit the choices and keep the conflict to a minimum," to "what am I doing wrong with this child?! I don't see ANY other kids act this way and what's worse, she only acts this way with me," to "I should never have had children… this kind of ability to freak out that Chloe does regularly comes directly from my bloodline. I had no business reproducing." Listening to these various responses, I had to regulate my own aversive feelings toward Anna's intense and fierce words and affects as she vented. In the heightened affective moments between Chloe and Anna, it was similarly hard for Anna to regulate her own affectivity. This challenged her to maintain her own sense of internal equilibrium. Anna often became overstimulated and unable to optimally respond to Chloe's over-stimulating behavior.

During our phone sessions, matching Anna's vocal rhythms or tonality while maintaining a focus on my internal equilibrium, I implicitly offered her a moment of recognition, the space to be mirrored. I worked hard to imbue her with a feeling of safety by matching her tone and rhythm, hoping to expand her response options beyond that of dissolving into a mass of unregulated, overwhelming emotions. As I listened to Anna's tales of frustration with Chloe and her unceasing needs, I found it helpful to focus on my own breathing. The following is an example of a familiar exchange between Anna and me on a "bad day" with Chloe:

Anna: I can't stand it→it's never enough with her→no matter *what* I do,[2] it's never enough and she is never satisfied and it's one crazy emotion after the next. (Extended pause[3]) I want to just scream at her to shut up.

Th.:   I can hear how frustrated you are→it's as though you can't ever get it right→no matter *what* you do. (Matching pause) And if she would zip it already, you wouldn't feel so totally overwhelmed.
        (Another extended pause)

Anna: Yeah!
        (Shorter switching pause)

Th.:   (*Pitched affectively softer by one or two notches.*) It is so difficult to manage how overwhelmed you feel with her when she is looking to you to help her with how overwhelmed she feels.
        (Therapist matches client's duration of pause)

---

[2] The arrows indicate continuous speech. The emphasis here is on the uninterrupted rhythm.

[3] Parenthetical descriptions of the nonverbal communication in this exchange are derived from Beebe et al. (2005).

Anna: (*matching my affective pitch*) Yeah (slightly longer pause. Client reflects on her own sense of being overwhelmed) and I just wish she could get herself together. (Pause) It's the meltdowns that kill me; they make me want to walk out of the house and leave her there.
        (Brief pause)
Th.:   (*a notch lower in affect*) Yes, because it's so difficult to know how to respond when nothing you do calms her down. (Pause) So I guess part of what makes this hard is that you are then left to feel a kind of anxiety of helplessness… can't seem to make it better.
        (Lengthy pauses)
A: (*following my notch lower*) I can't… I hate it. (Matches pause duration) I mean I know it's hard for her because I think she picks up on my anxiety……..[4]
Th.:   …….You both pick up on one another's…it's hard for you both……..

The above exchange represents a particular flavor of turn taking in which we both participate. In response to what I heard as a shallow chest breath accompanied by staccato-like rhythm, I deepened my breath but mirrored the rhythm. My staccato responses were slower than Anna's utterances, but they resonated a similar affectivity. I simultaneously made room for big affect by spontaneously connecting with my own emotions in the moment while also regulating my responses by carefully pitching my tone gradually lower than hers, hoping to encourage an underlying solidity that could hold the affect that felt so overwhelming to her. "We can hold these big emotions together" is the verbal representation of that function. It is noteworthy to emphasize that exchanges like those above unfolded in a nondeliberate, nonconscious way that was part of the process of procedural knowing. That is, I did not choose in the conscious sense of the word to respond in the way that I did. Rather, our familiarity with one another and my experience hearing from Anna the patterns of response that often occurred between her and Chloe began to make room for a new form of interaction around heightened affectivity and emotional overload. That being said, I did consciously monitor my own affectivity during those moments when Anna's was heightened. If I was too unresponsive, she was left alone with her own frustration in a way that reflected that early isolation; if I over-shot my response and became too caught up in my own reaction, then she remained hyper-stimulated and over-aroused without means of understanding how to mediate her own feelings in the presence of Chloe. The parallel to her relationship with her own mother is clear. When Anna's mother was anxious, frustrated, and angry, she was unable to regulate or modulate her emotions and would often fault Anna for causing her upset. Anna tended toward a similar pattern. As her therapist, it was imperative that I provide her with a means of holding and regulating powerful emotions in a way that her mother was never capable of offering. By doing so, I offered Anna another way of responding to Chloe's challenging affect states.

---

[4] This long ellipse signals a feeling of tapering reflection that occurs in this moment of our turn taking.

Knoblauch discusses this kind of interchange with an emphasis on what Lachmann and Beebe (1996) term "violation of expectancies."

> My approach suggests that violations of expected patterns of repeated interactions can be more precisely observed as shifts in the micromoment exchanges on rhythmic, tonal, and turn taking dimensions of the analytic exchange. These shifts represent anomalies in the patterning of nonverbal communication and constitute the feeling level that catalyzes the experience of a violated expectation. They represent the microbuilding blocks out of which a pattern of interaction is shifted. (Knoblauch, 2000, p. 48)

Thus, by not responding to Anna's distress in the way she came to expect her mother to respond, Anna and I began to shift the realm of the expected response to open to new forms of interaction.

Anna's mother's inability to respond to Anna's varying states as a child stemmed from her own traumatic history. This is keenly relevant as it reflects an important dimension of the pattern of trauma repetition and its deleterious effects from generation to generation. In his article, "Intergenerational Maternal Violent Trauma," Schecter (2003) makes an illuminating claim:

> Based on clinical observations by my research team we have noted that distress of the child under 4 years of age, who has not yet developed the capacity to regulate his or her own emotions, often becomes a posttraumatic reminder for caregivers who have memories of their helplessness, horror and outrage during a violent assault or memories of violent perpetrators who also had extreme difficulty modulating their negative affect and hostile aggression. (p. 126)

Similarly, Schore (2002) describes the manner in which early relational trauma imprints onto the right brain, which is responsible for personal or autobiographical memory. Early trauma, he suggests, can "create an enduring vulnerability to dysfunction during stress and a pre-disposition to PTSD" (p. 11). In this treatment, two generations present with a challenging interpersonal dilemma. From her relationship with her traumatized mother, Anna learned early on to discount and disconnect from her own needs and feelings, particularly those that created reactions of anxiety, helplessness, or fear in her mother. Thus, face-to-face with her preverbal child who is also constitutionally high energy and more emotionally precocious than she can manage on her own, Anna often feels jettisoned right back to her own feelings of helplessness and over stimulation. But she cannot retreat into isolation, as she knows she needs to respond to Chloe. By engaging outside of conscious awareness in a coordinated turn-taking exchange with me, she became more able to meet Chloe in a similar exchange. Again, as noted earlier, as she and I practiced this turn taking, more and more it became something automatic, a kind of procedural knowing. Just as in the case of Winnicott's (1953) "good-enough mother," the attunement became a part of a non-conscious process. At the same time, I thought it important to impart to Anna in a kind of psycho-educational fashion the impact of arousal, affect regulation, and inter-generational transmission of trauma. Not surprisingly, when Anna heard me talk about these dimensions of relating with others, her relief was almost audible. She so often feels like an island, alone with these problems with her daughter, isolated with this traumatic history. In these moments of understanding, her self critical tone dissipated, and in its place I could feel the beginning compassion for herself as well as for her daughter. What I did not interpret to her directly was how she and I engaged in this procedural knowing. That is the place where I felt it essential to provide her with an attuned, regulating experience without interpretation or explanation.

Discussion

As therapists, we rarely have moments of absolute assurance that what we do produces positive change for the client. It is hard to know with certainty what really changes or shifts, but we do have clues. In my telephone work with Anna, I had to look and listen very closely to our relationship to guide me. A few important markers of our mutual and progressive communication over the years had been steady throughout the treatment. Anna remained one of my most committed clients. Despite her very busy life as a mother, she called in regularly to our sessions, rarely missing, and always rescheduling if she was to be away for our appointed time. Further, despite Anna's early need to hide behind niceties, Anna revealed to me feelings that in the past she would have kept to herself for fear that they would have made her a "bad person." She grew to be able to disagree with me when she once would accept my words without question. She laughed with me and engaged her wonderful wit, all symbols to me that she increasingly inhabited herself in my presence; she stopped hiding out behind a smile of words. I also look to the life of the client outside the treatment room to tell me if growth is happening. She made friends with whom she shares genuine connection and she became far less isolated. Her relationship with Chloe continued to cause anxiety and frustration, but she learned to ride the waves, regulating her own and her daughter's affect with a little more confidence each time. And yet, she would never pretend that it is not hard for her to be Chloe's mom. Then there are those precious golden moments when the presence of growth is undeniable. Not long ago, while on a phone session with Anna, I was privy to an exchange between Anna and Chloe that reassured me again that our work together had truly created new options and modes of relating for Anna.

Chloe had come into the room while Anna was on the phone with me and asked Anna if she could lie on her lap. The following is the exchange I heard between them:

C: Mommy, I want to put my head in your lap.
Anna: Well, mommy is on the phone... remember, Mommy talks on the phone for an hour on Thursday mornings?
C: Uh-hun.
Anna: So if you can lay here with me and let me talk on the phone, you can stay here.
C: Ok.
        Anna resumes talking to me about the topic at hand and after about 30 seconds or so Chloe interjects:
C: No, mommy, you aren't patting my head the right way... do it like this.
Anna: [laughs lightly] Oh, ok, I wasn't doing it right.........is this better?
C: Uh-huh.
        Anna resumes talking to me and again about 30 seconds later...
C: No, mommy, you're moving your hand too slow... pet me like THIS.

Anna: Ooops, I can't get it right... ok, like this?
C: Yeah... uh-huh... like you're petting the kitty.
Anna: Oh, ok, like I'm petting the kitty... I think I got it.

As Anna resumed talking to me, I heard Chloe singing "rock-a-bye baby" softly in the background. I smiled as I sat back in my chair and I thought of sound again – the sound of Anna's voice in my ear, the sound of Chloe's voice singing to Anna. Resonant and melodic, these sounds filled the space between the three of us in a gentle rhythm of breath, movement, pause, and silence.

Study Questions

1. Define "reflective-verbal" and "implicit" domains of communication and give an example of each in a dyadic interaction between therapist and client OR caregiver and child.
2. Discuss countertransference issues in telephone treatment.
3. Explain the major functions of the right brain as it relates to attachment theory.
4. Describe the potential benefits of a telephone treatment for a client who may struggle with the closeness that can come from an in-person treatment setting.
5. Illustrate the relevance of intergenerational transmission of trauma as it relates to a child's affect regulation abilities.

References

Beebe, B., Jaffe, J., Lachmann, F., Feldstein, S., Crown, C., & Jasnow, M. (2002). Systems models in development and psychoanalysis: The case of vocal rhythm coordination and attachment. *Infant Mental Health Journal, 21*(1–2), 99–122.

Beebe, B., Knoblauch, S., Rustin, J., & Sorter, D. (2005). *Forms of intersubjectivity in infant research and adult treatment*. New York: Other.

Beebe, B., & Lachmann, F. (1992). The contribution of mother–infant influence to the origins of self and self- and object representations. In N. Skolnick & S. Warshaw (Eds.), *Relational perspectives on psychoanalysis* (pp. 83–117). Hillsdale, NJ: Analytic.

Beebe, B., & Lachmann, F. (2002). *Infant research and adult treatment: Co-construction interactions*. Hillsdale, NJ: Analytic.

Bennett, S. (2004). Viewing telephone therapy through the lens of attachment theory and infant research. *Clinical Social Work Journal, 32*(3), 239–250.

Boston Change Process Study Group. (2008). Forms of relational meaning: Issues in the relations between the implicit and reflective-verbal domains. *Psychoanalytic Dialogues, 18*, 125–148.

Brisch, K. (2000). Use of the telephone in the treatment of attachment disorders. In E. Aronson (Ed.), *Use of the telephone in psychotherapy* (pp. 35–395). Northvale, NJ: Jason Aronson.

Coen, S. J. (2005). Becoming comfortable with telephone therapy. *The Round Robin, 20*(2), 3–15.

Decety, J., & Chaminade, T. (2003). When the self represents the other: A new cognitive neuroscience view on psychological identification. *Consciousness and Cognition, 12*, 577–596.

Khan, H. I. (1996). *The mysticism of sound and music*. Boston, MA: Shambhala.

Knoblauch, S. H. (2000). *The musical edge of therapeutic dialogue*. Hillsdale, NJ: Analytic.

Lachmann, F., & Beebe, B. (1996). Three principles of salience in the organization of the patient–analyst interaction. *Psychoanalytic Psychology, 13*, 1–22.

Ludman, E. J., Simon, G. E., Tutty, S., & Von Korff, M. (2007). A randomized trial of telephone psychotherapy and pharmacotherapy for depression: Continuation and durability of effects. *Journal of Consulting and Clinical Psychology, 75*(2), 257–266.

Manosevitz, M. (2004). Panel: Analysis by phone. *Psychologist–Psychoanalyst, 24*(3), 38–39.

Merriam-Webster Dictionary. (2007). Springfield, MA: Merriam-Webster.

Moldawasky, S. (2004). Panel: Analysis by phone. *Psychologist–Psychoanalyst, 24*(3), 38–39.

Rotenberg, V. (1995). Right hemisphere insufficiency and illness in the context of search activity concept. *Dynamic Psychiatry, 150/151*, 54–63.

Schecter, D. S. (2003). Intergenerational communication of maternal violent trauma: Understanding the interplay of reflective functioning and post-traumatic psychopathology. In S. W. Coates, J. L. Rosenthal, & D. S. Schecter (Eds.), *September 11: Trauma and human bonds* (pp. 115–142). Hillsdale, NJ: Analytic.

Schore, A. N. (2001a). The effects of a secure attachment relationship on right brain development, affect regulation, and infant mental health. *Infant Mental Health Journal, 22*, 7–66.

Schore, A. N. (2001b). Dysregulation of the right brain: A fundamental mechanism of traumatic attachment and the psychopathogenesis of posttraumatic stress disorder. *Australian and New Zealand Journal of Psychiatry, 36*, 9–30.

Schore, A. N. (2002). Advances in neuropsychoanalysis, attachment theory, and trauma research: Implications for self psychology. *Psychoanalytic Inquiry, 22*(3), 433–484.

Schore, A. N. (2005). A neuropsychoanalytic viewpoint: Commentary on paper by Steven H. Knoblauch. *Psychoanalytic Dialogues, 15*, 829–854.

Stern, D. (1985). *The interpersonal world of the infant: A view from psychoanalysis and developmental psychology*. New York: Basic Books.

Winnicott, D. (1953). Transitional objects and transitional phenomena. *International Journal of Psychoanalysis, 34*, 89–97.

Chapter 7
Using a Mentalization-Based Framework to Assist Hard-to-Reach Clients in Individual Treatment

Christine H. Fewell

> *…You may give them your love but not your thoughts, for they have their own thoughts.*
> *You may house their bodies but not their souls, for their souls dwell in the house of tomorrow, which you cannot visit, not even in your dreams.*
> *You may strive to be like them, but seek not to make them like you.*
> *For life goes not backward nor tarries with yesterday…*

Gibran (1995, p. 17)

During a site visit in my role as faculty advisor for social work students, the supervisor began the discussion of a case by saying, "We are keeping an eye on this one. We think he's a psychopath." The female student then described a man who came to therapy so he could have a monogamous relationship. He described himself as having a sexual addiction, picking up men and women at a high-end department store, and using cocaine and Ecstasy on occasion. His presentation was narcissistic and grandiose, and he filled the therapy hour with expansive and disorganized stories. The student felt anxious and helpless as she attempted to engage him in discussing his presenting problem. This process seemed futile because he demonstrated no ability to reflect and seemed to convert every impulse into action. The concept of mentalization provides a useful framework for understanding and guiding interventions with clients like this one and assists with countertransferential reactions that may lead to therapeutic impasses (Fonagy, Gergely, & Target, 2008). The acquisition of a reflective mentalizing stance is a powerful developmental achievement that enables the individual to regulate affects, rather than using action and drugs to discharge feelings, as this client does.

This chapter will discuss the developmental origin of mentalization within the context of attachment relationships and the role it plays in affect regulation. Recently, *mentalization-based treatment* (MBT) has been developed for use in

C.H. Fewell (✉)
Silver School of Social Work, New York University, New York, NY, USA
and
Institute for Psychoanalytic Training and Research, New York, NY, USA
e-mail: christine.fewell@nyu.edu

S. Bennett and J.K. Nelson (Eds.), *Adult Attachment in Clinical Social Work*, Essential Clinical Social Work Series, DOI 10.1007/978-1-4419-6241-6_7, © Springer Science+Business Media, LLC 2010

various settings, including inpatient treatment programs for high achieving individuals from such diverse fields as medicine, the law, mental health, religion, and business (Allen & Fonagy, 2006; Bleiberg, 2006), individuals with borderline personality disorder (Bateman & Fonagy, 2007), and families (Fearon et al., 2006). In addition, facilitating the ability of parents to mentalize about the minds of their babies has been found to result in positive outcomes for first-time high-risk mothers (Sandler, Slade, & Mayes, 2006). While mentalizing is a part of many psychotherapeutic interventions, the focus on mentalizing in MBT can be considered to incorporate aspects of both psychodynamic and cognitive-behavioral approaches (Allen, Fonagy, & Bateman, 2008). These concepts can be used in individual treatment with clients who have difficulty in mentalizing, many of whom have suffered early trauma and are considered hard-to-reach or resistant.

The Definition and Development of Mentalization

Mentalization is a concept that describes the ability to envision mental states in one's self and in others. It is referred to as *reflective function* when measured by a scale developed to quantify mentalization in attachment-related contexts (Fonagy, Target, Steele, & Steele, 1998), and it is similar to the concept of *metacognitive monitoring* in the Adult Attachment Interview (Hesse, 2008; see Bennett and Nelson, Chap. 3). Mentalizing involves being able to interpret others' actions and one's own as being related to the particular mental state being experienced (Allen et al., 2008). It involves being aware of the nature of mental states and being willing to think about them. In addition to feelings, mental states include desires, beliefs, needs, thoughts, and dreams. Mentalizing also extends to cognitive operations, such as perceiving, describing, interpreting, and anticipating both spoken and nonverbal communication and states (Allen & Fonagy, 2006).

One example of mentalizing is when individuals show awareness that it is difficult to understand what is on another's mind and that there is a limit to what can be known. It includes the realization that it is necessary to work to understand another's state of mind, since mental states often are disguised by other emotions and need to be teased out to discover the underlying feelings and motivations. Mentalizing also involves recognizing that each person has a unique perspective and may have different feelings about a shared event. Finally, mentalization includes awareness that mental states precede behavior, resulting in a subsequent impact. Allen et al. (2008) capture the essence of the concept of mentalization by stating that it is the process of "holding mind in mind" (p. 3).

It should be noted that mentalization can be used to negative effect by children who tease and bully (Cutting & Dunn, 2002; Sutton, Smith, & Swettenham, 1999) and by adults who use awareness of vulnerabilities in others to attack or criticize. Hypermentalization occurs in people who are paranoid and constantly seek to attend to the meaning of their own and other's interventions (Bleiberg, 2006). Prisoners and others with psychopathic tendencies often use mentalization to understand how to gain advantage over their victims (Fonagy et al., 1998).

Individuals with borderline personality demonstrate impulsivity, deficits in affect regulation, and difficulties in relationships with others, particularly in the context of intimate attachment relationships. While they may be able to mentalize about other's thoughts and intentions in some situations, they experience failures in mentalizing when under stress. For this reason, understanding and providing a secure therapeutic attachment relationship where they can regain or learn mentalizing skills enables them to achieve stability and mastery over their internal states (Bateman & Fonagy, 2006). Substance misuse is often a way to inhibit mentalization and to stop from thinking about prior trauma (Bateman & Fonagy, 2006) or about the impact of substance abuse on others with whom an individual may have an intimate relationship (Allen & Fonagy, 2006).

Mentalization and Attachment

Fonagy and his colleagues have focused attention on the development of mentalization in the context of early attachment relationships and on the role that it plays in the organization of the self and the regulation of affects (Fonagy, Gergely, Jurist, & Target, 2002). They propose that mentalization grows out of the parent's ability to understand and reflect the infant's inner world and is fostered by the same conditions that promote secure attachment. Modern attachment theory has, in fact, been defined as the mutual regulation of affect (see Schore and Schore, Chap. 4).

There is increasing evidence that a parent's ability to mentalize about the child contributes to attachment security (Meins, Fernyhough, Fradley, & Tuckey, 2001; Oppenheim & Koren-Karie, 2002; Slade, Grienenberger, Bernbach, Levy, & Locker, 2005). The adaptation of the Reflective Function Scale (Fonagy et al., 1998) for use with the Parent Development Interview (PDI; Aber, Slade, Berger, Bresgi, & Kaplan, 1985) by Slade and her colleagues (Slade, Bernbach, Grienenberger, Levy, & Locker, 2004) has led to research measuring maternal reflective functioning toward her child. Slade et al. (2005) have shown that the mother's capacity for reflective functioning about her own child is related to adult attachment and to the infant's attachment classification and may be the means by which the intergenerational transmission of attachment occurs (Fonagy & Target, 2005). Parents with secure attachment classifications are able to understand what is on their infant's mind and accurately represent this, resulting in securely attached children. Similarly, parents with insecure attachment classifications are hampered by their anxious preoccupations or deactivating strategies and are thereby blocked from accurately understanding and responding to their child's desires and intentions.

While research has shown that there are strong correlations between the style of parenting that leads to both attachment security and mentalization, it is not certain how this occurs. According to Fonagy et al. (2008), "The process of acquiring mentalization is so ordinary and normal that it may be more correct to consider secure attachment as removing obstacles rather than actively and directly facilitating its development" (p. 796).

Social interactions common in parents with secure attachment may contribute to the development of mentalization. For example, how much the family values the role of talking about feelings and the reasons for people's actions may contribute to the development of mentalization (Fonagy & Target, 1997a, 1997b). When children are engaged in secure relationships with parents, they are better able to deal with emotional issues freely and interact in activities involving shared play and comforting and joking, which provide an atmosphere where parental explanations of mental states can be provided and absorbed (Fonagy et al., 2002).

There is also the possibility that securely attached children are able to use pretense and fantasy play more productively and that this promotes the understanding of mental states and emotions (Belsky, Garduque, & Hrncir, 1984). The parent's ability to play has been found to have implications for attachment security. While involved in play, the adult or even an older sibling joins in adopting the fantasy produced by the child's mind, while still keeping the framework of reality intact. Symbolic play permits the development of skills needed to imagine another's perception of reality (Fonagy et al., 2002).

Peer group interaction is a third possible contributor to reflective function. Interaction with peers provides the opportunity for imagining what others think and feel. Feeling safe enough to explore the meaning of others' actions is a precursor to the child's being able to find his or her own psychological experiences meaningful.

The Role of Parenting in Mentalization

The capacity for mentalization is acquired through the process of the primary caregiver's accurately attuning to and reflecting the child's mental states (Fonagy & Target, 1997a, 1997b). From the moment of birth, both infant and mother engage in a process of dyadic regulation at a nonverbal level. There is a reciprocal interaction of self-regulation and interactive regulation. This is reflected in tone of voice, touch, movements of the hands by both mother and child, widening of the eyes and mouth, and meeting or averting gaze (Beebe, Lachmann, & Jaffe, 1997). The caregiver's attuned responses serve to reflect back to the infant what he or she is feeling, at the same time that it is contained or soothed, or in the case of positive arousal, met in kind and appreciated. This nonverbal means of communication continues throughout life and is reflected in the therapeutic relationship.

When the mother is able to reflect on both her own and her child's mental states, whether upset or in pain, or playful and delighted, and to appropriately reflect back the reality of the child's internal experience, the child develops a representation of his or her inner self, which is internalized over time. The child learns through this process of attunement or mirroring what he or she is feeling and how to manage those affects.

Two conditions are essential to the reflecting or mirroring process. The mirroring must be "contingent." In other words, facial expressions, sounds, or behavior must be responded to within an optimally brief window of time so that the baby learns that the response came as a result of his or her effort. This enables the child to develop a sense of agency or of being able to influence others (Beebe, Knoblauch, Rustin, & Sorter, 2005). Mirroring must also be contingent in terms of emotional tone.

For example, if the mother's response to a baby's signal of distress is consistently one of depressed apathy, the child may develop a sense of helplessness and may come to depend on the self for coping with emotional regulation (Tronick, 2007).

It is crucial that the mirroring by the parent be what has been called "marked," which means that the infant's affect is mirrored, not exactly, but in a slightly distorted or transformed way by exaggerating, underplaying, or organizing it (Fonagy et al., 2008). If not marked, the infant may be unable to determine whose emotional state is being displayed. For example, if the mother's reflection mirrors a negative affect, such as anxiety, too closely, the reflection itself becomes a source of fear for the child. The caregiver's response to negative arousal must reflect the child's mental state and provide some form of soothing at the same time. In terms of positive arousal, the parent must attune in a playful manner and either increase or decrease the intensity of the positive arousal, appropriately reading or reflecting the child's affective state. In this process, the parent demonstrates a state of mind that is both the same and different from the child's mind. Thus, mirroring will fail if it is either too close to the infant's experience or too distant. As Fonagy and Target (1997a, 1997b) point out, this concept touches on Bion's conceptualization of "the mother's capacity to 'contain' the affect state intolerable for the baby and respond in terms of physical care in a manner that acknowledges the child's mental state yet serves to modulate unmanageable feelings" (p. 686). Positive and negative arousal may both need to be contained if they are intolerable for the child. This eventually results in the child's being able to understand the affects displayed by others, in addition to being able to regulate his or her own emotions (Fonagy et al., 2002).

Understanding the early nonverbal processes, including contingency and marked-ness, which are involved in developing the capacity to mentalize, is valuable for understanding the interactive patterns constructed in the therapy dyad. This under-standing is especially useful with "difficult-to-treat" clients who may have deficits in mentalizing and verbalizing their feelings.

Trauma and Mentalization

Among the most emotionally traumatic experiences abused children have are those in which their severe distress is caused by the caregivers, thus impairing the child's reflective capacities (Fonagy & Target, 1997a, 1997b). There are several reasons for this. First, in abusive families, the need for secrecy about the abuse brings about a sharp separation between the home environment and the public environment. Even if the child develops sensitivity in the public domain, the models for experiencing the self and others in the public and family worlds are likely to be rigidly applied to the particular context in which they are experienced (Fonagy & Target, 1997a, 1997b). Second, in abusive families, the meaning of people's behaviors may be denied or distorted. This prevents the child from testing out the true meaning of mental states. Finally, if the child tries to understand the thoughts and feelings of an abusive parent through the use of mentalization, he or she will be confronted by painful feelings about the self (Fonagy & Target, 1997a, 1997b). Frequently, in the process of rationalizing, the painful feelings resulting from contemplating the abusive parent's behavior, the child blames him or herself and internalizes the negative feelings, resulting in serious damage to the self-image (Fonagy et al., 2002).

It is also possible that the abused child's difficulty in mentalizing comes from the type of parenting rather than the abuse itself (Baumrind, 1971). Authoritarian parenting that demands obedience has been found to inhibit the development of mentalization, while parenting that reasons with the child and explains why rules must take into account others' points of view tends to facilitate mentalization (Baumrind, 1971).

For adults who have been maltreated as children, limited reflective functioning can be seen as an adaptive achievement within their early family context. However, their lack of ability to understand mental states causes difficulties with later interpersonal relationships (Fonagy et al., 2002). People who have been traumatized by their family environments thus face vulnerability from the original reaction to the trauma as well as to the handicap resulting from a nonmentalizing stance necessary to adapt to such a situation.

On the other hand, negative conflictual experiences may cause some individuals to develop or even over-develop mentalizing in order to cope with the situation (Newton, Reddy, & Bull, 2000). In a study of college age children of alcoholics (mean age=20.2), the adult children of alcoholics (ACOAs) (n=78) were significantly less secure in their attachment to their parents and had significantly higher psychological distress than those who did not have alcoholic parents (n=93) (Fewell, 2006). However, the ACOAs also demonstrated higher reflective functioning, especially toward their mothers, who were for the most part not the alcoholic parent. The emotional difficulties of growing up in alcoholic families appear to have drawn these college students to attempt to understand their mothers' minds and develop high reflective functioning, while not protecting them from high levels of psychological distress.

Adult Capacity for Mentalization

The adult who has the ability to mentalize has learned that reality can be interpreted in many different ways by different people (Fonagy & Target, 1996). Fonagy and Target (1996, 1997a, 1997b) describe a psychoanalytic model of the development of thought leading to mentalization. Although these stages are part of normal development, clients in the clinical situation may be using different levels of thought exclusively or simultaneously. Being able to determine what level of thought is being used provides a valuable way to gage interventions so that they will be most useful. The three levels of prementalizing experience are called the *psychic equivalence* or *actual mode*, the *pretend mode*, and the *teleological mode*.

In the psychic equivalence or actual mode, the client believes that others can read their thoughts and expects others to know what he or she is thinking and feeling (Fonagy et al., 2008). What the person thinks is perceived as reality. That is, what is in the individual's mind is the same or equivalent for all. A number of clients, for example, have not learned that they must tell others what they are thinking and feeling, or ask what others are thinking and feeling, rather than assuming that they know. Clients frequently express great distress in relationships when they think that others are intentionally not responding to their needs. Such problems may result from thinking in actual or psychic equivalence mode.

In the pretend mode, the individual is able to think about fantasy without having to be bound by the constraints of reality. In the adult, daydreaming and fantasizing are ways of using the pretend mode. It involves what Fonagy and Target (1996) have called "playing with reality" (p. 231). It is a way of acting "as if" reality did not exist and is a way to deal with parts of reality that are difficult to tolerate. This kind of thinking is positive when it allows a person to imagine new ways of acting, permits temporary escape from responsibilities so that it leads to rejuvenation, or allows creativity. It is negative if it shuts out important aspects of reality and results in a person who refuses to believe that he or she has a substance abuse problem, for example, that is impacting health and family life, or who is having an affair while disregarding the consequences this has for the marriage.

In addition to actual or pretend modes, there is the prementalizing teleological way of experiencing feelings in which an individual believes that only actions count. This may occur when an individual is under stress. In this mode of thinking, words and thoughts cannot contain or relieve painful feelings. A person who has experienced trauma such as physical and sexual abuse may feel that the only way to alter another person's thoughts and feelings is through action. This is demonstrated by the client encountered by the social work intern at the beginning of this chapter. An adolescent who bullies others as a way of communicating the pain he is feeling is thinking in a teleological mode. A client with borderline personality disorder who feels rage because of a perceived slight and cuts herself is saying in action what she cannot say with words (Allen et al., 2008). In the clinical situation, determining that a person is acting in teleological mode means that we must respond to the underlying painful attachment anxiety caused by the trauma.

When a mentalizing way of thinking is achieved, the person is able to integrate other ways of thinking and to be aware that the pretend way of viewing the world is subject to the constraints of reality. He or she cannot control things with omnipotent fantasy. Reality means that one's ideas are only one way of seeing the world. Other people have different ways of seeing the world. Ideas are just one way of representing reality in the mind and it is different for everyone. It involves recognition that people's actions are guided by underlying feelings, desires, beliefs, and intentions that are unique. Being able to mentalize includes a means to regulate arousal and distress. It also includes being able to evaluate the probable feelings behind emotional states and the likely consequences of expressing them in various situations. Thus, the individual is able to evaluate behavior prior to taking action.

Mentalizing is learned in the process of caregivers appropriately reflecting back the feelings and thoughts of the child so that the child can come to know the contents of his or her *own* mind and that he or she is unique and different from the caregiver. This occurs optimally within a secure attachment relationship. Having control over thoughts, feelings, and actions strengthens the sense of self, as described in early parent interactions. The therapeutic relationship attempts to provide a similar secure relationship, which promotes mentalizing so that affect regulation can be achieved.

Mentalization-Based Interventions

MBT has been developed and empirically validated as a means of assisting clients to achieve and maintain a mentalizing stance in the face of intense affect arousal (Allen & Fonagy, 2006). It combines an attachment-based psychodynamic understanding with elements of cognitive-behavioral therapy, including a focus on psychoeducation. Because of the developmental attachment context in which mentalizing is acquired, mentalizing interventions are also highly compatible with object relations theory (Fonagy, 2001). The development of a secure and safe therapeutic relationship is of importance for promoting mentalizing, just as the secure attachment to early caregivers is important in the development of the child's mentalization capacities (Allen & Fonagy, 2006). While mentalizing is a part of all therapy, MBT focuses specifically on the process of fostering the client's capacity to generate multiple perspectives and can be used as part of any theoretical construct. Allen et al. (2008) describe the aims of MBT as promoting mentalizing about oneself, about others, and about relationships. This process is accomplished with careful attention to the therapeutic relationship so that the emotional climate remains neither so tense and emotionally charged that mentalizing is strained, nor so distant and cold that rigid thinking and intellectualization dominate.

Transference is conceptualized in MBT as a reaction to the interaction between the client and the clinician that has been influenced by the past, but which is a new version of the internalized object relations of the mind being experienced in treatment in the present. Interpretations of transference based on the past are not given to clients with borderline personality disorder since they may experience them as unreal, which may lead to a dissociative experience and a belief that their own experience is invalid (Bateman & Fonagy, 2004). Instead, transference is regarded as a way in which the clinician can help to reveal different perspectives of mind.

Countertransference monitoring is considered critical in MBT and examined in the light of needing to "retain mental closeness" (Bateman & Fonagy, 2004, p. 210). This is necessary to maintain the therapeutic stance of accurately representing the internal mental state of the client in the way that a parent must in order to promote developmental progress. The clinician must differentiate between feelings the client may be inducing and those that arise from his or her own unresolved unconscious conflicts in order to stay attuned to the mental state of the client. The therapist, in other words, must be able to mentalize or reflect about both self and other.

In contrast to traditional psychoanalytic therapies, MBT does not promote free association, long monologs or silences, or active fantasy about the therapist. In such psychoanalytic therapies, these techniques are a means for understanding unconscious mental functioning, whereas mentalization-based therapy is concerned with preconscious and conscious aspects of thinking (Allen et al., 2008). MBT utilizes a more active and engaged stance than classical psychoanalytic methods, and the therapist conveys an attitude of authenticity through judicious self-disclosure about mental states in relation to the client's thoughts. In contrast to making interpretations based on the therapist's view of the client's thinking, the therapist maintains an inquisitive not-knowing stance that demonstrates that what is on the client's mind cannot really be known unless it is verbalized. Mentalizing interventions can be characterized as being more concerned with process, with the way a person is thinking, rather than with content, or finding the appropriate interpretations (Allen et al., 2008). This is because mentalizing interventions are conceived as a way to help the client develop skills that will enable the regulation of affects in times of high emotional arousal. An essential aspect of mentalizing interventions is to generate alternative perspectives on people's feelings and behaviors with an open mind that accepts the possibility of different outlooks (Allen et al., 2008).

Understanding the Client's Narrative

Assessing a client's narrative from the viewpoint of the type of thinking and level of mentalizing is a useful way to begin applying mentalizing interventions. Throughout the treatment, when perplexed by clients' distress over emotionally charged interactions and their inability to resolve their feelings, one useful intervention is to step back and contemplate what is happening to the client's mentalizing ability (Fonagy et al., 2008). Allen et al. (2008) describe the importance of gaging interventions along a continuum, with more supportive interventions used when high affect arousal causes mentalizing to be impaired and more interpretive interventions used when mentalizing capacity is stabilized. The developmental theory of the acquisition of mentalizing within the attachment relationship (Fonagy et al., 2008) provides a psychodynamic framework for understanding the application of interventions to help people resolve ambivalence about change (Prochaska & DiClemente, 1982).

Evaluating whether a client is using a psychic equivalence, pretend, or teleological mode of thinking, or is able to mentalize will allow the clinician to gage the type of interventions that will be most useful at that moment. For example, if someone is thinking in psychic equivalence mode and unable to envision alternative perspectives, it will be futile to introduce efforts to mentalize. The client is likely to feel invalidated and criticized. This approach entails keeping the client's state of mind at the forefront of the interaction (Allen et al., 2008).

An effort to promote mentalizing in clients would include asking questions to promote stepping back and thinking. However, a client who is using a psychic equivalence way of thinking is unable to do this because of thinking in a concrete manner. What is in the mind is held as the only perspective. Asking such a person to think about thinking will be futile and will increase resistance. Therefore, considering whether a client is capable of mentalizing before asking questions that require mentalizing is a useful framework for gaging interventions.

A person who is contemplating making a change or preparing to make a change may be seen as thinking in pretend mode. Interventions need to be geared to "playing with reality" (Fonagy & Target, 1996, p. 231) or discussing the possibility of change with the help of the therapist in a safe space where there is no expectation that it will be necessary to face reality immediately. The following case illustrates the usefulness of assessing the kind of cognitive psychic reality being used by the client.

Case of Regina

When Regina entered treatment in her late 20s, she expressed a great deal of self-hatred and hopelessness about herself, her weight, and her ability to maintain a relationship with a man. After a few months of treatment, she began to report drinking episodes that resulted in blacking out to the point of not remembering what she had been doing. Regina's narrative unfolded in a hypomanic way that allowed very little room for reflective thought and kept the interaction on a superficial basis. As the therapist, I felt anxious, somewhat helpless, and as if there were no room for my comments, feelings I recognized as being reflective of the way Regina felt. Problems were presented concretely and I felt challenged to provide a magical solution without any input from Regina. For example, Regina frequently stated that if only she could lose weight she would be able to find a man, without being able to mentalize about what other feelings might be involved in her difficulties. Initial sessions centered on her extreme disappointment with a 4-year relationship that had ended 3 years prior. This man had lied to her about being in college, which he pretended to attend during the time she was going to college. When he met a wealthy woman, he left Regina to marry the other woman. Regina was devastated by the betrayal of trust and abandonment.

Regina's mother was a practicing Roman Catholic who was concerned with social appearances. Her mother had a great deal of shame about the relationship she had with Regina's biological father, by whom she became pregnant when she was 19. The couple had married but divorced within the year due to his alcoholism. This experience led Regina's mother to convey the message that relationships with men were dangerous and to anxiously oversee Regina's dating experiences and curfews.

When Regina was one year old, her mother divorced, attended medical school, and married a physician who adopted Regina when she was five. A brother and sister were subsequently born into the family, and the first marriage was never mentioned again. Regina had no contact with her biological father and felt bereft about her mother's resistance to discussing him. However, her anger at her mother was accompanied by guilt and loyalty conflicts, since her stepfather was a warm person with whom she felt a more secure attachment than she felt with her mother. Although Regina's mother and father lived in another city at the time she began treatment, she was visiting them every 2 weeks for one social event or another.

Throughout the first year of treatment, Regina made occasional statements about how she would one day need to discuss her drinking but that she was not ready to do it yet. At this point she was alternating between a psychic equivalence or actual manner of thinking and a teleological manner and was not ready to contemplate another perspective. Since Regina presented with what seemed to be a preoccupied attachment with her mother for whom she served as an emotional caretaker, I was aware that I needed to respond in a way that would assist Regina to have a sense of herself as an intentional agent with her own feelings. Regina set her own goal to stop her frequent practice of getting drunk and going home with men for sex – a goal which I supported by validating that she was perceiving and responding with appropriate alarm. In addition, I observed that Regina had not developed the ability to mentalize based on my interpersonal experiences with her and her concrete ways of thinking. Therefore, I reflected back her feeling that she had things she wanted to change about her drinking and its effects but had not decided what to do about it. She gradually brought in more concerns about problematic behaviors related to drinking. Her accounts revealed a pattern of remaining at bars or parties with men after the women went home and drinking so heavily that she was unable to speak or walk. She had frequent blackout experiences of not remembering how she had gotten home.

While recounting one such occasion, Regina said that she was going to have to figure out a way to cut down or she would need to quit drinking completely. Wary of the need not to push her at this juncture, I asked which she felt she wanted to do, and she described a plan to try to control her drinking. Several social occasions passed where she was sometimes able to control her drinking and sometimes not. After another embarrassing and dangerous experience of excessive drinking that ended with her waking up in her apartment naked with the door open and no recollection of how she got home, Regina said that she would need to go to Alcoholics Anonymous meetings. When she returned to the next session, she announced that she had found the meeting very interesting and said she would go again. She had not spoken to anyone there, but added, "I think that they can pick up whether or not you want to talk." After a moment of reflection, she added, "I think I probably give off vibes to men that I don't want them to be involved. That's probably why I can't meet someone. I stay at the bars with the men because I feel as though I'm getting love and attention. When I'm drinking I am not afraid to be myself and let them know who I am."

Regina began treatment with tremendous difficulty regulating her affect. She used the prementalizing teleological or action-oriented way of dealing with her feelings by drinking and linking up with men for sex in order to feel loved and connected. Psychic equivalence thinking was evident in her concrete presentation of problems without an ability to perceive any other way of seeing them. She also made use of the prementalizing pretend mode of cognitive functioning. Having been invalidated in her inquisitiveness about her early childhood, she had many feelings she was unable to symbolize about her father and her early experiences. She had repeated this in her love relationship by finding an impostor boyfriend, which may have mirrored the experience she imagined her mother had with her father. Regina's attitude of naïveté also reflected the situation of victimization experienced by individuals who operate in pretend mode and are thus unable to perceive others' intentions and motives accurately.

While Regina continued to act as if the drinking was not affecting her, she was operating in a psychic equivalent mode of thinking. As she began to contemplate that one day she might do something about her drinking, she began to use a pretend mode of thinking where, in the safe space of the therapeutic relationship, she could envision what it would be like to make a change. In treatment I felt it important to enter into the pretend mode with her to provide a safe space where she could "play with reality." The experience of finally getting to the AA meeting demonstrated the dawning of the ability to mentalize. Her recognition that no one spoke to her at the meeting because she "gave out vibes to leave her alone," a pattern that was repeated in her other interactions with men, was demonstrating the important mentalizing function of seeing a causal relationship between her feelings and her behavior and other's feeling and behaviors.

Summary

The capacity for mentalizing begins with the attuned interventions of caretakers, who through their responses to the infant's negative and positive arousal, enable the infant to gradually learn the contents of his or her mind and develop a sense of the self as an intentional agent capable of influence and self-regulation (Fonagy et al., 2008). Secure attachment and mentalizing are fostered by the same capacities of parents for matching mental states to their babies in a manner that is neither too distant from, nor too close to, their experiences. The atmosphere of trust inherent in secure attachment permits optimal conditions for exploration and for learning about cooperation and competition, and it enables tolerance for both negative and positive emotions and novel experiences. In contrast, insecure attachment inhibits mentalization because the child must be concerned about the mind of the parent, who may be representing mental states that are either not an accurate representation or are frightening.

MBT provides a means for focusing on interventions to enable clients to develop skills in mentalizing. It devotes attention to creating a secure therapeutic environment that is neither too supportive nor too challenging, within which the therapist can help the client mentalize about the self, about relationships, and about the therapist. As part of this treatment process, it is important to assess the client's moment-to-moment changes in level of psychic functioning. When mentalizing fails in the face of stress, clients regress to prementalizing modes. Interventions must be geared to the level of psychic functioning the client is experiencing in order to be successful. For example, if someone is using a psychic equivalence or pretend mode of thinking and they are asked to think about the consequences or motivations of their behavior, they will react with resistance, dissociation, or even regress further in their level of psychic thinking.

A focus on mentalizing in psychotherapy builds on a foundation of attachment research to assist clients who have not developed or have lost the ability to self-regulate in the presence of psychological distress. As Slade (2008) points out in her review of attachment research, attachment organization does appear to play an important role in an individual's willingness and capacity to use treatment. However, there is still a great deal of work to be done in understanding how to integrate the findings of attachment research with clinical interventions. MBT holds promise for providing a means to focus on ways to assist individuals to understand mental states in the self and others and to experience more security in intimate relationships. This focus on the process of the therapeutic interaction, rather than the content, is what has made MBT especially relevant to the treatment of individuals with borderline personality disorder. Through the process of the clinician's keeping the client's mind and subjective experience at the forefront of the interaction, the client is helped to integrate his or her own subjectivity with the clinician's.

Study Questions

1. Think of a client who is upset with another person and assess whether the client's thinking reflects the psychic equivalence, pretend, teleological, or mentalizing mode.
2. Think of a situation where there is a disagreement or a misunderstanding between the social worker and a client. Discuss the mental processes that lead to different viewpoints.
3. How would the social worker intervene to help the client see that different viewpoints are possible and acceptable?
4. What characteristics are present in a client who is open to mentalizing or reflecting about his or her motivations, desires, and beliefs, and those of others?
5. What kinds of questions from the social work clinician promote mentalizing?

References

Aber, J. L., Slade, A., Berger, B., Bresgi, I., & Kaplan, M. (1985). *The Parent Development Interview*. Unpublished manuscript.

Allen, J. G., & Fonagy, P. (2006). *Handbook of mentalization-based treatment*. Chichester, England: John Wiley & Sons.

Allen, J. G., Fonagy, P., & Bateman, A. W. (2008). *Mentalizing in clinical practice*. Washington, D.C.: American Psychiatric Publishing.

Bateman, A., & Fonagy, P. (2004). *Psychotherapy for borderline personality disorder*. Oxford, England: Oxford University Press.

Bateman, A., & Fonagy, P. (2006). *Mentalization-based treatment for borderline personality disorder*. Oxford, England: Oxford University Press.

Bateman, A. W., & Fonagy, P. (2007). *Mentalization-based treatment for borderline personality disorder: A practical guide*. New York: Oxford University Press.

Baumrind, D. (1971). Current patterns of parental authority. *Developmental Psychology Monographs, 4*(1, Part 2), pp. 1–103.

Beebe, B., Knoblauch, S., Rustin, J., & Sorter, D. (2005). *Forms of intersubjectivity in infant research and adult treatment*. New York: Other Press.

Beebe, B., Lachmann, F., & Jaffe, J. (1997). Mother-infant interaction structures and presymbolic self- and object-representations. *Psychoanalytic Dialogues, 7*, 113–182.

Belsky, J., Garduque, L., & Hrncir, E. (1984). Assessing performance, competence and executive capacity in infant play: Relations to home environment and security of attachment. *Developmental Psychology, 20*, 406–417.

Bleiberg, E. (2006). Treating professionals in crisis: A mentalization-based specialized inpatient program. In J. G. Allen & P. Fonagy (Eds.), *Handbook of mentalization-based treatment* (pp. 233–247). Chichester, England: John Wiley & Sons.

Cutting, A. L., & Dunn, J. (2002). The cost of understanding other people: Social cognition predicts young children's sensitivity to criticism. *Journal of Child Psychology and Psychiatry, 43*, 849–860.

Fearon, P., Target, M., Sargent, J., Willimas, L., McGregor, J., Blieberg, E., et al. (2006). Short-term mentalization and relational therapy (SMART): An integrative family therapy for children and adolescents. In J. G. Allen & P. Fonagy (Eds.), *Handbook of mentalization-based treatment* (pp. 201–222). Chichester, England: John Wiley & Sons.

Fewell, C. H. (2006). *Attachment, reflective function, family dysfunction and psychological distress in college students with alcoholic parents*. Unpublished Doctoral Dissertation, New York University School of Social Work, New York.

Fonagy, P. (2001). *Attachment theory and psychoanalysis*. New York: Other Press.

Fonagy, P., Gergely, G., Jurist, E., & Target, M. (2002). *Affect regulation, mentalization, and the development of the self*. New York: Other Press.

Fonagy, P., Gergely, G., & Target, M. (2008). Psychoanalytic constructs and attachment theory. In J. Cassidy & P. R. Shaver (Eds.), *Handbook of attachment: Theory, research, and clinical applications* (2nd ed., pp. 783–810). New York: Guilford.

Fonagy, P., & Target, M. (1996). Playing with reality I: Theory of mind and the normal development of psychic reality. *International Journal of Psychoanalysis, 77*(2), 217–233.

Fonagy, P., & Target, M. (1997a). Playing with reality II: The development of psychic reality from a theoretical perspective. *International Journal of Psychoanalysis, 77*(3), 459–479.

Fonagy, P., & Target, M. (1997b). Attachment and reflective function: Their role in self-organization. *Development and Psychopathology, 9*, 679–700.

Fonagy, P., & Target, M. (2005). Bridging the transmission gap: An end to an important mystery of attachment research? *Attachment & Human Development, 7*, 333–343.

Fonagy, P., Target, M., Steele, H., & Steele, M. (1998). *Reflective functioning manual: Version 5. For application to adult attachment interviews*. London: University College London.

Gibran, K. (1995). *The prophet*. New York: Alfred A. Knopf.

Hesse, E. (2008). The adult attachment interview: Protocol, method of analysis, and empirical studies. In J. Cassidy & P. Shaver (Eds.), *Handbook of attachment: Theory, research, and clinical applications* (2nd ed., pp. 552–598). New York: Guilford.

Meins, E., Fernyhough, C., Fradley, E., & Tuckey, M. (2001). Rethinking maternal sensitivity: Mothers' comments on infants mental processes predict security of attachment at 12 months. *Journal of Child Psychology and Psychiatry, 42*, 637–648.

Newton, P., Reddy, V., & Bull, R. (2000). Children's everyday deception and performance on false-belief tasks. *British Journal of Developmental Psychology, 18*, 297–317.

Oppenheim, D., & Koren-Karie, N. (2002). Mothers' insightfulness regarding their children's internal worlds: The capacity underlying secure child-mother relationships. *Infant Mental Health Journal, 23*, 593–605.

Prochaska, J., & DiClemente, C. (1982). Transtheoretical therapy: Toward a more integrative model of change. *Psychotherapy: Theory, Research, and Practice, 19*, 276–288.

Sandler, L. S., Slade, A., & Mayes, L. C. (2006). Minding the baby: A mentalization-based parenting program. In J. G. Allen & P. Fonagy (Eds.), *Handbook of mentalization-based treatment* (pp. 271–288). Chichester, England: John Wiley & Sons.

Slade, A., Bernbach, E., Grienenberger, J., Levy, D., & Locker, A. (2004). *Addendum to Fonagy, Target, Steele & Steele reflective functioning scoring manual for use with the Parent Development Interview (Unpublished manuscript)*. New York, NY: The City College and Graduate Center of the City University of New York.

Slade, A., Grienenberger, J., Bernbach, E., Levy, D., & Locker, A. (2005). Maternal reflective functioning, attachment, and the transmission gap: A preliminary study. *Attachment and Human Development, 7*, 283–298.

Slade, A. (2008). The implications of attachment theory and research for adult psychotherapy. In J. Cassidy & P. R. Shaver (Eds.), *Handbook of attachment: Theory, research, and clinical applications* (2nd ed., pp. 762–782). New York: Guilford.

Sutton, J., Smith, P. K., & Swettenham, J. (1999). Bullying and "theory of mind": A critique of the "social skills deficit" view of anti-social behavior. *Social Development, 8*, 117–127.

Tronick, E. (2007). *The neurobehavioral and social-emotional development of infants and children*. New York: W.W. Norton.

Chapter 8
Attachment and Caregiving for Elders Within African-American Families

Susanne Bennett, Michael J. Sheridan, and Barbara Soniat

> *The forms of [attachment] behavior and the bonds to which they lead are present and active throughout the life cycle.*
>
> Bowlby (1980, p. 39)

Issues at the heart of clinical work with elders – loss, bereavement, and caregiving – are central to attachment theory. As Bowlby (1969/1982) famously proposed, attachment behavior plays a "vital role" in human life "from the cradle to the grave" (p. 208). Bowlby's theory and the subsequent research on attachment across the life cycle provide a framework for viewing relationships between elder adults and their caregivers. The theory clarifies coping strategies in times of stress in late life and suggests that the caregiving styles of adults are linked to the early attachment bonds they experienced with their parents. At this stage of life, attachment patterns established early in life become activated in ways that are unique to the cultural context of the family unit (Fiori, Consedine, & Magai, 2009). This chapter addresses some of the attachment issues and cultural manifestations that emerge in late adulthood, highlighting, in particular, African-American caregivers of elders.

Attachment's continuity throughout adulthood and its universality across cultures remain debatable tenets, although a wealth of research has clarified the origins of attachment through observational studies of infants and parental caregivers (Cassidy & Shaver, 2008). Despite the growing emphasis on adult attachments (Mikulincer & Shaver, 2007), longitudinal studies on attachment from childhood to adulthood have not progressed beyond middle age (Grossman, Grossman, & Waters, 2005). Limited research has explored attachments among adults in late life or the relationships between elders and caregivers, such as adult children caring for their parents (Magai, 2008). Studies of cultural differences in attachment among adults also are narrow in scope, leaving open questions about the theory's universality. Even in the pluralistic USA, few studies have focused on attachments within ethnically

S. Bennett (✉)
National Catholic School of Social Service, The Catholic University of America, Washington, DC, USA
e-mail: bennetts@cua.edu

S. Bennett and J.K. Nelson (Eds.), *Adult Attachment in Clinical Social Work*, Essential Clinical Social Work Series, DOI 10.1007/978-1-4419-6241-6_8, © Springer Science+Business Media, LLC 2010

diverse American families, especially nonwhite families with older adults (Fiori et al., 2009).

Although attachment researchers have only recently begun to examine the relational experiences of elder adults (Magai, 2008), this population has held the national spotlight for some time among health care providers, policy makers, and mental health clinicians. The increase in professional attention reflects pressing demographic shifts, since the aging of the US population is one of the major health care challenges of the twenty-first century. The number of persons 65 or older in age is expected to reach 79 million by 2050 – an increase of 20% from 1996 – and African-American elders are expected to quadruple from 2000 to 2050 (U. S. Bureau of the Census, 2007), with an estimated 14–20% of them in poor health by 2030 (National Center for Health Statistics, 1996). Currently, primary caregivers for older adults are generally family members, with an estimated 44.4 million individuals providing long-term care (National Alliance for Caregiving and the American Association of Retired Persons, 2007). National estimates indicate that nearly one in three caregivers of elders are men, with 40% of them caring for spouses (Kramer & Thompson, 2002), but it has been predicted that 50% of all women in families eventually will need to be caregivers to their dependent parents (Magai, 2008). Family caregivers are at risk for health problems themselves, since studies show that caregivers experience a variety of negative health-related consequences, including depression, anxiety, and other mental health problems (Vitaliano, Scanlon, Krenz, Schwartz, & Marcovina, 1996).

Given the urgency of these demographic trends, there is a need for social workers and health care providers to become knowledgeable about the relational characteristics and ethnic variations among elders and their families (Dilworth-Anderson & Goodwin, 2005; Gibson, 1982). For example, studies on African-American elders and their caregivers suggest that "religious beliefs may serve as a particularly important source of support and coping" (Montague, Magai, Consedine, & Gillespie, 2003, p. 208). In this chapter, we present the theoretical and empirical contributions of attachment theory for understanding caregiving within African-American families and examine how it is influenced by religious and cultural factors, mediated by attachment styles. Following a summary of attachment theory and research related to elders and caregivers, clinical examples of African-American caregivers are presented with recommendations for social workers who use an attachment-based approach to support elder clients and their families.

Theory About Adult Attachment and Caregiving

Caregiving has been a central part of attachment theory from the outset. Although Bowlby (1969/1982) placed initial emphasis on the development of infant attachment, the eventual measurement of adult attachment enabled validation of the significant link between the caregiver's attachment and the child's attachment (Main, Kaplan, &

Cassidy, 1985). Awareness emerged that infant attachment to the parent was shaped primarily by the parent's attachment experiences with his or her own early caregivers, suggesting a transgenerational transmission of attachment (Cassidy, 2008; Hesse, 2008). The answers to Bowlby's questions about the origins of attachment, say Mikulincer and Shaver (2007), "lay mostly on the parent's side of the relationship," because the "attachment behavioral system" in the infant was found to be shaped by the "caregiving behavioral system" in the parent (p. 324).

Like the attachment system, the caregiving system was viewed by Bowlby (1969/1982) as an outgrowth of an evolutionary process that emerged to assure survival of offspring. He proposed that humans are born with a biologically based capacity for goal-directed caregiving behaviors, designed to protect the more vulnerable from harm, alleviate distress and reduce suffering, and foster development and growth. In times of distress, the caregiver provides a *safe haven* to meet a dependent person's needs, and at other times, the caregiver supports that person's *exploration* through provision of a *secure base* (Bowlby, 1969/1982). Theoretically, the caregiving system becomes activated and a prospective caregiver becomes motivated to provide care when the caregiver discerns that another feels discomfort, distress or danger, or needs support or encouragement for exploration, mastery, or learning something new (Mikulincer & Shaver, 2007).

The manner in which care is provided is influenced by the caregiver's own personal and intrapersonal capacities for emotion regulation in the face of another's distress (Mikulincer & Shaver, 2007). For example, the caregiver may be someone who either distances or becomes overwhelmed with anxiety when confronted with another's need, leading to either the abdication of care or an overidentification with "the role of another needy person to soothe one's own feelings" (p. 328). Abdicating behaviors (a sign of an *avoidant* or *dismissing* attachment style) or needy responses (a sign of an *anxious* or *preoccupied* attachment style) emerge from the caregiver's own attachment system, which has been shaped by internalized representations of how the caregiver received care earlier in life. Caregivers with *secure* attachment styles "are ones who have generally witnessed good care provided by their attachment figures, and this gives them positive models for their own behavior" (p. 330). More importantly, they internalized the secure caregiving they received as young children, which was formative in shaping their future caregiving capacities. They are able to balance the demands of caregiving, respond with compassion while maintaining appropriate boundaries, and "flexibly chart a course between distance and closeness and between dominance and submissiveness" (p. 329). In contrast, Mikulincer and Shaver (2007) say,

> Excessive distance limits a caregiver's ability to attend to the other's needs and remain accessible and responsive to signals or calls for help. Excessive closeness leads to overidentification with the suffering person's emotional state, which can overwhelm a caregiver. Excessive closeness blurs the boundary between caregiver and careseeker, resulting in misinterpretations of the seeker's signals…effective care depends on the ability to distinguish between another person's welfare and one's own. (p. 329)

Although caregiving behaviors are the principal elements of parenting, they also exist as a "major component of romantic and marital relationships and in fact as a key constituent of all forms of prosocial behavior" (Mikulincer & Shaver, 2007, p. 324). These behaviors are also present among professional caregivers – such as psychotherapists with clients, health care providers with patients, or clergy with parishioners – or they can exist among adult friends and even strangers. The activation of the caregiving system for adult children in response to elder parents, however, can be a more complicated process because of the reversal of roles and the possibility that earlier parent–child conflicts remain unresolved. The demands of providing physical and emotional care for a needy parent may cause the adult child to long for a safe haven of support, while the original provider of that support – the parent – is now the one in need of the care. Magai (2008) predicts that when parents reach late adulthood, "men and women both will need to reengage psychologically with their parents in a way that activates attachment-related feelings and motivations" (p. 541), regardless of their childhood attachment systems. The following is an overview of the research relevant to attachment styles among elder adults and the caregiving system for adult children caring for them.

Research Relevant to Attachment in Later Life

There is a small, but growing, body of empirical literature on attachment styles among older adults and on parent–adult child relationships in later life, and a few of these studies have examined attachments among African-Americans and other ethnic groups (Connell & Gibson, 1997; Fiori et al., 2009; Magai et al., 2001; Montague et al., 2003). It is important to understand these studies on the attachment styles of elders to more fully appreciate the context of the caregiving experiences for their adult children.

Attachment Styles of Elder Adults

Attachment in adulthood is thought to evolve from the relationships initially established with primary caregivers (Mikulincer & Shaver, 2007). Over time, internalized memories of early relational experiences emerge into an *adult attachment style*, considered "a complex system of representations, expectancies, and beliefs about the self and others" (Fiori et al., 2009, p. 122). In general, a secure attachment style in adulthood is characterized by a positive view of self and others, resulting in a sense of self-worth, a comfort with intimacy, and a confidence that others can and will provide care and the ability to appropriately respond to the needs of others. In contrast, an avoidant or dismissing attachment style describes someone with a positive view of self but a negative view of others, which leads to strong independence and a reluctance to rely on others for assistance and a discomfort with providing care to others. Adults with an anxious or preoccupied attachment style hold a positive view of others, but a negative view of self, leading them to be overly dependent and clingy and to have a high level of anxiety in the face of their own or other people's distress. Some anxiously attached individuals become compulsive caregivers, transferring their clingy neediness into the caregiving realm. Although adults have general attachment styles reminiscent of their underlying attachment models of early childhood, adult styles of attachment may vary based on specific adult relationships and later life occurrences that counter earlier relational experiences (see Bennett and Nelson, Chap. 3, for further explanations of general and specific adult attachments).

Current research on the demographics of adult attachment reveals remarkable differences in the proportion of attachment styles, based on the race and age of the adults being studied. Magai (2008) says that the percentage of older adults with dismissing attachment is significantly higher compared with samples of younger adults in all self-report studies and in all studies using the Adult Attachment Interview (AAI). An early AAI meta-analysis (van IJzendoorn & Bakermans-Kranenburg, 1996), for example, showed that 58% of mostly young adult study participants were secure, 24% were dismissing, and 18% were preoccupied. Yet in a randomly drawn study (Magai et al., 2001) of 800 community-dwelling older Americans (mean age = 74) living in Brooklyn, NY, 83% of African-Americans (71% of the sample) were rated as dismissing compared to 65% of European Americans. The researchers suggested that the economic background of this urban sample (mean household income = $17,000) and their immigrant status (46% Caribbean born) may have contributed to the high rate of dismissing attachment among this group of African-Americans. That is, their immigrant status and strained economic circumstances may have led to a sense of self-sufficiency and mistrust of others. In the case of parents who had to work multiple jobs to survive economically, parents may have been unavailable and dismissing of their children by necessity, which shaped the child's attachment. A more recent study (Fiori et al., 2009) of ethnic differences in patterns of relating in late life found that 69.5% of the 616 participants, ranging in age from 50 to 70 years, had dismissing attachment, but there were *no* significant differences in the degree of dismissing (or avoidant) attachment among African-Americans compared with six other ethnic groups in the study, including European Americans. Nevertheless, all the studies on attachment in late adulthood clearly confirm that "the distribution of attachment styles in older adult samples is distinctly different from the distribution in samples of younger adults" (Magai, 2008, p. 534). Fiori et al.'s (2009) study further suggests that the socioeconomic context of older adults plays a role in shaping attachment style, though the importance of this variable differs among ethnic groups in complex ways.

The meaning of these differences is unclear, and Magai (2008) suggests that the high level of "dismissing attachment in older adults is grounds for some concern" (p. 534). She has proposed there may be birth cohort differences – that is, adults of a certain age may be more dismissing due to the more authoritarian child-rearing practices commonly experienced by their generation. We add that the sociohistorical context of growing up in poverty during the Great Depression and World War II may have left a residual effect on older adults, shaping the development of a self-sufficient style. In contrast, other researchers have suggested that attachment styles of older adults may have changed from early childhood. Dismissing attachment may have developed as a protective mechanism for older adults as they inevitably experience the death of family and friends and anticipate their own end of life (Grossman, 1996). However, in the absence of longitudinal research, there is no way to know the attachment style of these elders when they were young or if their attachment styles shifted over time in response to life experiences.

In terms of ethnic variations among older adults, it is important to remember that culture plays a salient role in influencing proximity to early attachment figures, and self-reliance and independence may have been highly valued among some ethnic groups, such as immigrants, as a means of survival (Weisner, 2005). Furthermore, the higher rates of dismissing attachment among older African-Americans, observed in a number of studies (Fiori et al., 2009), may have evolved from life-long experiences with racism and prejudice (Magai et al., 2001). Individuals who experienced emotional or physical abuse due to racial discrimination may have developed a prevalence of a dismissing attachment style to cope with the pain of oppression, or the style may be an outgrowth of culturally accepted child-rearing practices that encouraged "expressive control through physical means" (Fiori et al., 2009, p. 125).

Findings suggesting differences among adult cohorts stimulate further discussion about change versus stability in attachment styles among adults. Bowlby's (1973) theoretical model included the possibility of change in attachment styles based on relational experiences later in life, and the empirical literature is beginning to validate this occurrence. For example, one study of adults showed that 46% of the participants changed their attachment style due to the impact of acute stress (Cozzarelli, Karafa, Collins, & Tagler, 2003). Although there has been little research on stability and change in late adulthood, a recent longitudinal study examined 415 older adults (60% African-Americans; 40% European Americans), testing them first at age 72 and then again at age 78 (Consedine & Magai, 2006, as cited in Magai, 2008). The findings from this study showed that there was a decrease in both security and avoidance among these elders over the 6-year period. Magai (2008) suggests that some elders may have become less secure due to the deaths of their social support members. In contrast, others may have become less dismissing due to "the developmental tendency for older adults to place increasing value on intimate, emotionally rewarding relationships when they experience their time as limited" (Magai, 2008, p. 535).

Attachment Styles of Caregivers to Elder Parents

Similar to studies of older adults, attachment research on their caregivers is also limited. Although men are caregivers as well, most of the existing research has focused on the attachments of adult daughters taking care of parents with serious, chronic health problems, such as dementia (Carpenter, 2001; Cicirelli, 1995; Crispi,

Schiaffino, & Berman, 1997). These studies focus on the influence of attachment on caregiver burden, described as the subjective experiences and symptoms that result from the stress of caring for another individual. The findings predictably confirmed that the secure attachment of the caregiver and/or elder was associated with less caregiving burden (see Magai, 2008, for details of these studies). When a parent is viewed as secure prior to the health demands of later life, the adult child is protected from the stress of caregiving and tends to report lower caregiving burden (Magai, 2008). Crispi et al. (1997) has said:

> Once attachment has been established in childhood a system of protective behavior develops within the child's attachment system that is designed to protect the attachment figure, the aging parent, from harm. When the attachment figure is threatened by illness, the adult child will attempt to engage in caregiving behaviors to help protect the aging parent from harm and preserve the attachment bond. (p. 53)

Carpenter's (2001) study of attachment bonds of adult daughters caring for elder mothers explored a sample of 40 African-American women and 40 Caucasian women. Similar to other studies, Carpenter found that the daughters who were securely attached provided more emotional care to their mothers than the insecurely attached daughters, and secure daughters reported less caregiver burden. This study found no differences in ethnicity regarding caregiver burden or the attachment styles of the participants.

It should be underscored that the attachment of either the caregiver or the elder is just one of many factors that may contribute in some way to the presence – or the absence – of caregiver burden. Other factors include the context of the caregiving experience, such as the illness of the individual, the family's socioeconomic resources, and immediate family, social, and community supports. The presence of siblings who can combine forces to give care – or who regress into sibling rivalry and resentment in the caregiving process – also is a factor that affects the existence of caregiving burden. As Carpenter (2001) says, the caregiver is just "one part of a complex system of reciprocal interactions in which behavior is a result of many variables. Therefore, it is also important to consider that not only do these factors affect burden, but burden is also likely to affect those factors in a reciprocal manner" (p. 57). Similarly, race and ethnicity alone ought not be viewed as primary factors influencing either attachment or caregiving, but they are important factors to consider in understanding cultural differences related to social supports and the caregiving of elders. For example, Magai et al. (2001) compared African-American and European American elders and found that African-Americans scored higher on measures of affiliation with both family and nonkin because they had an extended network of social supports and a strong racial identity. It is possible that the social supports African-Americans experience serve to shape their perceptions of caregiving experiences and lessen their sense of caregiver burden.

Another factor that may affect African-American caregivers and lessens their sense of caregiver burden is their religious involvement, defined as religious practices and/or personal spirituality. Research findings show that African-American caregivers report that they consider God to be part of their informal support to the same extent as family, friends, and neighbors (Martin & Martin, 2002; Wood &

Parham, 1990) and that God is their most helpful source of support, even more than help with physical care (Koenig, 2005). Findings also consistently show that African-Americans report higher levels of both private and public religious practices and positive attitudes about their religious commitment, compared with European Americans (Montague et al., 2003). European Americans tend to use support from health care professionals or support groups, while African-Americans generally use their faith, prayer, help from clergy, or "religion as a coping strategy" (Montague et al., 2003, p. 193).

Attachments in African-American Caregiving: A Social Work Study

With this literature in mind, a recent mixed-method social work study examined a variety of factors affecting the health and mental health well-being of 250 (89% female) African-American caregivers of older adults living in the urban Washington, DC, area (Sheridan, 2009)[1]. Attachment was studied in terms of its link to several areas related to the caregiving experience, as well as the physical and mental health of the caregivers. The role of religious involvement was examined to explore its connection to the interrelationships of these variables. Attachment was measured using a modified version of the Measure of Attachment Quality (MAQ), which yields separate scores, using the terms *secure, ambivalent,* and *avoidant* for the attachment styles (Carver, 1997; Kim & Carver, 2007).[2] Different profiles emerged for scores on these three subscales in a number of areas (Sheridan, 2009).

First, different patterns in both positive and negative aspects of caregiving are illustrated in Table 8.1. Specifically, caregivers with higher scores on secure attachment showed higher levels of finding *meaning in caregiving* and *purpose in life*, and lower

Table 8.1 Attachment styles and caregiving rewards and stressors

Secure attachment	Ambivalent attachment	Avoidant attachment
Caregiving rewards		
↑ Meaning in caregiving	↓ Meaning in caregiving	↓ Meaning in caregiving
↑ Purpose in life	↓ Purpose in life	↓ Purpose in life
Caregiving stressors		
↓ Caregiver burden	↑ Caregiving burden	↑ Caregiving burden
↓ Financial stress	↑ Financial stress	↑ Financial stress
↓ Emotional/mental distress	↑ Emotional/mental distress	↑ Emotional/mental distress

[1]Research funded by the John Templeton Foundation and the Duke University Center for Spirituality, Theology, and Health.
[2]We are using the terminology of the research instrument. The terms "secure," "ambivalent," and "avoidant" parallel the terms "secure," "anxious" or "preoccupied," and "avoidant" or "dismissing," used earlier in this chapter.

levels of *caregiver burden, financial stress related to caregiving*, and *emotional/mental distress*. The opposite profile emerged for caregivers with higher scores on ambivalent attachment and avoidant attachment subscales.

The relationships between attachment styles and physical and mental health also were explored (see Table 8.2). Again, relatively consistent profiles emerged, and caregivers with secure attachment showed fewer *physical health problems* and lower numbers of *unhealthy physical and mental days* in a month compared to the other two attachment styles. No relationship was shown between ambivalent attachment scores and unhealthy physical days. In addition, both ambivalent and avoidant attachment scores were positively related with higher *depression scores*, with no relationship in this area revealed for scores on secure attachment.

Finally, the connections between attachment and involvement in religion and spirituality were examined. Three aspects of religion and spirituality were studied. One was involvement in *organized religion*, which included attendance at religious services and other activities offered by a religious institution. The second was engagement in *personal spiritual practices*, which involved the use of prayer, reading scripture and other religious/spiritual texts, watching or listening to religious/spiritual media, and saying grace or engaging in other rituals as part of meal times. Participants also responded to items that assessed *intrinsic religiosity*, which explored the internalization of religious or spiritual worldviews or principles into one's daily life.

Table 8.3 shows that attachment styles were related to some aspects of religion and spirituality, but not others. First, there was no significant relationship detected between any of the three attachment styles and involvement in organized religious activities. In terms of involvement with personal spiritual practices, a significant

Table 8.2 Attachment styles and physical and mental health

Secure attachment	Ambivalent attachment	Avoidant attachment
Physical health		
↓ Physical health problems	↑ Physical health problems	↑ Physical health problems
↓ Number unhealthy physical days reported monthly	No significant relationship	↑ Number unhealthy physical days reported monthly
Mental health		
No significant relationship	↑ Higher depression	↑ Higher depression
↓ Lower number of unhealthy mental days reported	↑ Higher number of unhealthy mental days reported	↑ Higher number of unhealthy mental days reported

Table 8.3 Attachment styles and religion and spirituality

Secure attachment	Ambivalent attachment	Avoidant attachment
Organized religion		
No significant relationship	No significant relationship	No significant relationship
Personal spiritual practices		
↑ Higher involvement	No significant relationship	No significant relationship
Intrinsic religiosity		
↑ Higher levels	No significant relationship	↓ Lower levels

positive relationship emerged with scores on secure attachment, but not for scores on the other two attachment styles. Additionally, higher scores on secure attachment were related to higher scores on intrinsic religiosity, while the opposite pattern was noted for higher scores on avoidant attachment, with no relationship detected between this variable and scores on ambivalent attachment.

Overall, findings from this research provide the most detailed information to date about the role of attachment styles in caregiving for elders among African-Americans. Compared to caregivers with one of the two insecure attachment styles, caregivers in the study with more secure attachment report more positive caregiving (or caregiving rewards), while showing lower levels of caregiving stressors. They also reveal better physical and mental health. Secure attachment was associated with higher engagement with personal spiritual practices and higher levels of intrinsic or internalized religiosity, which may partially explain more positive caregiving experiences and better health outcomes. These findings are consistent with the previous research that reports a critical role of religion and spirituality in the lives of African-American caregivers (Koenig, 2005; Montague et al., 2003; Wood & Parham, 1990). It is possible that caregivers with more secure attachment styles tend to have more internalized religiosity because of an ability to develop a strong attachment to their God or higher power, a proposition that needs to be explored in future research.

Clinical Illustrations of Attachments Within African-American Families

The following two examples demonstrate different responses to caregiving based on variations in the attachment styles of the adult children who shared their experiences of being caregivers of their mothers. The quotes are from qualitative interviews that explored the caregiver–care recipient relationships, the effects of caregiving on the physical and mental health of the caregivers, and the caregivers' use of spirituality to cope with their caregiving experiences. The stories reflect the importance of spirituality that is typical of African-American families engaged in care with elder parents.

Same Family, Different Attachments

Sharon, 36, and Monique, 32, are two single sisters involved in the caregiving of their mother, who was diagnosed with breast cancer at the age of 67. Their father died when Monique was 3 years old, but both sisters were raised by their widowed mother. From the moment her mother told them of the diagnosis, Sharon recalls that she knew "it was going to be okay" and that she would be able to facilitate her mother's care. A health care professional herself, Sharon relied on her experiences with other families and her knowledge of the health care system in her metropolitan area, yet she notes, "I had to transfer the same things I do every day to my mom, so that was a little difficult because I was more emotionally involved. But, I still had to remain focused.... those things came natural, but it was harder because it was my mom."

Monique, on the other hand, lives with their mother but has shown more resistance being involved with caregiving. Sharon described her sister as a "more passive person," who was not involved with the day-to-day caregiving process or the medical decision making. Reportedly, Monique suggested at one point that her mother should remain with a local hospital for medical care, rather than go to a highly recommended oncologist in a nearby city. Monique, who has a car, said to Sharon, "Mom needs to stay here because it's closer. If you can't take her to the doctor, at least she can catch the bus." Whenever Sharon asks Monique for assistance, such as picking up her mother's medical records or recent X-rays, Monique never follows through, saying she does not have the time. When their mother was undergoing chemotherapy treatment and lost her hair, she had a wig that she wore outside the house. At home, when their mother wanted to remove her wig, Monique said, "Oh, you have to put your wig back on. I can't stand to see you like that."

Confused about her sister's behavior, Sharon admits: "This is very difficult for me because I need somebody else to talk to me. Biologically, this is our mom. It isn't like Monique had a different mom. This is our mother and we shared the same parents, but I can't talk to my sister about what I am feeling or, you know, my fears of what might happen. I can't talk to her about any of this. So, basically, I have had to turn to my very close friend to share my thoughts. She listens to me because Monique can't – or won't. She isn't there to support me at all. And she acts as though she doesn't need any support for herself either." Sharon says she's leaning on Bible teachings to help her get past her anger with her sister and "let it go," as she wants to regain the closeness of their previous relationship.

In addition to her best friend, Sharon draws support from her coworkers and her pastor and church community, sharing that "the church board deacons, they constantly keep my mom and me in prayer." But most of all, she notes her daily conversations with God. She says, "Basically, relying on the Lord for all my energy is my main thing, and I really do think that praying for strength is not just for physical strength, but for mental strength. I think that my prayer is my nutrition, mentally and emotionally." Sharon has come to believe that her mother's cancer has helped her realize her life purpose, both professionally and spiritually. She says, "I figure the Lord blessed me with my gift for helping people. And when my mom became sick, I realized this is exactly what I'm here for. This is my purpose in life, so it is a blessing to me to have that knowledge and to be able to apply it to my mom. So, when I realized this, that helped, and I grew even more spiritually." Sharon also talks about her support of the Avon Walk for breast cancer, which began before her mother's diagnosis, as an important part of her odyssey. "I felt like everything was coming full circle for me, feeling like that's where I was supposed to be." She is concerned about the relative lack of involvement of African-Americans in programs like the Avon Walk and the need for doctors to reach out more to both African-American patients and caregivers. She concludes, "It has to be something that somebody's looking at."

Never Enough Care

Wanda is a 62-year-old grandmother who has been taking care of her 82-year-old biological mother for the past 16 years. Since a major stroke, her mother has required 24-hour care and has been wheelchair bound or bedridden. Wanda was raised in a variety of foster homes, though she says she always knew her real mother. Her memory of when her family fell apart was when she was a 4- or 5-year-old, after her brother died as a 1-year-old baby. "I remember them coming and picking him up; I can see it just plain – the black box and all." Her other siblings also were placed in foster care and have emphatically refused to be involved in their mother's care. "That's the ironic part of this," Wanda says. "People wonder why I'm taking care of her….but I knew, there was a spirit within me from years back, and it was almost like I was her mother instead of her being my mother. I knew we were poor – as old people used to say, 'poorer than dirt.' I knew what she went through trying to take care of us. I knew, not having any money myself when I raised my child. As Jesus said when they were getting ready to stone the prostitute, 'He with no sin cast the first stone.' To me, you just can't hold grudges, you've got to forgive and forget, and these are the type of things I say in my mind. I never look at my mother and say, 'Well, you didn't raise me.' I never look at it that way."

At this point, Wanda's mother has an additional diagnosis of Alzheimer's disease and is intermittently in the hospital. Wanda spends all her time attending to every aspect of her mother's care and will not consider the option of a nursing home for her mother, saying: "I'd feel guilty 'cause Black folk don't do that." She explains, "I have aides, but there are certain things the aides cannot do for her, and I have to be present." Although the aides are responsible for the medications and the bed changes, Wanda double checks everything ("I oversee that…I do it myself"). During the night, "I peep into my mama's room at 2:00 in the morning to make sure she's okay." Then, she awakens every day around 4:30 a.m., and "the first thing I do is go into her room to make sure she's okay. Second, I prep her as far as getting her changed, getting her teeth washed, and things like that, although that's the caregiver's responsibility." Although the aides are in the home until midnight most nights, Wanda says she *has* to work with them about what to do. In other words, she is constantly monitoring her mother's care. Even when the aides are present to go for medical appointments, Wanda goes along. "I'm there all the time to make sure they get the right information. I need to do it all myself, including the transportation."

When asked how she manages such constant care, she says: "I've learned – these burdens you can't carry yourself. God has to carry you through these. And as I tell people, God gives you that inner peace. That's what has carried me. I don't know about other people, but when you have to take care of somebody for 16 years, you can't do it on your own." Although she tries to read her Bible as she has done throughout her life, she says she does less of it now, "because I'm tired; you know, I need that rest." Wanda continues to attend her church, although she says she does not participate as much as she used to, saying, "I would let them know I do what

I can do, but my mother comes before my duties at church now – I still carry some duties, like I sell snacks after church for my flower ministry." When asked about what support she receives from her church community, she does not identify anything specific, saying "I could call one or two people, but what's the use, what could they do, you know?" She cites something she heard in a sermon, "When you reach the extreme of your life, and man can't help you, so you will come to God."

Clinical Discussion

The use of attachment theory to guide assessment and clinical interventions with older adults and their caregivers can enhance our understanding of the dynamics of these relationships, the origins of values and beliefs within the family system, and the diversity of caregiving experiences and outcomes. The families of Sharon and Wanda illustrate the complexity of giving care to elders and the relational and cultural matrix in which caregiving capacities develop. As social workers, we often look at adult caregivers and wonder how to assess whether they are doing a "good-enough" job with elders. Looking at families through the lens of attachment gives a deeper perspective of stories with rich sociohistorical contexts and cultural dimensions, as well as some guidelines for assessment. These stories suggest that the attachments developed in early childhood have much to do with one's capacity to be a caregiver in adulthood, particularly to elder parents.

A person with a secure attachment, such as Sharon, can respond to caregiving with openness and appropriate balance. Demonstrating her security, Sharon felt a calm confidence from the beginning that she could manage her mother's needs. Some of her self-assurance inevitably stemmed from career experiences as a health care professional, but her clarity revealed a sense of hope and a capacity to cope that went beyond professional experience. If she had been dismissive, as her sister Monique appears to be, she might not have explored better health care options in other locations, or turned to close friends for emotional support, or found such a sense of secure caregiving in her relationship with God. She would not have admitted her need for intimate conversations about her fatigue or her fears for her mother's future. She may have expressed more anger at her sister's lack of involvement. Although she was not living with her mother, she was able to arrange and monitor care in a balanced manner, maintaining connections with her friends and church community and preserving her own physical health and emotional well-being.

In contrast to an evenhanded and coherent *response* to caregiving, other individuals may *react* to caregiving demands through avoidance – as Monique did – or through hypervigilance, similar to Wanda. The caregiving behaviors of both these women demonstrate insecure attachment styles. As described, Monique's emotional reaction to her mother was one of dismissiveness, even though they lived together. She was unwilling to discuss her feelings about her mother's caregiving needs and revealed her discomfort with reminders of the reality of cancer, insisting that her mother hide behind her wig. Her resistance to seeking a second opinion from renowned oncologists exemplifies her reluctance to explore options and try new possibilities for care. Her statement that her mother could catch a bus to treatment – though Monique owned a car and lived with her mother – revealed a striking lack of empathy and an incapacity to reflect on her mother's health care reality. Though we know little about Monique's early years, we do know her father died when she was a toddler. This experience may have left the young child bereft at the loss of two parents – her father from death and her mother from grief. Such early childhood loss increases the possibility of attachment insecurity, which can lead to dismissing and unresolved attachment in adulthood. An adult with such an attachment history may not have the capacity (or desire) to give care to an elder parent who was not emotionally present when the adult was young.

Wanda's reaction to the unremitting caregiving needs of her mother illustrates a variation on the theme of insecure attachment – an anxiously attached person who becomes a *compulsive caregiver*. Wanda's mother was neither physically or emotionally present for her as a child, leaving her with memories of childhood poverty, a brother's death, and an upbringing in multiple foster homes. Perhaps in reaction to this deprivation, Wanda shows a determination to give her biological mother all the care this mother did not give her as a young child. She seems to have no awareness that her persistent, ever-present caregiving reveals a hypersensitivity to loss, so that she is hypervigilant and cannot leave her mother for even a moment under the care of someone else, including the paid aides. Although some may interpret her obsessive behavior as a sign of true caring for a dying parent, further reflection suggests that Wanda is responding in crisis mode to a long-standing, chronic health care challenge. She has not found a way to maintain balance in her life, to explore other options, and to ask and receive help from others. Instead, she is anxiously clinging to her mother as if to make up for the lack of care she received as a child.

These cases illustrate how sibling relationships, family challenges, and unresolved losses or trauma are contributing factors to the relational family matrix that shapes early attachments and influences adult caregiving. In African-American families, another significant influence is culture, which includes both spirituality and a history of racism and oppression. Spirituality and religious faith have long been recognized as critical sources of strength and coping with both personal difficulties and societal oppression within the African-American community (Gibson, 1982; Hill, 2003; Martin & Martin, 2002). Teaching matters of faith is most often transmitted through female family members as a way to transmit "respect for order in a world where life is threatened on a regular basis" (Dilworth-Anderson & Rhoden, 2000, p. 90). Within the context of caregiving, involvement in both organized religion and personal spirituality can be a significant aid in living with the demands and stressors of the caregiver role. This can include the use of religiously based coping strategies such as prayer and scripture reading, reliance on clergy and the larger faith community, and counting God as part of one's informal helping system and an attachment figure (Dilworth-Anderson, Williams, & Gibson, 2002; Morano & King, 2005; Wood & Parham, 1990; Wykle & Segall, 1991). All of these approaches are evident in Sharon's narrative of how she manages the caregiving of her mother. In particular, her close, personal relationship with God, reflected in what she calls her "daily conversations with Him," is experienced by her as a significant source of strength, guidance, and ongoing "nutrition." This personal resource is augmented by the support she receives from her pastor and her church.

Religious and spiritual involvement can also yield various caregiver rewards that emerge as unexpected benefits of this particular life challenge (Farran, Miller, Kaufman, & Davis, 1997; Picot, Debanne, Namazi, & Wykle, 1997; Pierce, 2001). These include an enhanced sense of meaning, purpose, and connection that often results in personal growth and development for the caregiver. Again, Sharon's story illustrates these spiritual fruits of caregiving as she describes a deepening awakening to a special purpose for her life, not only in caring for her mother, but also as a professional and engaged community member. She speaks of using her faith as a way to help her get past her anger with her sister, Monique, so that she can forgive her for her lack of involvement in their mother's care. Her spiritual journey of caregiving is connected to a larger, communal sense of care, as evidenced by her statements regarding the need for more awareness and involvement of African-Americans in efforts to tackle breast cancer and other health care issues within this population. In this way, she is embracing the "full circle" of self, family, community, and culture within a spiritual understanding of life that reflects an attachment style that is both secure and connected to a higher, collective good. She represents a person in the stage of *attachment reorganization*, where her anticipated loss and grief about her mother's eventual death are transformed into new attachments and behaviors (see Nelson, Chap. 5, this volume). Overall, Sharon has found several positive gifts through the caregiving experience, which have enriched her relationship with her God, furthered her own spiritual growth, and deepened her sense of responsibility and spiritual connections with others around her.

In Wanda's narrative, her faith also emerges as an important source of comfort, strength, and perseverance, and she is clearly turning to her God for help with her caregiving burdens. It is ironic that in talking about her reliance on God, she acknowledges that "you can't do it alone," but she seems unable to allow anyone else to help her with the substantial task she has embraced. There is no evidence of Wanda connecting her inner, religious beliefs to any type of external faith community or supports. Her engagement in her church seems to be more about fulfilling her previous roles as much as possible versus turning to her pastor or fellow congregants for support, either emotionally or instrumentally. Here, as in her caregiving role, she is attempting to "do it all herself." Nor do we see as many glimpses of spiritually based caregiver rewards from the experience of caregiving that are so apparent in Sharon's story. Although Wanda talks at one point about learning to have more patience in dealing with her mother, she does not place this within the context of spiritual growth. Wanda does affirm the African-American cultural value of caring for your own at home versus using facility-based care, or as she says, "Black folk don't do that." Her sense of "feeling guilty" about placing her mother in a nursing home suggests that her ongoing care may come more from a place of obligation or her unresolved, childhood deprivation, rather than an expanded sense of purpose or meaning in the caregiving role. Thus, unlike Sharon, whose spiritual connection and secure attachment have given her life deeper purpose and have enabled her to reach out to others in a more intimate way, Wanda's merged caregiving with a nonresponsive mother shows little signs of remittance, personal spiritual transformation, or expanded communal consciousness. Indeed, Wanda's obsessive, preoccupied caregiving activities and her inability to be calmed or comforted in her caregiving role – even through her spiritual connection – are classic signs of the insecure attachment she developed in her early childhood.

Conclusion

Attachment theory and research and the narratives of these women and their mothers provide glimpses into the influence of attachment in the complex caregiving relationships of adult children and their elder parents. It is apparent that the parent–child attachment bond in early childhood provides a foundation for adult relational styles, which then shape caregiving behaviors in later life. Empirical findings validate how important spiritual connection – and the use of God as the primary attachment figure – is for many African-American families. Faith often sustains elder adults approaching the end of their lives and the adult children providing their daily care. Yet, the attachment style of the adults and their attachment histories seem to be linked to the effectiveness of their religious activities as coping mechanisms.

For social work clinicians providing service to elder adults and their caregivers, it is essential to understand the complexity of this caregiving matrix. Often professionals focus on the financial issues and concrete services involved in meeting caregiving needs and overlook the attachment dynamics and cultural messages that underpin caregiving decision making for families. Based on our research and clinical experiences with this population, we suggest several recommendations to increase the understanding of the current adult child–parent relationship and improve clinical interventions through an attachment-based approach.

First, we recommend that social workers gain a deeper understanding of the caregiving matrix by exploring the family history and early attachment relationships through both individual and conjoint conversations with the caregiver and the recipient of care, if the elder is capable of conversation. Recognizing how the initial attachment bond is active in later life helps explain the complications involved in the adult child–elder parent relationship. Second, we suggest that social workers explore both the verbal and observed family messages about caregiving such as the history of who traditionally provided care for elders in the family. In the past, did elders have family homecare, paid homecare, facility-based care, hospice care, or a combination of these options? Was the caregiver raised in a home where her mother or a sister did all the caregiving of elders in the family? And, what complex stories are embedded in the fluid and complicated decisions that a family makes about caregiving? Third, we encourage social workers to explore the values and beliefs the family has received from its larger community to guide their decisions.

For example, many ethnic minority families, such as African-Americans, receive cultural messages that families *should* provide all the homecare, rather than use professional paid care. And, fourth, we suggest that social workers explore the role of spirituality in terms of understanding family obligations regarding elder care by asking what the caregiver does for spiritual growth and whether the caregiver partakes in activities that lessen the normal strain of caregiving, making it more manageable and meaningful.

Finally, all social workers and health care providers must pay special attention to their personal biases about the caregiving of elders, especially in crosscultural clinical work. In particular, European American social workers may have quite different values and caregiving experiences than African-Americans or other ethnic groups. European Americans often have less veneration of the elderly, have a more individualized approach to caregiving, and, as mentioned earlier, are more likely to depend on professional health care providers and support groups. It is critical to assess caregiving needs through the lens of the caregiver's belief system, rather than basing professional viewpoints on one's own cultural context. Just as attachment histories, cultural messages, and religious values need to be explored with clients, professionals should examine their own attachment styles and family messages to minimize their cultural countertransferences. Professionals should also recognize that the attachment style is not the sole contributing factor to caregiving dynamics. Instead, attachment interacts with other factors – including culture, family values, and spiritual beliefs – to influence the caregiver's capacity to give appropriate care, to find balance, and to experience a sense of purpose in the caregiving process.

Study Questions

1. Reflect on the specific cultural or family messages you received about family involvement with caregiving. Recall your own family history and who cared for (or currently cares for) your grandparents and other older relatives in the final years of their life. Where did they live, and did they have paid assistants or all-voluntary family caregiving?
2. How would you feel about caring for your mother or father in your home if they lived until late life and had chronic health problems that required care?
3. What are the different explanations for why more individuals in late life have dismissing attachment compared to people in early adulthood? What explanation would you give for these research findings?
4. As a clinician, how would you assess a client's spirituality or religious involvement and its role in caregiving? How might attachment styles interact with spiritual frameworks within the caregiver–care recipient relationship?
5. In this chapter, Wanda said, "Blacks don't do that," in reference to placing elders in nursing homes. What societal dynamics and structural constraints might be factors in this response to caregiving in the African-American community?

References

Bowlby, J. (1969/1982). *Attachment and loss: Vol. 1. Attachment*. New York: Basic Books.
Bowlby, J. (1973). *Attachment and loss: Vol. 2. Separation, anxiety, and anger*. New York: Basic Books.
Bowlby, J. (1980). *Attachment and loss: Vol. 3. Loss, sadness, and depression*. New York: Basic Books.
Carpenter, B. (2001). Attachment bonds between adult daughters and their older mothers: Associations with contemporary caregiving. *The Journals of Gerontology: Psychological Sciences, 56B*(5), 257–266.
Carver, C. S. (1997). Adult attachment and personality: Converging evidence and a new measure. *Personality and Social Psychology Bulletin, 23*, 865–883.
Cassidy, J. (2008). The nature of the child's ties. In J. Cassidy & P. Shaver (Eds.). *Handbook of attachment: Theory, research, and clinical applications* (2nd ed., pp. 3–22). New York: Guilford.
Cassidy, J., Shaver, P. (Eds.). (2008). *Handbook of attachment: Theory, research, and clinical applications* (2nd ed.). New York: Guilford.
Cicirelli, V. (1995). A measure of caregiving daughters' attachment to elderly mothers. *Journal of Family Psychology, 9*(1), 89–94.
Connell, C., & Gibson, G. (1997). Racial, ethnic, and cultural differences in dementia caregiving: Review and analysis. *The Gerontologist, 37*(3), 355–364.
Consedine, N. S., & Magai, C. (2006, July). *Patterns of attachment and attachment change in later life: Preliminary results from a longitudinal study of 415 older adults*. Paper presented at the third Biennial Conference of the International Association for Relationship Research, Rethymnon, Crete, Greece.
Cozzarelli, C., Karafa, J. A., Collins, N. L., & Tagler, M. J. (2003). Stability and change in adult attachment styles: Associations with personal vulnerabilities, life events, and global construals of self and others. *Journal of Social and Clinical Psychology, 22*, 315–346.
Crispi, E., Schiaffino, K., & Berman, H. (1997). The contribution of attachment to burden in adult children of institutionalized parents with dementia. *The Gerontologist, 37*(1), 52–60.
Dilworth-Anderson, P., & Goodwin, P. Y. (2005). A model of extended family support: Care of the elderly in African American families. In V. C. McLoyd, N. E. Hill, & K. A. Dodge (Eds.), *African American family life: Ecological and cultural diversity* (pp. 211–223). New York: Guilford Press.
Dilworth-Anderson, P., & Rhoden, L. (2000). Caregiving roles in older women. In N. J. Burgess, & E. Brown (Eds.), *African American woman: An ecological perspective* (pp 83–97). New York: Falmer Press.
Dilworth-Anderson, P., Williams, I. C., & Gibson, B. E. (2002). Issues of race, ethnicity, and culture in caregiving research: A 20 year review (1980-2000). *The Gerontologist, 42*(2), 237–272.
Farran, C. J., Miller, B.H., Kaufman, J. E., & Davis, L. (1997). Race, finding meaning, and caregiver distress. *Journal of Aging and Health, 9*, 316–333.
Fiori, K., Consedine, N., & Magai, C. (2009). Late life attachment in context: Patterns of relating among men and women from seven ethnic groups. *Journal of Cross Cultural Gerontology, 24*, 121–141.
Gibson, R. C. (1982). Blacks at middle and late life: Resources and coping. *Annals of the American Academy of Political and Social Science, 464*, 79–82.
Grossman, K. E. (1996). Ethological perspectives on human development and aging. In C. Magai, & S. H. McFadden (Eds.). *Handbook of emotion, adult development and aging* (pp. 43–66). San Diego, CA: Academic Press.
Grossman, K. E., Grossman, K., & Waters, E. (Eds.). (2005). *Attachment from infancy to adulthood: The major longitudinal studies*. New York: Guilford Press.
Hesse, E. (2008). The Adult Attachment Interview: Protocol, method of analysis, and empirical studies. In J. Cassidy, & P. Shaver (Eds.), *Handbook of attachment: Theory, research, and clinical applications* (2nd edn., pp. 552–598). New York: Guilford Press.

Hill, R. B. (2003). *The strengths of black families* (2nd Ed.). Lanham, MD: University Press of America.

Kim, Y., & Carver, C. S. (2007). Frequency and difficulty in caregiving among spouses of individuals with cancer: Effects of adult attachment and gender. *Psycho-Oncology, 16,* 714–723.

Koenig, H. G. (2005). *Faith and mental health: Religious sources for healing.* Philadelphia, PA: Templeton Foundation Press.

Kramer, B., &Thompson, E. (Eds.). (2002). Man as caregivers: Theory, research, and service implications. New York: Springer.

Magai, C. (2008). Attachment in middle and later life. In J. Cassidy, & P. Shaver (Eds.), Handbook of attachment: Theory, research, and clinical applications, (2nd ed., pp. 532_551). New York: Guilford Press.

Magai, C., Cohen, C., Milburn, N., Thorpe, B., McPherson, R., & Peralta, D. (2001). Attachment styles in older European American and African American Adults. *The Journals of Gerontology: Social Sciences, 56B*(1), S28–S35.

Main, M., Kaplan, N., & Cassidy, J. (1985). Security in infancy, childhood, and adulthood: A move to the level of representation. In I. Bretherton & E. Waters (Eds.), *Growing points of attachment theory and research. Monographs of the Society for Research in Child Development, 50* (1–2, Serial No. 209), 66–104.

Martin, E., & Martin, J. (2002). *Spirituality and the Black helping tradition in social work.* Washington, DC: NASW Press.

Mikulincer, M., & Shaver, P. (2007). *Attachment in adulthood: Structure, dynamics, and change.* New York: Guilford.

Montague, D., Magai, C., Consedine, N., & Gillespie, M. (2003). Attachment in African American and European American older adults: The roles of early life socialization and religiosity. *Attachment and Human Development, 5*(2), 188–214.

Morano, C. L., & King, D. (2005). Religiosity as a mediator of caregiver well-being: Does ethnicity make a difference? *Journal of Gerontological Social Work, 45*(1/2), 69–84.

National Center for Health Statistics (1996) *National health interview study: 2030 Data.* Atlanta, GA: Centers for Disease Control and Prevention.

Picot, S. J., Debanne, S. M., Namazi, K. H., & Wykle, M. L. (1997). Religiosity and perceived rewards of black and white caregivers. *Gerontologist, 37,* 89–101.

Pierce, L. L. (2001). Caring and expressions of spirituality by urban caregivers of people with stroke in African American families. *Qualitative Health Research, 11*(3), 339–352.

National Alliance for Caregiving and the American Association of Retired Persons (2007). *Family Caregiving in the U.S.* Retrieved from http://www.caregiving.org/data/Family%20 Caregiving%20in%20 the%20US.pdf.

Sheridan, M. J. (2009). *The spiritual rewards of caregiving: The role of religious and spiritual involvement in the lives of African American caregivers.* Paper presented at the DC Aging Network on Spirituality and Aging, Howard University, Washington, DC.

U.S. Bureau of the Census (2007). *Projections of the total resident population by 5-year age groups, race, and Hispanic origins with special age categories: Middle series 1999-2000.* Retrieved from http://census.gov/ipc.www.usinterimproj/natprojtabl02a.

van IJzendoorn, M. H., & Bakermans-Kranenburg, M. (1996). Attachment representations in mothers, fathers, adolescents and clinical groups: A meta-analytic search for normative data. *Journal of Consulting and Clinical Psychology, 64,* 8–21.

Vitaliano, P. P., Scanlon, J. M., Krenz, C., Schwartz, R. S., & Marcovina, S. M. (1996). Psychological distress, caregiving and metabolic variables. *Journals of Gerontology: Psychological Sciences and Social Sciences, 51,* 290–299.

Weisner, T. (2005). Attachment as a cultural and ecological problem with pluralistic solutions. *Human Development, 48,* 89–94.

Wood, J. B., & Parham, I. A. (1990). Coping with perceived burden: Ethnic and cultural issues in Alzheimer's family caregiving. *Journal of Applied Gerontology, 9,* 325–339.

Wykle, M., & Segall, M. (1991). A comparison of black and white family caregiving experiences with dementia. *Journal of the National Black Nurses Association, 5,* 29–41.

Chapter 9
Attachment in the Family Context: Insights from Development and Clinical Work

Janet Shapiro

Attachments lie at the heart of family life. They create bonds that can provide care and protection across the life cycle, and can evoke the most intense emotions – joy in the making, anguish in the breaking – or create problems if they become insecure.

Byng-Hall (1995, p. 45)

The formation of stable relational bonds that function to provide security and support developmental growth is described as a primary task of family development across cultures (Ainsworth, Blehar, Waters, & Wall, 1978; Bowlby, 1969/1982; Posada et al., 2002; Rothbaum, Rosen, Ujiie, & Uchida, 2002). Secure attachment bonds acquired within the family system confer developmental advantages on family members by providing safety, emotional security, adaptive mechanisms for the regulation of affective experience, the mediation of stress, and support for the development of autonomy and identity (Akister & Reibstein, 2004; Johnson, 2004; Schore & Schore, 2008; Siegel, 2001). Research on attachment relationships in families emphasizes the quality of psychological ties – whether secure or insecure – within the family as a more important mediator of developmental well-being than the particular structure of the family context (Shapiro, Shapiro, & Paret, 2001). This literature is particularly relevant to social work practitioners who seek to bring a strengths perspective to work with nontraditional families or parents and children in a broad range of social contexts and situations.

Attachment theory is an important lens through which to examine the relational context of family life. As Davies (2004) points out, current conceptualizations of attachment share ideas associated with family systems theory. Both family systems theory and attachment theory recognize the transactional nature of human development and the ways in which the quality of attachment relationships contributes to the intergenerational transmission of both risk and resiliency (Byng-Hall, 1995; Davies, 2004; Diamond, Siqueland, & Diamond, 2003; Hughes, 2007; Johnson, 2004; Rothbaum et al., 2004). Longitudinal research on attachment describes a strong correlation between the attachment style of parents and the attachment

J. Shapiro (✉)
School of Social Work, Bryn Mawr College, Bryn Mawr, PA, USA
e-mail: jshapiro@brynmawr.edu

S. Bennett and J.K. Nelson (Eds.), *Adult Attachment in Clinical Social Work*,
Essential Clinical Social Work Series, DOI 10.1007/978-1-4419-6241-6_9,
© Springer Science+Business Media, LLC 2010

patterns of children in their care, validating the clinical observation of the systemic nature of attachment across generations (George & Solomon, 2008).

As practitioners, we often come into contact with at-risk families in which psychological, social, and biological factors have combined to create vulnerability in the family's attachment system. When adults in the family have a state of mind with regard to attachment that is insecure or unresolved, they are more likely to become caregivers with limited capacities in the provision of sensitive and contingently responsive care (Lieberman, 2004; Lyons-Ruth, Bronfman, & Parsons, 1999). This is important because when children lack access to stable and empathically attuned care, many developmental vulnerabilities may emerge including difficulties with the capacity for affect regulation and an increased vulnerability to stress (Applegate & Shapiro, 2005; Gunnar, Bruce, & Grotevant, 2000; Hughes, 2007; McEwen & Seeman, 2003). Indeed, current research shows how the child's early relational experience is associated not only with the quality of attachment, but with many aspects of self-, affective-, cognitive-, and behavioral development (Schore, 2004; Schore & Schore, 2008).

This chapter describes the ways in which insight from the multidisciplinary study of attachment can be used to inform clinical work with families in order to create stable, satisfying attachment for all family members and enable the adults to meet the developmental needs of the children and adolescents in their care. A brief overview of the role of attachment processes between children and their caregivers and between adult partners in the family context provides a theoretical foundation for understanding the vulnerability of parent–child dyads characterized as "at risk" with regard to the formation of stable attachment bonds. Case vignettes exemplify challenges to the formation of secure attachment in a range of circumstances and family context including adolescent parenting, maternal depression, parental substance abuse, and the transition to adoption following traumatic early beginnings. Finally, this chapter describes how normative processes in the family life cycle can precipitate vulnerability in attachment relationships. To illustrate this, the family context of adolescent attachment and the ways attachment bonds must sometimes be reorganized to support mastery of new developmental phases and tasks in this phase will be used as an example. In both contexts – normative developmental tasks in families and at-risk families – insights from the field of attachment research can be used to inform models of preventive and clinical work, particularly infant mental health and family-based intervention (Carter, Osofsky, & Hann, 1991; Diamond et al., 2003; Dozier, Albus, Fisher, & Sepulveda, 2002; Hogue, Liddle, Becker, & Johnson-Leckrone, 2002; Liddle & Hogue, 2000; Lieberman, 2003; Lieberman, Van Horn, & Ghos Ippen, 2005; Slade, 2002).

Attachment and Direct Practice with Families: Insights from Clinical and Developmental Research

While a comprehensive review of attachment theory is beyond the scope of this chapter, it is important to begin with a brief review of concepts from attachment research that are most relevant to family-based assessment, prevention, and intervention.

Research on attachment has described the processes, in the first years of life, by which children develop internal representations, or working models, of their important attachment relationships (Ainsworth et al., 1978; Bowlby, 1969/1982; Main & Solomon, 1990). Variation with regard to the quality of primary attachment bonds has been described in the literature as *attachment patterns* (Ainsworth et al., 1978) or as *attachment styles. Secure attachments* are associated with important child competencies such as the ability to seek and utilize proximity to the caregiver when distressed, to modulate psychophysiological arousal, and to experience the caregiver as a *secure base* from which age-appropriate exploration and mastery experiences can occur. *Insecure attachments* are described as attachment systems that do not adaptively support the developmental goals of felt security, the need for self- and affect-regulation, and opportunities for exploration and mastery. Classified in childhood as *avoidant, ambivalent/resistant* or *disorganized*, these patterns of insecure attachment are associated with a range of developmental vulnerabilities over time. Infants classified as disorganized show the greatest vulnerability as this pattern is associated with caregiving environments in which the caregiver is experienced as unpredictable and frightening and thereby not available for the development of a consistent, regulatory mechanism within the attachment context (Madigan, Moran, & Pederson, 2006; Main & Solomon, 1990).

Longitudinal research on the nature of attachment has addressed questions of continuity and change with regard to patterns of attachment and internal working models of attachment (Hamilton, 2000). Studies on adolescent and adult attachment describe how early internal working models of attachment are carried forward into new relational contexts such as the formation of peer relationships in adolescence, adult relationships, and the parenting role (Allen, McElhaney, Kupermine, & Jodl, 2004; Johnson, 2004). Patterns of attachment in adolescence and adulthood are described as *secure/autonomous, dismissing, preoccupied*, or *unresolved/disorganized* (Hesse, 1999; Main, Kaplan, & Cassidy, 1985).

When adults become parents, their internal working models are reflected in their caregiving patterns (Cassidy & Shaver, 1999; George & Solomon, 2008). Secure-autonomous caregivers, for example, are able to be consistent, reliable, and available to their infants and children, effectively attuning to and regulating both negative and positive states of arousal. Parental caregivers with a preoccupied state of mind relative to attachment are inconsistent and unreliable, sometimes overattuning and hyperactivating in response to their infants' negative arousal. Caregivers with a dismissing state of mind underattune to their infants' negative arousal and thus necessitate the infant's deactivation of their attachment system leading to an overdependence on self-regulation before the infant is able to comfortably do so. Finally, unresolved/ disorganized caregivers are those whose own internal working models do not support organized caregiving. They either abdicate caregiving, as in the case of severe neglect, or fail to protect their infants and children from negative affective states, at times escalating it to intolerable levels, as in the case of physical or sexual abuse.

When romantic couple relationships become attachment relationships, as they do in the process of family formation, they are responsible for much of the most intense affect arousal, both positive and negative, in adult life (Mikulincer & Shaver, 2009).

The attachment system – and thus the internal working model of each partner – is easily activated by threats, disruptions, and separations within the context of the primary attachment. Under optimal circumstances, adult romantic/sexual partners also serve as caregivers for each other, providing a secure base for exploration and a safe haven for the successful regulation of affect. The internal working models of each member of the couple interact with the other's in ways that shape the couple's ability to function effectively in a variety of spheres, including work, social life, peer relationships, extended family networks and, of course, parenting. It is therefore imperative that couple relationships be included in the understanding, assessment, and intervention with parent/child relationship and attachment concerns.

When a new family is formed, or when developmental shifts occur in the context of an existing family, each member's internal working model of attachment can become activated within the new family structure (Johnson, 2004). Each person's internal working model of attachment particularizes the way relationships and the relational needs of others are experienced. As Johnson (2004) and Byng-Hall (1995) describe, research on attachment can help practitioners understand how the past is carried forward, creating the intergenerational transmission of attachment patterns and affect regulation within the family system.

Research on attachment has identified many biopsychosocial factors associated with the development of attachment security within the family system. These include access to adequate nutrition, freedom from abuse and neglect, and consistent access to caregiving that is empathic, warm, and infused with an understanding of the internal psychological world of the child and the adult partners (Slade, 2002; Stern, 1985). The ability to mentalize about, or have insight into, the child's psychological experience underlies the provision of care that is attuned, and contingently responsive, to the child's needs. Likewise, an adult's ability to mentalize about his/her partner's psychological experience is critical to the establishment of empathy and caring between adults in romantic relationships. This ability to imagine the mind of the other is referred to as *reflective functioning* (Slade, 2002). Reflective functioning supports secure attachment within the family system because it enables adult partners to respond to each other, and for the caregiver to respond to the child, in ways that are informed with an understanding of the internal world and psychological experience of other family members. For example, the way in which a caregiver understands, or thinks about, the child's mental states and behavior is important because it shapes the caregiver's responses to the child (Fraiberg, Adelson, & Shapiro, 1975; Slade, Grienenberger, Berbach, Levy, & Locker, 2005). From a clinical perspective, any factor that impairs the caregiver's ability for reflective functioning may be conceptualized as posing risks to the formation of secure attachment bonds and, consequently, to the well-being of the developing child or the family system.

It is important to recognize the ways in which disrupted early attachments and/or trauma in the context of an individual's attachment history may become manifest in the emotional life and behavior of adults and children both in the family context and in the external environment. In couples, when partners have experienced early childhood trauma that remains unresolved, the presenting problem is often related to this attachment history. For children who have experienced chronic stress in the context of early attachment relationships, presenting child or family problems are often reflective of this history and of the family's efforts to cope with various types of relational deprivation and stress. As clinicians, it is important to support the reflective function of parents in their efforts to increase parental insight into the emotional world of the child, or support the reflective function of partners to increase their empathic attunement to each other's needs. So too, practitioners' reflective functioning vis-à-vis children and families can be supported by understanding the ways in which behavior is linked to underlying mental states and experiences that are, perhaps, outside the family's awareness. Clinical and developmental studies on children who have experienced traumatic early beginnings highlight several areas discussed below as being important for both assessment and intervention (Applegate & Shapiro, 2005; Dozier, 2005; Dozier, Stovall, Albus, & Bates, 2001; McEwen & Seeman, 2003; Perry, 2004; Oppenheim & Goldsmith, 2007 Rutter, 2000; Shapiro et al., 2001; Siegel, 2001; Sroufe, Carlson, Levy, & Egeland, 1999). Understanding each of these areas is central to the practitioner's ability to have insight into how the family's current functioning may reflect elements of past relational experience, even if the family's current environment offers the possibility of recovery and repair. Many common presenting problems for the family can be assessed with the attachment history of the child and the parents in mind. These include difficulties in the following five areas:

1. *The experience, modulation, and/or expression of affect.* Normatively, during the first years of life children gradually broaden their ability to experience a widening range of affect (Greenspan & Porges, 1984) and an increasing ability to use language to describe internal feeling states (e.g., "I'm sad" or "I'm hungry"), linked to the caregiver's internal working model of attachment. In families where the parents are secure, children seek out and use support from the caregiver under conditions of stress or in an effort to share positive affect (e.g., look at my toy!). Yet, families with dismissive caregivers tend to have children who minimize affective experience and expression in an effort to decrease contact with the caregiver and may, depending on the circumstance, show a preference for withdrawal to the self. Preoccupied parents tend to have children who maximize affective expression and proximity to the caregiver, but without the ability to accept soothing and comfort in ways that support ongoing regulation and investment in exploration and mastery. Families in which one or more caregiver is unresolved/disorganized are at risk for having children develop disorganized attachment models as well. These adults and children do not show a consistent pattern, or repertoire, with regard to the experience and regulation of affect and thus lack effective strategies for managing stress. For example, families with domestic violence or child abuse histories suggest the presence of adults who lack the capacity for moderating stress or regulating affect, indicative of insecure or unresolved/disorganized attachments.

2. *Deficits in the capacity for mentalization.* The capacity to mentalize (Fonagy, Steele, Moran, Steele, & Higgitt, 1991; Fonagy & Target, 1998), or reflect, on the emotional and mental state of other people is an important developmental achievement and supports central adaptive capacities such as the reading of social cues and the ability

to understand the perspective of other people. Children and adults who lack access to stable, contingently responsive and warm care may develop more difficulties in identifying their own internal states and may be less able to think about the internal states of others, leading to the misreading of social cues. As children get older, deficits in this area create marked vulnerability because children are required to read cues in a broadening array of social environments such as day care, preschool, school, and community settings. Yet children originally develop these cues and the capacity to mentalize in the context of the family.

3. *Affective responses to new attachment relationships.* For adults and children who have experienced loss, disappointment, disruption, and/or trauma in early attachment relationships, the formation of new attachment bonds in a new family context may be associated with a range of affective states such as anxiety, anger, fear, or even despair. Such responses are common, for example, for adults in a new romantic relationship, which may activate old anxieties and fears. Similarly, children who move into a new living arrangement, such as a foster care family or a blended family formed by previously divorced parents with children, may experience a wide range of emotions. Their internal working models of attachment, formed in response to the relative lack of access to sensitive and attuned care, may lead children initially to either withdraw from, or resist, even the best intentioned offers of love and care. Over time, however, change can also work for the better if new attachment figures in families are more secure and/or emotionally available.

4. *Dysregulated affect and problems relating to exploration, learning, and mastery.* Adults who lacked access to stable and nurturing care as children may have difficulties in the area of supporting exploration and mastery experiences in their children or even their adult partners. Their strategies for the regulation of affect may lead them to be preoccupied with their own internal states and less able to focus on multiple aspects of the environment. If prior patterns of relating have led the adult to withdraw from the exploration of the environment, they may lack access to important opportunities for their child's early cognitive stimulation and learning. For example, a mother who was forbidden to develop friendships outside her family when she was a child, or who lacked a secure base for social exploration and outside friendships, may find it challenging to support her own child's exploration and may view his/her developmental achievements as a sign that the child no longer "needs" her and is abandoning her. Similarly, withdrawal from exploration may occur if a child's positive arousal – smiles, laughter, and play – is not met by an attuned parental response. The joint attention required for a child's "success" in an early learning environment such as preschool and day care may be challenging for parents and children who have not had positive experiences in the mutual regulation of affect and attention (Shonkoff & Phillips, 2000).

5. *Neuroendocrine dysregulation resulting from stress exposure.* When young children, like adults, have experienced chronic stress without access to the mediating buffer of supportive relationships, the stress response system may change in a "use dependent" manner (Perry, 2002) such that the "state" of "fight/flight" that is adaptive as a short-term response to threat becomes more "trait-like" with multiple deleterious consequences for the child's social, emotional, physical, and

neurological functioning (Davies, 2004). Studies on the neurobiology of stress and its impact on early childhood development reveal specific outcomes such as hypersensitivity to threat and a relative inability to differentiate minor threats, or experiences of deregulation, from previous levels of exposure to dysregulation. Studies on children in foster care show that the child's neuroendocrine response does not always "directly" map onto a child's more overt behavioral response (Dozier et al., 2006). For example, the secretion of cortisol (a stress hormone) may be elevated even in children who appear calm and quiet. Thus, studies in neurobiology confirm a common clinical observation that it is not always possible to infer the child's mental/emotional state from presenting behavior.

The neurobiological link between parent and child may be described as an inter-locking of their two nervous systems in that the parent's modes and methods of affect regulation become physiologically passed on to the infant, thereby shaping the infant's own ability to regulate affect. This occurs in regard to both positive and negative states of affect, meaning that whether an infant is crying, smiling, or laughing, the parental responses are key either for soothing the infant or for reinforcing the pleasure of connection and play. It is in this way that the intergen-erational transmission of attachment occurs, and it is for this reason that family treatment focuses on the parent/child dyad, the adult couple, and their interrelationship (Applegate & Shapiro, 2005; Schore, 2001).

Many of the consequences of disrupted and/or vulnerable early attachments are illustrated by the following family case vignettes. These vignettes address different types of family structures and relational contexts in which risk to the formation of secure attachment and, consequently, risks to family well-being exist. As always, patterns of risk and resiliency are particularized for any given family and deter-mined by a complex interplay of biopsychosocial factors.

Vulnerable Attachments: Direct Practice with Children in Different Family Contexts

Adolescent Mothers and Their Children

As with mothers of all age groups, great variation with regard to parenting competence exists among adolescent mothers. Still, the developmental vulnerability of adolescent mothers *and* their children has been carefully documented (Shapiro, 2009). As compared to older mothers, adolescent mothers have been described as less verbal in their interactions with their children, less contingently responsive, and more likely to expect either "too much too soon" or "too little too late" in terms of the social, emotional, cognitive, and physical development of their children (Osofsky, Eberhart-Wright, Ware, & Hann, 1992). In addition to the social, economic, and familial stress that may accompany early parenthood, adolescent mothers are developmentally vulnerable because the tasks of adolescence itself may conflict with the demands of parenthood. For example, the egocentrism associated with adolescent thinking may be in conflict with the parental task of understanding the infant's needs as separate from one's own (Applegate & Shapiro, 2005). The following case vignette describes how aspects of normative adolescent development may pose risks to the formation of stable and secure attachment bonds between an adolescent mother and her child.

Patrice and Frankie

Patrice is a 14-year-old adolescent mother who attends an alternative high school for adolescent mothers and their children. Her son, Frankie, is 13 months old. During the day, while Patrice attends classes, Frankie is cared for in the infant/toddler program located in the school building. Outside of school, Patrice and Frankie live with Patrice's mother, who sometimes provides additional parenting support.

As part of a developmental-clinical assessment, Patrice was observed playing with Frankie in the day care program. Patrice was asked by the developmental specialist to play with Frankie as she "normally would at home." This observation was intended to give the developmental specialist an opportunity to observe the social interaction between mother and child and to make an assessment regarding the quality of the attachment bond between Frankie and Patrice. Frankie and Patrice sat together on the floor in a quiet play area. Several age-appropriate toys were within reach. These toys included stacking rings, blocks, musical toys, and picture books. Patrice sat expressionless on the floor, at first staring at Frankie but then playing with the stacking rings by herself. When Frankie reached for a ring, Patrice said "get your own toys." Rebuffed, Frankie continued to show interest in exploring the toys and, for a while, made continued efforts to engage his mother in the interaction by looking up at her and "showing" her his toys. For example, when Frankie first picked up the musical blocks and noticed the sounds made by tapping them together, he looked up expectantly at his mother. Patrice was unresponsive, showing neither verbal nor gestured responses to Frankie. At first, Frankie looked away and continued to play. As the minutes passed, Frankie's play became diminished in its exploratory quality. His smile faded and, when his next bid for interaction with his mother was ignored, soft signs of anxiety began to emerge. Frankie began to drool and also began a slight rocking back and forth on the play mat. Quickly, the developmental specialist joined Frankie and Patrice on the play mat and quietly began to engage Frankie by offering him toys and commenting positively. In response, Frankie began to brighten, seeking out eye contact with the developmental specialist and venturing glances at his mother as well. Eventually, a bell rang indicating it was time for Patrice to return to class. She got up to leave saying "he won't even know that I'm gone" and left the room.

Discussion of Patrice and Frankie

From an attachment perspective, the case of Frankie and Patrice describes some of the risks to attachment associated with adolescent parenthood. A paradox of adolescent parenthood is that the nature of adolescence itself may be in conflict with the primary tasks of parenthood and attachment formation. Normative adolescent characteristics such as egocentrism, variation with regard to the capacity for abstract thinking, and psychological conflict relating to separation and individuation processes may, though age-appropriate, create barriers to attachment formation via their impact on the quality of maternal sensitivity, capacity for empathy, and the ability to accurately perceive the internal world of the infant and young child.

From an intervention perspective, there are several factors that are important to consider. First, it is important to remember that adolescent mothers are often not the only primary caregiver in the child's relational experience. In Frankie's case, his initial sense of enjoyment and expectation for interaction, indicated by reaching toward his mother, suggests that he has experienced positive caregiving interactions. As it turned out, Frankie spent a good deal of time in the care of his maternal grandmother. A full assessment of his attachment experiences would have to include an observation of this important relationship as well. Additionally, in working with young mothers such as Patrice, it is important to remember that the "deficits" observed in the parent–child interaction may stem not from maternal pathology, but from aspects of typical adolescent development that are in conflict with the developmental tasks of parenthood. The adolescent's developmental stage is relevant to the type of intervention likely to support more optimal parent–child interactions. Many parent education programs are didactic in nature and may not meet the needs of adolescents who, in general, require hands-on, trial and error learning opportunities. The adolescent's own history of attachment and loss, as well as the adolescent's current developmental needs (e.g., for education and support), must be attended to as well. In this way, the attachment quality of the dyad is dependent on the ongoing developmental well-being of both parent and child.

Maternal Depression

Clinical and developmental research on attachment has shown that children of depressed mothers are at risk for many presenting problems including (1) developmental delays, (2) regulatory deficits in relationship to affect, attention, and behavior, (3) higher rates of childhood anxiety and affective disorders, and (4) relational difficulties in primary attachment and peer relationships (Campbell, Cohn, & Neyers, 1995; Dawson et al., 1999).

An important question for clinicians is how to think about the impact of maternal depression on the relational context of early development. Research on maternal depression suggests that depressed mothers are less contingently responsive and sensitive, display more negative mood states and less augmentation of positive affect, express more negative attributions about infant behavior, demonstrate less positive gaze and touch, and are slower to respond to the young child's bids for attention and interaction (Dawson et al., 1992; Field, 1995; Lyons-Ruth et al., 1999; Tronick and Weinberg, 1998). Children of depressed mothers may come to be developmentally at risk, in part, because the symptoms of depression may inhibit the caregiver's capacity for reflective functioning, thereby limiting their capacity for attunement with the child's emotional state and needs. The case vignettes below describe different manifestations of maternal depression in the caregiving environment.

Heather and Mary

Heather is a 9-month old infant, born full term into an economically stressed family context. Heather's parents live together but are struggling to create economic stability as each of them holds several part-time jobs. The family was being seen because a well-baby check-up revealed a slow pattern of weight gain and delays in motor development. Additionally, the pediatrician expressed concern that Heather's mother was herself showing signs of depression and exhaustion, having little energy for interaction with Heather or others.

Upon observation by a developmental specialist, Heather appeared listless, withdrawn, and far less active than one would expect of a physically healthy, full-term 9-month old infant. When presented with toys as part of a developmental assessment, Heather neither reached for the toys nor showed interest in visual stimuli or human interaction. The specialist reported that even though she was in a room with several people, she "felt as though she were alone" as almost no affective response was forthcoming from either Heather or her parents. When asked if this behavior was typical of Heather or perhaps if Heather was either tired or ill on the day of the assessment, Heather's mother, Mary, responded that "she's always like this." Further, she indicated that they were "lucky to have such a good baby." Heather's mother described that other babies she has seen were "too nosy" and "always trying to get attention from other people." When asked for a more complete description of a typical day for Heather, the mother described that Heather will often lie awake in her crib during the day, for "3 or 4 hours until she gets really hungry" and that after eating, "she's happy to go right back in there." A structured developmental assessment revealed that Heather's fine and gross motor development was delayed and that a noticeable bald spot was present on the back of her head, suggesting that she had indeed been lying relatively motionless on her back much of the time. A more in-depth developmental, pediatric assessment found no underlying vision, hearing, or neurological deficits. Over many visits, Heather did begin to show mild affective responses to her interactions with the developmental specialist, turning toward the sounds of musical toys, reaching for objects, sustaining joint attention, and self-feeding small crackers. As she ate the crackers during one visit, her mother commented, "if you keep giving her those crackers, she'll just want more and it will never stop."

Discussion of Heather and Mary

The case vignette of Heather and Mary describes a relational pattern in which the mother's untreated depression left her with little energy for interaction with her infant, and it shows how parental attribution of infant behavior can be shaped by a lack of knowledge of child development. Heather's mother interpreted her baby's silence and listlessness as "good" qualities, requiring little response or attention from the baby's overwhelmed parents. To the extent that Heather began to show some affective response to the developmental specialist, Mary began to show concern that the baby's needs would have no end, which revealed the mother's underlying sense that she would not be able to meet these needs. As the caregiver began to engage the infant, Heather showed some increased capacity for responsiveness over time. When this occurs, it is critically important that the practitioner try to direct the infant's responsiveness to the parent and to support the parent in noticing how the infant responds to the parent's efforts at engagement, even if the infant's response is muted.

Deanna and Anthony

Anthony is a physically healthy 11-month old boy born to Deanna, a 21-year old mother who struggles with a major depressive disorder. Born physically and neurologically intact, Anthony met most of the major developmental milestones during his first 6-months of life. During this time, Deanna experienced stress relating to the transition to parenthood but was able to utilize a range of family and social network supports, buffering both her and Anthony from the vulnerability of her mental health history. During the last several months, however, Deanna has experienced another major depressive episode resulting in the deterioration of Deanna's affect, coping ability, and cognitive functioning, which, in turn, has impaired her parenting behavior in many ways.

Upon observation, Deanna showed little interest in Anthony's bids for attention and interaction. Additionally, Deanna seemed unaware of her frequent lapses into a "still face" and/or into highly negative states of facial expression. From Anthony's perspective, this is very anxiety provoking because he seeks out his mother's face as a point of social referencing. It may often seem to him that the mother he had come to rely on is "lost." Rather than a shared experience of joint attention, or the opportunity to gain important situational information from his mother's facial expression, Anthony's gaze is instead often met with blank stares or expression of sad/angry affect. Steadily, Anthony has begun to show less age-appropriate exploratory behavior and seems to have become more preoccupied, or even vigilant, with his mother's affective state. At the age of 11 months, one normatively expects to see an infant "check back" with their caregiver as they explore elements of the environment, as if to receive the "all clear" sign from the caregiver or a sense of mutually shared pleasure in the exploration of the environment itself. In Anthony's case, the developmental specialist observed Anthony's behavior to be less and less exploratory, with Anthony increasingly preoccupied with searching his mother's face. Additionally, when met with a lack of affective expression from his mother, Anthony showed signs of anxiety such as drooling, less mature quality of vocal expression, and less interest in play and exploration. The developmental specialist also noted that, over time, it became more difficult to soothe Anthony following these episodes.

Discussion of Deanna and Anthony

The case of Anthony shows how states of depression in the caregiver can create challenges to the child's ability to regulate affect. Anthony attempts to cope with his mother's unpredictable affective state, by paying increased attention to her facial cues of affect. This can be understood as representing his efforts to create pattern and predictability where, in fact, less and less contingent responsivity in the caregiving environment exists. While Anthony's mother is present in the room with Anthony, her lack of emotional availability represents loss to Anthony. At the age of 11 months, access to an emotionally attuned caregiver is an important element of the young infant's coping repertoire. As Anthony "loses" his empathic connection to his mother, he turns away from the developmental tasks of exploration and learning as he becomes more preoccupied with efforts to regulate his increased state of affective distress. When a young infant's caregiver is emotionally unavailable to this degree, the infant loses an important source of information about *his/her own* internal state. Anthony's relational environment, or attachment bond, is not functioning to provide him with the type of mirroring that provides both gestural and verbal cues about his own internal state. As she struggles with major depression, Deanna is preoccupied with her own affective state and is not predictably able to accurately read and/or respond to Anthony's cues.

Substance Abuse and Parenting

Many questions exist regarding the impact of parental substance abuse on child development. One subset of this literature has focused on the direct influence of prenatal exposure to illicit drugs on the short- and long-term development of the child (Chasnoff et al., 1998). It is important to recognize that children born to substance abusing parents are at risk not only because of the possible effects of prenatal exposure, but because of the ways in which the parents' drug use may shape the caregiving environment. The National Clearinghouse on Child Abuse and Neglect (NCCAN, 1993) summarized the ways in which parental drug usage can negatively impact parenting behavior, parent–child attachment formation, and, consequently, child development outcomes. First, parental drug use likely strains the financial and social resources of the family unit and can impact contextual factors such as housing stability, access to food and medical care, and parental employment stability. Second, if a parent is overwhelmed by issues relating to addiction, the reflective function or sensitivity of the parent is likely to be diminished, leaving the parent less able to correctly perceive and/or respond to the child's cues regarding their needs. Third, if a parent's drug use began as an effort to self-medicate states of prolonged, dysregulated affective experience, it may portend poorly for the parent's ability to help the infant/young child learn to recognize and regulate their own affective experience. This is particularly problematic because young children rely almost entirely on the auxiliary support of the primary caregiver for the augmentation of positive affect and the mediation of negative affective states. Without access to such support, the developing child can become overwhelmed and experience affective dysregulation and stress.

Jackie and Her Children

Jackie is a 28-year-old mother of two who is currently in recovery from her addiction to methamphetamine. During the active phase of her addiction, her two children (ages 2 and 4) were cared for by a foster family. Prior to their placement in foster care, Jackie's children experienced great instability and disruption of their attachment bonds. Jackie would often leave the children alone to fend for themselves. The day the children were removed from her care, a neighbor found the older child wandering in the street looking for food. Upon placement in foster care, the children showed little emotion and were not at all oriented toward adults. The older child evidenced no expectation that the foster parents would provide for basic needs such as food, warmth, interaction, and shelter. The older of the two children was very protective of the younger sibling, wanting to stay with his younger sister both day and night. Any effort to separate the two siblings was met not only with resistance, but signs of panic.

Jackie worked hard to recover from her addiction, attending an inpatient program and working to attain a stable living situation for herself and her children. Over time, the children began to have visits with Jackie. A developmental specialist periodically observed Jackie interacting with her children as part of an effort to work toward reunification. During one of these visits, Jackie expressed frustration and worry that her children act like "they don't even know me," and "it's like I'm no big deal." Jackie expressed a sense that the children should have more of an understanding of what she is going through and how hard she is working while they just "play all the time." It is especially painful for Jackie to see her children turn to their foster mother and/or to the case worker when they fall, have a question, or want to share a toy or a book. Indeed, when one of the children cries or expresses anxiety/concern, Jackie finds their affect very difficult to tolerate. As she put it herself, "what do they have to worry about?" or, "when I was their age nobody helped me at all."

Discussion of Jackie

The case of Jackie and her children highlights some commonly observed dynamics in the attachment relationship between parents recovering from drug addiction and their children. In Jackie's case, her insight into the cause of her addiction is not well developed. As with all addictions, hers was multidetermined but one factor that emerged is her relative inability to use other strategies for affect modulation. Additionally, Jackie herself was a child of neglect, often having to fend for herself at a very early age. Jackie has great difficulty in recognizing the emotional needs of her children, much like she has great difficulty in tolerating her own affective experiences for long enough to reflect on them or on their meaning. From an attachment perspective, it is important that Jackie receive empathic support that might allow her, over time, to safely experience more of the affect associated with her own past losses as this may enable her to recognize, tolerate, and respond more effectively to her children's affective experience. Additionally, Jackie will need tremendous support to understand her children's "rejection" of her. Having had little support for understanding the meaning, *to her*, of her own trauma in the context of her early attachment relationships, Jackie is not well prepared emotionally to empathically understand the meaning, *to her children*, of their disrupted attachment to her.

Post Foster Care Adoption

When a family adopts a child from foster care, many challenging relational tasks exist in supporting the development of new attachment relationships and opportunities for more stable family bonds (Hughes, 2007; Shapiro et al., 2001). The advent of a new family structure presents the hope of safety, stability, and new opportunities for attachment. Still, the child's early experiences of separation, trauma, and loss may reverberate across time, posing challenge to the formation of new family bonds. Adoptive parents have great hopes that their offers of external stability, love, and affection will ease the child's preadoptive experiences of attachment disruption, trauma, and loss. Adoptive parents may themselves experience disappointment and a sense of loss as they find that the child's internal fragility may persist, even as the external stability of a new relational context is provided (Davies, 2006; Perry, 2002; Shapiro & Applegate, 2005). Adoptive parents may benefit from supportive guidance in understanding the relational vulnerability of children who have early histories of neglect, attachment disruption, trauma, and loss. For some of these children, a much longer than anticipated period of time will be necessary in order to form new relational bonds not infused with the anxiety and grief of past attachment relationships (Dozier, Dozier, & Manni, 2002; Hughes, 2007).

At the time of adoption, foster children vary tremendously with regard to many characteristics such as age, the quality of their early caregiving experiences, the type and number of attachment-related losses, the degree of trauma they may have experienced, the length of time spent in foster care, and the number of moves they may have made within the foster care system (Shapiro et al., 2001). The preadoptive attachment history of each foster child is important because it can be utilized by practitioners and by parents to create a more empathically informed understanding of the child's developmental needs and vulnerabilities. In particular, knowledge of the child's preadoptive history supports the parents' ability to have insight into the newly adopted child's internal world and relational capacity. This is important as parents may face the daunting task of reaching out repeatedly to a child who may seem disinterested or even rejecting. Supportive intervention can help the adoptive parents to understand the ways in which a child's early relational context and history have shaped the child's internal working model of relationships and the child's belief system about the trustworthiness of adults. The child's experience may have taught him/her that relationships are associated, not with mutually regulated experiences of connection, disruption, and repair, but with disorganization, rejection, indifference, and unregulated states of anxiety and sadness. Adoptive parents seeking to keep the needs of their children "in mind" may need support in understanding the child's attachment behavior, not as a personal reaction to them but as a reflection of the child's past relational history, sense of self, and capacity for affect regulation in the context of attachment relationships (Dozier, Albus, et al., 2002; Hughes, 2007).

In extreme cases, children who have not had access to organized and stable care and children who have experienced abuse and neglect may show symptoms of *reactive attachment disorder (RAD)*. According to the American Academy of Child and Adolescent Pediatrics (2005), children with RAD "have a history of being reared in atypical environments characterized by extreme neglect, and they manifest abnormal social behaviors such as lack of responsiveness, excessive inhibition, hyper vigilance, indiscriminate sociability, or pervasively disorganized attachment behaviors" (p. 1209). Researchers have identified two subtypes of RAD that are referred to as *emotionally withdrawn/inhibited* and *indiscriminate/uninhibited* (Zeanah, Boris, Bakshi, & Lieberman, 2000). These two subtypes, though different, share in common descriptions of children who show great vulnerability in their behavioral functioning and in their capacity to relate to others. Adoptive parents can be "overwhelmed" by the demands of managing the complex array of interpersonal and behavioral problems including, in severe cases, a seemingly "remorseless aggression" (AACAP, p. 1211), protracted reluctance to engage in dyadic interaction, or dismissal of the importance of the family's offer of a new attachment bond.

Ms. Williams and Her Grandchildren: Skipped Generation Kinship Foster Care

Three young children, ages 2, 3, and 5, had been living with their parents. Both mother and father had volatile histories, including multiple arrests for drug usage and violence. Dramatically, both parents were arrested simultaneously, leading to the involvement of social services and the placement of all three children in foster homes. Eventually, in an effort to keep the siblings together, the children were transferred to a kinship care placement and their 52 year-old grandmother, Ms. Williams, became their legal guardian and foster mother.

Ms. Williams lived alone and, while she worked full time, had little in the way of economic support and suffered from an array of physical problems, including high blood pressure and arthritis. At the time of placement, Ms. Williams expressed a desire to care for her grandchildren but, at the same time, quickly became overwhelmed by what she viewed as children who were "out of control" and who "just didn't care who they hurt," both symptoms of RAD. Ms. Williams attempted to parent the children in the way that she knew best – setting limits and attempting to soothe their upset. From her perspective, the children "made everything harder than it had to be" by resisting her efforts to engage them in the "simple" tasks of feeding, bathing, and play. Ms. Williams took the initiative in asking for a more in-depth assessment and support as she was concerned about the ways in which "any little thing" could send the children into rages that she was unable to help them contain. These were not the children she "had in mind" when she agreed to care for them. While Ms. Williams had been aware of her daughter's social and legal problems, she had no way of fully understanding the meaning of the children's traumatic preplacement experiences. Ms. Williams reported that she thought she would "be able to love the children" but that they "had no love for her at all."

Discussion of Ms. Williams

Immediate intervention was necessary to help Ms. Williams to see that the behavior of her grandchildren represented not a rejection of her, but a representation of their past attachment history. Specifically, these were children who had been left on their own to cope with overwhelming affects associated with neglect, such as prolonged states of hunger, anxiety, and fear. These children had spent years in a chaotic care-giving environment of neglect, deeply affecting their capacity to experience trust in relationship to caregiver and/or to rely on primary attachment figures for the modu-lation of strong states of affect. Rather, the offer of a new relationship from their grandmother may have precipitated overwhelming states of anxiety as such rela-tionships were associated with fear and perhaps with danger for these children. In addition to helping Ms. Williams understand the children's behavior and needs from an attachment perspective, of central importance would be an ongoing assessment of the children's psychological and physical well-being, as well as the physical safety and psychological well-being of Ms. Williams herself.

The Family Context of Adolescent Attachment: Life Cycle Development and Challenges to Attachment Security

During adolescence, families face the normative but difficult task of renegotiating aspects of the attachment system with the developing adolescent (Diamond et al., 2003; Johnson & Whiffen, 2003). The family of the adolescent has the complex task of maintaining the psychological tie with the developing adolescent while, at the same time, finding ways to facilitate new attachment experiences in relationship to the adolescent's emerging identity, need for autonomy, capacity for affect regulation, and growing cognitive abilities (Diamond, 2005; Liddle & Hogue, 2000).

Bowlby's conceptualization of attachment as serving the dual goals of *security/ proximity seeking* and *mastery/exploration* is relevant to the age-related, develop-mental tasks of adolescence. Even as adolescents take on adult physiology and characteristics, developmental research has made clear that the ongoing developmental tasks of adolescents in cognitive, emotional, and neurobiological spheres are most optimally achieved when adolescents have continued access to adult attachment figures (Werner-Wilson, 2001). Adolescent development requires that earlier conceptualizations of security and exploration expand to reflect the adolescent's "internal sense of connection" as a marker of proximity and understanding that, for adolescents, "exploration occurs not only in the adolescent's behavior, but in the adolescent's thinking" (Allen et al., 2004).

What does a securely attached adolescent "look like?" Securely attached adolescents are likely to approach new developmental experiences with an internalized sense of self-efficacy and an internalized belief that the psychological tie with the caregiver(s) remains a secure base from which they are able to risk exploring a more independent and autonomous state of being. These adolescents are able to tolerate a range of affect, both positive and negative, with the security that comes from a view of the self as able to recover and reorganize following disappointment, anxiety, and other potentially negative affective states. In contrast, adolescents with insecure working models of attachment may be more likely to utilize attachment strategies that are either dismissing in nature, associated with an avoidance of familial closeness and risky exploration of the external world, *or* strategies that reflect a preoccupation with parental attachment figures, resulting in increased negative styles of engagement that interfere with the adolescent's ability to autonomously explore a wider social environment. Indeed, the extremes of these insecure models of attachment are often central to the conflicts within families of adolescents. In either case, insecure working models of attachment are associated with attachment strategies that may both reflect and result in a lack of the access to parenting that is sensitive, warm, and infused with an appreciation of the adolescent's developmental needs.

Adolescents who lack access to consistent, contingently responsive and developmentally informed attachment figures may have difficulty in many spheres, particularly in relationship to executive functioning and the control of both impulsivity and affect. Clinically, we are familiar with adolescents described by a range of difficulties including substance abuse, eating disorders, social/emotional disruption, risk-taking vulnerabilities and, in extreme cases, violence directed either toward others or towards the self, as in the case of adolescent suicide. Thus, understanding the need for transformation of the attachment relationship during this life phase is critically important in work with adolescents and their families (Allen & Manning, 2007; Allen et al., 2004).

For parents, the psychological experience of the attachment relationship shifts as the adolescent may seek to meet more of their attachment needs outside the family system via contact with peers, teachers, coaches, and other interested adults. Adults may misinterpret this shift as a sign that adolescents are not in need of the secure base provided by their primary attachment relationships. A lack of understanding in this regard can lead to negative parental states of mind and disruptions in the attachment system. The need for intervention models focused on supporting and repairing the attachment system, even as it broadens to incorporate the changing development needs associated with adolescence, is important to family-based work designed to support the developmental competence of adolescents.

Byng-Hall (1995) describes the secure family context as "a family that provides a reliable and readily available network of attachment relationships, and appropriate caregivers, from which all members of the family are able to feel sufficiently secure to explore their potential" (p. 627). Parents with secure working models of attachment are more likely to perceive the adolescent's increased desire for autonomy, self-direction, and new experiences as part of an important step toward adulthood and *not* as a rejection of the parent–child attachment.

When parents and adolescents share a relatively secure model of attachment, it is more likely that adolescents will have developmentally appropriate opportunities to "test out" burgeoning capacities such as self-expression, the experience and modulation of a widening range of affect, and interest in more independent and autonomous functioning. The security of the adolescent's internal working model of attachment may not always be simplistically inferred from direct behavioral observation. For example, securely attached adolescents may be more likely to express differences of opinion and anger in relationship to adult attachment figures. While this may appear as an increased level of conflict, such interactions may also reflect an abiding trust that supports the adolescent's ability to practice emerging skills of abstract reasoning, the utilization of language to express internal states, and a capacity to question sense of self in relationship to adult authority figures. When the family attachment context is not as secure, the adolescent's movement toward psychological separation and individuation may be perceived as more threatening to the stability of the attachment relationships within the family. In this context, the attachment system can be compromised as a negative cycle of interaction emerges in which the attachment needs of the adolescent are not understood, and parenting behavior may no longer be infused with an accurate understanding of the child's developmental needs (Werner-Wilson, 2001).

Attachment-Based Family Therapy

In writing about clinical work with adolescents, Diamond et al. (2003) describes the nature of family dynamics and processes that can impair the family attachments so important to the adolescent's ongoing developmental trajectory. Among the factors cited are (1) communication patterns that reflect high levels of tension and conflict and low levels of family cohesion, (2) parental mental health difficulties such as affective/mood disorders, substance use and dependence, (3) traumatic stress in the family's social ecology, and (4) a relative inability on the part of the parent(s) to reframe the interaction with adolescents to allow the adolescent more autonomy while at the same time continuing to show love and affection to the developing child. Together, these factors can create a context in which "keeping the needs of the child in mind" is hampered by the parents' own state of mind with regard to parenting behavior and attachment, as well as the parents' own unresolved attachment experiences and needs (Madigan et al., 2006).

Diamond's work identifies developmental goals that support the adolescent ability to renegotiate the attachment system and the parental ability to successfully expand the attachment model in ways that include the adolescent's maturational change.

For adolescents, important skills include (1) the ability to use words to represent important elements of ongoing family challenges, (2) developmentally appropriate broadening of the capacity to identify and regulate a range of affective experiences, and (3) increasing capacity for perspective taking that is supported by ongoing cognitive development in terms of abstract thinking capacity. The adolescent's growing ability to "hold a mirror" up to the family system can be challenging for parents. As adolescents have developed internal working models of important attachment relationships, so too have they developed the observed and "internalized other" aspects of the family context. The growing cognitive, reflective, and linguistic ability of adolescents makes it possible for them to confront adult attachment figures with their observations of the family system and family dynamics. Yet often adolescents lack the capacity to regulate their affect when confronting authority figures with newly developed observations, and parents similarly experience dysregulation when challenged by their teens.

For parents, renegotiating the attachment system in ways that sustain the psychological tie to the adolescent and, at the same time, encourage increased autonomy and independence requires specific abilities as well. Diamond summarizes these as including (1) the importance of the ongoing commitment of the caregiver to keeping the developmental needs of the adolescent in mind even as the adolescent's behavior may be difficult to tolerate, (2) recognizing the dual needs of affiliation and independence on the part of the adolescent, (3) using empathic understanding to insightfully reflect on the emotional experience of the adolescent including the nature of ambivalence and uncertainty so typical of adolescent psychosocial development, and (4) becoming aware of the parental state of mind with regard to unresolved issues from one's own adolescence and current thoughts and affects with regard to the changing nature of the parent–child relationship.

Diamond's model of *Attachment Based Family Therapy* (*ABFT*) (Diamond et al., 2003) combines concepts from earlier models of family intervention with core elements of attachment theory to support the well-being of at-risk adolescents by helping the family to reframe the attachment relationship in more developmentally optimal and supportive ways. Similarly, Johnson (2004) describes attachment theory as informing work with families by encouraging family members to think about problem behaviors as either "hyperactivations" of the attachment system or as "defensive withdrawal and numbing" in relationship to unmet attachment needs. These models reflect the roots of attachment theory in that all patterns of attachment are conceptualized as behavioral adaptations to the caregiving environment as they relate to the dual needs of felt security and the developmental push toward autonomy, exploration, and mastery.

As an example, Diamond writes about the use of ABFT to address the adolescent crisis of suicidal ideation and behavior. From an attachment theory perspective, the adolescent's suicidal ideation/gesture is considered to be a critical activation of the attachment system, requiring a focus on the adolescent's need for protection and support. Particularly in family contexts characterized as either dismissive and avoidant, or in family contexts described as ambivalent and high in conflict, the suicidal behavior of the adolescent is conceptualized as an opportunity to address unresolved attachment issues in the family and to move the relational system of the parent(s) of the adolescent toward a more secure model of attachment organization and functioning. As summarized in the literature, ABFT targets multiple problem domains including overly harsh family criticism, adolescent withdrawal, problems in the area of affect regulation of parents and adolescents, high levels of family conflict, high levels of family stress, lack of information about adolescent development, and lack of access to successful strategies for limit setting with the developing adolescent. These problem domains can limit the flexibility of the attachment system with regard to meeting the developmental needs of security and safe exploration as they are represented in the experience of adolescence as a life phase.

Intergenerational Transmission of Attachment Patterns

The clinical case of Nancy, Paul, and Tommy illustrates the intergenerational transmission of attachment patterns and exemplifies concepts from Diamond's model of family treatment with an adolescent. Nancy was the youngest of three children who grew up with her family in the rural South. Her mother had spent part of her own childhood in foster care and was often critical and rejecting, yet at other times smothering and anxious with her two daughters. Nancy's father, a farmer, was withdrawn and sullen, ignoring his daughters and physically abusive to Nancy's older brother. The mother gave preferential treatment to Nancy's brother, who was sexually abusive to his sisters when they were preadolescents. Nancy's older sister eventually told their mother about the abuse, but the mother did not believe her. When her sister went away to college, her brother started sexually abusing Nancy, who was 9-years old at the time. The family was isolated from the wider world; the mother refused to allow her daughters to have friends or a social life outside the home and she called Nancy a "slut" because of the way she dressed. Having witnessed her mother's lack of belief regarding her sister's abuse, Nancy never confided in her parents about her own abuse and spent her adolescence alone and in silence, reading books in order to maintain some sense of stability. When she left for college, she was the target of her parent's anger and disapproval for leaving home and she experienced this step toward adult development as deep disruption in her relationship to her parents. At the time Nancy began therapy, both her parents had died, and her unmarried older sister had spent most of her adult life in and out of psychiatric hospitals with mental illness. Nancy had no contact with her brother, who was in prison due to dealing drugs. At the time of her initial visit to a therapist, Nancy had been married for 11 years to Paul and had a 5-year old son, named Tommy. Her first foray into therapy focused on significant symptoms of depression and prolonged grief due to the death of her infant daughter to congenital heart disease, 2 years earlier. She and Paul were experiencing marital stress, and Tommy had begun to show symptoms of serious emotional problems soon after his sister's death. Nancy entered into long-term weekly psychotherapy with a social worker and received medication from a consulting psychiatrist. By the time he was in first grade, Tommy began treatment with a child psychologist and was hospitalized due to hallucinations and extreme tantrums.

By fifth grade, Tommy was labeled as "emotionally disturbed" or ED by the school system and was gradually moved into a restrictive classroom setting; he was in a full-time ED school by eighth grade. He continued to have problems in both his school work and social life, despite the psychiatric care he and his mother were receiving. By the time he reached adolescence, Tommy had become explosive at home and experienced his mother as overprotective and "too worried." He had frequent verbal, and sometimes physical, fights with his father. At 14, he was hospitalized for 6 months at a nearby private treatment facility after he pulled a knife on a classmate at school. Nancy and Paul felt at a loss regarding how to help their son, and at the same time, Nancy described being emotionally and sexually withdrawn from her husband except for periods of argument over Tommy.

Following Tommy's hospitalization, the family entered biweekly family therapy, alternating with marital treatment for the couple. Nancy continued her individual psychotherapy for her depression and intermittent suicidality, and Tommy continued individual treatment with a medicating child psychiatrist who believed the teen was showing signs of conduct disorder. Through individual and family treatment, Nancy was able to reflect on, and revise, her thoughts about Tommy's emotional development. When she first entered treatment, Nancy believed that Tommy's problems were primarily a result of his father's insensitivity and overly strict parenting. As she felt supported to reflect on her own childhood and the ways in which she had been parented, she was able to think about the impact of her anxiety, her overprotection, and sometimes even intrusive parenting of her son. As Nancy experienced empathic understanding from the therapist about her own history of trauma and loss, she became better able to think about Tommy's experience of his relationship with her.

Tommy's therapists at the treatment center believed that he and Nancy were in a pathologically enmeshed dyadic relationship and that he had received the covert message that their relationship would not be able to withstand his growing up or the adolescent processes of separation and individuation. Nancy had perceived herself as Tommy's only protector over the years, and he hers, providing her with the only emotional intimacy in her life. Tommy felt too anxious to function without his mother's constant reassurance and approval, yet he had also grown angry about his degree of dependence on her. Family and individual treatment focused actively on transgenerational issues, offering empathic support to Paul and Nancy in a way that enabled them to see how they had been parenting Tommy in the only way they knew. Tommy's attachment relationship with Nancy mirrored the one she had with her own mother, and his relationship with Paul was like Nancy's relationship with her brother and Paul's aggressive and controlling relationship with his own father.

The family therapy eventually became a secure base for the parents and Tommy to explore areas of their relationship they had not been able to examine or resolve in earlier years of treatment. The therapeutic space became a place for Nancy and Paul to process their own unresolved feelings of loss about the death of their daughter and for Tommy to process his personal feelings of guilt about his unspoken wish for his baby sister's death. Therapy enabled the normalization of Tommy's developmental strivings toward individuation and the regulation of the angry affect that had emerged in the context of his relationship with his parents. The couple's private treatment afforded them a safe haven to express the shame and anguish they had felt about their "failures" as parents. They also could begin to see that the sexual dysfunction in their relationship was connected to Nancy's childhood sexual abuse. Through their multifaceted treatment, the parents were able to utilize the therapeutic relationship as a secure base from which they were able to explore their own histories. As Nancy and Paul explored their individual attachment histories, they were able to form a more empathic understanding of their childhood experiences as well as increased empathy for the developmental needs of their own son. As a result, the parents began to regulate their affect more successfully and provide developmentally appropriate support for Tommy's adolescent development.

Conclusion

This chapter has described the ways in which developmental and clinical research on attachment can be used to inform direct practice with children and families in a range of contexts. The multidisciplinary study of attachment addresses important questions relating to continuity and change with regard to adaptive capacity in children and families. As the literature on attachment expands to describe the role of attachment processes to a wide group of relational competencies, such as the capacity for affect regulation, practitioners are increasingly able to inform their work with an understanding of how attachment relationships can be important mechanisms of prevention and change. Forming and sustaining attachment bonds is a primary developmental task of family life. When children have experienced traumatic early beginnings with regard to primary attachment relationships, multiple areas of developmental vulnerability may exist. Practitioners can offer support to parents as they work to understand the impact of the child's attachment history and to create more stable bonds of attachment within the family context. For families of adolescents, in particular, the normative tasks of growth and development present the need to reconfigure the attachment system to reflect the changing needs of the developing child with regard to connection and autonomy. In cases of both young children and adolescents, an understanding of the developmental consequences of various patterns of attachment supports the development of preventive and clinical interventions in family based work in multiple contexts.

Study Questions

1. How does an understanding of attachment in the family context support a strengths perspective in social work with children and families?

2. Describe how an attachment perspective on work with children, couples, and families can be used in a variety of clinical settings including child welfare, domestic violence, substance abuse, couples, children, and adolescents.
3. Describe the connection between the quality of attachment relationships and the capacity for affect regulation.
4. How does adolescence, as a life phase, pose challenges to attachment relationships in the family context?
5. How does helping adults gain insight into their own attachment experiences help them to have more empathy for adult partners and more empathic understanding of their children's needs?

References

Ainsworth, M., Blehar, M., Waters, E., & Wall, S. (1978). *Patterns of attachment: A psychological study of the strange situation*. Hillsdale: Erlbaum.

Akister, J., & Reibstein, J. (2004). Links between attachment theory and systemic practice: Some proposals. *Journal of Family Therapy, 26*, 2–16.

Allen, J., & Manning, N. (2007). From safety to affect regulation: Attachment from the vantage point of adolescence. *New Directions for Child and Adolescent Development, 117*, 23–39.

Allen, J., McElhaney, K., Kuperminc, G., & Jodl, K. (2004). Stability and change in attachment security across adolescence. *Child Development, 75*(6), 1792–1805.

American Academy of Child and Adolescent Psychiatry. (2005). Practice parameter for the assessment and treatment of children and adolescents with reactive attachment disorder of infancy and early childhood. *Journal of the American Academy of Child and Adolescent Psychiatry, 44*(11), 1206–1220.

Applegate, J., & Shapiro, J. (2005). *Neurobiology for clinical social work: Theory and Practice*. New York: Norton.

Bowlby, J. (1969/1982). *Attachment and loss* (Vol. 1). New York: Basic Books.

Byng-Hall, J. (1995). Creating a more secure family base: Some implications of attachment theory for family therapy. *Family Process, 34*, 45–58.

Campbell, S., Cohn, J., & Neyers, T. (1995). Depression in first-time mothers: Mother-infant interaction and depression chronicity. *Developmental Psychology, 31*, 349–357.

Carter, S., Osofsky, J. D., & Hann, D. M. (1991). Speaking for baby: Therapeutic interventions with adolescent mothers and their infants. *Infant Mental Health Journal, 12*, 291–302.

Cassidy, J., & Shaver, P. (Eds.). (1999). *Handbook of attachment: Theory, research and practice*. New York: Guilford Press.

Chasnoff, I., Anson, A., Hatcher, R., Stenson, H., Iaukea, K., & Randolph, L. (1998). Parental exposure to cocaine and other drugs: Outcome at four to six years. In J. Harvey & B. Kosofsky (Eds.), *Cocaine: Effects on the developing brain* (pp. 314–328). New York: Annals of the New York Academy of Science.

Davies, D. (2004). *Child development: A practitioner's guide* (2nd ed.). New York: Guilford Press.

Davies, D. (2006). Parent–child therapy for traumatized young children in foster care. In R. Lee & J. Whting (Eds.), *Handbook of relational therapy for foster children and their families*. Washington: Child Welfare League of America.

Dawson, S., Frey, K., Self, J., Panagiotides, D., Hessl, D., Yamada, E., et al. (1999). Frontal brain electrical activity in infants of depressed and nondepressed mothers: Relation to variations in infant behavior. *Development and Psychopathology, 11*, 589–605.

Dawson, S., Grofer-Klinger, L., Panagiotides, H., Hilld, D., Spieker, S., & Frey, K. (1992). Infants of mothers with depressive symptoms: Electrophysiological and behavioral findings related to attachment status. *Development and Psychopathology, 4*, 67–80.

Diamond, G. (2005). Attachment-based family therapy for depression: Theory and case study. *The Family Psychologist, 21*(2), 4–9.

Diamond, G., Siqueland, L., & Diamond, G. M. (2003). Attachment-based family therapy for depressed adolescents: Programmatic treatment development. *Clinical Child and Family Psychology Review, 6*(2), 107–127.

Dozier, M. (2005). Challenges of foster care. *Attachment and Human Development, 7*, 27–30.

Dozier, M., Albus, K., Fisher, P., & Sepulveda, S. (2002). Interventions for foster parents: Implications for developmental theory. *Development and Psychopathology, 14*, 843–860.

Dozier, M., Dozier, D., & Manni, M. (2002). Recognizing the special needs of infants' and toddlers' foster parents: Development of a relational intervention. *Zero to Three Bulletin, 22*, 7–13.

Dozier, M., Manni, M., Gordon, M. K., Peloso, E., Gunnar, M. R., Stovall-McClough, K., Eldreth, D., & Levine, S. (2006). Foster children's diurnal production of cortisol: An experimental study. *Child Maltreatment*, Vol. 11, 189–197.

Dozier, M., Stovall, K. C., Albus, K. E., & Bates, B. (2001). Attachment for infants in foster care: The role of caregiver state of mind. *Child Development, 72*, 1467–1477.

Field, T. (1995). Infants of depressed mothers. *Infant Behavior and Development, 18*, 1–13.

Fonagy, P., Steele, H., Moran, G., Steele, M., & Higgitt, A. (1991). The capacity for understanding mental states: The reflective self in parent and child and its significance for security of attachment. *Infant Mental Health Journal, 13*, 200–217.

Fonagy, P., & Target, M. (1998). Mentalization and the changing aims of child psychoanalysis. *Psychoanalytic Dialogues, 8*, 87–114.

Fraiberg, S., Adelson, E., & Shapiro, V. (1975). Ghosts in the nursery: A psychoanalytic approach to the problems of impaired mother-infant relationships. *Journal of the American Academy of Child Psychiatry, 14*, 387–421.

George, C., & Solomon, J. (2008). The caregiving system. In J. Cassidy & P. Shaver (Eds.), *The handbook of attachment: Theory, research, and clinical applications* (2nd ed., pp. 833–856). New York: Guilford Press.

Greenspan, S. I., & Porges, S. W. (1984). Psychopathology in infancy and early childhood: Clinical perspectives on the organization of sensory and affective-thematic experience. *Child Development, 55*, 49–70.

Gunnar, M., Bruce, R., & Grotevant, H. (2000). International adoption of institutionally reared children: Research and policy. *Development and Psychopathology, 12*, 677–694.

Hamilton, C. (2000). Continuity and discontinuity of attachment from infancy through adolescence. *Child Development, 71*, 690–694.

Hesse, E. (1999). The adult attachment interview: Historical and current perspectives. In J. Cassidy & P. Shaver (Eds.), *Handbook of attachment: Theory, research and clinical applications* (pp. 395–433). New York: Guilford Press.

Hogue, A., Liddle, H., Becker, D., & Johnson-Leckrone, J. (2002). Family based prevention counseling for high risk young adolescents: Immediate outcomes. *Journal of Community Psychology, 30*(1), 1–22.

Hughes, D. (2007). *Attachment-focused family therapy*. New York: W.W. Norton.

Johnson, S., & Whiffen, V. (Eds.). (2003). *Attachment processes in couple and family therapy*. New York: Guilford Press.

Johnson, S. M. (2004). *The practice of emotionally focused couples therapy: Creating connection*. New York: Brunner-Routledge.

Liddle, H. A., & Hogue, A. T. (2000). A family-based, developmental-ecological preventive intervention for high-risk adolescents. *Journal of Marital and Family Therapy, 26*(3), 265–279.

Lieberman, A. (2004). Child-parent psychotherapy: A relationship-based approach to the treatment of mental health disorders in infancy and early childhood. In A. Sameroff, S. McDonough, & K. Rosenblum (Eds.), *Treating parent-infant relationship problems: Strategies for intervention* (pp. 97–122). New York: Guilford Press.

Lieberman, A. F. (2003). The treatment of attachment disorder in infancy and early childhood: Reflections from clinical intervention with later-adopted foster care children. *Attachment and Human Development, 5*(3), 279–282.

Liberman, A. F., Van Horn, P., Ippen, C. G. (2005). Toward evidence-based treatment: Child-parent psychotherapy with preschoolers exposed to marital violence. *Journal of the American Academy of Child and Adolescent Psychiatry, 44*(12), 1241–1248.

Lyons-Ruth, K., Bronfman, E., & Parsons, E. (1999). Maternal frightened, frightening or atypical behavior and disorganized attachment patterns. *Monographs of the Society for Research in Child Development, 64*, 67–96.

Madigan, S., Moran, G., & Pederson, D. R. (2006). Unresolved states of mind, disorganized attachment relationships, and disrupted mother-infant interactions of adolescent mothers and their infants. *Developmental Psychology, 4*(2), 293–304.

Main, M., Kaplan, N., & Cassidy, J. (1985). Security in infancy, childhood and adulthood: A move to the level of representation. In I. Bretherton & E. Waters (Eds.), Growing points of attachment theory and research. *Monographs of the Society for Research in Child Development, 50*, 66–104.

Main, M., & Solomon, J. (1990). Procedures for identifying infants as disorganized/disoriented during the Ainsworth strange situation. In T. Greenberg, D. Cicchetti, & E. Cummings (Eds.), *Attachment in the preschool years: Theory, research and intervention* (pp. 121–160). Chicago: University of Chicago Press.

McEwen, B. S., & Seeman, T. (2003). Stress and affect: Applicability of the concepts of allostasis and allostatic load. In R. J. Davidson, K. R. Scherer, & H. H. Goldsmith (Eds.), *Handbook of affective sciences* (pp. 1117–1137). New York: Oxford University Press.

Mikulincer, M., & Shaver, P. (2009). *Attachment in adulthood.* New York: Guilford Press.

National Clearinghouse for Child Abuse and Neglect. (1993). *Child abuse: Intervention and treatment issues.* Washington: Department of Health and Human Services.

Oppenheim, D., & Goldsmith, D. (Eds.). (2007). *Attachment theory in clinical work with children: Bridging the gap between research and practice.* New York: Guilford Press.

Osofsky, J., Eberhart-Wright, A., Ware, L., & Hann, D. (1992). Children of adolescent mothers: A group at risk for psychopathology. *Infant Mental Health Journal, 13*(2), 119–131.

Perry, B. (2002). Childhood experience and the expression of genetic potential: What childhood neglect tells us about nature and nurture. *Brain and Mind, 3*, 79–100.

Perry, B. (2004). Neurobiological sequelae of childhood trauma: Post-traumatic stress disorders in children. In M. Murberg (Ed.), *Catecholamine function in post-traumatic stress disorder: Emerging concepts* (pp. 233–255). Washington: American Psychiatric Press.

Posada, G., Jacobs, A., Richmond, M., Carbonell, O., Alzate, G., Bustamante, M., et al. (2002). Maternal caregiving and infant security in two cultures. *Developmental Psychology, 38*, 67–78.

Rothbaum, F., Rosen, K., Ujiie, T., & Uchida, N. (2002). Family systems theory, attachment theory and culture. *Family Process, 41*(3), 328–350.

Rothbaum, F., Rosen, K., Ujiie, T., & Uchida, N. (2004). Family systems theory, attachment theory and culture. *Family Process, 41*(3), 328–350.

Rutter, M. (2000). Clinical implications of attachment concepts: Retrospect and prospect. *Journal of Child Psychology and Psychiatry, 36*, 1179–1198.

Schore, A. (2001). Effects of a secure attachment relationship on right brain development, affect regulation and infant mental health. *Infant Mental Health Journal, 22*, 7–66.

Schore, A. (2004). *Affect regulation and the organization of self: The neurobiology of emotional development.* Hillsdale: Erlbaum.

Schore, A., & Schore, J. (2008). Modern attachment theory: The central role of affect regulation in development and treatment. *Clinical Social Work Journal, 36*, 9–21.

Shapiro, J. (2009). The developmental context of adolescent motherhood. In N. Farber (Ed.), *Adolescent pregnancy: Policy and prevention services* (pp. 38–52). New York: Springer.

Shapiro, J., & Applegate, J. (2005). *Neurobiology for clinical social work: Theory and Practice.* New York: Norton Publishing Company.

Shapiro, V., Shapiro, J., & Paret, I. (2001). *Complex adoption and assisted reproductive technology: A developmental approach to clinical practice.* New York: Guilford Press.

Shonkoff, J., & Phillip, D. (Eds.). (2000). *From neurons to neighborhoods: The science of early childhood development*. Washington: National Academy Press.

Siegel, D. (2001). Toward an interpersonal neurobiology of the developing mind: Attachment relationships, "mindsight," and neural integration. *Infant Mental Health Journal, 22*, 67–94.

Slade, A. (2002). Keeping the baby in mind: A critical factor in prenatal mental health. *Zero to Three, June/July*, 10–16.

Slade, A., Grienenberger, J., Bernbach, E., Levy, D., & Locker, A. (2005). Maternal reflective functioning, attachment and the transmission gap: A preliminary study. *Attachment and Human Development, 7*, 283–298.

Sroufe, L. A., Carlson, E., Levy, A., & Egeland, B. (1999). Implications of attachment theory for developmental psychopathology. *Development and Psychopathology, 11*, 1–13.

Stern, D. (1985). *The interpersonal world of the infant*. New York: Basic Books.

Tronick, E., & Weinberg, M. (1998). The impact of maternal psychiatric illness on infant development. *Journal of Clinical Psychiatry, 59*, 53–61.

Werner-Wilson, R. (2001). *Developmental systemic and family therapy with adolescents*. New York: Haworth Press.

Zeanah, C., Boris, N., Bakshi, S., & Lieberman, A. (2000). Disorders of attachment. In J. Osofksy & H. Fitzgerald (Eds.), *WAIMH handbook of infant mental health*. New York: Wiley.

Chapter 10
Applications of Attachment Theory to Group Interventions: A Secure Base in Adulthood

Timothy F. Page

> *In all social species that have been observed in their natural environment, it is clear that the group itself possesses a protective function for the individuals that comprise it.*
>
> Ainsworth (1989, p. 713)

Attachment theory is at heart a theory of intimacy. The developmental accomplishment of attachment security depends on a relational context of deep understanding and love between the growing child and his/her attachment figures, the specific individuals who are consistently involved in providing for the child's most basic needs (Ainsworth, 1989). Qualities first established in childhood attachment relationships become characteristic of the ways in which individuals engage in intimate relationships in later life, particularly those relationships where the partner assumes the function of attachment figure, which is usually the case in sexual pair bonds, between parents and children, and often in friendships (Ainsworth, 1989). This chapter explores applications of attachment theory to group interventions with adults, focusing especially on interventions directed at problems concerning the experience of intimacy in the two major relational domains of sexual pair bonds and parenting.

Social work practice, going back to its roots in the settlement houses of the nineteenth and early twentieth centuries, has been integral to the development of group work. Our professional perspective has always emphasized the importance of social relationships and contexts for human problems. Group modalities are particularly valuable because they are reflective of resources in a vitally influential social ecological niche, that of a community of social peers. The potency of group interventions derives from the systems of mutual regulation that are created in groups, the experiences of belonging, and the safety that they provide. This chapter's integration of attachment theory into social work practice, particularly group

T.F. Page (✉)
School of Social Work, Louisiana State University, Baton Rouge, LA, USA
e-mail: tpage2@lsu.edu

S. Bennett and J.K. Nelson (Eds.), *Adult Attachment in Clinical Social Work*,
Essential Clinical Social Work Series, DOI 10.1007/978-1-4419-6241-6_10,
© Springer Science+Business Media, LLC 2010

practice, provides a new way to understand familiar group dynamics and those interpersonal processes responsible for growth-oriented change, from a developmentally informed, multisystem perspective. In addition, emerging literatures on applications of attachment theory to therapeutic group processes and to group interventions aimed at relief of psychiatric symptoms will be discussed, followed by a clinical example from an attachment-based treatment group with high-risk parents.

The Social Ecology of Group Affiliations and Attachment

The social bonds comprised of affection and care that are associated with group memberships in families and communities are central to the evolutionary legacy of our species (Baumeister & Leary, 1995). Memberships in intervention groups are based on commonly shared personal and/or social experiences that help to create a sense of community and belonging, in effect reenacting an important aspect of our evolutionary tribal legacy. It should be pointed out that the bond that can develop toward a group does not necessarily involve attachment. Bowlby (1982) acknowledged that in adulthood, people can experience "a measure of attachment behavior" toward "groups and institutions other than the family" (p. 207). He was clear, however, that the "hallmark of attachment behavior" is that it is "directed towards one or a few particular figures" (p. 229). Attachments associated with group affiliations, according to him, are probably "mediated, at least initially, by attachment to a person holding a prominent position within that group" (p. 207). To disregard this can distort the actual complexity of individual relationships that occur within groups. Not all relationships within groups should be expected to be equally affectionate or close. Attachment experiences, nevertheless, do influence group behavior in important ways, as the following review of literature shows.

Review of Attachment-Based Group Interventions for Adults

Group interventions for adults that are explicitly based on attachment theory and incorporate essential attachment concepts in their interventions have been generated at a remarkable rate in recent years. The following review of this literature is divided into four categories: Group processes, psychiatric symptom relief, intimate relationships in sexual pair-bonds, and parenting. Of these categories, the literature on parenting is the largest and longest established, a reflection of the interest in improving attachment security in developing children through interventions aimed at strengthening parenting capacities.

Much of the research on attachment in adulthood relies on the use of self-report survey instruments, including, most notably: the Parental Bonding Instrument

(Parker, Tupling, & Brown, 1979), the Adult Attachment Scale (Collins & Read, 1990), Griffin and Bartholomew's (1994) Relationship Scales Questionnaire, the Attachment Styles Questionnaire (Feeney, Noller, & Hanrahan, 1994), and the Experiences in Close Relationships Scale (Brennan, Clark, & Shaver, 1998) (for a review of self-report survey instruments, see Bennett and Nelson, Chap. 3). Rather than producing attachment categories per se, these instruments primarily assess dimensions of relational experience considered integral to attachment organization, particularly *anxiety* and *avoidance*. The major limitation of reliance on these measures is that they are best at capturing conscious models of dimensions of attachment relationships and weakest at capturing unconscious or defensive models (Crowell, Fraley, & Shaver, 1999), which are typically key elements of attachment experience. The attachment measure designed to specifically capture unconscious models of attachment organization, the Adult Attachment Interview (Hesse, 2008), has yet to be used in group intervention research as an outcome measure.

Many important group interventions for adults have been informed by or address basic attachment-related constructs such as parental sensitivity or infant/child self-regulatory characteristics. For this review, however, only those explicitly based in attachment theory are included. Two major criteria were used for inclusion: (a) whether the study was based on a conceptual foundation explicitly informed by attachment theory, and (b) whether major outcome measurements were reflective of attachment theory to a substantial degree. This second criterion was given relatively greater weight in the selection of studies because it indicates that attachment quality was the focus for the intervention.

Attachment Applications to Group Processes

A limited, though growing area of group intervention research concerns the understanding of how individual differences in attachment qualities in adulthood may be associated with the development of group processes thought to be essential for effective treatment. For example, the interactive processes of self-disclosure, intimate expressiveness, empathic responsiveness, and active exploration of thought and feeling were studied by Shechtman and Rybko (2004) in interactional counseling groups among 436 Israeli, female, university students (average age 29). Securely attached participants (measured with the Relationship Scales Questionnaire) were significantly higher on each assessed dimension of group functioning, compared to those identified as insecure ambivalent and avoidant.

According to most theories of group dynamics and development, group "cohesion," the sense of belonging and sharing of a common mission of mutual benefit (see, e.g., Yalom, 2005), is believed to be an essential process for effective intervention. As one might expect, some evidence has been provided from this research showing that the attachment dimensions of avoidance and ambivalence can be influential in the development of cohesion and other group development processes.

Lindgren, Barber, and Sandhal (2008) found that among 18 professional class people participating in a group intervention for depression, those with dismissing/avoidant attachment profiles, as assessed with the Relationship Scales Questionnaire, were most likely to feel weak alliance (a dimension of cohesion) to the group early on. The same people, however, also tended to show an increase in their sense of alliance to the group in the beginning stages, indicating that dismissing-avoidant people can become effectively engaged – and may especially benefit from – this therapeutic group process.

Tasca, Balfour, Ritchie, and Bissada (2007b) also measured change in group alliance in relation to attachment security among 65 women with binge-eating disorders, randomly assigned to either a psychodynamic or cognitive-behaviorally oriented treatment group. Of the 33 women in the psychodynamic group, those with dismissing/avoidant attachment styles, unlike other participants, and in contrast to Lindgren et al. (2008, cited above), experienced no increase in group alliance over the course of the group. They also presented some evidence that dismissing/avoidant women were more likely to drop out. They concluded that group context – in this case psychodynamic vs. cognitive-behavioral – may differentially activate attachment-related interactive styles, depending on the sort of interpersonal demands presented by the intervention. The authors speculate that their psychodynamic intervention model presented a high level of interpersonal demands, including affective exploration and here-and-now focus, which proved to be overwhelming for some avoidant participants.

Rom and Mikulincer (2003) studied the experiences of young Israeli adults (some undergraduates, some young men entering military service) in task-oriented groups in a series of four studies involving a total of over 750 participants. They found that insecurely attached participants (assessed by scales for attachment anxiety and avoidance developed by the authors) had more negative appraisals of their groups' processes, across several dimensions. Avoidant people tended to respond to stress by withdrawing emotionally, "deactivating" attachment-related behavior anxious/ambivalent people tended to engage in hyperarousal and extreme desire for engagement. Both strategies interfered with group functions by impairing instrumental performance in the group anxious/ambivalent people, however, tended to be more helpful in creating cohesive groups involving mutual support. The authors concluded that avoidant people may be especially threatened and resistant to cohesive groups, echoing the findings above.

Mallinckrodt and Chen (2004) studied 71 psychology graduate students (76% female) who participated in 11 interpersonal growth groups. They used attachment theory as a framework to understand the process of intra-group transference (i.e., perceptions held by a group member about fellow group members' dispositions toward them), a phenomenon that is central to major theories of personal growth in group interventions (e.g., Yalom, 2005). Perceptions of fellow group members as friendly tended to vary positively with memories of mothers as emotionally responsive, and negatively with attachment avoidance. Group members reporting high adult attachment anxiety tended to be perceived by other group members as friendly and low in hostility. Group members who self-reported parents as intrusive and controlling or fathers as often threatening to withdraw love (characteristics associated with insecure attachment) tended to perceive fellow group members as hostile, and they were themselves perceived by other group members as hostile. The strongest finding for consensual group ratings of "target" group member behavior was found specifically for consensual judgment of a target group member as hostile and domineering toward fellow group members and that target group member's self-reported memories of a nonnurturing father.

The attachment styles of group leaders, and their influence on client treatment outcomes, is another important and emerging area of scholarship. Berson, Dan, and Yammarino (2006) studied 127 American undergraduate management students assigned to task groups as part of a class assignment. Groups were composed of between three and six members, and assessments were conducted at the end of the academic semester. They found that securely attached participants (as measured with a self-report attachment survey) were viewed as more effective leaders by others, than were insecurely attached participants.

Extending a similar line of inquiry specifically to clinical settings, Marmarosh et al. (2006) studied 76 group therapists to determine whether their "group attachment" orientation was associated with their perceptions of group participants, an important indicator of the potential quality of the therapeutic alliance. Although not, strictly speaking, a measure of attachment organization, their measure of "group attachment," the Social Group Attachment Scale, is an index of an individual's perceptions of the importance of various social groups in the person's life, consisting of anxiety (i.e., concern about acceptance and rejection) and avoidance (i.e., rejection of intimacy) scales. They found a positive association between therapists' self-ratings of group attachment anxiety and their anticipation of negative beliefs held by clients such as the inferiority of group services. Such negative preconceptions held by a group therapist would be likely to be obstacles to the establishment of group alliance, cohesion, and positive working relationships.

In summary, attachment relational styles, secure and insecure (anxious/preoccupied/ambivalent and dismissing/avoidant) types, appear to influence some important group change processes, particularly group alliance and cohesion, as well as mutual perceptions of support and hostility. These findings are particularly intriguing for their consistency with internal working model theory. Knowledge of attachment styles thus could be a significant aid to assessment and intervention. Discomfort with interpersonal emotional demands, difficulty in joining in cohesion-building activities, and expressed hostility and dominance by group members may be artifacts of attachment insecurity. Initial evidence also points to the relevance of group leaders' attachment organization to participants' perceptions of them, and perhaps to their expectations of clients' beliefs regarding the value of their services. Group leaders would do well to be sensitive to attachment history, including their own, when addressing important interactive characteristics such as these.

Attachment-Focused Interventions Addressing Symptom Relief

Bowlby's original intention in developing attachment theory was to find a theory of psychiatric practice that could explain personality development and psychopathology (Ainsworth & Bowlby, 1991). As yet, this remains an emerging area of research. The idea that attachment organization in adulthood plays an important role in group interventions targeted at specific symptoms has been advanced at a theoretical level in limited areas. Flores (2001), for example, has discussed the relevance of attachment style for understanding the power of group affiliations experienced in Alcoholics Anonymous, and de Zuleta and Mark (2000) have discussed the relevance of attachment organization for group interventions for patients with borderline personality disorder.

Empirical studies of attachment in adulthood and symptom relief in group interventions are as yet few. Changes in attachment security and depressive symptoms among women with binge-eating disorders who participated in group interventions have been examined by Tasca, Balfour, Ritchie, and Bissada (2007a). They found significant pre-post changes in attachment insecurity ("anxiety" and "avoidance," measured with the Attachment Styles Questionnaire) for women ($n=66$) randomly assigned to two group treatments (psychodynamic and cognitive-behavioral). Changes in attachment security were associated with improvements in binge-eating episodes, irrespective of treatment modality. Improvement in depressive symptoms was found for anxiously attached (not avoidant) women, but only for those in the psychodynamic treatment group. They, thus, provide some evidence that the effects of treatment type on depressive symptoms may vary with type of attachment insecurity. One of the important implications of this study is that psychodynamic and cognitive-behavioral group interventions may be relatively more effective for some people with different attachment profiles. Furthermore, although a large clinical literature now supports cognitive-behavioral interventions as the treatment of choice for depression (see, e.g., Beck & Alford, 2008), cognitive-behavioral group treatment may not be as effective for some people with more anxious (not avoidant) attachment insecurity. Clearly, more needs to be learned about these possible variations.

Muller and Rosenkranz (2009) studied the impact of inpatient group treatment on adults with post-traumatic stress disorder in relation to changes in attachment security, as assessed with the Relationship Scales Questionnaire. Subjects were middle-class, primarily white, female Canadians, 61 of whom completed follow-up measures. Several intervention groups were offered daily, over 5 weeks, the content of which included understanding the impact of patients' traumatic experiences on their daily lives, coping with trauma-related effects, and recreational activities. Psychiatric symptoms were assessed with two instruments, one for global symptoms and one specifically for trauma symptoms. The post-test following the intervention revealed significantly more secure attachments and fewer anxious/preoccupied attachments compared to controls, and these gains were maintained at the 6-month follow-up assessment. Attachment security varied negatively with the measure of overall psychiatric symptoms, and these effects were maintained at the follow-up. Trauma symptoms were predicted by attachment security (negatively) at follow-up only. It, thus, appears that changes in trauma symptoms associated with improvements in attachment security, brought about through group therapy, are likely to be observable only after considerable time has passed. This would seem logical, given that the nature of these changes is profound, involving no less than altering basic characteristics such as affect arousal and affect regulation. As the authors speculate, it is likely that the influence of attachment security on improvement in trauma-related symptoms is cumulative, building on incremental improvements in functioning.

In a recent study, Kirchmann et al. (2009) have examined the relationship between attachment organization and symptom relief following intensive group intervention, and the mediational effect on this relationship of group processes. Attachment organization was measured with both interview and survey measures, the only group study to date where this approach has been taken. Patient symptoms were measured by a global severity rating of a broad range of symptoms. Their sample consisted of 289 psychiatric inpatients in six hospitals in Germany, who received psychodynamic group treatment (average of 10.7 weeks). Group climate/cohesion was positively associated with symptom improvement for all attachment groups, but this was especially important to insecure ambivalent patients.

The existing literature on the role of attachment in group interventions with respect to symptom relief indicates that dimensions of attachment organization appear to be associated with the relief of psychiatric symptoms, including binge eating, trauma, and, to a lesser extent, depression, and it is likely that group modalities and processes influence these associations differentially, depending on the individual's attachment style. This growing literature thus contributes to recent empirical investigations into the important role, predicted by theory (see, e.g., Crittenden & Claussen, 2000), of attachment security in the development, maintenance, and amelioration of some psychiatric symptoms.

Attachment-Focused Interventions Addressing Intimacy with a Romantic Partner

Intimacy with a romantic partner is a signature developmental achievement of young adulthood. A small but growing literature supports the relevance of attachment organization in young adulthood for group interventions targeted at problems in intimacy with romantic partners.

Kilmann et al. (1999) and Kilmann, Urbaniak, and Parnell (2006) studied a brief "attachment focused" group intervention they developed for young adults "at risk for relationship distress," which targets current expectations in romantic relationships and reflection on how parental relationships influenced participants' own relationship expectations and relationship strategies. In one study (Kilmann et al., 2006), participants were randomly assigned to either their attachment-focused group ($n = 14$), which emphasized comparatively more reflection on relationship style and family history, a cognitive-oriented relationship skills group ($n = 15$), or no-treatment control ($n = 14$). At post-test, attachment-focused participants showed improvements in self-esteem and anger management, and relationships skills participants showed improvement in total interpersonal problems, compared to controls. At their follow-up observation, however, 15–18 months after the intervention, no differences among the three conditions were observed.

Lawson, Barnes, Madkins, and Francios-Lamonte (2006) studied a group intervention for men adjudicated for violent partner abuse ($n = 33$) in relation to changes in attachment organization as measured with the Adult Attachment Scale. The group intervention reflected an eclectic blend of feminist, cognitive-behavioral, and psychodynamic perspectives. Men who changed from insecure to secure ($n = 13$) self-reported more comfort with closeness in relationships and less anxiety and depression after the group intervention. No distinctions among attachment classifications were found for reductions in partner violence, although all participants reported less violence.

This limited body of work is a promising beginning to the use of attachment as an organizing framework for group interventions aimed at improving intimate relationships in adulthood. While far from conclusive, the evidence suggests that adults with insecure attachment histories are amenable to change via group intervention processes and that risk for relationship distress may be reduced. Much more, however, remains to be learned about these approaches.

Attachment-Focused Interventions Addressing Parenting Capacities

A modest but impressive evidence base now exists, spanning over 20 years, attesting to the value of attachment theory for parenting group interventions. Despite this growing body of literature, these approaches have yet to be widely disseminated to social work audiences. A vital opportunity thus exists for the profession to further integrate this body of knowledge into practice with vulnerable children and families.

What may be the first use of a group intervention incorporating concepts from attachment theory is reported by Minde, Shosenberg, Thompson, and Marton (1983). They devised a support and educational group for 55 mothers of premature infants (28 intervention/27 controls), to strengthen parenting capacities, cope with stress, and facilitate bonding. This study is notable for its use of innovative observational measures of interactive behavior in participants' homes. They found that intervention mothers demonstrated more direct engagement, social stimulation, physical support, such as when feeding, and support for their children's autonomy. At a 1-year follow-up, they attempted to assess attachment quality using nonstandardized measures from their home observations but found no differences between groups.

Perhaps the best known of early parenting interventions, based explicitly in attachment theory and incorporating a group format, is the steps toward effective and enjoyable parenting steps toward effective and enjoyable parenting (STEEP) Program, developed by Egeland and Erickson (2004). The STEEP Program is notable for many reasons, foremost because it grew out of Egeland and Erickson's experience with the Minnesota Longitudinal Study, the first and to date longest running longitudinal study of attachment among families in high-risk circumstances (Sroufe, 2005).

STEEP focuses on impoverished, high-risk mothers and their infants. Mothers are recruited into the program in the fifth or sixth month of pregnancy, to begin a process of relationship building with treatment staff, as the mother begins her relationship with her child. STEEP is a multifaceted program that is highly individualized to the particular needs, personal and environmental, of the parent and family. Participation in the program lasts for 2 years or more. Group interventions with approximately seven to nine parents alternate every other week with home visits, facilitated by the same person, typically a paraprofessional. Home visits include guided discussion of relationship challenges and incorporate extensive videotaping of mothers in interaction with their children (e.g., feeding) (Egeland & Erickson, 2004). The group intervention consists of several activities, including mother–child interaction time, a shared meal, and group discussion among mothers while the children are cared for by providers, the focus of which includes examination of experiences with parents in families of origin.

The results of a randomized controlled trial ($n = 154$), with post-intervention measurement observations at 1 month and approximately 6 months, showed that treatment group participants had a better understanding of infant development and of their relationships with their infants, had lower depression and anxiety, and were more competent in managing daily lives compared to controls. No differences between treatment and control groups were found for children's attachment security at either time, however (Egeland & Erickson, 2004).

In what was essentially a replication of the STEEP program, Heinicke, Fineman, Ponce, and Guthrie (2001) randomly assigned 31 young mothers in their third trimester of pregnancy to their treatment condition (33 others were controls), each of whom was identified as at risk for inadequate parenting as indicated primarily by poverty and low social support. They found that their home visiting/group intervention participants demonstrated higher maternal sensitivity and responsiveness and greater support for children's autonomy, their children were assessed with significantly more attachment security compared to controls, and these effects strengthened over the 2 year course of study. One important implication of these findings is that major changes in qualities such as maternal responsiveness and child attachment security may only be observable after a considerable period of time has passed, in this case 1–2 years.

Constantino et al. (2001) also studied impoverished mothers, recruited from urban public health clinics and social services offices, with random assignment to treatment ($n = 52$) or controls ($n = 39$). They evaluated the effects of an attachment-influenced group intervention on parents' sensitivity and responsiveness to children, including emotional engagement, children's behavior problems, and parents' voluntary participation in home visitation. Parents and their children participated in groups of 8–10 dyads in ten weekly sessions, organized around didactic and interactive activities involving developmentally related themes, including attachment and autonomy, the experience of separation for infants and for parents, and the development of children's capacities to communicate. Emotional engagement with children during group sessions was emphasized. Participants also jointly shared experiences in parenting with each other, and were encouraged to reflect on how their parenting was influenced by experiences in families of origin. Their major finding was that group participation facilitated voluntary participation in the home visiting program. Some improvements were noted in capacities for emotion communication in treatment participants, and a trend was noted for the intervention group toward increasing capacities for emotion recognition and interpretation.

Right From The Start (RFTS; Niccols, 2008) is an attachment-based group intervention consisting of large (12–40) groups of parents meeting in one community setting, divided into small work groups of four to six people. In each work group, videotapes are viewed of model parents demonstrating exaggerated examples of poor parenting in specific dimensions. A total of eight 2-hour sessions are offered, meeting once per week. Group meetings are also used for didactic instruction on topics such as attachment, parent sensitivity to children's cues, and temperament. Subjects, who were Canadian and mostly middle-class, were randomly assigned to RFTS ($n=27$) or an established home visiting program ($n=28$). RFTS participants who attended four or more sessions had significantly larger pre-post change scores on the Responsivity scale of the H.O.M.E. assessment (Caldwell & Bradley, 1984) compared to controls and larger changes at the 6-month follow-up on the Attachment Q-Set (Waters, 1995).

Feinberg and Kan (2008) incorporated dimensions of attachment security in their study of Family Foundations, a group intervention designed to provide support for the transition to parenthood through focus on coparenting skills, particularly support and closeness, coordination, and conflict management. They randomly assigned 169 heterosexual, expectant couples (primarily white, middle-class) to groups consisting of six to ten couples. Four of the eight class sessions were provided prior to the birth of the couples' children. Posttest assessments were conducted when children were 6 months old. The study evaluated associations among adult attachment (assessed with the Relationship Scale Questionnaire), couple response to treatment, and subsequent regulatory capacities of children.

They found that fathers' attachment insecurity, to a greater degree than that of mothers, moderated relationships between the program effect and several of the mother-related variables, including coparental support, depression, and dysfunctional interaction with the child. That is, mothers with insecure husbands tended to fare worse on these outcomes. Fathers' attachment insecurity also predicted fathers' own tendencies to undermine support and dysfunctional interactions with children. The authors conclude that fathers' attachment security is a key factor in successful adaptations of families making the transition to parenthood, especially because of the relatively greater needs of mothers during this time.

Case studies with qualitative data concerning the organization and impact of group interventions based on attachment theory are provided by Harwood (2006), Polansky, Lauterbach, Litzke, Coulter, and Sommers (2006), and Reynolds (2003). In each of these interventions, emphasis is placed on strengthening parents' capacities for perspective taking (i.e., understanding the child's experience from the child's viewpoint), empathic responsiveness, and reflection on the ways in which current cognitive models of parenting are derived from experiences with parents in families of origin. Polansky et al. (2006) applied attachment-related constructs, with particular emphasis on reflection of the influence of families of origin, to an intervention group for seven drug-addicted mothers living in a residential facility, involving 6 weekly sessions of approximately 90 min each. The authors report that group participants gained in empathic responsiveness, more child-centered discipline, and better verbal communication with their children.

Harwood's Prevention of Insecure Disorganized Attachment (PIDA) group (Harwood, 2006) and Reynolds' Mindful Parenting (Reynolds, 2003) are two additional models of parent–child interactive group therapy specifically targeting the promotion of secure attachment through coaching and group support. Both are designed to promote children's secure attachments by sharpening parents' observational abilities of children in group sessions and using modeling and on-the-spot feedback to teach affective attunement and perspective-taking.

The literature to-date on applications of attachment theory to parenting group interventions indicates several consistencies in program elements thought to be essential for strengthening parenting skills and improving children's attachment security. These include sharpening of observational abilities to discern children's needs, facilitation of perspective-taking toward better understanding of children's experiences, focus on sensitive and empathic responsiveness, open communication of emotion and mutual emotion regulation, and reflection on attachment "internal working models," specifically how beliefs and expectations toward parenting have been influenced by experiences in families of origin. Actual observations of, and feed-back on, dyadic interactive qualities are essential to achieving these goals.

An additional group treatment model that focuses on enhancing parental capacities of observation and responsiveness is The Circle of Security (CoS; Marvin, Cooper, Hoffman, & Powell, 2002), a model based explicitly on attachment theory. The following discussion describes this 20–26 week manualized group intervention for parents.

The Circle of Security

Overview of CoS Group Model

In the CoS intervention, approximately six to eight participants per group are trained to recognize and respond to their children's alternating expressions of autonomous/exploratory behavior and intimate/attachment behavior, conceptualized as a continuous circle. Parents learn by watching themselves in interaction with their children on videotape, created from footage obtained with the assessment (pre-test) Preschool Strange Situation Procedure (PSSP; Cassidy & Marvin, 1992). The PSSP is, thus used for several purposes: It is an assessment upon which individual intervention treatment plans are formed; excerpts from it, viewed in group sessions, constitute the basis of the intervention; and it is the major evaluation outcome variable. The relationship strengths and weaknesses in each parent–child dyad are conceptualized in terms of the relative balance between exploration and attachment.

The central relationship problem for each dyad, the so-called "lynch-pin issue," is the focus for the most intense of three video review sessions provided to each parent, and this typically occurs at the mid-point of the course of the group. A dyad with its primary problems in the area of attachment intimacy, for example, might have this problem demonstrated in a video segment where the child is upset about being alone in the observation room; the parent responds not with comfort, but with a frightening toy, presumably to distract the child from her distress. Such a video segment of the dyad then becomes the basis for important discussion with the parent in the group about relationship dynamics, specifically the emotional obstacles that are barriers to the parent in sensitively recognizing the child's need and effectively responding to it.

The empirical base of support for the Circle of Security is, to date, limited though promising. Two published studies, both by the originators of the intervention, support its efficacy with families involved in Early Head Start programs (Hoffman, Marvin, Cooper, & Powell, 2006; Marvin et al., 2002). These studies have shown that following the intervention, attachment classifications of children and caregivers ($n = 65$ dyads; attachment ratings were assessed with the PSSP and the companion Caregiver Coding System [Britner, Marvin, & Pianta, 2005]) tended to improve, from disordered/disorganized and organized insecure classifications (i.e., avoidant and ambivalent) to organized insecure and secure classifications. These studies, however, have included neither random assignment nor control groups.

The Child Welfare Circle of Security Demonstration Project

At this time, our research team is pilot-testing the Circle of Security with parents involved in the child welfare system as a result of substantiated child maltreatment. In our first trial, we enrolled eight participants, all mothers, referred to us randomly, following normal procedures used by the child welfare agency to refer parents to services. Attachment security of children and mothers was assessed using the preschool PSSP and the companion Caregiver Coding System (Britner et al., 2005). Of these, four dyads were found to change attachment classifications from pre- to post-test in expected directions: two dyads (both parent and child) improved from disorganized classifications to secure; one parent improved from insecure-ambivalent to secure (this child was classified secure); one child improved from disorganized to insecure-avoidant (the mother was also classified as avoidant). Of those where no change was observed, one dyad was rated secure at both pre- and post-test, and the other three were rated insecure-disorganized at both observations.

The following is a vignette from this group, involving a mother of one of the dyads that changed attachment classification from disorganized at pre-test to secure at post-test (see Page & Cain, 2009). "Mary" was 23 years old at the time of the intervention. Her family became involved with child welfare as a result of child neglect related to her and her husband's substance abuse. Her son (the focus for the intervention), Aaron, was 4.5 years old at the time the group began. He had been placed in foster care from ages 2 to 3 (a total of 18 months). Due to a relapse, Mary was not permitted in the home for 2 months following Aaron's return home from foster care. At this time Aaron lived in the family home with his father and two siblings. Mary returned home 5 months prior to the start of the group. At the start of the group, Aaron was exhibiting externalizing behavioral problems in preschool. By the time of the following vignette, which took place in session 17 (of 26), Aaron's behavior problems had escalated to the point where he was forbidden to ride the school bus.

In previous sessions, Mary had expressed strong frustrations with Aaron about his argumentativeness and her inabilities to control him, a "never-ending battle," which often left her feeling defeated, incompetent as a parent, and increasingly angry. She revealed unrealistic expectations of him ("He gets all the love he needs, he gets all the time he needs. He needs to be a little bit more helpful and stop acting like a 2-year-old."). She also revealed her awareness that the model of parenting she learned from her own parents, especially with respect to the communication of caring, interfered with the intimacy she wished to have with her son. As she put it, "My dad…was very intimidating while we were kids. We were scared of him…I keep my distance from my dad because of the way he treated us when we were kids…I do the same thing to mine…I still have that wall there because I am going to protect me…It is like if you leave me tomorrow, I will live. I have to keep the wall there. It is horrible. Of course, I don't feel like that, but I feel like I have to protect myself."

In session 17, Mary had her "Phase II" video review, where seven short vignettes were chosen to illustrate her "lynch-pin" struggles with her son, totaling only 4 minutes, 12 seconds of videotape. The vignettes were taken from continuous tape, starting with the segment of the Strange Situation where Mary had left the room for the second time, and showing her return and their subsequent interactions. These were characterized mostly as escalating coercive and argumentative exchanges where each sought to exert control over the other. The following group session transcript excerpt picks up after Mary has viewed the first chosen segment of the review, where she is out of the room. In the video clip, Aaron reacts to his mother's absence from the room with extremely strong protest – activated attachment behavior – to the point where he could not be left alone and the research assistant had to be called in to join him.

First, a note about the interactive process in a Circle of Security tape review session: Group practitioners will notice in the following dialog between the facilitator and client that there is very little of what is commonly known as larger "group process" involved. Unlike therapy groups that rely to a great extent on interactive processes among group members, the Circle of Security relies primarily on the interaction between facilitator and the client who is identified for the tape review session. This reflects our understanding that attachment relationships involve specific interactive histories; intervention, therefore, must focus on specific relational issues in each parent–child dyad, and accomplish this in a very limited time-frame. One might fairly question if this is so, what the advantage of even holding meetings among other group members might be – why not just do individual therapy? The answer to this is to recall that the entire intervention consists of only three sessions dedicated to each individual member, and it lasts for up to 26 weeks, for eight participants – far fewer sessions than would normally be expected in individual treatment for the same number of people. Experience thus far supports the assertion that clients learn a considerable amount about their own relationships in watching the tape reviews of their fellow group members and derive considerable support from the presence of others as they engage in this process.

(Note: "F" = facilitator)

F: Let's imagine that he is going to be completely honest with you and tell you what he was feeling when you were away. What would he say?

Mary: Mom, I don't like it when you leave, I get scared.

F: That is exactly what he would say.

Mary: You were gone too long.

F: If he said that to you, what would be your response?

Mary: I am sorry. I would have picked him up and hugged him and told him not to be scared because I would always be there.

F: In this clip, it is a different kind of tango...You say that you know the feeling that is under there, and that is easy to miss...It takes a while to get to the point of "Let's be honest about what you are feeling and I will comfort you." We think we have this dance in the short sequence here.

         (The next video clip shows Aaron approaching Mary with a toy to look at. Mary's response to the facilitator demonstrates her use of Circle of Security terminology, a recognition of Aaron needing to "come in" to her as his "safe haven.")

F: What do you think is going on?

Mary: He was coming in for comfort, to make sure it was okay to come in for comfort. Trying to get me involved in what he was doing...

         (A following video clip shows escalation of coercive and controlling exchanges.)

F: Let's pay attention to this right here, what is he doing?

Mary: Ignoring me again.

F: Yeah. One thing I am wondering about is, does he do the ignoring thing to you, and does it push your buttons?

Mary: Yes, it makes me mad.

A (other group member): I think all kids do that.

Mary: When I am calling you, you don't come and you are just standing there looking at me like I am dumb. That makes me mad, too.

F: Right on. Think about A's comments, that all kids do this.

Mary: It is one of their only defenses to us because they are so small and they can't do a lot of things. We make them angry, so they are going to find ways to make us angry.

F: I don't think we can understand this clip without understanding everything we already watched. "I need to be close to you, but I am also going to ignore you because I am pissed off"…So at the feeling level, let's track what is going on inside of you.

Mary: I want to know why, what are you doing? Then it starts to make me angry, especially the way he keeps acting, and he is arguing with me about it.

F: Right. The dance is escalating, this sense of getting mad at each other. "I am going to ignore you and disobey you." I was wondering how familiar that seems to you.

Mary: That is every day…He didn't act no different here than he would at home….I am doing a lot of things different now…Now I would definitely approach that differently.

F: Right, let's keep in mind that it takes two to dance. It is important for everybody to think about their exit strategy from the dance.

Mary: Yeah, my exit strategy…I found when I start to get angry, I stop and say, "What is wrong?" I am, like, while I am angry because of this…I will start talking to him, you know, asking him questions for him to tell me how he feels, so we can fix it.

F: That is a new dance.

Mary: Yeah, we are trying to do it differently. It seems to be working.

F: Can you give an example of something that has happened in the past couple weeks?

Mary: It seems like lately, every time the case worker comes over, Aaron wants to act out… [Now], I get down and look him eye to eye, I don't just bend over, I get down. Most of the time I will wrap my arm around him and I will hold his hands, not pulling him back like I just did (*Mary references the video clip just watched, where in her anger, she aggressively grabbed Aaron's arm*), but holding his hands, and I will just tell him, "You know, you are really making me upset, and you really need to calm down because acting like this isn't going to get you what you want. It is just going to make mommy madder and then everybody is going to be upset," and saying, "What do you want me to do?" Then he will tell me. That is the main thing that I say, "What do you want me to do?"

We were particularly impressed with Mary's ability, especially on seeing the first video clip of Aaron's intense activation of attachment behavior in the Strange Situation, to bring forth great reserves of empathic caring for him, with new insights into the depth of his need for her. As she said in the sessions, she had been taught to keep her emotional distance from those she loved, and her reflections on this in the group helped her to see Aaron's need for her in a new way and respond to him with a degree of caring that she had previously denied him. She became able to identify the familiar cycle of coercion and conflict that typified their daily interactions and very consciously step outside this to focus on what he needed from her, seeing his experience from his vantage point, even to a literal degree, as we see in her physically lowering herself to meet him at eye level. As she reflected on her old interactive "dance" with Aaron in the final group session, "…it was difficult watching me arguing back with him like I am his age…like, I am acting like *a kid.* Oh, my God. That was a little annoying." She came to assume the role of, as we say, the "bigger, stronger, wiser, and kind" parent. Sometime after this review, Mary reported that Aaron's behavior problems at school had ceased, and they did not reappear during the rest of the course of the group.

Despite the fact that the majority of work in Circle of Security group sessions focuses on individual parent–child dyads, and involves primarily interaction between group facilitator and individual client, according to their anecdotal reports to us, group members learn valuable lessons relevant to their own relationships and derive much-needed support and reassurance by watching and listening to their peers. The group format thus enables members to examine their behavior with less defensiveness and sense of stigma than might be the case in individual treatment. This community of peers is designed to be, and thus becomes, to use Winnicott's (1965) term, a "holding environment" that creates the therapeutic conditions necessary for change.

Conclusion

The ways in which we learn to be intimate are an inheritance of our early attachments, and these are brought forward and reenacted in later life, particularly in relationships with the greatest emotional significance, between romantic partners and with our children. Group interventions addressing these issues can provide a uniquely potent corrective experience because they involve the protective function of a community of peers functioning as a safe haven and secure base. Applications of attachment theory to group interventions have become a vibrant area for research and practice in recent years, and we can expect to see this trend accelerating. This is a vital area for social workers to lend their expertise, particularly because of our dedication to improving the well-being of vulnerable children and families. Expanding our expertise in applications of attachment theory to practice should be embraced as an essential part of this professional commitment.

Study Questions

1. To what extent are connections felt between group members considered to be "attachment bonds?"
2. What major areas in group intervention research for adult clients have incorporated attachment theory?

3. What are some of the ways in which attachment organization in adulthood can influence individual behavior in small groups?
4. What are common elements of attachment-influenced group interventions for parents and how do they reflect major tenets of attachment theory?
5. Reflect on your various past and current group memberships and discuss your attachments to the group members, leader, and the group as a whole. Have you ever belonged to a group that gave you a sense of safety and protection or sought out a group membership that could provide this?

References

Ainsworth, M. D. S. (1989). Attachments beyond infancy. *American Psychologist, 44*(4), 709–716.

Ainsworth, M. D. S., & Bowlby, J. (1991). An ethological approach to personality development. *American Psychologist, 46*(4), 333–341.

Baumeister, R. F., & Leary, M. R. (1995). The need to belong: Desire for interpersonal attachments as a fundamental human motivation. *Psychological Bulletin, 117*(3), 497–529.

Beck, A. T., & Alford, B. A. (2008). *Depression: Causes and treatment* (2nd ed.). Philadelphia: University of Pennsylvania.

Berson, Y., Dan, O., & Yammarino, F. J. (2006). Attachment style and individual differences in leadership perceptions and emergence. *The Journal of Social Psychology, 146*(2), 165–182.

Bowlby, J. (1973). *Attachment and loss, II: Separation, anxiety, and anger*. New York: Basic Books.

Bowlby, J. (1982). *Attachment and loss, Vol. I: Attachment* (2nd ed.). New York: Basic Books.

Brennan, K. A., Clark, C. L., & Shaver, P. R. (1998). Self-report measurement of adult attachment: An integrative overview. In J. A. Simpson & W. S. Rholes (Eds.), *Attachment theory and close relationships* (pp. 46–76). New York: Guilford Press.

Britner, P. A., Marvin, R. S., & Pianta, R. C. (2005). Development and preliminary validation of the caregiving behavior system: Association with child attachment classification in the preschool Strange Situation. *Attachment & Human Development, 7*(1), 83–102.

Caldwell, B., & Bradley, R. (1984). *Home observation for measurement of the environment*. Little Rock: University of Arkansas at Little Rock.

Cassidy, J. & Marvin, R.S. (1992). *Attachment organization in preschool children: Procedures and coding manual* (5th ed.). Unpublished manuscript, MacArthur Working Group on Attachment, Seattle.

Collins, N. L., & Read, S. J. (1990). Adult attachment, working models and relationship quality in dating couples. *Journal of Personality and Social Psychology, 58*, 644–663.

Constantino, J. N., Hashemi, N., Solis, E., Alon, T., Haley, S., McClure, S., et al. (2001). Supplementation of urban home visitation with a series of group meetings for parents and infants: Results of a "real world" randomized, controlled trial. *Child Abuse & Neglect, 25*, 1571–1581.

Crittenden, P. M., & Clausson, A. H. (2000). *The organization of attachment relationships: Maturation, culture, and context*. Cambridge: Cambridge University.

Crowell, J. A., Fraley, R. C., & Shaver, P. R. (1999). Measurement of individual differences in adolescent and adult attachment. In J. Cassidy & P. R. Shaver (Eds.), *Handbook of attachment: Theory, research, and clinical applications* (pp. 434–465). New York: The Guilford.

de Zulueta, F., & Mark, P. (2000). Attachment and contained splitting: A combined approach of group and individual therapy to the treatment of patients suffering from borderline personality disorder. *Group Analysis, 33*, 486–500.

Egeland, B., & Erickson, M. F. (2004). Lessons from STEEP: Linking theory, research, and practice for the well-being of infants and parents. In A. J. Sameroff, S. C. McDonough, & K. L. Rosenblum (Eds.), *Treating parent–infant relationship problems* (pp. 213–242). New York: Guilford Press.

Feeney, J. A., Noller, P., & Hanrahan, M. (1994). Assessing adult attachment. In M. B. Sperling & W. H. Berman (Eds.), *Attachment in adults* (pp. 128–151). New York: Guilford Press.

Feinberg, M. E., & Kan, M. L. (2008). Establishing family foundations: Intervention effects on coparenting, parent/infant well-being, and parent–child relations. *Journal of Family Psychology, 22*(2), 253–263.

Flores, P. J. (2001). Addiction as an attachment disorder: Implications for group therapy. *International Journal of Group Psychotherapy, 51*(1), 63–81.

Griffin, D. W., & Bartholomew, K. (1994). Models of the self and other: Fundamental dimensions underlying measures of adult attachment. *Journal of Personality and Social Psychology, 67*(3), 430–445.

Harwood, I. (2006). Head start is too late: Integrating and applying infant observation studies, and attachment, trauma, and neurobiological research to groups with pregnant and new mothers. *International Journal of Group Psychotherapy, 56*(1), 5–28.

Heinicke, C. M., Fineman, N. R., Ponce, V. A., & Guthrie, D. (2001). Relation-based intervention with at-risk mothers: Outcome in the second year of life. *Infant Mental Health Journal, 22*(4), 431–462.

Hesse, E. (2008). The adult attachment interview. In J. Cassidy & P. R. Shaver (Eds.), *Handbook of attachment: Theory, research, and clinical applications* (2nd ed., pp. 552–598). New York: Guilford Press.

Hoffman, K. T., Marvin, R. S., Cooper, G., & Powell, B. (2006). Changing toddlers' and pre-schoolers' attachment classifications: The circle of security intervention. *Journal of Consulting and Clinical Psychology, 74*(6), 1017–1026.

Kilmann, P. R., Laughlin, J. E., Carranza, L. V., Downer, J. T., Major, S., & Parnell, M. M. (1999). Effects of an attachment-focused group preventive intervention on insecure women. *Group Dynamics: Theory, Research, and Practice, 3*(2), 138–147.

Kilmann, P. R., Urbaniak, G. C., & Parnell, M. M. (2006). Effects of attachment-focused versus relationship skills-focused group interventions for college students with insecure attachment patterns. *Attachment & Human Development, 8*(1), 47–62.

Kirchmann, H., Mestel, R., Schreiber-Willnow, K., Mattke, D., Seidler, K. P., Daudert, E., et al. (2009). Associations among attachment characteristics, patients' assessment of therapeutic factors, and treatment outcome following inpatient psychodynamic group psychotherapy. *Psychotherapy Research, 19*(2), 234–248.

Lawson, D. M., Barnes, A. D., Madkins, J. P., & Francios-LaMonte, B. M. (2006). Changes in male partner abuser attachment styles in group treatment. *Psychotherapy: Theory, Research, Practice, Training, 43*(2), 232–237.

Lindgren, A., Barber, J. P., & Sandahl, C. (2008). Alliance to the group-as-a-whole as a predictor of outcome in psychodynamic group therapy. *International Journal of Group Psychotherapy, 58*(2), 163–184.

Mallinckrodt, B., & Chen, E. C. (2004). Attachment and interpersonal impact perceptions of group members: A social relations model analysis of transference. *Psychotherapy Research, 14*(2), 210–230.

Marmarosh, C. L., Franz, V. A., Koloi, M., Majors, R. C., Rahimi, A. M., Ronquillo, J. G., et al. (2006). Therapists' group attachments and their expectations of patients' attitudes about group therapy. *International Journal of Group Psychotherapy, 56*(3), 325–338.

Marvin, R., Cooper, G., Hoffman, K., & Powell, B. (2002). The Circle of Security project: Attachment-based intervention with caregiver–pre-school child dyads. *Attachment & Human Development, 4*(1), 107–124.

Minde, K., Shosenberg, N., Thompson, J., & Marton, P. (1983). Self-help groups in a premature nursery – follow-up at one year. In J. D. Call, E. Galenson, & R. L. Tyson (Eds.), *Frontiers of infant psychiatry* (Vol. I, pp. 264–272). New York: Basic Books.

Muller, R. T., & Rosenkranz, S. E. (2009). Attachment and treatment response among adults in inpatient treatment for posttraumatic stress disorder. *Psychotherapy Theory, Research, Practice, Training, 46*(1), 82–96.

Niccols, A. (2008). 'Right from the start': Randomized trial comparing an attachment group intervention to supportive home visiting. *Journal of Child Psychology and Psychiatry, 49*(7), 754–764.

Page, T., & Cain, D. S. (2009). "Why don't you just tell me how you feel?" A case study of a young mother in an attachment-based group intervention. *Child and Adolescent Social Work Journal, 26*(4), 333–350.

Parker, G., Tupling, H., & Brown, L. B. (1979). A parental bonding instrument. *British Journal of Medical Psychology, 52*, 1–10.

Polansky, M., Lauterbach, W., Litzke, C., Coulter, B., & Sommers, L. (2006). A qualitative study of an attachment-based parenting group for mothers with drug addictions: On being and having a mother. *Journal of Social Work Practice, 20*(2), 115–131.

Reynolds, D. (2003). Mindful Parenting: A group approach to enhancing reflective capacity in parents and infants. *Journal of Child Psychotherapy, 29*(3), 357–374.

Rom, E., & Mikulincer, M. (2003). Attachment theory and group processes: The association between attachment style and group-related representations, goals, memories, and functioning. *Journal of Personality and Social Psychology, 84*(6), 1220–1235.

Shechtman, Z., & Rybko, J. (2004). Attachment style and observed initial self-disclosure as explanatory variables of group functioning. *Group Dynamics: Theory, Research, and Practice, 8*(3), 207–220.

Sroufe, L. A. (2005). Attachment and development: A prospective, longitudinal study from birth to adulthood. *Attachment & Human Development, 7*(4), 349–367.

Tasca, G., Balfour, L., Ritchie, K., & Bissada, H. (2007a). Change in attachment anxiety is associated with improved depression among women with binge eating disorder. *Psychotherapy: Theory, Research, Practice, Training, 44*(4), 423–433.

Tasca, G., Balfour, L., Ritchie, K., & Bissada, H. (2007b). The relationship between attachment scales and group therapy alliance growth differs by treatment type for women with binge-eating disorder. *Group Dynamics: Theory, Research, and Practice, 11*(1), 1–14.

Waters, E. (1995). Appendix A. The Attachment Q-Set (Version 3.0). *Monographs of the Society for Research in Child Development, 60*(2–3, Serial No. 244), 234–246.

Winnicott, D. (1965). *The maturational processes and the facilitating environment.* Madison: International Universities.

Yalom, I. (2005). *The theory and practice of group psychotherapy.* New York: Basic Books.

Part III
Attachment Applications to Policy, Research, and Education

Chapter 11
Policy Implications of Attachment Processes in Adulthood: Caregiving and Family Preservation

Joyce E. Everett

> *There is in consequence a great danger that we shall adopt*
> *mistaken norms. For, just as a society in which there is a*
> *chronic insufficiency of food may take a deplorably inadequate*
> *level of nutrition as its norm, so may a society in which parents*
> *of young children are left on their own with a chronic insuffi-*
> *ciency of help take this state of affairs as its norm.*
>
> Bowlby (1988, pp. 2–3)

Attachment theory originated from Bowlby's (1969/1982) clinical observations about the real life experiences of institutionalized children, and the initial policy changes that emerged out of his concerns focused on improving child care (Rutter, 2008). In collaboration with his social work colleague, John Robertson, Bowlby's early work had major impact on public health when his analysis of Robertson's films of hospitalized children was presented to the World Health Organization (WHO) in 1951. Public policy was eventually altered in response to the presentation's emphasis on the negative reactions of children separated from parents for medical treatment or residential care (Bowlby, 1951; Robertson & Robertson, 1971). Subsequent attachment research has continued to influence the development of child welfare policies over the past half century (Rutter, 2008), and primary focus has remained on the needs of children. Little attention has been given to the attachment needs of adults, yet all family policies inevitably affect the emotional well-being and attachment systems of adults as well. This chapter highlights the interface of attachment and current social welfare policies from the standpoint of adults.

One strategy for understanding the implications of policy on attachment processes is to examine specific instances in which attachment relationships and behaviors are affected by policy. The five case scenarios described below illustrate the ways social welfare policy interacts and affects the attachment relationships in the lives of ordinary citizens. Bowlby's (1958) theory of attachment is based on the assumption that "the patterns of attachment established in early life are relatively stable across development"

J.E. Everett (✉)
Smith College School for Social Work, Northampton, MA, USA
e-mail: jeverett@smith.edu

S. Bennett and J.K. Nelson (Eds.), *Adult Attachment in Clinical Social Work*,
Essential Clinical Social Work Series, DOI 10.1007/978-1-4419-6241-6_11,
© Springer Science+Business Media, LLC 2010

(Austrian, 2008, p. 365) and become guides for future behavior. Each vignette describes potential disruptions in attachment bonds and is illustrative of the range of situations or circumstances in which aspects of social welfare policy impact, positively or negatively, the development of the attachment between adults and children or adults and other adults. Although social welfare policies generally focus on the needs of children, these scenarios underscore how the attachment styles of adults and attachment dynamics within families are linked to the issues addressed by these policies.

Vignette 1. John and Kevin have been in a committed gay relationship for more than 9 years. Both are employed, earn fairly good salaries, and live a more than comfortable lifestyle. They want to adopt the three foster children they have cared for during the last 4 years. The children, ages 4, 6, and 9, have been placed in their home since they were removed from their birthparent, due to substance use.

Vignette 2. Five police officers entered the living room of the apartment that Keith, age 5, shared with his mother, Jessica, and 6-month old breast-fed baby sister Andrea. After a brief conversation, Jessica was handcuffed and taken away by four of the officers, while the children watched and cried. One officer remained to find someone to come for Keith and Andrea. The next time they saw their mother was a year and a half later. At the time, they were living with their aunt and calling her "Mom" (Greenberg, 2006, p. 168).

Vignette 3. Ellen and Elaine have been together for over 12 years, during which Ellen gave birth to their only child, Ann. Ann thinks she's very lucky to have two moms, because she gets to do different things with each of them. She cooks with Ellen and rides her bike with Elaine. From the beginning, the two moms shared everything in raising Ann, from feeding, diapering, to signing school forms. Now, Ellen and Elaine have decided to end their longstanding relationship, but Ellen has filed a petition to sever Elaine's future relationship with Ann.

Vignette 4. Elizabeth, age 32, is an Army reservist who completed one tour of duty in Iraq about 18 months ago. Her first child was born 12 months before her first 15-month deployment. While she was away, her husband cared for their son with the help of her mother. She returned from Iraq to reunite with her son, spending more than 11 months with him. However, she recently learned that her unit was scheduled to be deployed again in 6 months. As a reservist, she has few, if any, options to get out of this second deployment with her unit.

Vignette 5. Alana, a college professor, age 48, began caring for her elderly mother, age 83, in Alana's home about 6 months ago when she realized her mother's health was deteriorating, making it difficult for her mother to manage living alone. Her mother Ann is completely unhappy with these arrangements because she fears she will lose her independence and become a burden on her daughter.

The purpose of this chapter is to assess the implications and relevance of attachment theory for social welfare policy, especially those policies in the areas of child protective services, foster care, family preservation, adoption, child care, alcohol or substance abuse treatment, military service, imprisonment, adult caregivers of the elderly or disabled, and gay and lesbian families. The chapter begins with a general overview of the functions of social welfare policy in our society and a brief summary of attachment theory. The remainder of the chapter describes pertinent policies that affect the development of attachment relationships illustrated in each of the previous case vignettes. The implications of these policies for adult attachment processes are assessed at the end of the chapter.

Overview of Social Welfare Policy and Attachment

While social welfare policy is not specifically designed to facilitate or foster attachment relationships, it can inadvertently impact attachment relationships, whether positively or negatively. Social welfare policies function as a mutual aid system or social safety net that comes into play when human needs are not being met through the family, religious institutions, the economy, or the polity. Usually social welfare activities take place outside the market system and are designed to relieve or ameliorate social problems that affect relatively large numbers of individuals. How the social problem is defined is a significant factor in determining a policy response. Many of the activities associated with social welfare overlap with the activities of other institutions. For example, income support is provided to poor families through the Temporary Assistance for Needy Families program (TANF), a public assistance program. The United States tax system also provides support to working-class families through the Earned Income Tax Credit. In this case, social welfare policy and fiscal policy overlap in the pursuit of one goal, namely providing an alternative income source for low income families.

Attachment theory, as described in previous chapters, presumes that human infants are born with a predisposition to become attached to their caregivers, and from this attachment between the child and the caregiver, the child develops an internal working model of the relationship with the principal attachment figures, based on their availability and responsiveness (Austrian, 2008; Schneider, 1991). The child's expectation about this primary attachment relationship builds up similar expectations about future relationships. Early disruptions in the primary attachment relationship lead to lifelong feelings of insecurity and a distorted capacity to develop and sustain meaningful relationships (Austrian). The primary relationship becomes the model for future relationship development. It is important, however, to emphasize that internal working models are not static and can be restructured.

Child Welfare and Attachment

The Child Welfare League of America (CWLA) reports that in fiscal year 2006, there were 301,358 children who entered out of home care in the USA, and 137,873 children under the age of 16 were reported by state child welfare agencies to be free for adoption (CWLA, 2009). These children and their birth parents, regardless of the reasons for their separation from each other, were affected by child welfare policies that lead to separation and/or loss and activate attachment processes within their families. Such parents and children must restructure or repair the breach in their attachment bonds to successfully reunite or to develop future attachment relationships apart from each other.

In the first two case vignettes, foster fathers John and Kevin and biological mother Jessica illustrate attachment issues that frequently arise for adults in the child welfare system. John and Kevin's vignette suggests that they have been fulfilling their need to nurture and are seeking greater attachment security for their foster children by adopting children who have been determined free for adoption. Jessica's vignette illustrates the challenges a biological parent experiences when reunited with children who have been temporarily placed in foster care due to parental imprisonment, resulting in weakened attachment ties with their mother. Child welfare policies and judicial standards are particularly applicable to these case vignettes, and the adults, as well as their children, are affected by these policies.

The Federal Adoption Assistance and Child Welfare Act of 1980 revolutionized child welfare practice by establishing *permanence* as the ultimate goal of foster care placement by mandating that such placements become temporary arrangements. The law also required the state to make *reasonable efforts* to prevent or eliminate the need for the child to be removed from his/her home and make it possible for the child to return home (Moye & Rinker, 2002). To meet this mandate, states are required to provide preplacement and postplacement services to keep children in their own homes or reunite them with their families as soon as possible. Each child must have a case plan that is periodically reviewed to ensure that consistent efforts are made to achieve the permanency goals for that child. The Federal Adoption and Safe Families Act of 1997 shifted the focus of child welfare services from family preservation to the child's health and safety in determining what is reasonable and consistent with the plan for timely, permanent placement of a child. The Act further specifies the circumstances in which the reasonable efforts requirement could be waived (Pecora et al., 1992). For example, a waiver could be granted if the parent had committed a felony assault causing serious bodily injury to the child or sibling; committed or attempted murder or voluntary manslaughter of a sibling; aggravated circumstances including abandonment, torture, chronic abuse, or sexual abuse; or if the parental rights to a sibling had been terminated involuntarily (Welte, 1997). Subsequent legislation (Keeping Families and Children Safe Act, 2003) reaffirmed these principles.

Neither the Adoption Assistance and Safe Families Act nor any of the subsequent bills reauthorizing child welfare services address the question of "whether gay and lesbian prospective parents can adopt" (Kenyon, Chong, Enkoff-Sage, Hill, Mays, & Rochelle, 2003, p. 572). None of these laws offers a definition of family, which leaves states the option of interpreting on a case-by-case basis what constitutes an appropriate family for adoption. Uniform standards across states regarding adoption by gay men and lesbians do not exist. Each state's policies are dictated by state statutes, agency regulations, and court opinions (Kenyon et al.), but state laws have been in flux over the past decade. According to the most recent Human Rights Campaign (HRC, 2010b) summary on the subject of adoption, single and coupled gay men and lesbians are prohibited from adopting in Florida, Mississippi, and Utah. Currently, however, ten states (California, Connecticut, Illinois, Indiana,

Maine, Massachusetts, New Jersey, New York, Oregon, Vermont) and the District of Columbia explicitly permit lesbian and gay couples to *adopt jointly* – the same adoption process permitted by heterosexual couples – and two states (Nevada and New Hampshire) allow same-sex couples to adopt jointly in some jurisdictions (HRC). In addition, *second-parent adoption* (each partner in the couple adopts the child individually) is a statewide option in nine states, and in 15 other states, second-parent adoption has been permitted in some jurisdictions. Although 47 states allow consideration of a gay or lesbian person as an adoptive parent, some states have adopted or have considered administrative policies that prohibit gay men and lesbians from adopting children in the state's custody. These practices "ignore evidence that family form does little to ensure success in adoption" (Ryan, Pearlmutter, & Groza, 2004, p. 86). Despite the personal biases, fear, and discrimination they have experienced, gay men and lesbians have adopted children for many years. Lesbian and gay male parents are as emotionally healthy, socially well adjusted, and flexible as heterosexual parents and therefore are just as capable of providing a permanent home for children as heterosexual parents (Evan B. Donaldson Institute, 2006; Patterson, 1994; Wainwright, Russell, & Patterson, 2004).

Permanency planning is defined as a systematic planning process of setting goal-directed activities designed to help children live within permanent families (i.e., adoptive families, reunification with birth parents, kinship care, or foster care families) that occur within a brief, time-limited period. Permanence is not defined by statute, nor is it determined by the child's attachment relationships. Instead it is defined in terms of *best interest* standards. The best interest standard, derived from US family law (Xu, 2005) and popularized by Goldstein, Freud, and Solnit (1973, 1979), encompasses traditional goals of the physical protection and the psychological well-being of children (Banach, 1998). The best interest standard as determined by a family court is based on a prediction as to which parent and environment is likely to ensure the protection, happiness, and continuity of care for a child.

The *psychological parent*, the parent to whom the child attaches feelings of love, security, and identity, may be a surrogate with whom a child is placed when removed from a biological parent (Goldstein et al., 1973). In legal terms, the psychological parent is considered a *de facto parent*. A de facto parent is someone who has assumed the role of parent on a day-to-day basis, someone who has provided emotional support, has taken care of the child's physical needs, and has given the child affection for a substantial period of time, just as the biological parent would do. The first two case vignettes of John and Kevin and Jessica illustrate the significance of a psychological parent on attachment behaviors and the potential change in the child's attachment bond. In John and Kevin's case, they have become the psychological parents for the three foster children who have been in their care. Similarly, though Jessica is prepared to reunite with her biological children, it appears that her sister has become the psychological parent to the children during Jessica's separation from them.

Despite the relative consensus among professionals working in the family court arena, the meaning of the best interest standard "is highly contested and has been criticized for its vagueness" (Xu, 2005, p. 752). There is no universally recognized operational definition of the best interest standard: "the standard means different things to different people" (Banach, 1998, p. 331). There are no uniform factors to consider in decisions based on best interests. Only limited common guidelines concerning the standard are applied. Some states have adopted statutes that identify factors to be considered by judges, thus limiting judicial discretion. For example, the Uniform Marriage and Divorce Act recommends considering relevant factors, including the wishes of the child's parents and the child's wishes as to his/her custody; the interaction and interrelationship of the child with parents, siblings, and any other person who may significantly affect the child's best interests; the child's adjustment to home, school, and community; and the mental and physical health of all involved individuals (Pruett, Hogan-Bruen, & Jackson, 2000).

Critics of the best interest standard argue that its vagueness and its reliance on judges to evaluate psychological assessments in making abstract decisions about the fate of a child may be influenced by their personal biases. In the third vignette above, Ellen and Elaine's situation illustrates the potential for judicial bias. Elaine is viewed as a psychological parent by her daughter Ann. Yet in the child custody battle between these coparents, there is the possibility Elaine may have her parental rights terminated because she has no legal or biological ties to their child. The judge's opinions about Ann's "best interests" potentially could be biased by his personal views about same-sex parenting. Recently, the American Law Institute (ALI, 2002), a national nonprofit group of lawyers and legal scholars, proposed a number of reforms for a uniform law of child custody. ALI's intent in making reform recommendations is to serve the best interests of children involved in custody disputes (Willemsen, Andrews, Karlin, & Willemsen, 2005). The ALI guidelines provide incentives for parents to design a parenting plan that specifies the custodial and decision-making responsibilities of the parents or other contending parties and mechanisms for resolving future disputes. Failing to reach an agreement, ALI guidelines recommend that the court issue a plan that details residential time, transfer arrangements, and who participates in which decisions about the child(ren) (Willemsen et al., 2005, p. 199).

Another ALI reform, the *approximation rule*, is based on attachment theory. According to the approximation rule, physical custody decisions should be based on the time each parent devoted to caretaking prior to separation. This proposal is intended to avoid the prolonged conflict and uncertainty frequently associated with the best interest test by suggesting that the caregiving and decision-making responsibility allocated within the intact family before its disruption should be roughly the same proportion of the caregiving and decision-making responsibility following family breakup. The approximation rule addresses some of the criticisms of the best interest standard by incorporating observable and identifiable evidence of parent–child attachment into deliberations, thereby reducing the potential for bias in decision-making among judges.

The approximation rule is consistent with attachment theory in three basic areas. First, it recognizes the importance of caregiving. Second, it considers the ability to form attachments with multiple caregivers, and finally, it acknowledges the consistency of attachment relationships (Kelly & Ward, 2002). Supporters of the approximation rule argue that the time spent with a child equals parental ability, emotional security, and security of attachment (Riggs, 2005). However, time spent in caregiving by either parent may be dictated by external factors such as work schedules and work responsibilities, all of which could unfairly favor a stay-at-home parent and discriminate against a working parent. Critics counter-argue that time spent in caregiving may foster the formation of an attachment bond, but it does not necessarily foster a secure bond. An insecure avoidant, resistant/ambivalent, or disorganized attachment bond between the child and a parent may negatively impact child outcomes (Fonagy, 2003; Gauthier, Fortin, & Jeliu, 2004; Putnam, 2005; Teisl & Cicchetti, 2008) as better child outcomes are associated with the child's security in attachment relationships with the parent/caregiver. ALI guidelines also specify a list of factors that cannot be considered by the court when ordering parenting plans. These include "the race or ethnicity of the child, parent, or other household member; the sex of the parent or child; the religious practices of a parent or child; the sexual orientation of the parent; the parent's extramarital sexual conduct; and the parents' relative earning capacity or financial circumstances" (Willemsen et al., 2005, p. 201). Prohibiting these factors from the court's consideration is designed to shorten or eliminate litigation that arises when one parent prolongs the decision-making process because of concerns about the sexual orientation, race, or economic status of the other parent.

Neither the best interest standard nor the approximation rule assumes that attachment behaviors are the sole criteria upon which custody decisions are based. Other factors such as the child's adjustment to the environment and the physical and mental health of all parties involved are given significant consideration as well. Neither standard takes into account the grief and loss that the biological parent, the foster/adoptive, or the noncustodial parent may experience as a result of a separation from the child. These standards are designed to protect the child and not the parent. Few, if any, recourses, including treatment programs, are available to address the attachment loss that biological parents, foster parents, or adoptive parents experience following their separation from a child with whom they have formed a strong attachment bond.

Maternal Incarceration and Attachment

The intersection between child welfare and criminal justice policy, especially prison policy, is illustrated through the second vignette of Jessica, Keith, and Andrea. Jessica's arrest in their home and her later imprisonment created a sudden interruption in her attachment with her two children, placing Keith and Andrea at risk of feelings of abandonment, physical and emotional loss, an interruption in the attachment process and possibly later adverse developmental and mental health outcomes. Similarly, Jessica, who has lost her children, is at high risk of guilt, depression, anxiety disorders, posttraumatic stress disorder, and other serious mental illnesses. The social stigma of parental incarceration exacerbates the psychological and emotional difficulties children experience during separation. The children of incarcerated mothers are often virtually invisible to the professionals who work with children and families (Greenberg, 2006). Yet a growing number of children are affected by maternal incarceration, in part because of mandatory sentencing requirements resulting in longer periods of incarceration that impact low-income women at a higher rate.

According to a Department of Justice special report (Glaze & Maruschak, 2008), an estimated 809,800 inmates in the nation's prisons were parents at midyear 2007. This same report indicates that 52% of state inmates and 63% of federal inmates reported having an estimated 1,706,600 minor children, accounting for 2.3% of the US resident population under age 18. Forty-one percent of women in state prison reported having more than one child, and 36% of those in federal prisons reported having two children on average (Glaze & Maruschak). Women made up 7.2% of the prison population on June 30, 2006, compared with 6.1% at year end 1995 (Sabol, Minton, & Harrison, 2007). The incarcerated mother, in this case Jessica, is in an unfortunate situation of forced or legally mandated separation from her children.

Park and Clarke-Stewart (2003) estimate that one in five children is present at the time of the arrest and witness when their parent is taken away by authorities. According to one report in California (Nieto, 2002), a majority of the law enforcement agencies surveyed did not have a written policy to guide the arresting officers about whether or how they should assume responsibility for the minor children present during a parent's arrest. Communication and coordination between the child protective and law enforcement agencies about how to respond in an arrest situation involving children is often one of the neglected policy areas with detrimental trauma effects for children, including nightmares and flashbacks to the arrest incident. While the way to manage explaining parental arrest and incarceration is controversial, the failure to disclose or maintaining a conspiracy of silence undermines the child's ability to cope and may impact his or her parental attachment bond. Children should be provided with reliable and dependable information that allows them to make sense of their situation, begin to grieve the loss of their parent, and cope with their new life circumstances (Park & Clarke-Stewart, 2003).

For the arrested parent, the immediate and unresolved issues during incarceration are the living arrangements for children during their imprisonment, frequency of visitation or contact with the children during incarceration, and coordination of parenting expectations with the caregivers of the children. Department of Justice data show that mothers in state prisons most commonly identified the child's grandmother (42%) or other relatives (23%) as the current caregiver of their children (Park & Clarke-Stewart, 2003). Kinship providers such as grandparents and other relatives are less likely to separate siblings during a parent's absence and if financially able, are more likely to maintain parental contact. Separation of siblings during maternal incarceration may be especially traumatizing for young children. Some research shows that some siblings, especially if they continue to live together, function as subsidiary attachment figures for each other during a parent's incarceration (Teti & Ablard, 1989). Finally, mothers in prison (11%) were five times more likely than fathers in prison (2%) to report that their children were in the care of a foster home, agency, or institution (Teti & Ablard).

The Adoption and Safe Families Act of 1997 (ASFA) requires states to file for termination of parental rights for children who have been in out-of-home care for 15 of the past 22 months. The aim of this legislation was to create permanency for children by freeing them for adoption, which requires termination of parental rights. Luke (2002) recommends revisiting the concept of permanency, particularly for children of incarcerated mothers. While ASFA and subsequent child welfare laws were designed to address the needs of abused and neglected children and their families, it was not designed for parents in a situation of separation due to incarceration. Children of incarcerated mothers may benefit from maintaining a relationship with an incarcerated mother rather than severing legal connections with the mother and seeking permanency in a new family. Luke further recommends "exempting time spent in jail from the cumulative termination of parental rights timeline for this specific population" (p. 943).

Incarcerated mothers with children in foster care are in jeopardy of losing their parental rights because (1) their past conduct may imply parental unfitness, (2) imprisonment does not allow them to perform their parental duties, and (3) imprisonment restricts access to the services required to fulfill the case plan for reunification with their children. Sametz (1980) indicates that the basis of court custody decisions should include the fitness of the mother and the *best interest* or the *least detrimental interests* of the child. The best interest standard refers to the child's physical well-being and overall welfare, while the least detrimental interest means the alternative that would have the least long-term negative impact on the child and safeguards the child's growth and development. The key principles associated with the least detrimental alternative are (1) the child's sense of time and (2) continuity of care. The first principle places emphasis on the child's age. The younger the child, the more urgent the need for permanent placement. The second principle underscores the importance stability plays in the development of secure parent–child relationships (Goldstein, Solnit, Goldstein, & Freud, 1996). The court's use of this alternative standard maximizes placement according to the child's biological and emotional needs and acknowledges the court's limited ability to predict the child's future relationship with an adult who is not the biological parent. The least detrimental interest standard views the rights of all parties on an equal basis, rather than weighting the child's rights against the adult's rights. The maintenance of a stable, intimate parent–child relationship may be in the best interests of the child. The least detrimental standard is more likely to be evoked in those circumstances where the child is younger and there is sufficient evidence to suggest an attachment bond has been formed with a psychological parent.

Maintaining contact between the incarcerated parent and the child is challenging even though face-to-face contact between the female prisoners and their children is likely to result in more positive maternal perceptions of the mother–child relationship and likely ease the child's fears (Poehlmann, Shlafer, Maes, & Hanneman, 2008). The barriers affecting visitation include distance (jails and prisons are frequently located in remote geographic areas), costs associated with transportation, lack of child-appropriate visitation space, inconvenient visiting hours, prison rules regarding physical contact with visitors, including children, and a reluctance to expose children to the prison setting (Young & Smith, 2000). In addition, prison rules about who is eligible to visit, the number of visitors, the physical layout of the visiting room, and lack of privacy deter family visitations (Park & Clarke-Stewart, 2003). Although telephone contact occurs more frequently than visits, according to some research, this method of contact has less meaning for young children, and prison policies on telephone privileges vary. Some prisons allow inmates to place outgoing telephone calls if they are billed to the receiver – a cost to caregiver families that may become a potential barrier to maintaining attachment relationships between the parent and child and the parent and the caregiver.

Communication between kinship providers and incarcerated mothers about parenting expectations is necessary for the continuity of care for children. However, the relationship between the caregiver and the incarcerated parent is often strained and accompanied by anger about the imprisoned parent's action, resentment, guilt, disappointment, and the demands of providing care for children. For the incarcerated mother, there is guilt, low self-esteem, increased levels of stress directly attributed to child separation, doubts about parenting skills, and fear of losing attachment to the child. Park and Clarke-Stewart (2003) indicate that several women's prisons have developed visiting programs for inmates that feature special play areas for parents and children, extended visits, flexibility in scheduling visits, and special housing for children in the institution. The Sesame Street program opened special playrooms adjacent to the visitation room in a number of prisons where children can participate in educational and entertaining activities when they become restless. The Girl Scouts Beyond Bars Program provides transportation for children and regular Scout troop meetings for mothers and daughters at the prison. Girls participate in other regular Girl Scout activities such as field trips and meetings without their mothers and some offer counseling services to girls as well (Park & Clarke-Stewart). In addition, many correctional facilities have instituted interventions such as prisoner parenting programs for incarcerated parents. These programs range from prison infant nurseries, parent education classes, and supportive and therapeutic services (see Young & Smith, 2000, for descriptions of these programs). Loper and Tuerk (2006) recommend including issues related to the caregiver in prisoner parenting training programs, in order to offer guidance to inmates about the stressors in the caregivers' experience. Such training would help incarcerated mothers empathize and establish more realistic expectations about the caregiver's parenting role. The skills to be taught in this training include relationship building and communication skills.

Child Custody, Lesbian and Gay Parents, and Attachment

When same-sex couples coparent and then end their relationship, like Ellen and Elaine in the third vignette, child custody and visitation rights are much more complicated. The central legal question in such cases is "who has the most legitimate claim to be the parent of the child?" (Hare & Skinner, 2008, p. 367). The best interest of the child principle applies in cases such as these, though it may be applied in different ways. The circumstances that might lead to custody disputes involving gay couples include those between a former spouse and a formerly married parent now identified as homosexual; the biological and nonbiological mothers in a gay couple who had agreed to coparent following adoption or artificial insemination, but subsequently separate; or a gay custodial parent and some other caregiver who would qualify as a psychological parent (Willemsen et al., 2005). The effect of a parent's homosexual relationship on custody decisions varies from state to state. In these cases, the prevailing community attitudes regarding homosexuality have everything to do with what happens to children. In such circumstances, the court imposes one of two legal approaches in denying custody: the *nexus* approach or the *per se* approach. Since state laws vary, some require evidence that the parent's conduct as lesbian or gay is harmful to the child (Stein, 1996). In these instances the court only considers a parent's homosexuality if there is evidence to show that it is harmful to the child. The nexus approach places the burden on the nonhomosexual parent to show or prove that the child is being harmed by parental behavior (Willemsen et al., 2005). Interestingly, if two lesbian or gay parents separate, the courts frequently revert to the biology approach, wherein the parental rights of the partner who conceived and bore the child are recognized and no rights of the other lesbian or gay parent are heard in court. The homosexuality of the two women or men is usually ignored if the *biology wins* approach is invoked (Willemsen et al.).

Conversely, the per se approach can be used in custody disputes involving a gay parent. In some jurisdictions, the court appears to presume that homosexuality is a reason to deny custody. The court may or may not presume that the parent is an unfit parent, but instead presumes that sexual conduct inherent in lesbian or gay lifestyles is "an important consideration in determining a mother's [or father's] fitness for custody of the child" (Stein, 1996, p. 441). When courts categorically apply a per se approach and ignore existing evidence that counters stereotypes, the decision is little more than state-sanctioned discrimination and does not reflect the spirit of the best interest standard (Stein). The ALI proposed guidelines would greatly reduce the application of the nexus and per se approaches to resolving custody disputes involving gay parents.

Gay and lesbian parents who separate have few of the protections offered by legal marriage. In the last 5 years, however, there have been significant developments in advancing gay marriage. By the end of 2009, gay marriage had been legalized in five states (Massachusetts, Connecticut, Vermont, New Hampshire, and Iowa) and the District of Columbia, with six additional states (California, Maine, New Jersey, Nevada, Oregon, and Washington) offering legal alternatives known as civil unions or domestic partnerships (Human Rights Campaign, 2010a). With these developments, presumably the courts will approach custody decisions involving gay and lesbian parents who separate using the best interest standard in the same manner as they do heterosexual couples. In doing so, the attachment bonds between same-sex couples and their children will receive the same consideration in custody disputes as given to heterosexual couples who end their relationships. In short, the parent–child attachment bond in same-sex relationships will be granted greater significance in custody decisions than the parent's sexual conduct.

Military Service and Attachment

The most common situations that affect attachment relationships and family life among military personnel include "domestic and international relocation, deployment and family separation, and the reunion and reorganization of families after separation" (Drummet, Coleman, & Cable, 2003, p. 280). Prior research indicates that approximately one third of military families relocate annually. Among military families, international moves are four times higher than in the general population, and longer distances are required for domestic moves of military families than those experienced by nonmilitary families. Deployment, which is distinctly different from relocation because it seldom involves the family unit, occurs on average for a total of 15 months or less annually. Reunification of families following a military separation or deployment involves a great deal of adjustment. Renegotiating family roles, boundaries, household management, social supports, parental rejection and anxiety, and the physical and mental toll on family service members are the most frequently cited stressors during family reunion.

The fourth case vignette of 32-year-old Elizabeth illustrates one way military service affects family life. A child's attachment behavior is built from experiences of their primary caregiver's reliable availability and responsiveness to their signals. This early relationship functions as a secure base that the child uses to explore and develop competence in new activities. Although interruptions in this relationship bond due to separation are important, they are less crucial if the attachment figure is perceived as available and responsive to the child's needs (Schneider, 1991). Recent research (van IJzendoorn & Sagi-Schwartz, 2008), as well as Ainsworth's (1973) initial research in Uganda, suggests that children can develop attachment relationships with other caregivers, though the child's internal working models are formed from the relationship with the principle attachment figure. Elizabeth's case vignette focuses attention on the effects of separation on the child's attachment behaviors, especially when these separations are long and the reunions are complicated by the principle attachment figure's emotional availability upon return. In times of war, returning soldiers are frequently distracted by symptoms of posttraumatic stress that include nightmares, flashbacks, withdrawal from activities, and detachment from others (Drummet et al., 2003), which undoubtedly affects the attachment figure's availability and responsiveness to the child's needs.

Women constitute roughly 15% of the armed services. According to a 2002 report by the Government Accountability Office, as many as one in ten active duty women become pregnant each year. Until July 2009, all branches of the military gave servicewomen 6 weeks maternity leave before they were called back to service. But according to a National Public Radio broadcast (Mann, 2008), if servicewomen are headed into a war zone, they are required, depending on the branch of the military they serve, to deploy as early as 4 months after their babies are born. Each of the four military services has a different policy on post-birth deployment deferment for military mothers. The Army, for example, has the longest deployments (averaging 15 months), and the shortest deployment deferments for servicewomen (only 4 months). In July 2009, the Army announced a change in policy, lengthening the current deployment deferment period to 6 months for military mothers of newborns and soldiers adopting a child. The policy applies to women in the military who are new mothers, single soldiers who adopt a child, or to one member of a dual-military couple who adopts a child. The deferment period begins on the date the child is born or placed in the home as part of the adoption process.

Military deployment practices in Elizabeth's case play a central role in her predicament. Shortly after the September 11 attacks in the USA and the beginning of the Iraq War, Secretary of Defense Robert Gates implemented a policy that extended deployment from 12 to 15 months to ensure an adequate number of military personnel in Iraq and Afghanistan, continuity in leadership, cohesion within military units, and retention of soldiers with the skills needed in these units. In effect, active military and reservists were required to serve an extra 3 months during each deployment overseas. At the same time, "dwell time" – the time at home between deployments – was less than ideal. "The Army and Marine Corps both aim for a period at home that is equal to about twice the amount of time deployed, but neither have achieved that yet" (Lubold, 2009, csmonitor.com/2009/0320/p03s05-usmi.html). Coupled with this, the Bush Administration activated an executive order (known as the "stop loss policy," signed in 1990) that authorized the Defense Secretary to hold onto and/or bring discharged or retired military personnel deemed essential to national security back into service. The stop loss policy kept soldiers in service if their units were deployed within 90 days of the end of the soldier's enlistment contract. Officials report that the time soldiers were held on in service averaged 5–8 months (Jelinek, 2009). Critics, as well as Secretary Gates, call the stop loss policy a back-door draft that keeps troops in the military beyond the end of their enlistment or retirement dates (Jelinek). The stop loss policy also meant that soldiers who had planned to remain in service, but who intended to change positions within the military or attend a military school, were unable to do so (Shanker, 2009).

Estimates are that 1% of the Army's forces have been affected by the forced extensions. As of January 2009, roughly 13,000 soldiers have been prevented from leaving the service, including 7,300 active duty Army soldiers, about 4,450 in the Guard and 1,450 reservists (Jelinek, 2009). Some have indicated that as many as 185,000 troops had been affected by the stop loss policy since the September 11, 2001 terrorist attacks. On March 18, 2009, Secretary Gates announced plans to suspend the unpopular stop loss policy, cutting the number of soldiers forced to stay in service by half by mid-2010 and eliminating the policy altogether by March 2011 (Lubold, 2009). Veterans groups praised the change in policy.

Military policies governing maternity leave have a direct effect on the formation of a mother–child attachment bond during infancy. Ainsworth (1968), who identified five phases of the attachment process, found that newborns between 8 weeks and 6 months of age show signs of knowing and preferring their mothers. The infant at birth through 8 weeks behaves in characteristic ways toward people, but is unable to discriminate one person from another. A 6-week (i.e., 1½ months) maternity leave for military personnel is insufficient time for the newborn to form an attachment bond with her mother based on Ainsworth's (1973) research. Under the Family and Medical Leave Act (1994), parents are allowed 12 weeks maternity leave without pay – far more than that offered to military personnel. The more time a caregiver has to develop an attachment relationship with an infant, the better. A 12-week maternal leave allows a greater opportunity to establish consistency and continuity in caregiving, thereby increasing the likelihood of a secure attachment bond between caregiver and infant.

Disruptions in attachment bonds due to deployment policies, especially those that are extended beyond the normal 12 month deployment, also potentially have detrimental effects on parent–child and adult attachment relationships, as evidenced by the re-entry difficulties experienced by soldiers returning from the Iraq and Afghanistan wars. Among the psychological difficulties returning soldiers face are posttraumatic stress in the form of reoccurring nightmares, flashbacks, and hyper-arousal, suppression of emotions, isolation, mistrust of others, shame, irritability, and survivor guilt. Symptoms of this nature are compounded among female returning vets, making attachment issues more prominent for parent–child and adult attachments. These psychological challenges impact the consistency, stability, and continuity of adult attachment bonds, as well as parent–child attachments. Although cognitive behavioral interventions have been used with returning soldiers, they do not affect attachment relationship problems as well as other interventions.

Elder Care and Attachment

Interestingly, each of the case vignettes described in this paper addresses different aspects of caregiving, though formal definitions of the term seldom refer to the care of young children. According to Moroney (1998): "Caregiving is a human service transaction that is built on a relationship between caregivers and care recipients. There is a process of communication through which resources are transferred and through which the emotional process of caring develops" (p. 50). His definition implicitly suggests that an essential element of caregiving involves attachment, since he defines it as an "emotional process." This process is not limited to the caregiving of parents to young children, however. It may also involve instances in which the care provider is an adult child and the care receiver is an elderly parent, as portrayed in the fifth vignette of Alana. "Caregiving is not only a form of labor; it constitutes a relationship" (Garey, Hansen, Hertz, & MacDonald, 2002, p. 709), with a multiplicity of emotional dimensions ranging from anger, guilt, resentment, love, pity, sympathy, embarrassment, frustration, shame, grief, and disappointment. In Alana's case, one can imagine the anger, resentment, pity, and sympathy she may feel toward her mother and the mother's feelings of embarrassment, frustration, shame, grief, and disappointment that she is no longer able to care for herself in the manner to which she had become accustomed.

The Alana vignette is illustrative of the thousands of other adult children today who are caring for elderly parents. The percentage of older adults in the country is expected to double between now and 2030, and given the state of US medical care, the elderly will continue to live longer; some will live healthier active lives, while others will become frail and increasingly dependent on family members and the larger society. "It is predicted that by the middle of the twenty-first century, a majority of the US population will be over the age of 65 and many may need family and institutional care" (Beckett, 2008, p. 5).

Fortunately, efforts to protect the integrity, health, and welfare of older adults began as early as 1935 with the passage of the Social Security Act. The Act is the largest cash assistance program in the USA, providing benefits to some 46 million people and covering more than 154 million workers. To be eligible for Old Age Survivors Disability benefits, workers must have contributed to the fund through a payroll tax for a minimum of 40 quarters (10 years). Through monthly cash payments, retired workers like Alana's mother are assured a minimally secure income. Along with a basic income source, the 1965 Social Security Amendments establishing the Medicare program, some 40 million seniors are assured medical care for a minimal deductible for hospital coverage and a premium for the cost of physician fees. Other policies in the area of housing provide low income housing for the elderly. To round out income, health and housing services, the Older American Act also passed in 1965 provides funding for senior citizen centers, transportation, homemaker, home health care, and nutrition programs.

Family caregivers have received far less attention than they deserve. Twenty-two percent of caregivers are assisting two individuals, while 8% are caring for three or more. Almost half of all caregivers are over age 50, making them more vulnerable to a decline in their own health, and one-third describe their own health as fair to poor (http://www.aoa.gov/AoARoot/AOA_Programs/HCLTC/Caregiver/index.aspx#purpose). Often these 50-year-old and older caregivers, caught between raising their own children and caring for elderly family members, respond emotionally to changes and demands that occur as they give help and support to the older person, a phenomena referred to as caregiver burden. Caregiver burden encompasses all of the stressors associated with being a care provider. Recognizing the effects of caregiver burden, the National Family Caregiver Support Program was established in 2000 providing $125 million of federal funding to state offices of aging. The program offers access to information, education, counseling, support groups, daytime and overnight respite services through adult day care, residential care and other options to family caregivers of elders. "Despite an increasing availability of caregiver supports in all 50 states, there is also a great unevenness in services and service options for family caregivers across the states and within states" (Feinberg & Newman, 2006, p. 95).

The lack of sufficient services to assist with the care of the elderly and their care providers is one of many factors that have lead to an increase in elder abuse. An estimated 2.1 million elderly Americans are victims of physical, psychological, or other forms of abuse and neglect (American Psychological Association, n. d.). All 50 states have enacted legislation regarding elder abuse prevention. While there is considerable variation in the provisions of these laws and their definitions of elder abuse, all 50 states have systems for reporting elder abuse. Elder abuse is described as the willful infliction of physical pain or injury, sexual abuse, mental or emotional anguish, financial or material exploitation, neglect on the part of a caregiver, or behavior of an elder that threatens his/her own health or safety (self-neglect). Adult protective service (APS) agencies receive and screen reports of suspected elder abuse and assign a case worker to conduct an investigation of the report to substantiate the allegation. If the allegations are substantiated and the elder agrees or has not been declared incapacitated by the court and a guardian has been appointed, APS works with community agencies to provide services that ensure the safety and health of the elder. A 1998 National Elder Abuse Incidence Study (US Department of Health and Human Services) funded by Administration on Aging (AOA) found that 551,011 persons aged 60 and over experienced abuse, neglect, and/or self-neglect in a 1-year period and that in 90% of the cases, the perpetrator was a family member.

Caregiving, as indicated previously, involves an ability to form an adult relationship with the elderly that may be associated with adult attachment style (see Bennett, Sheridan, and Soniat, Chap. 8). For example, Hazan and Shaver (1990) found that "adult attachment style predicts adult relationship styles" (Austrian, 2008, p. 398). They found that adults with a secure style find found it easy to get close to others, were comfortable depending on others, and comfortable having others depend on them. Conversely, adults with avoidant attachment styles were uncomfortable with closeness, avoid intimacy, and found it hard to trust or depend on others, while those with anxious ambivalent attachment styles found that others were reluctant to get close to them even though they sought unqualified closeness, commitment, and affection. These findings suggest that individuals with avoidant or anxious ambivalent attachment styles are far less likely to form effective adult relationships and thus are likely to be less effective caregivers to the elderly.

Discussion

Five case vignettes were used to illustrate policy implications of attachment processes affecting adults. The cases are fairly typical of the circumstances in which policies in child welfare, military service, criminal justice, elder services, and gay and lesbian families touch the lives of adults. Analyses of legislative, administrative and judicial standards differ. In the case of legislation governing child welfare and elder services, it is fairly common to assess their impact using criteria such as *equity*, *equality*, and *adequacy*. Equity refers to a conventional sense of fair treatment. It is defined as the extent to which "situations in similar circumstances are dealt with similarly" (Flynn, 1985, p. 54). Using equity as an evaluation criterion, one would expect that attachment issues in the case of an incarcerated mother would be handled in a similar fashion as in the case of any other parent who has been separated from a child for other reasons such as neglect or physical abuse. In both instances, the child's return would be dependent upon the parent's ability to fulfill the requirements specified in a case plan.

What, if anything, makes the circumstances that lead to the separations in these two situations different? In both situations, a forced separation has occurred; in one instance the separation happens because of the intervention by a law enforcement agency and in the other the separation has been forced by a child welfare agency acting on behalf of the state. While the reasons leading to the separation differ, it is the parent's access and ability to fulfill the conditions under which the child may be returned that differs. If child welfare services are equitable, then all children should receive the same combination of services, should exit, and should achieve permanency at the same rate (Chipungu, 1997). Children of incarcerated mothers are unlikely to receive services, exit, or achieve permanency at the same rate as children of parents who abuse or neglect them. Incarcerated parents are unable to comply with the conditions specified in the case plan and are therefore more likely to have their parental rights and attachment relationship terminated. Their experience suggests that the legislation is inequitable.

Equality implies the same treatment to all, however as Gilbert and Terrell (2005) point out, a distinction must be made between numerical and proportional equality. *Numerical equality* implies that all receive an equal share (i.e., the same treatment of everyone), while *proportional equality* implies the same treatment of all who are similar – "to each according to merit or virtue" (p. 79). For example, numerical equality would require that the attachment styles of all adults be treated in the same way, while proportional equality would require that the attachment styles of anxious ambivalent, avoidant, or secure adults be treated differently to achieve overall equality. While the distinction is somewhat subtle, the implications can have significant effects on the distribution of services and benefits for adult caregivers of the elderly. For adult caregivers with secure attachment styles, the National Family Caregiver Support Program might be enormously beneficial, but for adult caregivers with anxious ambivalent or avoidant attachment styles, more intensive services may be required. Because no such distinction is made in the provision of support groups, daytime or overnight respite services available through the National Family Caregiver Support Program, the impact of the program is uneven. The issue of equity can also be applied to child welfare laws. Current child welfare law imposes the same timelines for termination of parental rights after separation for a set period of time regardless of circumstances. The implementation of the law treats all parents the same, yet a case could be made that the court exempt time spent in jail or prison from the cumulative timeline for terminating parental rights in cases involving the incarceration of mothers, thereby increasing the proportional equality in child welfare legislation. Using equality as an evaluation criterion requires an assessment of the sameness in the distribution of services to all, as well as the sameness of services to those with similar characteristics. The attachments between adult children and their elderly parents have been until recently completely ignored, and even with the passage of legislation designed to offer some assistance, the policy does not fully acknowledge the significance of these attachment relationships.

Adequacy, another evaluation criterion, is defined as the degree to which the benefits provided meet some predetermined level. For example, are Social Security benefits adequate to ensure economic sufficiency for the elderly and disabled? Since the number of elders living below the poverty line has decreased over the years, it would appear that benefits are adequate. The range of services available to parents separated from their children due to neglect, abuse or incarceration is inadequate, largely because waiting lists for public housing, substance abuse treatment, counseling, and other services are so long that it causes delays in the provision of services and frequently results in the termination of parental rights and permanent disruptions in the parent–child attachment relationship. Adequacy is an appropriate criterion for evaluating the effects of administrative standards such as military deployment and maternal leave. Previous descriptions of these standards in relation to attachment issues show their detrimental effects on the parent–child and other adult attachment relationships. The attachment issues that arise for women in the military with children are compromised by the conflict between the interests of the child and those that pertain to protecting the military interests of the country. These interests collide and are only now being addressed with more liberal policies.

Chambers (2005) has proposed that evaluation of the effect of judicial rulings and standards, such as the best interest standard, requires a different set of evaluation criteria that should include the following;

1. "The extent to which the judicial decision is a departure from legislation passed by a freely elected assembly
2. The extent to which the decision concerns a due process or procedural issue or a substantive policy issue
3. The extent to which the decision represents a departure from prior judicial precedent
4. The extent to which the court delegated the responsibility to other agencies or officials or took responsibility to make general policy to create their own." (p. 45)

It would appear that custody decisions categorically based on the per se approach, such as cases involving gay or lesbian partners who separate, constitute what might be considered a departure from prior judicial precedent, in that they allows the court to act on the basis of personal or community bias. Such bias ignores existing evidence that counteracts stereotypes about lesbian and gay parents and sanctions discrimination. State sanctioned discrimination in these cases may be more likely to occur because these couples do not have the legal protections associated with marriage. State laws and judicial decision-making standards make it difficult to recognize the attachment relationships among these couples.

Conclusion

The five case vignettes discussed in this chapter – far from an exhaustive collection of possible illustrations – demonstrate the lack of equity, equality, and adequacy inherent in many policies that impact attachment relationships in contemporary American families. This situation likely exists because attachment behavior is not generally the salient factor in the policies that affect adult family relationships. While the well-being of the child in judicial decision-making and agency practice *does* consider attachment relationships, attachment is not *explicitly* considered the primary goal or objective. Issues of the fitness of the mother, the interests of the adult, and the best interests of the child converge, sometimes resulting in a breach in the mother–child attachment relationship. Resolving the conflicting interests that arise in custody decisions within foster care and adoptive families, lesbian and gay families, and families with incarcerated mothers, as well as current policies regarding military deployment and elder care, may require a reexamination of all the aspects of family law. Exceeding the scope of this chapter, such a reexamination should be based on a new set of premises that takes the significance of attachment behaviors of adults and children into account. With that objective in mind, a closer examination of the equity, equality, and adequacy inherent in policies impacting families might prevent what Bowlby (1988) suggested was a "great danger" in our society of adopting "mistaken norms" that ignore attachments and, consequently, provide "…a chronic insufficiency of help" (pp. 2–3) to families in need.

Study Questions

1. What are the key elements of the best interest standard and why do some criticize it?
2. What arguments might you present to the court about the importance of the non-custodial gay parent's attachment relationship to a child in a custody hearing?
3. Some have advocated revisiting the concept of permanency, particularly for children of incarcerated mothers. What if any modifications might you recommend for the timelines established in the Adoption and Safe Families Act regarding the termination of parental rights?
4. A recent case illustrates the conflicting situation women in the military sometimes encounter. Alexis Hutchinson refused to report for deployment to Afghanistan. Hutchinson is a single mother of an infant and was unable to find suitable care for her son before she was deployed. She had initially turned to her own mother who found it impossible to care for the child because of prior caregiver commitments. Without reasonable accommodations, Hutchinson chose not to deploy. Hutchinson's son was temporally placed in foster care, and she faces charges and possible jail time. What are your opinions of the case? Should Alexis' child be placed in foster care? What are the implications for parent–child attachment?
5. Identify a social policy that affects attachment relationships and analyze its effects using the concepts of equity and equality.

References

Ainsworth, M. (1968). Object relations, dependency, and attachment: A theoretical view of the infant-mother relationship. *Child Development, 40*, 969–1025.
Ainsworth, M. (1973). The development of infant-mother attachment. In J. L. Gewirtz (Ed.), *Attachment and dependency* (pp. 97–137). Washington, DC: V. H. Winston.

American Law Institute (ALI). (2002). *Principles of the law of family dissolution: Analysis and recommendations*. Newark, NJ: LexisNexis.

American Psychological Association. (n.d.) *Elder abuse and neglect: In search of solutions*. Retrieved from http://www.apa.org/pi/aging/eldabuse.html

Austrian, S. (2008). *Developmental theories through the life cycle* (2nd ed.). New York, NY: Columbia University Press.

Banach, M. (1998). The best interests of the child: Decision-making factors. *Families in Society, 79*(3), 331–339.

Beckett, J. (2008). *Lifting our voices: The journeys into family caregiving of professional social workers*. New York, NY: Columbia University Press.

Bowlby, J. (1951). *Maternal care and mental health*. Geneva: World Health Organization.

Bowlby, J. (1958). The nature of the child's tie to his mother. *International Journal of Psycho-Analysis, 39*, 350–373.

Bowlby, J. (1969/1982). *Attachment and loss: Vol. 1. Attachment*. New York, NY: Basic Books.

Bowlby, J. (1988). *A secure base: Parent-child attachment and healthy human development*. New York, NY: Basic Books.

Chambers, D. (2005). *Social policy and social programs: A method for the practical public policy analyst* (4th ed.). New York, NY: Macmillan Publishing.

Child Welfare League of America (CWLA). (2009). *National Data Analysis System*. Retrieved from http://ndas.cwla.org/data_stats/access/predefined/Report.asp

Chipungu, S. (1997). A value-based policy framework. In J. Everett, B. Leashore, & S. Chipungu (Eds.), *Child welfare: An africentric perspective* (pp. 290–305). New Brunswick, NJ: Rutgers University Press.

Drummet, A., Coleman, M., & Cable, S. (2003). Military families under stress: Implications for family life education. *Family Relations, 52*(3), 279–287.

Evan B. Donaldson Institute (March, 2006). *Expanding resources for children: Is adoption by gays and lesbians part of the answer for boys and girls who need homes?* Retrieved from http://www.adoptioninstitute.org/publications/2006

Feinberg, L., & Newman, D. (2006). Preliminary experiences of the states in implementing the National Family Caregiver Support Program: A 50-state study. *Journal of Aging and Social Policy, 18*(3), 95–113.

Flynn, J. (1985). *Social agency policy: Analysis and presentation for community practice*. Chicago, IL: Nelson-Hall.

Fonagy, P. (2003). The development of psychopathology from infancy to adulthood: The mysterious unfolding of disturbance in time. *Infant Mental Health Journal, 24*(3), 212–239.

Garey, A., Hansen, K., Hertz, R., & MacDonald, C. (2002). Care and kinship: An introduction. *Journal of Family Issues, 23*(6), 703–712.

Gauthier, Y., Fortin, G., & Jeliu, G. (2004). Clinical application of attachment theory in permanency planning for children in foster care: The importance of continuity of care. *Infant Mental Health Journal, 25*(4), 379–396.

Gilbert, N., & Terrell, P. (2005). *Dimensions of social welfare policy* (6th ed.). Boston, MA: Pearson.

Glaze, L., & Maruschak, L. (2008). *Parents in prison and their minor children (NCJ 222984)*. Washington, DC: US Department of Justice.

Goldstein, J., Freud, A., & Solnit, A. (1973). *Beyond the best interests of the child*. New York, NY: Free Press.

Goldstein, J., Freud, A., & Solnit, A. (1979). *Before the best interests of the child*. New York, NY: Free Press.

Goldstein, J., Solnit, A., Goldstein, S., & the Estate of Anna Freud. (1996). *Best interests of the child. The least detrimental alternative*. New York, NY: Free Press.

Government Accountability Office. (2002, September 18). *Military personnel: Active duty benefits reflect changing demographics, but opportunities exist to improve* (GAO Publication No. GAO-02-935). Washington, DC: Government Printing Office.

Greenberg, R. (2006). Children and families: Mothers who are incarcerated. *Women and Therapy, 29*(3/4), 165–179.

Hare, J., & Skinner, D. (2008). "Whose child is this?": Determining legal status for lesbian parents who used assisted reproductive technologies. *Family Relations, 57*(3), 365–375.

Hazan, C., & Shaver, P. (1990). Love and work: An attachment-theoretical perspective. *Journal of Personality and Social Psychology, 52*(3), 511–524.

Human Rights Campaign (HRC). (2010a). *Marriage equality and other relationship recognition laws*. Retrieved from http://www.hrc.org/documents/Relationship_Recognition_Laws_Map.pdf

Human Rights Campaign (HRC). (2010b). *Parenting laws: Joint adoption*. Retrieved from http://www.hrc.org/documents/parenting_laws_maps.pdf

Jelinek, P. (2009, March 18). Pentagon phasing out "stop-loss" policy. *Huffington Post*. Retrieved from http://www.huffingtonpost.com

Kelly, R., & Ward, S. (2002). Allocating custodial responsibilities at divorce: Social science research and the American Law Institute's approximation rule. *Family Court Review, 40*(3), 350–370.

Kenyon, G., Chong, K., Enkoff-Sage, M., Hill, C., Mays, C., & Rochelle, L. (2003). Public adoption by gay and lesbian parents in North Carolina: Policy and Practice. *Families in Society, 84*(4), 571–575.

Loper, A., & Tuerk, E. (2006). Parenting programs for incarcerated parents: Current research and future directions. *Criminal Justice Policy Review, 17*(4), 407–427.

Lubold, G. (2009, March 20). Gates lightens load for war-worn forces. *Christian Science Monitor*. Retrieved from http://www.csmonitor.com

Luke, K. (2002). Mitigating the ill effects of maternal incarceration on women in prison and their children. *Child Welfare, 81*(6), 929–948.

Mann, B. (2008, May 26) Military moms face tough choices. *National Public Radio*. Retrieved http://www.npr.org

Moroney, R. (1998). *Caring and competent caregivers*. Athens, GA: University of Georgia Press.

Moye, J., & Rinker, R. (2002). It's a hard knock life: Does the Adoption and Safe Families Act of 1997 adequately address problems in the child welfare system. *Harvard Journal on Legislation, 39*(2), 375–394.

Nieto, M. (2002). *In danger of falling through the cracks: Children of arrested parents*. Sacramento, CA: California Research Bureau, California State Library.

Park, R., & Clarke-Stewart, A. (2003). The effects of parental incarceration on children: Perspectives, promises and policies. In J. Travis & M. Waul (Eds.), *Prisoners once removed* (pp. 189–232). Washington, DC: The Urban Institute Press.

Patterson, C. (1994). Children of the lesbian baby boom: Behavioral adjustments, self-concepts and sex role identity. In B. Green & G. M. Herek (Eds.), *Lesbian and gay psychology: Theory, research and clinical applications* (pp. 156–75). Thousand Oaks, CA: Sage.

Pecora, P., Whittaker, J., & Maluccio, A. (1992). *The child welfare challenge: Policy, practice and research*. New York, NY: Aldine de Gruyter Publishers.

Poehlmann, J., Shlafer, R., Maes, E., & Hanneman, A. (2008). Factors associated with young children's opportunities for maintaining family relationships during maternal incarceration. *Family Relations, 57*, 267–280.

Pruett, M., Hogan-Bruen, K., & Jackson, T. (2000). The best interests of the child: Parents' versus attorney's perspectives. *Journal of Divorce & Remarriage, 33*(1/2), 47–63.

Putnam, F. (2005). The developmental neurobiology of disrupted attachment: Lessons from animal models and child abuse research. In L. Berlin, Y. Ziv, L. Amaya-Jackson, & M. Greenberg (Eds.), *Enhancing early attachments: Theory, research, intervention, and policy* (pp. 79–99). New York, NY: Guilford Press.

Riggs, S. (2005). Is the approximation rule in the child's best interests? A critique from the perspective of attachment theory. *Family Court Review, 43*(3), 481–493.

Robertson, J., & Robertson, J. (1971). Young children in brief separation: A fresh look. *Psychoanalytic Study of the Child, 26*, 264–315.

Rutter, M. (2008). Implications of attachment theory and research for child care policies. In J. Cassidy & P. Shaver (Eds.), *Handbook of attachment: Theory, research, and clinical applications* (2nd ed., pp. 958–974). New York, NY: Guilford Press.

Ryan, S., Pearlmutter, S., & Groza, V. (2004). Coming out of the closet: Opening agencies to gay and lesbian adoptive parents. *Social Work, 49*(1), 85–95.

Sabol, W., Minton, T., & Harrison, P. (2007). Prison and jail inmates at midyear 2006. *Bureau of Justice Statistics Bulletin (NCJ 217675)*. Washington, DC: US Department of Justice.

Sametz, L. (1980). Children of incarcerated women. *Social Work, 25*(4), 298–303.

Schneider, E. L. (1991). Attachment theory and research: Review of the literature. *Clinical Social Work Journal, 19*(3), 251–266.

Shanker, T. (2009, March 18). 'Stop-loss' will all but end by 2011, Gates says. *The New York Times*. Retrieved from http://www.nytimes.com

Stein, T. (1996). Child custody and visitation: The rights of lesbian and gay parents. *Social Service Review, 70*(3), 435–450.

Teisl, M., & Cicchetti, D. (2008). Physical abuse, cognitive and emotional processes, and aggressive/disruptive behavior problems. *Social Development, 17*(1), 1–23.

Teti, D., & Ablard, K. (1989). Security of attachment and infant-sibling relationships: A laboratory study. *Child Development, 60*, 1519–1528.

U. S. Department of Health and Human Services. (1998). *National Elder Abuse Incidence Study. (Grant No. 90-AM-0660)*. Washington, DC: U.S. Government Printing Office.

van IJzendoorn, M., & Sagi-Schwartz, A. (2008). Cross-cultural patterns of attachment: Universal and contextual dimensions. In J. Cassidy & P. Shaver (Eds.), *The handbook of attachment: Theory, research, and clinical applications* (2nd ed., pp. 880–905). New York, NY: Guilford Press.

Wainwright, J., Russell, S. T., & Patterson, C. J. (2004). Psychosocial adjustment, school outcomes, and romantic relationships of adolescents with same-sex parents. *Child Development, 75*(6), 1886–1898.

Welte, C. (1997). *Detailed summary of the Adoption and Safe Families Act*. Retrieved from http://www.casanet.org/references/asfa-summary.htm

Willemsen, E., Andrews, R., Karlin, B., & Willemsen, M. (2005). The ethics of the child custody process: Are the American Law Institute's guidelines the answer? *Child and Adolescent Social Work Journal, 22*(2), 183–211.

Xu, Q. (2005). In the "best interest" of immigrant and refugee children: Deliberating on their unique circumstances. *Child Welfare, 84*(5), 747–770.

Young, D., & Smith, C. (2000). When moms are incarcerated: The needs of children, mothers, and caregivers. *Families in Society, 81*(2), 130–142.

Chapter 12
Attachment Research: Contributions of Social Workers

Joanna E. Bettmann and Rachael A. Jasperson

> *Currently, attachment theory and research are moving forward along several major fronts, inspired by...methodological advances, and by the infusion into attachment theory of complementary theoretical perspectives.*

> Bretherton (1992, p. 26)

Attachment theory and research have created exciting new ways for clinical social workers to bridge understanding of human development and clinical work, particularly in the area of early relational experiences that influence personality development and disrupt healthy psychological development (Bowlby, 1947). Early social work interest in attachment theory focused on understanding the influence of the mother–child relationship on the child's overall emotional and psychological development, with particular interest on foster home placements, traumatic separations from parents, and child neglect and abuse. In the 1970s, attachment theorists generally began to integrate a clinical approach, and around this time attachment articles began to appear in the social work literature (McMillen, 1992). Shortly thereafter, social work scholars also began to design, implement, and publish attachment-focused research, including research related to adult attachment.

Much of social work attachment research aims at increasing insight in order to advance casework and treatment applications. Ranging from foster care placement to the treatment of psychopathology, attachment-focused social work research has allowed practitioners to incorporate research findings into practice. This growing focus of attachment theory in social work research has contributed to the use of attachment-based interventions in the field of clinical social work. This chapter aims to provide an overview of the various aspects of attachment theory that social work researchers investigate and their contribution to the growing body of research on attachment theory.

J.E. Bettmann (✉)
College of Social Work, University of Utah, Salt Lake City, UT, USA
e-mail: Joanna.Bettmann@socwk.utah.edu

S. Bennett and J.K. Nelson (Eds.), *Adult Attachment in Clinical Social Work*,
Essential Clinical Social Work Series, DOI 10.1007/978-1-4419-6241-6_12,
© Springer Science+Business Media, LLC 2010

Method

Three major search engines were used: Ebsco, Social Work Abstracts, and Social Services Abstracts. The original search included all Ebsco databases with no publication date or publication type restrictions. Keywords "attachment" and "social work" were used, generating 1,668 results. However, "author affiliation" was not among the selections for search options. Ebsco's PsychInfo is the only Ebsco database that allows for this option. Therefore, PsychInfo only was used within the Ebsco search engine. Once "author affiliation" was used, many more relevant articles surfaced. After excluding book-reviews, editorials, comments/replies, and allowing for peer-reviewed journal articles and dissertations only, this search generated 304 hits. Ovid's Social Work Abstracts was searched next. For the subject term, "attachment" was used, and for the institution, "social work". This search generated 24 results. After cross referencing these results with Ebsco's PsychInfo, this search identified 11 new articles. Finally, CSA Illumina's Social Services Abstracts was searched also using subject term "attachment" and institution "social work." This search resulted in 169 hits and after cross referencing with Ebsco's PsychInfo generated 63 new articles. Finally, in order to make the findings more manageable, the date range for publication was narrowed to a 10-years span of 1997–2007.

It is important to note that this was not an exhaustive search. Thousands of articles looking at attachment have been published by social workers. The purpose of this chapter is to give the reader a glimpse into what social work researchers perceive as important areas to examine using an attachment perspective. Articles from this search were secured if one or more of the authors had an affiliation with a school of social work and if the articles reported quantitative or qualitative empirical data. This chapter reviews 40 articles and 7 dissertations that emerged from the search. Organized based on population, the following discussion presents the contribution of these studies to the field of attachment and identifies some of the existing gaps in the research.

Results

Studies fell naturally into five groups by population studied: children, adolescents, young adults, adults, and families. With the exception of longitudinal studies, most authors focused on selected age groups, examining attachment phenomenon in specific populations.

Children

Social workers have explored several important domains of child attachment, notably attachment in foster care populations, intergenerational transmission of attachment, attachment in divorced families, and attachment in young children. We identified nine social work studies that examined child attachment. Of these, four considered children in foster care (Andersson, 2005; Chang, 2007; Cole, 2005a, 2005b). See Table 12.1 for

Table 12.1 Summary of social work research on child attachment

Source	Population and study purpose	Measures	Outcome
Andersson (2005)	• Children placed in a children's home in Sweden during the early 1980s • Used attachment theory and developmental psychopathology to analyze perceptions of birth parents, foster parents, and family	• Semi-structured interviews • Standardized questionnaires (i.e. SCL-90) • Review of social welfare files • Review of clinical journals • Attachment assessed through observation by child care workers, questioning of contact people (i.e., Foster mother), weekly observation by psychologist	• Those who had "good" social adjustment as adults were securely attached to their biological mothers early in life, maintained positive relationships with their mothers later, and had contact with them throughout the foster care experience • Those in the "moderate" and "bad" social adjustment groups had insecure attachments with mothers early in life and did not maintain contact with their birth families while in foster care
Cole (2005b)	• 46 infants and 46 foster caregivers • Looked at patterns of attachment in infants in foster care and examined environmental and relational factors affecting these patterns	• Caregiver Interview Form (Wells, 1999) • Infant Toddler Symptom Checklist (De Gangi, Poisson, Sickel, & Wiener, 1995) • Minnesota Infant Development Inventory (Ireton & Thwing, 1980) • Support Functions Scale (Dunst & Trivette, 1986) • Parenting Stress Index-Short Form (Abidin, 1995) • Home Observation for the Measurement of the Environment (Caldwell & Bradley, 1984) • Strange Situation Procedure (Ainsworth, Blehar, Waters, & Wall, 1978) • Childhood Trauma Questionnaire (van IJzendoorn, Schuengel, & Bakermans-Kranenburg, 1999)	• The majority of the infants studied were securely attached • Predictors of insecure attachment: Caregiver childhood trauma and level of involvement with the infant • Predictors of secure attachment: Environmental organization and age-appropriate learning materials

(continued)

Table 12.1 (continued)

Source	Population and study purpose	Measures	Outcome
Cole (2005a)	• Same as Cole (2005b) • Examined the correlation between foster caregiver motivation and infant attachment	• Same measures as Cole (2005b)	• Secure attachment was correlated with caregivers' motivations to increase family size, as well as social concern for the community • Insecure attachment was correlated with the intent to adopt, the motivation to foster as a means of spiritual expression, and to foster as a means to replace a grown child
Chang (2007)	• 84 preadolescents adopted in the previous year • Examined the relationship between attachment security and psychological adjustment	• The Security Scale (Kerns, Klepac, & Cole, 1996) • The Child Behavior Checklist for ages 6–18 (Achenbach, 2001)	• Youth who perceived themselves as securely attached to their adoptive mothers showed fewer externalizing or internalizing behavior problems
Finzi-Dottan, Cohen, et al. (2006)	• 168 subjects; 56 families with drug using fathers in recovery • Examined how children of drug using fathers are impacted by family characteristics and family attachment	• Adult Attachment Style Classification Questionnaire (Mikulincer, Florian, & Tolmacz, 1990) • FACES III (Olson, 1986) • Children's Attachment Style Classification Questionnaire (Finzi, Cohen, & Ram, 2000; Finzi, Har-Even, Weizman, Tyano, & Shnit, 1996)	• Found no difference between perception of family cohesion or adaptability and the family norm around these variables, a strong representation of securely attached mothers and children in these families, and an over-representation of avoidant attachment among the fathers
Finzi-Dottan, Manor, et al. (2006)	• 65 Israeli children diagnosed with ADHD • Explored the impact of childhood temperament and parental styles on attachment patterns of children with ADHD	• Temperament Survey for Children: Parental Ratings (Buss & Plomin, 1984) • Parent's Report Questionnaire (Dibble & Cohen, 1974) • Children's Attachment Style Classification Questionnaire (Finzi et al., 1996; Finzi, Ram, Har-Even, Shnit, & Weizman, 2001)	

Study	Description	Measures	Findings
Page and Bretherton (2003)	• 27 preschool aged girls • As part of a larger study, this study compared differences in representation of attachment behavior between two groups of girls: those who enacted the lowest frequencies and those who enacted the highest frequencies of narrative representations of attachment behavior toward the father	• Attachment Story Completion Task-Revised (Bretherton et al., 1990) • The Preschool Competence Questionnaire (Olson, 1985; Olson & Lifgren, 1988) • The Preschool Behavior Questionnaire (Behar & Stringfield, 1974; Behar, 1977)	• Girls who demonstrated strong attachment to their father in their narratives also showed evidence of anxious attachment towards their mothers • These same girls were also rated lower in social competence by their teachers
Hart (2006)	• 13 5-year-old children from a Head Start Program • Descriptive analysis of young children's attachment security, and coping strategies when presented with stressful story stems	• Direct observation • Modified version of the story stem procedure (Bretherton et al., 1990)	• Analysis revealed themes of self-agency, nurturance, authority, violence and mood • Most children reported confidence in their environment and parents to be kept safe • Separation did not appear to be a particularly anxiety-provoking event for these children • Feeling words were rarely used • Coping strategies used by these children were fairly typical of 5-year old development
Bennett (2001)	• 15 lesbian couples with 1 internationally adopted child • Explored the attachment process between: lesbian coparents and their adopted children	• In-depth interviews • U.S. Census information • "Who Does What"? (Cowan & Cowan, 1988, 1990)	• All children in this study developed attachment to both mothers, with most demonstrating an initial primary bond to one mother • Lesbian couples and heterosexual couples with internationally adopted children have a remarkable similar parent–child attachment process • These families' differences were most notable when looking at the additional challenges that the lesbian families faced in regards to diversity

a description of the populations, instruments, findings, and outcomes of the articles described in this section.

Investigating attachment in foster care populations is a natural fit for social work researchers, since the environmental context of attachment is critically important and child welfare has historically been the purview of the social work profession. Andersson's (2005) longitudinal study of children placed in foster care at a young age makes a particularly important contribution. This study examined longitudinal data from 26 children in Sweden placed in foster care when they were under 4 years old. Andersson reinterviewed these children, now aged 20–25, and categorized them as having "good," "moderate," or "bad" social adjustment. The author created these categories using his assessment of interview data, as well as the Symptom Checklist SCL-90, a Swedish version of the SCL-90 (Derogatis, 1994). After considering longitudinal data from previous studies with the same sample (Andersson, 1984, 1988, 1999a, 1999b), Andersson concludes that those who had "good" social adjustment as adults were securely attached to their biological mothers early in life, maintained positive relationships with their mothers later, and had contact with them throughout the foster care experience. By contrast, Andersson found that those in the "moderate" and "bad" social adjustment groups had insecure attachments with mothers early in life and did not maintain contact with their birth families while in foster care.

Cole (2005b) examined infants in foster care, considering the relational and environmental factors which impact attachment security. This study of 46 infants used the Strange Situation procedure, as well as numerous measures of infant and caregiver mental health. The author concludes that a number of factors, including a well-organized home environment and the presence of age-appropriate learning materials, are positively correlated with infants' secure attachment to foster caregivers. Notably, infants' insecure attachment was positively correlated with the foster caregivers' childhood experience of abuse as well as their hypervigilant involvement with the infant.

Cole (2005a) considered the same sample in a different study that examined the correlation between foster caregiver motivation and infant attachment. In this study, infants' secure attachment was correlated with caregivers' motivations to increase family size, as well as social concern for the community. Caregivers who expressed that they were fostering infants driven by concern for their communities were six times more likely to have a securely attached foster infant than those who did not express this motivation. Interestingly, infants' insecure attachment was correlated with caregivers who expressed motivations including the intent to adopt, the motivation to foster as a means of spiritual expression, and the motivation to foster as a means to replace a grown child. Such findings have important implications for child welfare workers as they assess caregiver motivation prior to placement. Such consideration may help prevent troubled foster placements that may contribute to insecure attachments.

Finally, Chang's (2007) exploratory dissertation considered 84 preadolescents who had been adopted in the previous year. She examined the relationship between attachment security and psychological adjustment, concluding that youth who perceived themselves as securely attached to their adoptive mothers showed fewer externalizing or internalizing behavior problems.

All four of the above studies explored the environmental and familial factors that weigh on client mental health, a focus that seems particularly representative of social work's distinctive approach of "person in environment." Five other social work studies that consider child attachment explore familial contributors to childhood attachment. Finzi-Dottan, Cohen, Iwaniec, Sapir, and Weizman (2006) and Finzi-Dottan, Manor, and Tyano (2006) examined parental contributions to child attachment. Page and Bretherton (2003) examined girls' attachment representations of their fathers, and Hart's (2006) dissertation investigated 5-year-olds attachment security in times of stress. Finally, using a mixed methods design, Bennett (2001) explored the attachment processes between lesbian coparents and their adopted children. Each of these studies will be explored below.

Finzi-Dottan, Cohen, et al. (2006) studied the impact of family cohesion, family adaptation, and parental attachment styles on the attachment of children with drug-abusing fathers. In this study of 56 Israeli families after the fathers had gone through drug treatment, the authors found no difference between their sample's perception of family cohesion or adaptability and the Israeli family norm around these variables. Similarly, the authors found a strong representation of securely attached mothers and children in these families. The authors did find an over-representation of avoidant attachment among the fathers, suggesting the importance of using clinical interventions aimed towards supporting parents with particular insecure attachment styles.

Finzi-Dottan, Manor, et al. (2006) explored the relationship between childhood temperament, parental styles, childhood attachment, and children's ADHD. This study of 65 Israeli children diagnosed with ADHD explored how parental style contributes to children's abilities to self-regulate and behave inattentively or impulsively. The authors conclude that certain parenting styles combined with certain child temperaments may exacerbate children's tendencies towards problematic self-regulation, leading to insecure attachment patterns and greater attention problems. Specifically, children's anxious attachment was correlated with parental behavior promoting excess child autonomy and a childhood temperament of intense affect arousal. The findings from this study suggest that inadequate parental practices might worsen difficulties in self-regulation and lead to insecure attachment in children with ADHD. Such findings are helpful to clinicians who may begin to reconceptualize inattentive symptoms as problems in the attachment system, specifically problems in the affect regulation system unconsciously taught by parent to child (see Schore & Schore, Chap. 4, this volume).

Page and Bretherton (2003) investigated attachment representations of fathers in 27 preschool children in postdivorce families where the child was living with the mother. Using the Attachment Story Completion Task-Revised, an assessment measure which uses story stems and family dolls to elicit children's narratives, the authors found that girls who demonstrated strong attachment to father in narrative also showed evidence of anxious attachment towards their mothers. Additionally, the girls who described children's attachment to the father in the Task were rated lower in social competence by their teachers. These complex findings have important implications for clinical social workers. In postdivorce families, social workers need to facilitate the critically important attachment relationship between the primary custodial parental and child. Such work may involve reinterpreting the child's behavior for the parent, helping parents view children's complex behavior as often driven by attachment needs.

Hart's (2006) dissertation also considered young children's attachment, 5-year-olds attachment security, and coping strategies when presented with stressful story stems. This qualitative study of 13 children used a modified version of Bretherton, Ridgeway, and Cassidy's (1990) story stems and contextual analysis methodology. This approach uses prompt questions that allow the child to provide their own details and conclusions to a story. The author coded responses to indicate security of attachment according to seven predetermined categories: sense of self agency, nurturing and protection, denial, authority, violence, relationship with others, and mood. Each story stem was evaluated in the context of these categories and definitions of attachment were used to understand the responses in relation to their perceptions of attachment. Findings were discussed in the context of each child's story response and perception of attachment. There were noticeable similarities in coping strategies by most of the children. Most children created story stems that demonstrated a sense of self-reliance or trust that their caregiver would aid them with the problem presented. In addition, they were typically able to solve the problems in a logical and coherent manner. The results here point to the importance of story stems as a clinical tool to be used with this difficult-to-assess age-group.

Finally, Bennett (2001) explored the attachment process between lesbian coparents and their internationally adopted children. This primarily qualitative study looked at 15 lesbian couples each with an internationally adopted child. She found that all children in this study developed attachment to both mothers. However, a large percentage exhibited a hierarchy of attachment. Despite the nontraditional nature of the family structure, lesbian couples and heterosexual couples with internationally adopted children have a remarkably similar parent–child attachment process. Differences were most notable when looking at the additional challenges that the lesbian families faced in regards to diversity. All of these studies focused on children and attachment consider the critically important context of such attachment: family and environment. It is clear that social workers have made an important contribution to our understanding of childhood attachment.

Adolescents

We identified seven social work studies that consider adolescent attachment, three of which focus particularly on relationships between parent and teen. See Table 12.2 for a description of the populations, instruments, and outcomes of the articles described in this section.

Hahm, Lahiff, and Guterman (2003) explored Asian-American adolescents' risk of alcohol use correlated with two factors: acculturation and parental attachment. The study used a nationally representative subsample of data from the National Longitudinal Adolescent Health data set, analyzing data from 712 Asian-American adolescents. The authors concluded that greater acculturation was associated with greater alcohol use, but attachment moderated the findings. Very acculturated adolescents with moderate or high attachment (the only designations used in the study)

Table 12.2 Summary of social work research on adolescent attachment

Source	Population and study purpose	Measures	Outcome
Hahm et al. (2003)	• 714 Asian-American boys and girls from the National Longitudinal Adolescent Health dataset • Examined the role acculturation plays in predicting alcohol use and tests the moderating effect of parental attachment	• Instruments designed by the authors for the National Longitudinal Study of Adolescent Health (Harris et al., 2008).	• Greater acculturation was associated with greater alcohol use • Very acculturated adolescents with moderate or high attachment to parents had no greater risk of alcohol use than less acculturated adolescents with the same levels of attachment to parents • Having a nonresidential father, problems in relating to him, less attachment to him, less caregiver monitoring as well as less spirituality were predictive of adolescent alcohol use
Jones and Benda (2004)	• 3,395 high school students • Investigated what assets and deficits predict adolescent alcohol use, and mediate the relationship between families with a nonresidential biological father and youthful alcohol use • Examined if certain assets and deficits moderated the relationship between these same families and adolescent alcohol use	• Short Michigan Alcoholism Screening Test (Selzer, Vinokur, & van Rooijen, 1975) • Childhood Trauma Questionnaire (Bernstein & Fink, 1998) • The Beck Depression Inventory (Beck & Steer, 1993) • Beck Hopelessness Scale (Beck & Steer, 1993) • Peer association with delinquents is measured by 5 items (5-pointLikert scale from none to four or more) (Akers, 2000) • Problems with Father subscale of the Multi-Problem Screening Inventory (Hudson, 1990) • Attachments were measured with four questions about each caregiver and Caregiver monitoring is measured by 5 items asking how closely caregivers supervise: These scales have been used in numerous studies (e.g., Benda, 2002; Benda & Corwyn, 2002; Benda & Toombs, 2002) • Spiritual Well-Being Scale (Ellison, 1983) • Resilience Scale (Wagnild & Young, 1993) • The Ego Identity Scale (Erikson, 1968)	

(continued)

Table 12.2 (continued)

Source	Population and study purpose	Measures	Outcome
Turnage (2004)	• 105 urban twelfth grade adolescent African American girls • Examined global self-esteem	• The HARE General and Area-specific (School, Peer, and Home) Self-Esteem Scale (Hare, 1996) • The Inventory of Parent and Peer Attachment (Armsden & Greenberg, 1987) • Multigroup Ethnic Identity Measure (Phinney, 1992)	• Found a positive direct relationship exists between the global self-esteem score and trust of mother score • Found participants who scored high on global self-esteem also scored high on ethnic identity achievement
Bettmann (2006)	• 93 adolescents in a wilderness therapy program in Utah • Examined the shifts in adolescents' perceptions of attachment with parents and peers over the course of a 7-week residential program	• Adolescent Attachment Questionnaire (West, Rose, Spreng, Sheldon-Keller, & Adam, 1998) • Adolescent Unresolved Attachment Questionnaire (West, Rose, Spreng, & Adam, 2000) • Inventory of Parent and Peer Attachment (Armsden & Greenberg, 1987)	• Found that adolescents became less angry at parents by end of treatment but not more trusting • Found similarly mixed results with peer relationships
Schofield and Brown (1999)	• 5 adolescent females referred to a family centre (location not specified) • A case exploration of five adolescent females, exploring attachment themes and attachment-oriented interventions with adolescents in the child welfare system	• Case examples: No assessments used in this study	• It is critically important for workers to understand attachment themes with this population and to consider workers' own roles as secure bases for relationally wounded adolescents
Heran (2006)	• 31 male adolescent sex offenders in a court-ordered residential treatment program • Explored the impact of a 6-week training on attachment styles, social competencies and empathy	• Adult Attachment Inventory • Interpersonal Reactivity Index (Davis, 1983) • Child Molester Empathy Measure • The Teenage Inventory of Social Skills (Inderbitzen & Foster, 1992)	• Found no statistically significant findings, but raw scores did show increases in empathy and social skills from pre to post test

| Schwartz et al. (2004) | • 25 pregnant and parenting teens
• Considered the experiences and support networks of adolescents who were pregnant or parenting and living in a transitional living facility for formerly homeless women | • No formal attachment measure-Attachment assessed through various sources:
 o Data obtained through initial admission assessment
 o Narrative data from life plans, case summaries, discharge summaries
 o Interviews
• Beck's Depression Inventory II (Beck, Steer, & Brown, 1987)
• Child Abuse Potential Inventory (Milner, 1984)
• Emotional Autonomy Scale (Steinberg & Silverberg, 1986) | • Close to one-third of the participants lacked a significant relationship with someone who could have functioned in a parental role
• Participants displayed a strong desire for romantic attachments. However, romantic attachments were typically insecure and characterized by violence and unsafe sexual practices
• Participants struggled with low self-esteem and depression |

to parents had no greater risk of alcohol use than less acculturated adolescents with the same levels of attachment to parents.

Similarly, Jones and Benda (2004), considering a stratified random sample of 3,395 adolescents in a mid-western state, found that having a nonresidential father, problems in relating to him, less attachment to him, less caregiver monitoring as well as less spirituality were predictive of adolescent alcohol use. In both studies, we see that parental attachment mediates adolescent alcohol use, a significant finding for clinicians working with adolescent populations.

The third study to examine adolescent–parent relationships is Turnage (2004), which explored the African-American mother–daughter relationships in 105 urban teenagers attending a Catholic high school. The author found a correlation between adolescents' reported self-esteem and trust in mothers, qualities that relate to security of attachment, though attachment was not measured specifically. They also found that participants who scored high on global self-esteem also scored high on ethnic identity achievement. This finding too is important for clinicians, underscoring the importance of working to support the parent–adolescent relationship as clearly it serves as a protective factor throughout adolescence. Their findings also suggest a link between high self-esteem and positive ethnic identity.

Bettmann (2006) similarly studied parent–adolescent relationships, as well as peer–adolescent relationships. Her study considered the impact of a 7-week wilderness therapy program on 93 adolescents' attachment relationships with parents and peers. Studying self-reported attachment relationships pre and post treatment, Bettmann concluded that adolescents became less angry at parents by the end of treatment but not more trusting. She found similarly mixed results with peer relationships, and concluded that adolescents in residential care may need targeted interventions in order to support improved attachment relationships in out-of-home care.

The other three studies in which social workers focused on adolescent attachment all examine adolescents in the context of particular settings: a counseling center for adolescents in the child welfare system, a court-ordered residential treatment, and a transitional living center. The first of these, Schofield and Brown (1999), presents a case exploration of five adolescent females, exploring attachment themes and attachment-oriented interventions with adolescents in the child welfare system. The authors conclude that it is critically important for workers to understand attachment themes with this population and to consider workers' own roles as secure bases for relationally wounded adolescents.

Heran's (2006) dissertation explored the impact of a 6-week empathy training group on the attachment narratives, social competencies and empathy problems of 40 adolescent male sex-offenders in a court-ordered residential treatment program. This study found no statistically significant findings, but raw scores did show increases in empathy and social skills from pre to post test.

Schwartz, McRoy, and Downs (2004) considered the experiences and support networks of adolescents who were pregnant or parenting and living in a transitional living facility for formerly homeless women. Using case records, interview data, and quantitative measurements, the authors examined 25 adolescent women. They concluded that these women's attachment relationships with parents, partners, and children were "fragmented, distant and, at times, abusive" (Schwartz et al., 2004, p. 105), suggesting insecure attachment styles. The authors assert that participants' personal relationships, as well as relationships with staff, appeared indicative of insecure attachment styles, a finding which may be enlightening to staff working with such populations.

Young Adults

College students are a unique population. Made up of individuals in late adolescence through all levels of adulthood, the struggles of college students are distinctively different from those of most other age groups. Developmentally, the attachment process for these individuals may be at very different stages. Some students are experiencing their important peer attachment relationships for the first time living away from home, while others already have spouses and children of their own. From 1997 to 2007, there were four articles published by social work researchers looking at attachment with this population from very distinct perspectives. See Table 12.3 for a description of the population, instruments, and findings of the studies discussed in this section.

Lonergan (2003) investigated psychological separation and parental attachment in learning disabled and nondisabled students who attended college away from home. He also examined whether these differences would predict grade point average and/or college retention. Subjects were 84 graduating high school seniors, 43 learning disabled, and 41 nondisabled. He found that neither psychological separation from mother or father nor parental attachment to mother or father significantly affected GPA or college retention for either group. Notably, the learning disabled students were significantly different than nondisabled students on subscales of parental attachment. The learning disabled students reported more trust and less alienation with their mothers and better communication with both parents. In addition, the nondisabled students showed a higher functional and emotional independence from both parents than did the learning-disabled students (Lonergan, 2003).

In her 1997 study, Chassler examined individuals with bulimia nervosa and anorexia nervosa through the lens of attachment theory. She hypothesized that anorexic and bulimic patients would manifest a greater degree of attachment difficulties than their controls. Both the eating disordered and control groups were administered an attachment assessment. Chassler found significant differences in attachment between the eating disordered and control groups. The eating disordered group scored significantly lower in secure attachment and significantly higher in insecure attachment, supporting the research hypothesis (Chassler, 1997).

In a very different area of study, Sim and Loh (2003) explored the application of attachment theory to the religious experience. Sim and Loh developed and tested a measure of the attachment to God construct. Their overall goal was to develop an accurate means of assessing an individual's relationship to his/her God, irrespective of how the individual expresses this attachment. The authors found good internal consistency of the measure items demonstrated in both the measure itself and in terms of the specific aspects

Table 12.3 Summary of social work research on college student attachment

Source	Population and study purpose	Measures	Outcome
Lonergan (2003)	• 84 graduating high school seniors • 43 learning disabled and 41 nondisabled • Investigated psychological separation and parental attachment in learning disabled and nondisabled students who attended college away from home and examined whether differences would predict grade point average and/or college retention	• Psychological Separation Inventory (Hoffman, 1984) • Inventory for Parental and Peer Attachment (Armsden & Greenberg, 1987)	• Neither psychological separation from mother or father nor parental attachment to mother or father significantly affected GPA or college retention for either group • The learning disabled students were significantly different than nondisabled students on subscales of parental attachment • Nondisabled students showed a higher functional and emotional independence from both parents then did the learning-disabled students
Chassler (1997)	• 30 female anorectic and bulimic inpatients • 31 primarily female social work students • Examined whether there is a connection between anorexia and bulimia and early childhood attachment relationships	• Attachment History Questionnaire (Pottharst, 1990)	• The eating disordered group scored significantly lower in secure attachment and significantly higher in insecure attachment

| Sim and Loh (2003) | • 241 university students in Singapore
• Explored the attachment to God construct
• Attempted to validate a measure of attachment to God | • Attachment to God (measure developed for this study)
• Attachment to father and mother (measure developed for this study)
• Religious belief (measure developed for this study)
• Religious practice (measure developed for this study)
• Optimism assessment (measure developed for this study) based on Life Orientation test (Scheier, Carver, & Bridges, 1994)
• Satisfaction assessment (measure developed for this study) based on Satisfaction with Life Scale (Diener, Emmons, Larsen, & Griffin, 1985)
• Rosenberg Self-Esteem Scale (Rosenberg, 1965)
• Negative affect (measure developed for this study) | • Found good internal consistency of the measure items
• Found that God attachment could be distinguished from religious belief and practice and from father and mother attachments |
| Ben-Ari (2004) | • 64 Arab social work students at a university in Israel
• Examined the relationship between attachment style and utilization of sources of support | • Assessment developed for this study | • Found that first choice for support was not always the family. Participants utilized best friends more often for relationship problems and depressive issues |

of attachment assessed. They also found that God attachment could be distinguished from religious belief and practice and from father and mother attachments.

In 2004, Ben-Ari explored attachment theory by examining the relationship between attachment style and utilization of sources of support among Israeli and Arab students. This author found that contrary to expectation the first choice for support was not always the family. In fact, participants utilized partners and best friends more often for relationship problems and depressive issues. Such findings support those who envision adolescence and early adulthood as a time of shifting primary attachments from family of origin to peers (Allen & Land, 1999).

Adults

Social work researchers have considered adult attachment in many contexts. Whether examining the attitudes of foster fathers (Inch, 1999) or evaluating marital relationship quality (Ben-Ari & Lavee, 2005), adult attachment is visible in many facets of social work research. Some studies concentrate on attachment as a central variable, while for others the focus is more peripheral. Several studies looked specifically at the role of attachment in the development of violent behaviors (Bond & Bond, 2004; Buttell, Muldoon, & Carney, 2005; Carney & Buttell, 2005; Corvo, 2006), while other researchers used attachment theory as a basis to explore specific phenomena (Andersson & Eisemann, 2004; Benda, 2003; Landolt, Bartholomew, Saffrey, Oram, & Perlman, 2004; Rodell, Benda, & Rodell, 2003). Others consider attachment patterns as a predictive, contributing, or distinguishing variables (Cohen & Finzi-Dottan, 2005; Hamama-Raz & Solomon, 2006; Lyn & Burton, 2004; Stalker, Gebotys, & Harper, 2005; Zakin, Solomon, & Neria, 2003). See Table 12.4 for a listing of the populations, instruments, and findings of these studies described in more detail below.

In their study, Bond and Bond (2004) looked at attachment style as a predictor of marital violence. They collected data from 41 couples measuring attachment style, violence, and marital satisfaction. They found that attachment style was a predictive variable in marital violence. Specifically, the authors found that significant predictors of marital violence were the combination of female-anxious and male-dismissing attachment patterns in the couple, along with poor problem-solving and communication skills.

Similarly, Corvo (2006) examined the role of attachment in an intergenerational transmission model of domestic violence. He gathered information on separation and loss, erratic caregiving, and violence, both in the family of origin and in current relationships. Subjects were 42 men currently in a domestic violence treatment program. He found a correlation between early life separation and loss and current spousal family violence, pointing to the need to expand the intergenerational transmission model of domestic violence to include attachment variables.

Both these studies looked at the role attachment plays in spousal violence. Two similar studies examine interpersonal dependency, an indicator of an anxious or preoccupied insecure attachment style, in court-mandated batterers (Buttell et al., 2005;

Table 12.4 Summary of social work research on adult attachment

Source	Population and study purpose	Measures	Outcome
Inch (1999)	• 15 foster fathers from mid-western, multipurpose, nonprofit, child welfare organizations • Examines the views and experience of foster fathers on becoming foster parents	• Individual interviews	• Found a relationship between the foster father's view of his functions, his attitude toward the child's birth family, and issues of separation, loss, and abuse
Ben-Ari and Lavee (2005)	• A subsample of 248 Jewish and Arab couples randomly selected from a random sample from a larger study • Looked at couple types based on attachment security and neuroticism and examines how they relate to a global evaluation of relationship quality and dyadic closeness–distance	• Neuroticism subscale of the Eysenck Personality Questionnaire – Revised (Eysenck, Eysenck, & Barrett, 1985) • Experience in Close Relationships questionnaire (Brennan, Clark, & Shaver, 1998) • Modified version of the short Enriching Relationship Issues, Communication, and Happiness scale (Fowers & Olson, 1993)	• Found 3 types of dyadic attachment configurations (secure, fearful avoidant, and insecure–mixed) • Found 4 types of dyadic neuroticism (low couple neuroticism, high couple neuroticism, wife neuroticism, and husband neuroticism) • Found significant differences among attachment and neuroticism dyadic types in marital quality
Bond and Bond (2004)	• 41 couples from several family treatment facilities in Montreal • Looked at individual and couple's attachment styles and examined if they predicted violence within the marriage • Explored whether other variables moderated the risk of violence	• The Marital Satisfaction Inventory Revised (Snyder, 1997) • The Partner Abuse Scale-Physical (Hudson, 1997) • The Physical Abuse of Partner Scale (Hudson, 1997) • The Relationship Questionnaire (Bartholomew & Horowitz, 1991) • The Experiences in Close Relationships Scale (Brennan et al., 1998)	• Found that significant predictors of marital violence were the combination of female-anxious and male-dismissing attachment patterns with poor problem-solving and communication skills within the context of a longer relationship

(continued)

Table 12.4 (continued)

Source	Population and study purpose	Measures	Outcome
Corvo (2006)	• 74 men in a domestic violence treatment program • Explored the intergenerational transmission of domestic violence from the perspective of attachment theory	• The Conflict Tactics Scale (Straus, 1979) • Separation and loss was operationally defined through questions about death of family members, divorce of parents, parental absence, and respondent's removal or absence from the home	• Compared to exposure to family of origin violence, separation and loss were found to have greater of comparable effects on the violent behavior of participants
Buttell et al. (2005)	• 158 male batterers court-ordered into treatment for domestic violence • 25 men with no history of domestic violence • Examined interpersonal dependency among men court-mandated into domestic violence treatment	• The Interpersonal Dependency Inventory (Hirschfeld et al., 1977)	• Compared to the nonviolent group, batterers reported significantly elevated levels of interpersonal dependency
Carney and Buttell (2005)	• 75 women in a court-mandated batterer intervention program (BIP), 39 completers and 36 drop outs • Investigated interpersonal dependency (ID) and violence among women entering a court-mandated, batterer intervention program(BIP) • Examined associations between ID and violence • Investigated differences in demographic variables and psychological variables between treatment completers and drop-out • Evaluated the treatment effect of a standard BIP in altering levels of ID among treatment completers	• Interpersonal Dependency Inventory (Hirschfeld et al., 1977) • The Revised Conflict Tactics Scale (Straus, Hamby, Boney-McCoy, & Sugarman, 1996)	• Study participants reported elevated levels of ID to their partner, an indicator of insecure attachment style • Drop-outs were significantly more abusive than treatment completers • Reported levels of ID were directly related to domestic violence • ID was an important variable in predicting treatment completion • For treatment completers, levels of ID were higher following participation in a BIP

| Benda (2003) | • 650 homeless male Vietnam veterans in a substance abuse program
• Examine what factors discriminate between nonsuicidal veteran, those with suicidal ideation, and individuals who have attempted suicide | • Multi-Problem Screening Inventory (Hudson, 1990)
 o The family relationship problems of this assessment were considered as a measure of familial attachment
• Self-Efficacy Scale (Sherer, 1982)
• Multidimensional Scale of Perceived Social Support (Zimet, Dahlem, Zimet, & Farley, 1988)
• The Addiction Severity Index (McLellan, Kushner, Metzger, & Peters, 1992) | • Discriminators between suicide attempters and both other groups: psychiatric comorbidity, early abuse, severity of substance abuse, and longevity of drug use
• Discriminators between nonsuicidal homeless substance abusers and others: elements of attachment and commitments such as marriage, employment, and religiosity |
| Rodell et al. (2003) | • 188 homeless male veterans in a substance abuse program
• Examine predictors of suicidal thoughts | • The Addiction Severity Index (McLellan et al., 1992)
• Multi-Problem Screening Inventory (Hudson, 1990)
 o The family relationship problems of this assessment were considered as a measure of familial attachment | • Early attachments to caregivers had inverse relations to suicidal thoughts, low self-esteem, less self-efficacy, depression, and being unmarried and in less than full-time employment were positively related to suicidal thoughts
• Sexual abuse before 18 years of age had a long-term positive relationship to suicidal thoughts
• Attachments and sexual abuse significantly interacted with both intensity and duration of alcohol and other drug abuse |

(continued)

Table 12.4 (continued)

Source	Population and study purpose	Measures	Outcome
Landolt et al. (2004)	• 191 gay and bisexual men • Explored the associations between gender nonconformity, rejection by parents and peers, attachment anxiety, and attachment avoidance	• Boyhood Gender Conformity Scale (Hockenberry & Billingham, 1987) • Recollections of Early Childrearing (Perris, Jacobsson, Lindstrom, von Knorring, & Perris, 1980) • The Mother–Father–Peer Scale (Epstein, 1983) • The Inventory of Peer Attachment (Armsden & Greenberg, 1987) • History of Attachment Interview (Designed for this study)	• Gender nonconforming behavior in childhood was associated with maternal, paternal, and peer rejection • Paternal rejection independently predicted adult attachment anxiety and was associated with adult attachment avoidance • Peer rejection largely mediated the associations between parental rejection and both attachment anxiety and avoidance • Paternal and peer rejection largely mediated the associations between gender nonconformity and adult attachment orientation • Gender nonconformity was not related to attachment avoidance in adult relationships • Childhood rejection was more strongly and consistently related to adult anxiety than avoidance
Andersson and Eisemann (2004)	• 662 healthy subjects from different schools in Sweden • 319 patients from a Methadone Maintenance Program in Stockholm City • Investigated dysfunctional parental rearing in order to evaluate cognitive self-protective strategies	• The Bowlby Scale • The Attachment Style Questionnaire (Fenney, Noller, & Hanrahan, 1994) • Reciprocal Attachment Questionnaire (West, Sheldon, & Reiffer, 1987) • The Dysfunctional Attitudes Scale (Weissman, 1979; Weissman & Beck, 1978) • The Dysfunctional Working Models Scale (Perris, 1988; Perris, Fowler, Skagerlind, Olsson, & Thorsson, 1998)	• Found insecure attachments among addicts and secure attachment among controls • The influence of the pathological pattern "Compulsive self-reliance" on the personality factor "Confidence in self and others" was significantly higher for addicts • The content of schemas in substance-related disorders showed an individual susceptibility to decreased social competence and high risk for the development of various types of psychopathology • Findings from the control subjects showed a "normal" organization of self-protective strategies and behavior patterns consistent with secure attachment

Hamama-Raz and Solomon (2006)	• 300 Israeli survivors of malignant melanoma • Examined the contributions of hardiness, attachment style, and cognitive appraisal to the psychological adjustment	• Mental Health Inventory (Veit & Ware, 1983) Hebrew version (Florian & Drory, 1990) • Cognitive Appraisal of Health Scale (Kessler, 1998) translated into Hebrew by the first author and two native English speakers, using back translation, and modified in accord with Lazarus and Folkman (1984) • The Hardiness Scale (Kobasa & Puccetti, 1983) Hebrew version (Orr & Westman, 1990) • The Multi-Item Measure of Adult Attachment (Brennan et al., 1998). Hebrew version (Mikulincer & Florian, 2000)	• The best predictors of adjustment were personal resources and cognitive appraisal not features related to their illness or sociodemographic variables that were measured
Zakin et al. (2003)	• 164 prisoners of war from the 1973 Yom Kippur war • 189 comparable controls who fought in the same war • Examined the role of hardiness and attachment style, as personal resources in adjustment to stress	• Attachment style was assessed using an instrument based on Hazan and Shaver's (1987) descriptions of how people typically feel in close relationships (Mikulincer et al., 1990) • The Hardiness Scale (Kobasa & Puccetti, 1983) Hebrew version (Orr & Westman, 1990) • Symptom Checklist–90 (Derogatis, 1977) • The current version of the PTSD Inventory is a self-report scale based on the DSM-III-R criteria (American Psychiatric Association, 1987)	• Among both groups greater hardiness and secure attachment style were separately associated with reduced vulnerability to PTSD, symptoms of depression, anxiety and somatization • Found a compensatory interaction between hardiness and attachment style: the attachment resources of subjects with low level of hardiness were more effective, while the hardiness of insecure subjects provided them with more protection

(continued)

Table 12.4 (continued)

Source	Population and study purpose	Measures	Outcome
Cohen and Finzi-Dottan (2005)	• 49 Jewish Israeli recently divorced couples • Examined attachment style, parenting style, perception of own parents' parenting, and the ex-spouse's assessment of the quality of the parent's parenting as predictors of parental satisfaction following a divorce	• Satisfaction was measured on a self-report questionnaire developed for this study • Relationship Questionnaire (Bartholomew & Horowitz, 1991) • Parental Bonding Instrument (Parker, Tupling, & Brown, 1979) • Parent's Report questionnaire (Dibble & Cohen, 1974) • Perception of other parent's assessment of the quality of one's parenting was measured by a single question, constructed by the authors	• Among mothers, satisfaction predictors were: dismissing attachment style and centrality of the child in her own parenting style • Among fathers, great satisfaction predictors were: more education, perception of their own mother as less overprotective, and perceptions of their ex-wife's approval of the quality of their fathering
Stalker et al. (2005)	• 134 women who reported histories of child abuse • Investigated insecure attachment as a predictor of outcome for inpatient treatment for traumatic stress	• Trauma Assessment for Adults–Self–Report (Resnick, Best, Kilpatrick, Freedy, & Falsetti, 1993) • Symptom Checklist–90 (Derogatis, 1992) • Modified PTSD Symptom Scale–Self-Report (Falsetti, 1997; Falsetti, Resnick, Resick, & Kilpatrick, 1993) • Traumatic Stress Institute Belief Scale-Revision L (Pearlman, 1996) • Rosenberg Self–Esteem (Rosenberg, 1965) • Social Provisions Relationship Questionnaire (Cutrona & Russell, 1987) • Reciprocal Attachment Questionnaire (West & Sheldon-Keller, 1994) • The Avoidant Attachment Questionnaire (West & Sheldon-Keller, 1994)	• For participants in this study, the variables with the highest effect on treatment outcome were high levels of insecure attachment and current perceived social support from friends

| Lyn and Burton (2004) | • 184 inmates from a Midwestern prison: 144 sexual offenders and 34 nonsexual offender
• Investigated the relationship between attachment style and sexual offending | • Modified version of the Self-Report Delinquency Scale (Elliot, Huizinga, & Ageton, 1985)
• Experiences in Close Relationships Inventory (Brennan et al., 1998)
• Carlson Psychological Survey (Carlson, 1981) | • Insecure attachment was significantly associated with sex offender status
• With the exception of victim age, insecure attachment was not related to the characteristics of the sexual offenses |

Carney & Buttell, 2005). Buttell et al. (2005) gathered data from 158 court-mandated male batterers and 25 men with no history of domestic violence. In this study, the authors found that court-ordered batterers displayed significantly higher rates of interpersonal dependency than did men with no history of domestic violence. Their findings also indicated that court-mandated batterers are similar to batterers that volunteer for treatment in that they tend to be exceedingly dependent on their intimate partners. Carney and Buttell (2005) found similar results with their study looking at court-mandated female batterers. Their secondary analysis of pretreatment data of 75 women referred to a batterer intervention program found that the women in their sample were overly dependent on their partners. Similar to the men, these women demonstrated elevated levels of interpersonal dependency relative to a nonviolent comparison group. In all four studies, researchers strove to understand the link between violence and attachment. Interpersonal violence is clearly relational in nature. Understanding this connection can have a significant impact on treatment approach and development for this population.

Other social work researchers have used attachment theory as a basis for exploring entirely different phenomena. In 2003, two studies examined suicidal and nonsuicidal substance-abusing homeless military veterans through the lens of attachment theory. Both studies considered determining factors for suicidal thoughts and gestures (Benda, 2003; Rodell et al., 2003). In his exploratory study, Benda used attachment theory as a basis to distinguish potential elements that may contribute to suicidal thoughts. Deviating slightly from this, Rodell et al. (2003) used attachment theory to examine predictors of suicidal thought. Both found that caregiver attachment and attachment elements such as self-efficacy and self-esteem played a significant role in discriminating between nonsuicidal homeless substance abusers and those who were thinking about or who had attempted it (Benda, 2003; Rodell et al., 2003).

Grounding their study in attachment theory, Landolt et al. (2004) investigated the adult relationship experiences of gay men by exploring childhood gender nonconformity and parental and peer rejection. They found that childhood gender nonconformity was associated with maternal, paternal, and peer rejection. In addition, paternal rejection predicted adult attachment anxiety and was associated with adult attachment avoidance, but maternal rejection did not.

In another study, Andersson and Eisemann (2004) examined patients diagnosed with heroin addiction from the perspective of attachment theory. They assessed patients' self-protective strategies, or internal working models, developed from dysfunctional parenting. Results found insecure attachment styles among the participant addicts. In contrast to the addicts, control subjects demonstrated an organization of self-protective strategies and a pattern of behavior mainly based on secure attachment strategies.

Exploring these phenomena through the lens of attachment theory guided the focus of these researchers in their attempt to identify mental health phenomena. However, other researchers explore the role of attachment as contributing to the dynamic of particular emotional states or behaviors. For example, Hamama-Raz and Solomon (2006) considered hardiness, cognitive appraisal, and attachment style as possible factors in the psychological adjustment of Israeli cancer survivors. The authors found that survivors' adjustment was better predicted by self-reported personal resources and cognitive appraisal than any sociodemographic variables, with the exception of marital status. They also found that, of all variables, attachment style was the best predictor of adjustment. Secure attachment predicted survivors' self-reported well-being and lower distress.

Also exploring hardiness and attachment style, Zakin et al. (2003) considered which variables are personal resources for prisoners of war and combat veterans. They found that attachment style was a mitigating factor for dealing with traumatic stress. Among both groups, greater hardiness and secure attachment style were associated with reduced vulnerability to PTSD, symptoms of depression, anxiety, and somatization. Additionally, the authors found a compensatory interaction between hardiness and attachment style: the attachment resources of subjects with low levels of hardiness were more effective, while the hardiness of insecure subjects provided them with more protection.

Several researchers considered attachment style when seeking to find predictors of emotional or behavioral outcomes for their adult participants. Cohen and Finzi-Dottan (2005) explored possible predictors of parental satisfaction for recently divorced couples. They found that for mothers, the less dismissing the attachment style and the more central the child was in her parenting style, the greater her parental satisfaction tended to be. Among mothers, satisfaction predictors were dismissing attachment style and centrality of the child in her own parenting style. Among fathers, great satisfaction predictors were more education, perception of their own mother as less overprotective, and perceptions of their ex-wife's approval of the quality of their fathering.

In another study, Stalker et al. (2005) looked at insecure attachment as a predictor of treatment outcome for women with histories of trauma. They found that, after controlling for other variables, an insecure attachment style and perceived social support from friends were significant predictors of poorer outcome. Such findings have strong implications for social workers whose knowledge of clients' attachment styles should have significant impact on treatment planning.

Seeking to investigate insecure attachment as a distinguishing factor, Lyn and Burton (2004) examined whether attachment status of sexual offenders and non-sexual offenders was distinct and speculated that for sexual offenders, attachment status would be reflected in characteristics of their offense. Their results indicated that insecure attachment status was more specific to the sexual offending population, that offenders who sexually abused children were more likely to be classified as insecurely attached than those who victimized adults, but that there was no significant relationship between attachment status and familiarity with victim, means to commit the offense, or offense severity.

Families

We located four studies which considered the impact of attachment in family settings and across time. See Table 12.5 for a listing of the populations, instruments, and findings of the studies described in this section. Two of these four family studies consider attachment specifically in a family context: Ispa, Sable, Porter, and Csizmadia (2007) examined the toddler attachment, maternal sensitivity, and parenting stress of 173 low-income African-American mothers. Using a range of observational and quantitative

Table 12.5 Summary of social work research on family attachments

Source	Population and study purpose	Measures	Outcome

Ispa et al. (2007)	• 173 young, low income, African American, primiparous mothers
	
	• Explored relations between pregnancy acceptance and later maternal and child outcomes
		• Pregnancy acceptance assessed with 2 questionnaires:
		  o First: Items used in the 1995 National Survey of Family Growth to measure ambivalence (London, Peterson, & Piccinino, 1995)
		  o Second: Items developed by Early Head Start staff
		• Parenting Stress Index (Abidin, 1990)
		• Maternal warmth based on mothers' behavior during videotaped play sessions
		  o Scored according to scales adapted from National Institute of Child Health and Human Development Study of Early Child Care (NICHD Early Child Care Research Network, 1997)
		• Attachment Q-Sort (Waters, 1987)
		• Rothbart Infant Behavior Questionnaire (Rothbart, 1981)
		• Social support assessed by a scale adapted from previous surveys by Mathematica Policy Research, Inc.
		• Multidimensional Personality Questionnaire (Tellegen, 1982)
			• Found no significant relations between pregnancy acceptance and maternal warmth
			
			• Pregnancy acceptance predicted toddler attachment security and maternal feelings that parenting was burdensome

McCarthy (2007)	• 61 families: 61 children and 61 adult kinship, foster, or adoptive caregivers • Examined relationships between caregiver attachment status and child functioning	• Qualitative Interviews guided by the Adult and Child Interview Guide (McCarthy, 2003) • Experiences in Close Relationships-Revised (Fraley, Waller, & Brennan, 2000) • Adult Attachment Scale (Cicirelli, 1995) • Child Behavior Checklist (Achenbach, 1992) • Behavioral Assessment Score System for Children(McCarthy, 2003; Reynolds & Kamphaus, 1992)	• Caregivers' attachment status matters for the well-being of children in care • Children with unfavorable resiliencies-to-risk status were more likely to do poorly, with those who were in the care of adults with insecure attachments doing worst of all

Iwaniec and Sneddon (2001)	• 31 failure-to-thrive children identified between 1977 and 1980 who were investigated, assessed, and provided with social work intervention and treatment
	• 20-year follow up: Examined stability of internal working models
		• Strange Situation Test (Ainsworth et al., 1978)
		• The Attachment Style Classification Questionnaire (Hazan & Shaver, 1987)
			• Changes from childhood to adulthood were as follows:
			  o Increase in secure attachment classification from 14 to 22
			  o Decrease in anxious ambivalent classification from 9 to 1
			  o Avoidant remained the same at 8

Leifer et al. (2004)	• 99 nonoffending African American mothers; 106 grandmothers of the same children • Investigated histories of attachment relationships, abusive experiences, and current functioning	• Semi-structured interviews • Inventory of Supportive Figures (Burge & Figley, 1982, adapted by Runyan, Hunter, & Everson, 1992) • Trauma Symptom Checklist-40 (Briere & Runtz, 1988, 1989) • Relationship Scales Questionnaire (Bartholomew & Horowitz, 1991; Griffin & Bartholomew, 1994)	• 3 factors best predicted childhood sexual abuse: maternal problems in adult functioning (i.e. domestic violence, substance abuse, etc), current negative relationship between the grandmother and mother, and a disrupted pattern of caregiving during the mother's childhood

measurements collected over a period of 2 years, the authors concluded that pregnancy acceptance predicted toddler attachment security. This finding indicates the importance of working with all pregnant populations towards pregnancy acceptance, as such acceptance has important implications for the child's later attachment.

The other study considering family attachment is McCarthy's (2007) mixed-method dissertation. This study considered 61 foster, kinship and adoptive caregivers' attachment and their children's functioning, attempting to identify risk and resilience factors in children's lives. She found that caregivers' attachment insecurity predicted children's low functioning, while social and community supports for caregivers were sources of resilience, predicting children's higher functioning. This study is important for its identification not only of risk, but also of resiliency factors for children and the role of attachment in this.

Two other studies by social workers contribute to the important literature considering family and individual attachment across time. Iwaniec and Sneddon (2001) followed 44 nonorganic failure-to-thrive children and their families for 20 years after identification and treatment. Thirty one of the original children participated in this 20-year follow up study, which considered differences in attachment classification from childhood to adulthood. Notably, many insecurely attached failure-to-thrive children were classified as securely attached adults (30%), while 50% of the sample experienced no change in attachment. The authors point to the importance of attachment-oriented interventions in such populations, as well as the impact of major life events on changes in attachment style.

Leifer, Kilbane, Jacobsen, and Grossman (2004) examined the attachment and abuse histories and current functioning of 199 African-American mothers and 106 grandmothers of sexually abused and nonsexually abused children. Notably, the mothers of abused children "reported more severe histories of childhood abuse and neglect, more serious problems in their family of origin, and less positive relationships with their mothers" (Leifer et al., 2004, p. 670), as well as more problems in current functioning. Interestingly, the authors found no difference between the two groups of mothers in terms of attachment style. However, grandmothers' opinions of currently poor or ambivalent relationships with their daughters were associated with the sexual abuse of the grandchild. The findings that a mother's childhood disruptions and family of origin attachment difficulties are significantly associated with daughters' sexual abuse are important, suggesting that there are important intergenerational vulnerabilities to sexual abuse which attachment histories may help to predict.

Conclusion

As this brief review makes clear, social workers have made an important contribution to the field of attachment research. Because of the natural match between social work practice and attachment concepts, social workers are increasingly producing original articles, creative applications, and research designs that contribute to the body of attachment knowledge as a whole. Attachment research has long been conducted primarily by psychologists, despite the fact that attachment theory fits well with social workers' person in environment perspective. The dearth of attachment research by social workers is perhaps due to the preponderance of MSWs rather than PhDs in social work. Since the MSW is considered the terminal degree for practice, there has not been as much emphasis on conducting empirical research within social work. Now, however, social workers are beginning to recognize the utility of attachment as a theoretical basis for both practice and research, and they are contributing significantly to the literature of both.

Social workers have explored several important domains of attachment across all ages. In the field of childhood attachment research, some areas that social work researchers examine are attachment in foster care populations, the impact of parental attachment, attachment in divorced families, and attachment in young children. Studies focused on adolescents and attachment often consider the family and environmental contexts of such attachment. Social work researchers also examine attachment in younger adults through later adulthood from various perspectives. Some have sought to understand predictive patterns of attachment, while others have explored mental health phenomena or treatment outcomes using attachment as a variable. Studies used both quantitative and qualitative methodologies, utilizing primarily exploratory research designs. There are still some gaps in the literature. Future social work research should consider geriatric populations, as well as experimental designs with all populations, bringing greater rigor to this literature.

Attachment theory's contribution to our understanding of human development has assisted clinicians in practical application. Much of social work research seeks to build upon these contributions in order to advance clinical intervention strategies. With implications ranging from infant–caregiver attachment to the treatment of psychological disorders, social work research in the field of attachment provides practitioners with information that is easily integrated into practice. This developing focus of attachment theory in social work research has resulted in the important and growing use of attachment-based interventions in the field of clinical social work.

Study Questions

1. What are some of the gaps in the attachment literature written by social workers? Design a study that would fill one of the existing gaps.
2. What does the social work attachment literature tell us about the impact of the foster caregiver's attachment style on the adjustment of children in foster care? How should this information inform or modify current child welfare practices?
3. What does the social work attachment literature tell us about the intergenerational transmission of attachment? How should this knowledge inform our work with families?
4. Since attachment issues are central to social work practice, why has the contribution of the social work profession to attachment research lagged behind that of other mental health professions?
5. How have social work researchers been leaders in the examination of attachment processes within diverse and oppressed populations?

References

Abidin, R. R. (1990). *Parenting Stress Index/Short Form*. Charlottesville, VA: Pediatric Psychology Press.

Abidin, R. R. (1995). *Parenting Stress Index: Professional manual* (3rd ed.). Odessa, FL: Psychological Assessment Resources.

Achenbach, T. M. (1992). *Child behavior checklist for ages 4–18*. Burlington, VT: University of Vermont.

Achenbach, T. M. (2001). *Manual for the Child Behavior Checklist for ages 6–18 and 2000 profile*. Burlington, VT: University of Vermont, Department of Psychiatry.

Ainsworth, M. D. S., Blehar, M., Waters, E., & Wall, S. (1978). *Patterns of attachment: A psychological study of the Strange Situation*. Hillsdale, NJ: Lawrence Erlbaum.

Akers, R. L. (2000). *Criminological theories: Introduction and evaluation* (3rd ed.). Los Angeles, CA: Roxbury.

Allen, J. P., & Land, D. (1999). Attachment in adolescents. In J. Cassidy & P. R. Shaver (Eds.), *Handbook of attachment: theory, research and clinical applications* (pp. 319–335). New York: Guildford Press.

American Psychiatric Association. (1987). *Diagnostic and statistical manual of mental disorders* (3rd ed., rev.). Washington, DC: American Psychiatric Press.

Andersson, G. (1984). *Barn på barnhem (Small children in a children's home)*. Unpublished Doctoral, Department of Psychology, Lund University, Lund.

Andersson, G. (1988). *En uppföljning av barn som skilts från sina föräldrar (A follow-up of children separated from their parents)*. Lund: School of Social Work, Lund University.

Andersson, G. (1999a). Children in residential and foster care – a Swedish example. *International Journal of Social Welfare, 8*(4), 253–266.

Andersson, G. (1999b). Skolsituationen för barn i familjehem (The school situation for children in foster care). *Socionomen, 8*, 19–29.

Andersson, G. (2005). Family relations, adjustment and well-being in a longitudinal study of children in care. *Child & Family Social Work, 10*(1), 43–56.

Andersson, P., & Eisemann, M. (2004). Parental rearing and substance related disorders – A multifactorial controlled study in a Swedish sample. *Clinical Psychology & Psychotherapy, 11*(6), 392–400.

Armsden, G. C., & Greenberg, M. T. (1987). The Inventory of Parent and Peer Attachment: Individual differences and their relationship to psychological well-being in adolescence. *Journal of Youth and Adolescence, 16*(5), 427–454.

Bartholomew, K., & Horowitz, L. M. (1991). Attachment styles among young adults: A test of a four-category model. *Journal of Personality and Social Psychology, 61*(2), 226–244.

Beck, A. T., & Steer, R. A. (1993). *Manual for the Beck Hopelessness Scale*. San Antonio, TX: Psychological Corporation.

Beck, A., Steer, R., & Brown, G. (1987). *Beck Depression Inventory*. San Antonio, TX: The Psychological Corporation.

Behar, L. B. (1977). The preschool behavior questionnaire. *Journal of Abnormal Child Psychology, 5*(3), 265–275.

Behar, L., & Stringfield, S. (1974). A behavior rating scale for the preschool child. *Developmental Psychology, 10*(5), 601–610.

Ben-Ari, A. (2004). Sources of social support and attachment styles among Israeli Arab students. *International Social Work, 47*(2), 187–201.

Ben-Ari, A., & Lavee, Y. (2005). Dyadic characteristics of individual attributes: Attachment, neuroticism, and their relation to marital quality and closeness. *American Journal of Orthopsychiatry, 75*(4), 621–631.

Benda, B. B. (2002). Religion and violent offenders in boot camp: A structural equation model. *Journal of Research in Crime and Delinquency, 39*(1), 91–121.

Benda, B. B. (2003). Discriminators of suicide thoughts and attempts among homeless veterans who abuse substances. *Suicide and Life-Threatening Behavior, 33*(4), 430–442.

Benda, B. B., & Corwyn, R. F. (2002). The effect of abuse in childhood and in adolescence on violence among adolescents. *Youth & Society, 33*(3), 339–365.

Benda, B. B., & Toombs, N. J. (2002). Two preeminent theoretical models: A proportional hazard rate analysis of recidivism. *Journal of Criminal Justice, 30*(3), 217–228.

Bennett, S. (2001). Two mothers and their child: A multimethod study of parenting bonds and division of labor within lesbian adoptive families. *Dissertation Abstracts International Section A: Humanities and Social Sciences, 62*, 1582–1582.

Bernstein, D. P., & Fink, L. (1998). *Childhood Trauma Questionnaire: A retrospective self-report questionnaire and manual.* San Antonio, TX: The Psychological Corporation.

Bettmann, J. (2006). Shifts in attachment relationships: A quantitative study of adolescents in brief residential treatment. *Dissertation Abstracts International Section A: Humanities and Social Sciences, 66*(9-A), 3458.

Bond, S. B., & Bond, M. (2004). Attachment styles and violence within couples. *Journal of Nervous and Mental Disease, 192*(12), 857–863.

Bowlby, J. (1947). The study of human relations in the child guidance clinic. *Journal of Social Issues, 3*, 35–41.

Brennan, K. A., Clark, C. L., & Shaver, P. R. (1998). Self-report measurement of adult attachment. In J. A. Simpson & W. S. Rholes (Eds.), *Attachment theory and close relationships* (pp. 46–76). New York: Guilford Press.

Bretherton, I. (1992). The origins of attachment theory: John Bowlby and Mary Ainsworth. *Development Psychology, 28*, 759–773. Retrieved from http://www.psychology.sunysb.edu/attachment/online/inge_origins.pdf.

Bretherton, I., Ridgeway, D., & Cassidy, J. (1990). Assessing the internal working models of the attachment relationship: An attachment story completion task for 3-yearolds. In M. T. Greenberg, D. Cicchetti, & E. M. Cummings (Eds.), *Attachment in the preschool years: Theory, research, and intervention* (pp. 273–308). Chicago: University of Chicago Press.

Briere, J., & Runtz, M. (1988). Symptomatology associated with childhood sexual victimization in a nonclinical adult sample. *Child Abuse & Neglect, 12*, 51–59.

Briere, J., & Runtz, M. (1989). The Trauma Symptom Checklist (TSC-33): Early data on a new scale. *Journal of Interpersonal Violence, 4*, 151–163.

Burge, S., & Figley, C. (1982). *The social support scale.* Unpublished manuscript, Purdue University.

Buss, A. H., & Plomin, R. (1984). *Temperament: early developing personality traits.* Hillsdale, NJ: Lawrence Erlbaum Associates, Publishers.

Buttell, F., Muldoon, J., & Carney, M. (2005). An application of attachment theory to court-mandated batterers. *Journal of Family Violence, 20*(4), 211–217.

Caldwell, B., & Bradley, R. (1984). *Home observation for the measurement of the environment.* Little Rock, AK: University of Arkansas.

Carlson, K. A. (1981). A modern personality test for offenders: The Carlson Psychological Survey. *Criminal Justice and Behavior, 8*(2), 185–200.

Carney, M. M., & Buttell, F. P. (2005). Exploring the relevance of attachment theory as a dependent variable in the treatment of women mandated into treatment for domestic violence offenses. *Journal of Offender Rehabilitation, 41*(4), 33–61.

Chang, A. C. (2007). Perceived attachment security and psychological adjustment in recently adopted pre-adolescents. *Dissertation Abstracts International Section A: Humanities and Social Sciences, 67*(12-A), 4700.

Chassler, L. (1997). Understanding anorexia nervosa and bulimia nervosa from an attachment perspective. *Clinical Social Work Journal, 25*(4), 407–423.

Cicirelli, V. G. (1995). A measure of caregiving daughters' attachment to elderly mothers. *Journal of Family Psychology, 9*(1), 89–94.

Cohen, O., & Finzi-Dottan, R. (2005). Parent-child relationships during the divorce process: From attachment theory and intergenerational perspective. *Contemporary Family Therapy: An International Journal, 27*(1), 81–99.

Cole, S. A. (2005a). Foster caregiver motivation and infant attachment: How do reasons for fostering affect relationships? *Child & Adolescent Social Work Journal, 22*(5), 441–457.

Cole, S. A. (2005b). Infants in foster care: Relational and environmental factors affecting attachment. *Journal of Reproductive and Infant Psychology, 23*(1), 43–61.

Corvo, K. (2006). Violence, separation, and loss in the families of origin of domestically violent men. *Journal of Family Violence, 21*(2), 117–125.

Cowan, C. P., & Cowan, P. A. (1988). Who does what when partners become parents: Implications for men, women, and marriage. *Marriage & Family Review, 12*(3), 105–131.

Cowan, C. P., & Cowan, P. A. (1990). Who does what? In J. Touliatos, B. Permutter, & M. Straus (Eds.), *Handbook of family measurement techniques* (pp. 447–448). Beverly Hills, CA: Sage.

Cutrona, C. E., & Russell, D. (1987). The provisions of social relationships and adaptation to stress. In W. H. Jones & D. Perlman (Eds.), *Advances in personal relationships* (Vol. 1, pp. 37–68). Greenwich, CT: JAI Press.

Davis, M. H. (1983). Measuring individual differences in empathy: Evidence for a multidimensional approach. *Journal of Personality and Social Psychology, 44*(1), 113–126.

De Gangi, G., Poisson, S., Sickel, R., & Wiener, A. S. (1995). *Infant Toddler Symptom Checklist.* Tuscon, AZ: Therapy Skill Builders, the Psychological Corporation.

Derogatis, L. R. (1977). *The SCL-90 manual F: scoring, administration & procedures for the SCL-90.* Baltimore: John Hopkins University, School of Medicine, Clinical Psychometrics Unit.

Derogatis, L. R. (1992). *SCL–90–R: Administration, scoring & procedures manual–II.* Towson, MD: Clinical Psychometric Research.

Derogatis, L. R. (1994). *Symptom Checklist-90-R: Administration, scoring and procedure manual for the revised version of the SCL-90a.* Minneapolis, MN.: National Computer Systems.

Dibble, E., & Cohen, D. J. (1974). Companion instruments for measuring children's competence and parental style. *Archives of General Psychiatry, 30*(6), 805–815.

Diener, E., Emmons, R. A., Larsen, R. J., & Griffin, S. (1985). The satisfaction with life scale. *Journal of Personality Assessment, 49*(1), 71–75.

Dunst, C. J., & Trivette, C. M. (1986). *Support Functions Scale: Reliability and validity.* Asheville, NC: Winterberry Press.

Elliot, D., Huizinga, D., & Ageton, S. (1985). *Explaining delinquency and drug abuse.* Beverly Hills, CA: Sage.

Ellison, C. W. (1983). Spiritual well-being: Conceptualization and measurement. *Journal of Psychology & Theology, 11*(4), 330–340.

Epstein, S. (1983). *The mother–father–peer scale.* Unpublished manuscript, University of Massachusetts, Amherst.

Erikson, E. (1968). *Identity: Youth and crisis.* New York: Norton.

Eysenck, S. B., Eysenck, H. J., & Barrett, P. (1985). A revised version of the Psychoticism scale. *Personality and Individual Differences, 6*(1), 21–29.

Falsetti, S. A. (1997). *A review of the modified PTSD symptom scale.* Paper presented at the 13th Annual Meeting of the International Society of Traumatic Stress Studies, Montreal, Canada.

Falsetti, S. A., Resnick, H. S., Resick, P. A., & Kilpatrick, D. G. (1993). The modified PTSD symptom scale: A brief self–report measure of posttraumatic stress disorder. *Behavior Therapist, 16*, 161–162.

Fenney, J. A., Noller, P., & Hanrahan, M. (1994). Assessing adult attachment. In M. B. Sperling & W. H. Berman (Eds.), *Attachment in adults* (pp. 128–152). New York: Guilford.

Finzi, R., Cohen, O., & Ram, A. (2000). Attachment and divorce. *Journal of Family Psychotherapy, 11*(1), 1–20.

Finzi, R., Har-Even, D., Weizman, A., Tyano, S., & Shnit, D. (1996). The adaptation of the Attachment Styles Questionnaire for latency-aged children. *Psychologia: Israel Journal of Psychology, 5*(2), 167–177.

Finzi, R., Ram, A., Har-Even, D., Shnit, D., & Weizman, A. (2001). Attachment styles and aggression in physically abused and neglected children. *Journal of Youth and Adolescence, 30*(6), 769–786.

Finzi-Dottan, R., Cohen, O., Iwaniec, D., Sapir, Y., & Weizman, A. (2006). The child in the family of a drug-using father: Attachment styles and family characteristics. *Journal of Social Work Practice in the Addictions, 6*(1), 89–111.

Finzi-Dottan, R., Manor, I., & Tyano, S. (2006). ADHD, temperament, and parental style as predictors of the child's attachment patterns. *Child Psychiatry & Human Development, 37*(2), 103–114.

Florian, V., & Drory, Y. (1990). Mental Health Inventory (MHI) – Psychometric properties and normative data in the Israeli population. *Psychologia: Israel Journal of Psychology, 2*(1), 26–35.

Fowers, B. J., & Olson, D. H. (1993). ENRICH Marital Satisfaction Scale: A brief research and clinical tool. *Journal of Family Psychology, 7*(2), 176–185.

Fraley, R. C., Waller, N. G., & Brennan, K. A. (2000). An item response theory analysis of self-report measures of adult attachment. *Journal of Personality and Social Psychology, 78*(2), 350–365.

Griffin, D. W., & Bartholomew, K. (1994). The metaphysics of measurement: The case of adult attachment. In K. Bartholomew & D. Perlman (Eds.), *Advances in personal relationships: Vol. 5. Attachment processes in adulthood* (pp. 17–52). London: Jessica Kingsley.

Hahm, H. C., Lahiff, M., & Guterman, N. B. (2003). Acculturation and parental attachment in Asian-American adolescents' alcohol use. *Journal of Adolescent Health, 33*(2), 119–129.

Hamama-Raz, Y., & Solomon, Z. (2006). Psychological adjustment of aelanoma survivors: The contribution of hardiness, attachment, and cognitive appraisal. *Journal of Individual Differences, 27*(3), 172–182.

Hare, B. R. (1996). The HARE General and Area-Specific (School, Peer and Home) Self-Esteem Scale. In R. L. Jones (Ed.), *Handbook of tests and measures for Black populations* (Vol. 2, pp. 199–206). Hampton, VA: Cobb & Henry Publishers.

Harris, K. M., Halpern, C. T., Entzel, P., Tabor, J., Bearman, P. S., & Udry, J. R. (2008). *The National Longitudinal Study of Adolescent Health: Research design.* Retrieved September 8, 2009, from http://www.cpc.unc.edu/projects/addhealth/design.

Hart, M. B. (2006). What five-year-old children say about their attachment security and their coping strategies when presented with stressful situations in story form: An exploratory study. *Dissertation Abstracts International Section A: Humanities and Social Sciences, 66*(9-A), 3463.

Hazan, C., & Shaver, P. (1987). Romantic love conceptualized as an attachment process. *Journal of Personality and Social Psychology, 52*(3), 511–524.

Heran, W. J. (2006). The effects of global empathy training on attachment styles, social competencies and empathy deficits with male adolescent sex offenders in court-ordered residential treatment. *Dissertation Abstracts International Section A: Humanities and Social Sciences, 66*(9-A), 3463.

Hirschfeld, R., Klerman, G., Gough, H., Barrett, J., Korchin, S., & Chodoff, P. (1977). A measure of interpersonal dependency. *Journal of Personality Assessment, 41*(6), 610–618.

Hockenberry, S. L., & Billingham, R. E. (1987). Sexual orientation and boyhood gender conformity: Development of the Boyhood Gender Conformity Scale (BGCS). *Archives of Sexual Behavior, 16*(6), 475–492.

Hoffman, J. A. (1984). Psychological separation of late adolescents from their parents. *Journal of Counseling Psychology, 31*(2), 170–178.

Hudson, W. W. (1990). *The MPSI technical manual.* Tempe, AZ: Walmer Publishing Company.

Hudson, W. (1997). *Walmyr Assessment Scales Scoring Manual.* Tallahassee, FL: Walmyr Publishing Co.

Inch, L. J. (1999). Aspects of foster fathering. *Child & Adolescent Social Work Journal, 16*(5), 393–412.

Inderbitzen, H. M., & Foster, S. L. (1992). The Teenage Inventory of Social Skills: Development, reliability, and validity. *Psychological Assessment, 4*(4), 451–459.

Ireton, H., & Thwing, E. (1980). *Minnesota Infant Development Inventory.* Minneapolis, MN: Behavior Science Systems.

Ispa, J. M., Sable, M. R., Porter, N., & Csizmadia, A. (2007). Pregnancy acceptance, parenting stress, and toddler attachment in low-income black families. *Journal of Marriage and Family, 69*(1), 1–13.

Iwaniec, D., & Sneddon, H. (2001). Attachment style in adults who failed to thrive as children: Outcomes of a 20 year follow-up study of factors influencing maintenance or change in attachment style. *British Journal of Social Work, 31*(2), 179–195.

Jones, K. A., & Benda, B. B. (2004). Alcohol use among adolescents with non-residential fathers: A study of assets and deficits. *Alcoholism Treatment Quarterly, 22*(1), 3–25.

Kerns, K. A., Klepac, L., & Cole, A. (1996). Peer relationships and preadolescents' perceptions of security in the child-mother relationship. *Developmental Psychology, 32*(3), 457–466.

Kessler, T. A. (1998). The Cognitive Appraisal of Health Scale: Development and psychometric evaluation. *Research in Nursing & Health, 21*(1), 73–82.

Kobasa, S. C., & Puccetti, M. C. (1983). Personality and social resources in stress resistance. *Journal of Personality and Social Psychology, 45*(4), 839–850.

Landolt, M. A., Bartholomew, K., Saffrey, C., Oram, D., & Perlman, D. (2004). Gender nonconformity, childhood rejection, and adult attachment: A study of gay men. *Archives of Sexual Behavior, 33*(2), 117–128.

Lazarus, R., & Folkman, S. (1984). *Stress, appraisal, and coping*. New York: Springer Publishing.

Leifer, M., Kilbane, T., Jacobsen, T., & Grossman, G. (2004). A three-generational study of transmission of risk for sexual abuse. *Journal of Clinical Child and Adolescent Psychology, 33*(4), 662–672.

London, K., Peterson, L., & Piccinino, L. (1995). The National Survey of Family Growth: Principal source of statistics on unintended pregnancy: Supplement to Chapter 2. In S. S. Brown & L. Eisenberg (Eds.), *The best intentions. Unintended pregnancy and the well-being of children and families* (pp. 286–295). Washington, DC: Institute of Medicine, National Academy Press.

Lonergan, M. R. (2003). Parental attachment, psychological separation and learning-disabled and non-disabled students' success in a college away from home. *Dissertation Abstracts International Section A: Humanities and Social Sciences, 64*(5-A), 1849.

Lyn, T. S., & Burton, D. L. (2004). Adult attachment and sexual offender status. *American Journal of Orthopsychiatry, 74*(2), 150–159.

McCarthy, G. D. E. (2003). The clinician's guide to the Behavior Assessment System for Children (BASC): A review. *Clinical Social Work Journal, 31*(4), 440–443.

McCarthy, G. D. E. (2007). *Doing well and doing poorly in care: Caregivers' attachment status and other risk and resilience predictors of children's outcomes in kinship, foster, and adoptive placements*. US: Smith College School of Social Work.

McMillen, J. C. (1992). Attachment theory and clinical social work. *Clinical Social Work Journal, 20*(2), 205–218.

McLellan, A. T., Kushner, H., Metzger, D., & Peters, R. (1992). The fifth edition of the Addiction Severity Index. *Journal of Substance Abuse Treatment, 9*(3), 199–213.

Mikulincer, M., & Florian, V. (2000). Exploring individual differences in reactions to mortality salience: Does attachment style regulate terror management mechanisms? *Journal of Personality and Social Psychology, 79*(2), 260–273.

Mikulincer, M., Florian, V., & Tolmacz, R. (1990). Attachment styles and fear of personal death: A case study of affect regulation. *Journal of Personality and Social Psychology, 58*(2), 273–280.

Milner, J. (1984). *CAP Inventory Form IV*. De Kalb, IL: Psytec Corporation.

NICHD Early Child Care Research Network. (1997). The effects of infant child care on infant-mother attachment security: Results of the NICHD study of early child care. *Child Development, 68*(5), 860–879.

Olson, S. L. (1985). *The preschool competence questionnaire: Factor structure, longitudinal stability, and convergence with ratings of maladjustment*. Unpublished Manuscript, University of Michigan, Ann Arbor, MI.

Olson, D. H. (1986). Circumplex model VII: Validation studies and FACES III. *Family Process, 25*(3), 337–351.

Olson, S. L., & Lifgren, K. (1988). Concurrent and longitudinal correlates of preschool peer sociometrics: Comparing rating scale and nomination measures. *Journal of Applied Developmental Psychology, 9*(4), 409–420.

Orr, E., & Westman, M. (1990). Does hardiness moderate stress, and how? A review. In M. Rosenbaum (Ed.), *On coping skills, self-control, and adaptive behavior* (pp. 64–94). New York: Springer-Verlag.

Page, T., & Bretherton, I. (2003). Representations of attachment to father in the narratives of preschool girls in post-divorce families: Implications for family relationships and social development. *Child & Adolescent Social Work Journal, 20*(2), 99–122.

Parker, G., Tupling, H., & Brown, L. B. (1979). A parental bonding instrument. *British Journal of Medical Psychology, 52*(1), 1–10.

Pearlman, L. A. (1996). The Traumatic Stress Institute Belief Scale, Revision L. In B. Stamm (Ed.), *Measurement of stress, trauma and adaptation* (pp. 415–417). Lutherville, MD: Sidran Press.

Perris, C. (1988). A theoretical framework for linking the experience of dysfunctional parental rearing attitudes with manifest psychopathology. *Acta Psychiatrica Scandinavica, 78*(344), 93–109.

Perris, C., Fowler, D., Skagerlind, I., Olsson, M., & Thorsson, C. (1998). Development and preliminary application of a new scale for assessing dysfunctional working models of self and others (DWM-S) in severely disturbed patients. *Acta Psychiatrica Scandinavica, 98*(3), 219–223.

Perris, C., Jacobsson, L., Lindstrom, H., von Knorring, L., & Perris, H. (1980). Development of a new inventory for assessing memories of parental rearing behaviour. *Acta Psychiatrica Scandinavica, 61*(4), 265–274.

Phinney, J. S. (1992). The multigroup ethnic identity measure: A new scale for use with diverse groups. *Journal of Adolescent Research, 7*(2), 156–176.

Pottharst, K., & Kessler, R. (1990). Appendix A: Attachment History Questionnaire. In K. Pottharst (Ed.), *Research explorations in adult attachment* (pp. 338–353). New York: Peter Lang Publishing.

Resnick, H. S., Best, C. L., Kilpatrick, D. G., Freedy, J. R., & Falsetti, S. A. (1993). *Trauma Assessment for Adults–Self–Report*. Charleston, SC: The National Crime Victims Research and Treatment Center, Medical University of South Carolina.

Reynolds, C. R., & Kamphaus, R. W. (1992). *Behavior Assessment System for Children*. Circle Pines, MN: American Guidance Services.

Rodell, D. E., Benda, B. B., & Rodell, L. (2003). Suicidal thoughts among homeless alcohol and other drug abusers. *Alcoholism Treatment Quarterly, 21*(2), 57–74.

Rosenberg, M. (1965). *Society and the adolescent self-image*. Princeton, NJ: Princeton University Press.

Rothbart, M. K. (1981). Measurement of temperament in infancy. *Child Development, 52*(2), 569–578.

Runyan, D., Hunter, W., & Everson, M. (1992). *Maternal support for child victims of sexual abuse: Determinants and implications*. Final report (Grant No. 90-CA-B68). Washington, DC: National Center on Child Abuse and Neglect.

Scheier, M. F., Carver, C. S., & Bridges, M. W. (1994). Distinguishing optimism from neuroticism (and trait anxiety, self-mastery, and self-esteem): A reevaluation of the Life Orientation Test. *Journal of Personality and Social Psychology, 67*(6), 1063–1078.

Schofield, G., & Brown, K. (1999). Being there: A family centre worker's role as a secure base for adolescent girls in crisis. *Child & Family Social Work, 4*(1), 21–31.

Schwartz, A. E., McRoy, R. G., & Downs, A. C. (2004). Adolescent mothers in a transitional living facility: An exploratory study of support networks and attachment patterns. *Journal of Adolescent Research, 19*(1), 85–112.

Selzer, M. L., Vinokur, A., & van Rooijen, L. (1975). A self-administered Short Michigan Alcoholism Screening Test (SMAST). *Journal of Studies on Alcohol, 36*(1), 117–126.

Sherer, M. (1982). The Self-efficacy Scale: Construction and validation. *Psychological Reports, 51*(2), 663–671.

Sim, T. N., & Loh, B. S. M. (2003). Attachment to God: Measurement and dynamics. *Journal of Social and Personal Relationships, 20*(3), 373–389.

Snyder, D. K. (1997). *Marital Satisfaction Inventory, Revised (MSI-R) manual.* Los Angeles, CA: Western Psychological Services.

Stalker, C. A., Gebotys, R., & Harper, K. (2005). Insecure attachment as a predictor of outcome following inpatient trauma treatment for women survivors of childhood abuse. *Bulletin of the Menninger Clinic, 69*(2), 137–156.

Steinberg, L., & Silverberg, S. B. (1986). The vicissitudes of autonomy in early adolescence. *Child Development, 57*(4), 841–851.

Straus, M. A. (1979). Measuring intrafamily conflict and violence: The Conflict Tactics (CT) Scales. *Journal of Marriage & the Family, 41*(1), 75–88.

Straus, M. A., Hamby, S. L., Boney-McCoy, S., & Sugarman, D. B. (1996). The revised Conflict Tactics Scales (CTS2): Development and preliminary psychometric data. *Journal of Family Issues, 17*(3), 283–316.

Tellegen, A. (1982). *Brief manual for the Multidimensional Personality Questionnaire.* Unpublished manuscript, University of Minnesota, Minneapolis.

Turnage, B. F. (2004). African American mother- daughter relationships mediating daughter's self-esteem. *Child & Adolescent Social Work Journal, 21*(2), 155–173.

van Ijzendoorn, M. H., Schuengel, C., & Bakermans-Kranenburg, M. J. (1999). Disorganized attachment in early childhood: Meta-analysis of precursors, concomitants, and sequelae. *Development and Psychopathology, 11*(2), 225–249.

Veit, C. T., & Ware, J. E. (1983). The structure of psychological distress and well-being in general populations. *Journal of Consulting and Clinical Psychology, 51*(5), 730–742.

Wagnild, G. M., & Young, H. M. (1993). Development and psychometric evaluation of the Resilience Scale. *Journal of Nursing Measurement, 1*(2), 165–178.

Waters, E. (1987). *Attachment behavior Q-set: Revision 3.0.* Unpublished manuscript, State University of New York, Stony Brook.

Weissman, A. N. (1979). *The Dysfunctional Attitude Scale: A validation study.* US: ProQuest Information & Learning.

Weissman, A. N., & Beck, A. T. (1978). *Development and validation of the Dysfunctional Attitude Scale: A preliminary investigation.* Paper presented at the meeting of the American Educational Research Association, Toronto, Canada.

Wells, K. (1999). *Caregiver Interview Form (6/6/99 ed.).* Cleveland, OH: Mandel School of Applied Social Sciences, Case Western Reserve University.

West, M., Rose, S., Spreng, S., & Adam, K. (2000). The Adolescent Unresolved Attachment Questionnaire: The assessment of perceptions of parental abdication of caregiving behavior. *Journal of Genetic Psychology, 161*(4), 493–503.

West, M., Rose, M. S., Spreng, S., Sheldon-Keller, A., & Adam, K. (1998). Adolescent Attachment Questionnaire: A brief assessment of attachment in adolescence. *Journal of Youth and Adolescence, 27*(5), 661–673.

West, M., Sheldon, A., & Reiffer, L. (1987). An approach to the delineation of adult attachment: Scale development and reliability. *Journal of Nervous and Mental Disease, 175*(12), 738–741.

West, M., & Sheldon-Keller, A. (1994). *Patterns of relating: An adult attachment perspective.* New York: Guilford Press.

Zakin, G., Solomon, Z., & Neria, Y. (2003). Hardiness, attachment style, and long term psychological distress among Israeli POWs and combat veterans. *Personality and Individual Differences, 34*(5), 819–829.

Zimet, G. D., Dahlem, N. W., Zimet, S. G., & Farley, G. K. (1988). The Multidimensional Scale of Perceived Social Support. *Journal of Personality Assessment, 52*(1), 30–41.

Chapter 13
Implications of Attachment Theory for Social Work Education

Susanne Bennett and Kathleen Holtz Deal

> *The major function of attachment theory is to guide further research, which in turn will extend and refine our theoretical understanding.*

Ainsworth (1989, p. 715)

Historically, attachment theory has been an explanatory theory of human behavior applied to child development and, more recently, adult pair–bond relationships, personality structure, and psychopathology. In previous chapters, this book has demonstrated the current upsurge of the application of attachment theory to adult treatment processes and clinical relationships as well. Research studies on these topics have maintained a "micro" or "mezzo" center of attention, but over the past decade, attachment research has extended into institutional settings, adding an organizational focus to the theory (Mikulincer & Shaver, 2007). This new focus is useful for educators in the helping professions in understanding relationships between students and their instructors and for conceptualizing the development of professional identity and leadership.

Attachment theory's relevance for social work education is explored in this chapter, with applications to the classroom setting, the fieldwork internship, supervision relationships, academic learning, and professional development. An overview of the growing body of research germane to these topics will be examined. Although to date there are no studies on the association of attachment styles and critical thinking skills, a conceptual overlap exists between metacognitive monitoring, a hallmark of secure attachment (Hesse, 2008), and critical thinking, considered salient for social work education (Clark, 2002; Kersting & Mumm, 2001; Plath, English, Connors, & Beveridge, 1999). This too will be examined as a foundation for developing theory about attachment and cognitive processes in professional education.

S. Bennett (✉)
National Catholic School of Social Service, The Catholic University of America, Washington, DC, USA
e-mail: bennetts@cua.edu

S. Bennett and J.K. Nelson (Eds.), *Adult Attachment in Clinical Social Work*, Essential Clinical Social Work Series, DOI 10.1007/978-1-4419-6241-6_13, © Springer Science+Business Media, LLC 2010

The Academic Group and Agency Field Internship

Attachment and Academic Groups

Early in his writings, Bowlby (1969/1982) proposed: "During adolescence and adult life a measure of attachment behavior is commonly directed not only towards persons outside the family but also towards groups and institutions other than the family" (p. 207). He added that "a school or college" or "a work group" could "constitute for many people a subordinate attachment 'figure,' and for some people a principal attachment 'figure'" (p. 207). His ideas seem pertinent to adults being educated in careers such as the helping professions that call for strong relational skills, empathy, and self-awareness.

During the educational process, students often feel challenged by the emotional intensity of the training, as well as the complexity of the academic content. The challenging demands of professional graduate education generally lead them to rely on a cohort of fellow students as a safe haven and secure base. Indeed, research on group cohesion suggests that during demanding times, "groups can be attractive and effective sources of support, comfort, and relief" (Mikulincer & Shaver, 2007, p. 434; for more discussion of groups, see Page, Chap. 10). Through supportive relationships with instructors and classmates, adults develop a professional self or symbolic bond to a professional identity, similar to the child's personal self that unfolds through relationships with parents and family.

Research suggests that attachment styles influence adult reliance on social groups and institutions for support and on the relationships adults have with institutional leaders who serve attachment-related functions (Davidovitz, Mikulincer, Shaver, Izsak, & Popper, 2007; Mayseless & Popper, 2007; Rom & Mikulincer, 2003). As adolescents begin to deidealize and separate from parents, they lessen the use of parents as primary attachment figures and take on alternative figures through reliance on peers or romantic partners. Yet adult partners may not provide the full attachment function for each other, though they do provide support, because adults realize their partners are fallible, equal, and in need of mutual reassurance (Mayseless & Popper). As a result, they tend to look for an added sense of security and protection in their social institutions, such as a close group of friends or community, their work environment, or their church. They also turn to institutional leaders such as political and religious leaders, managers and supervisors, or they rely on a spiritual being or God (Kirkpatrick, 2005). Times of intense crisis and challenge especially present "fertile soil to the desire for a leader who is capable of giving reassurance and relieving deep anxieties" (Mayseless & Popper, p. 79). When adults embark on a career change and are under the academic demands of graduate training, for instance, they often turn to instructors, academic advisors, supervisors, and sometimes psychotherapists in search of "stronger and wiser" leaders who can provide the attachment functions of calming anxiety, empowering and motivating, and increasing self-esteem. When such leaders are found, they help to facilitate the development of the student's professional identity.

Research on attachment and leadership suggests that attachment styles play a significant role for both leaders and followers in the context of institutions (Davidovitz et al., 2007). A leader's incapacity or unwillingness to be sympathetic with followers' needs is thought to "heighten followers' anxiety, demoralization, or rebellion ('protest')" (Mikulincer & Shaver, 2007, p. 441). This phenomenon can be observed among students who perceive an instructor as unsympathetic or indifferent, so they reject the instructor's advice or guidance. From an attachment perspective, Mikulincer and Shaver propose that "the key factor in a leader's failure to empower followers is the development of an insecure attachment bond, because of the leader's lack of sensitivity and responsiveness to followers' genuine and legitimate needs" (p. 441). If a leader has an *anxious* or *preoccupied* attachment style (i.e., fearful of rejection and separation), the risk is that followers become unnecessarily dependent and healthy development is precluded. "Nervous but narcissistic teachers who draw too much attention to themselves, monopolize the 'air space' and cause their students to feel helpless rather than increasingly capable are examples" (Mikulincer & Shaver, p. 442). Other examples are *avoidant* or *dismissing* teachers (i.e., uncomfortable with dependency) who might use their leadership status to reinforce their inflated self-esteem, keep distance from emotional intimacy with students, and fail to provide an optimal classroom environment for student growth and professional development.

In considering the attachment style of followers, such as graduate students, adults with attachment insecurities are unable to benefit from comfort when it is offered in times of stress or have difficulty asking for support when they need it. They may reject the leader as a safe haven, even when the leader tries to be responsive and facilitating. Clearly, the attachment styles of both leaders and followers, and instructors and students, interact and mutually influence relationships. Keller (2003) has proposed that the discordant combinations of avoidant leader with anxious followers, or anxious leader with avoidant followers, can be the most challenging of institutionally based relationships. When followers are part of a group, such as students in an academic classroom, group cohesion organized around insecurity can become an overpowering force against an instructor who is perceived as uninformed and weak, rather than wiser and stronger.

Attachment and the Workplace

Because social work graduate education is designed for professional development and training, much emphasis is placed on experiential learning in field internships, in addition to academic coursework in classrooms. The agency field work experience usually runs concurrent with coursework and is considered central to the student's learning (Kadushin & Harkness, 2002; Munson, 2002). Consequently, research on attachment and work is applicable to a discussion of social work field education.

Hazan and Shaver (1990) were the first to examine the idea of work as a form of adult exploration, and they proposed that persons with secure attachment have secure work orientations. Their study of 670 men and women who answered a self-report survey in a Colorado newspaper confirmed that securely attached respondents reported high work satisfaction, while those with anxious or preoccupied attachments felt job insecurity and low appreciation from coworkers. Those with avoidant or dismissing attachments were satisfied with their job security – similar to securely attached respondents – but they were dissatisfied with their coworkers, focusing more on work activities than on relationships. Predictably, securely attached respondents had better work–relationship balance, but they placed higher value on their relationships than on their work. In other words, the findings of this study supported original theories of infant attachment regarding the balance between attachment and exploration in the securely attached (Ainsworth, Blehar, Water, & Wall, 1978). Hazan and Shaver note that "the balance between attachment and exploration associated with healthy functioning early in life is, in important respects, similar to the love/work balance that marks healthy functioning in adulthood" (p. 270).

The Hazan and Shaver (1990) findings have been conceptually replicated by a number of recent cross-sectional and longitudinal studies on attachment and work, looking at job dissatisfaction, burnout and distress at work, and job performance (see Mikulincer & Shaver, 2007, for an overview). "Taken together," state Mikulincer and Shaver, "these studies indicate that attachment insecurities contribute to poor adjustment in the workplace" (p. 240). These findings are important to consider when evaluating students in their field internships. Though many variables influence student adjustment to the field agency, attachment style may shape how easily students enter the agency setting, balance internship demands with personal relationships, prefer individual work vs. team work, and explore unfamiliar work assignments that could help them develop new skills. Attachment also may be associated with how secure and confident students feel as they interact with their clients in direct practice, their professional colleagues, and their field supervisors.

Attachment and Field Supervision

Though no study to date has examined student–instructor attachment in the classroom setting or student attachment in the field agency as an institution, a small number of empirical studies have evaluated the role of attachment in supervisory relationships of both social work and psychology students-in-training. Psychologists were the first to conceptualize the influence of student attachment styles on the student–supervisor relationship (Neswald-McCalip, 1995; Pistole & Watkins, 1995; Watkins, 1995). They proposed that the stress and novelty of learning to do psychotherapy activates the student's attachment behavioral system. Secure students generally use supervision as a secure base, but, suggested Watkins, insecure students may form pathological supervision attachments that are either too dependent on the supervisor or too dismissive.

More recently, social work educators Bennett and Saks (2006) proposed that students and supervisors are mutually influenced by their attachment styles in an interactive relationship. They suggested that attachment affects the supervisor's style of professional caregiving, and supervision becomes a *supervisory circle of security* that fluctuates based on the student's needs. At times the student comes to the supervisor as a safe haven for clarification, reassurance, and organization, and at other times, the student moves from the secure base of supervision to explore new activities in the field. When the supervisor has a secure attachment style, the student and supervisor are more likely to form a positive supervisory relationship. On the other hand, when the two have similar insecure attachment styles or there are discordant styles in the dyad, supervision becomes less effective, more challenging, and at times problematic. For example, if a supervisor's attachment is avoidant/ dismissive, while the student's attachment is anxious/preoccupied, a major supervision rupture may develop. The student's clinginess may trigger the supervisor's dismissiveness, while the supervisor's avoidance may heighten the student's sense of abandonment. In contrast, an anxious/preoccupied supervisor who is intrusive and over involved may trigger dismissiveness in an avoidant/dismissive student, who then refuses to use the supervisor's help. An insecure supervisor also may trigger anxiety or avoidance in an otherwise secure student because of the power that the supervisor has over the student.

Empirical studies on supervision have examined student attachment styles and their association with the *supervisory working alliance*, Bordin's (1983) concept defined as the goals, tasks, and bonds of supervision. Two studies of psychology doctoral students found a weak, but significant association between the attachment styles of students and their perceptions of the supervisory working alliance (Riggs & Bretz, 2006; White & Queener, 2003). In a similar cross-sectional study, Bennett, Mohr, BrintzenhofeSzoc, and Saks (2008) examined 72 master's level foundation social work students and their perceptions of field supervisors. This study expanded previous research by differentiating *general attachment* and *supervision-specific attachment*. Attachment research has made a distinction between an individual's global interpersonal style of relating across all close relationships (i.e., general attachment) and a relationship-specific attachment style that shifts, based on the individual's particular relationship, and has noted that the two interact (Cozzarelli, Hoekstra, & Bylsma, 2000; Creasey & Ladd, 2005; Klohnen, Weller, Luo, & Choe, 2005; Pierce & Lydon, 2001). Unlike an earlier study of psychology, counseling, and social work students that found similar attachment styles in both interpersonal and supervisory relationships (Foster, Lichtenberg, & Peyton, 2007), Bennett et al. found that a student's relationship-specific attachment with a field supervisor was a strong predictor of the supervisory working alliance, while general attachment was primarily unrelated. One exception was that students with higher levels of general avoidance were more likely to have insecure attachment-related perceptions of their supervisors.

A follow-up study of social work field supervision examined the interaction of attachment styles of students and supervisors as part of research that evaluated an attachment-based supervision training program (Deal & Bennett, 2009; Mohr, Bennett, & Deal, 2009). Titled a "Developmental-Relational Approach to Field Supervision," the training was an outgrowth of Bennett and Deal's (2009) conceptualization of the interface of attachment processes and student development. The effects of the 16-hour training were examined using a two-group, experimental design, with a sample of 100 supervisors and 65 students from two universities. Surveys administered three times over the academic year evaluated the supervisors and their students regarding their general attachment styles, their affect in relation to supervisory sessions, their perceptions of the supervisory working alliance, and their perceptions of student competencies. Students also evaluated their relationship-specific attachments to their supervisors.

Although preliminary findings in this study showed a mixed and complex picture, they did confirm a link between attachment and a number of variables in supervision. For example, students who scored with highly anxious general attachments experienced high negative affect about supervision at the beginning of their field placement and at mid-year. Similarly, supervisors with highly anxious attachments also reported high negative affect at the beginning of students' placements. Another significant association was the relationship between the supervisory working alliance and general attachments for both students and supervisors. At mid-year, two factors predicted supervisors' perceptions that they had a negative working alliance with their students – when supervisors had highly avoidant general attachments and when individual students had highly anxious general attachments. These associations disappeared by the end of the academic year. These findings suggest that positive alliances may be more difficult to develop or they develop more slowly when supervisors have a generally avoidant style. Likewise, supervisors may take longer or have more difficulty establishing a positive alliance when students have a generally anxious attachment style. It is important to note that this negative supervisory alliance was present at the time of year when these supervisors were performing their first formal evaluation of their students. Nevertheless, no associations existed between supervisor attachment and supervisor perceptions of student competencies at mid-year or at the end of the academic year. In other words, there is no evidence that supervisors rated their students more critically even when a negative alliance existed.

For students, there were a few significant associations between attachment and student perceptions of their own competencies. Students with avoidant supervisors were more likely to rate themselves as highly motivated at mid-year and at the end of the academic year. Anxious students saw themselves as having less self- and other awareness, less motivation, and more dependency at the beginning of the year, while avoidant students rated themselves as less motivated at mid-year. Overall, the findings from this study suggest a need for further research on the interface between attachment and the supervisory alliance and attachment and student competencies based on the perceptions of supervisors and students.

Attachment Styles and the Learning Process

How Attachment Affects Learning

Theoretically, attachment is believed to affect student learning because security in exploration, which is crucial to the learning process, differs based on attachment style. Moss and St-Laurent (2001, as cited in Larose, Bernire, & Tarabulsy, 2005) suggest that toddlers' secure exploratory style becomes internalized by middle childhood so that the child feels motivated, competent to learn, and values learning. Secure attachment in toddlers has been found to be related to greater effectiveness in solving tasks and in understanding others' minds, while longitudinal studies of children into adolescence have found positive relationships between securely attached children and the development of formal operational reasoning and academic achievement (see Larose et al. for a review of this literature). Geddes (2003, 2005) studied how insecurely attached elementary and secondary students behave in the classroom. As expected, she found that anxious/preoccupied students tended to cling to the teacher and experience learning tasks as irrelevant intrusions, resulting in poor academic performance, while avoidant/dismissing students resisted seeking assistance and had problems learning new material and being creative.

Studies of young adults also reveal the impact of attachment style on learning. Larose et al. (2005) studied students transitioning to college, a vulnerable time that could trigger attachment-related behaviors that might interfere with learning. The authors found that learning dispositions (emotional, cognitive, and behavioral resources) of secure autonomous students either remained stable or improved during their transition to college. Avoidant/dismissing students, by comparison, had lower grades for their first three college semesters and "reported lower levels of test preparation and attention in class, gave less priority to studies, and had more difficulty seeking teachers for help" (p. 287). The authors hypothesize that "the negative internal model held by dismissing students with regards to parental availability interferes with the student's attention capabilities" (p. 288). Elliot and Reis (2003) found that securely attached university undergraduates were less fearful of failure and more oriented toward mastery and performance than either avoidant or anxious students. In other studies, students with secure attachments who were seeking a GED were more likely to have positive friendships with peers, helpful relationships with their instructors, and the ability to complete their GED, in contrast to either avoidant or anxious students (Reio, Marcus, & Sanders-Reio, 2009).

Overall, the literature supports the proposition of Grossmann, Grossmann, and Zimmermann (1999, as cited in Larose et al., 2005) that attachment security results in an open-minded and careful but curious approach to reality, which favors competent exploration and leads to academic achievement. These research findings are important for educators at all academic levels because they help explain the advantages of a secure attachment in learning processes and outcomes. The next section will highlight some of the particular abilities that social work students need to learn and the connection of these abilities to attachment styles.

Mentalization, Empathy, and Critical Thinking Skills

Strengthening both interpersonal and critical thinking skills is important for successful social work student development. Interpersonal skills include the ability to form and maintain relationships, demonstrate empathy, and utilize self-and other awareness in relationships. Fonagy (2003) posits that securely attached individuals are well equipped to engage in interpersonal relationships because they have a strong capacity to *mentalize*, that is, "to attribute independent mental states to self and others to explain and predict behavior" (p. 226). Attachment style and mental-izing have been found to be highly correlated in a diverse sample of early adolescents (Humfress, O'Connor, Slaughter, Target, & Fonagy, 2002). Within a classroom setting, the strategy of withdrawing from interpersonal exchanges characteristic of individuals with an avoidant/dismissing style may lead to reluctance to seek needed help from a teacher or other students, while the dependency of those with anxious/preoccupied attachment styles may lead to overvaluing the teacher's opinions and a desire to be liked at the expense of self-direction and exploration.

Secure attachment and the ability to empathize are partially connected through the function of effortful control, a self-regulation skill acquired through the infant–caregiver attachment relationship which enables a child to focus attention based on internal priorities, independent of surroundings (Fonagy & Target, 2002). Effortful control has been linked to "social competence, empathy, sympathy, low levels of aggression, and the development of conscience" (Fonagy & Target, p. 319). In addition to the implications of the role played by effortful control in the self-direction required for learning, this function has particular relevance for social work students' development of empathic capacity. "The self-regulation capacity achieved though effortful control assists in the establishment of a sense of separateness. This allows the individual to attain a psychological closeness that enables him to be in touch with the feelings and thoughts of another person without being overwhelmed by that person's distress" (Fonagy & Target, pp. 319–320). The ability to empathize while maintaining personal boundaries, therefore, is theoretically and empirically connected to effortful control that develops within a secure attachment relationship. Without empathic capacity, social work students may either have difficulty connecting with instructors and/or clients because of an inability to perceive and interpret the inner world of another or feel overwhelmed in interpersonal relationships because of difficulty in experiencing themselves as separate.

Critical thinking has been identified by the Educational Policy and Accreditation Standards (EPAS) of the Council of Social Work Education (CSWE) (2008) as one of the ten core competencies social work students must master during their professional education. Critical thinking has been described by The Critical Thinking Delphi Project as follows:

> In critical thinking a person gives reasoned consideration to evidence, context, theories, methods, and criteria in order to form a purposeful judgment. At the same time, one uses these skills to monitor, correct, and improve the process one is using to form that judgment. The expert consensus includes this metacognitive self-regulation as a core critical thinking skill.

> as cited in Gendrop and Eisenhauer (1996, p. 330)

This description of critical thinking is relevant to social work education because it includes metacognition, or the ability to reflect on and evaluate one's thinking process, and it identifies decision-making as an outcome. Although interpersonal skills and critical thinking have often been studied separately, some empirical evidence shows that persons who think critically are more empathic (Belenky, Clinchy, Goldberger, & Tarule, 1986; Benack, as cited in Kurfiss, 1988; Goldberg, 1974).

The connection between attachment, mentalization, and critical thinking is largely conceptual at this point. The single study of BSW students that examined relationships between these variables showed mixed results. Padykula (2008) found that the capacity for mentalization of insecurely attached students was significantly lower than for those who were securely attached. However, she found no association between attachment style and reflective thinking, using a scale (Level of Reflective Learning Questionnaire) whose highest level represents the use of critical reflection. In a study exploring critical thinking skills and personality traits, Deal and Pittman (2009) found that social work students with higher levels of critical thinking were significantly more likely to be open-minded. This personality characteristic, as measured by the Neuroticism Extraversion Openness – Five Factor Inventory (NEO-FFI; Costa & McCrae, 1992), includes openness to feelings and new ideas, creativity, and a willingness to examine one's values – all qualities consistent with the capacity for exploration seen in secure attachment.

The exploration of connections between attachment and critical thinking offers a promising area for future research, because of the conceptual link between these two variables through the concept of mentalization. In order to think critically, an individual must be able to clearly identify a problem, differentiate her perspective from the perspectives of others, evaluate competing evidence using relevant criteria, and arrive at a considered judgment (Kurfiss, 1988; Paul, 1992). Thus, the capacity for mentalization prepares an individual to both engage in interpersonal relationships, as mentioned earlier, and also to understand that individual perspectives differ about what is "known" or "true," a capacity essential to the critical thinking process.

A related concept is that of *metacognitive monitoring*, which has been found to be associated with adult secure autonomous attachment (Hesse, 2008). Metacognitive monitoring, as used in attachment theory, includes the ability to recognize several kinds of distinctions, i.e., between reality and appearances, representations held by self and others, and changes over time (Forguson & Gopnik, 1988, as cited in Hesse). The ability to understand that knowledge is contextual and dependent on individual perception is particularly important for social work students whose learning constantly involves the ability to take the perspectives of others, including clients, classmates, field instructors, and other professionals.

Conclusion

Attachment theory has now expanded into areas of research not likely envisioned by Ainsworth and Bowlby when they began their collaborations over 40 years ago. Yet the extension of attachment theory into the organizational domains of higher education – especially academic programs that train professional social workers – seems to be a logical, appropriate fit. Attachment theory's concept of exploration applies to understanding adults in their development of new skills and professional identities. The concept of a secure base depicts the relationships students develop with professors, supervisors, and colleagues to motivate and support their exploration. Distinguishing the differences in attachment styles of students and educators enhances our understanding of why some students succeed while others struggle in the process of learning. Recognizing the connection between mentalization and critical thinking adds insight into reflective thinking, open-mindedness, and empathy. Indeed, because social work is a profession that values strong interpersonal skills and openness to differences, the capacity for mentalization – an outgrowth of secure attachment – is central to professional development.

Although limited research – the beginning studies on supervision – directly links higher education with attachment, attachment theory presents the opportunity to "extend and refine our theoretical understanding" (Ainsworth, 1989, p. 715). As previously stated, the theory offers a framework for discerning the interpersonal processes that are present in the instructional and practicum environments of social work education. However, incorporating this theory into the curriculum also holds promise. Students can benefit from knowledge of an attachment perspective on human behavior, child development, and family relationships, as well as attachment's empirical findings on personality formation, psychopathology, and psychotherapy. Social work educators can benefit from attachment-based training programs to improve their relational teaching skills and their insight into classroom and supervisory dynamics. In other words, weaving together the theoretical and empirical findings on attachment provides numerous opportunities for expanding the knowledge base of social workers and clarifies some of the educational processes of becoming a professional. Furthermore, emphasis on attachment theory renews appreciation for what is at the heart of social work – the importance of the relationship in clinical interventions and in professional education.

Study Questions

1. In considering your relationship with your primary supervisor in your agency, what interactions have taken place that lead you to think of this person as a "secure base" for exploring new professional activities?
2. Have you had any interactions that lead you to experience your supervisor as dismissing/avoidant or anxious/ambivalent in the way you relate to each other?
3. How does your understanding of attachment theory inform your experience of social work education and supervision?
4. What factors contribute to the differences or similarities you experience when you compare your general interpersonal style of relating with close family members in contrast to your relationships with specific professionals in your academic training or work environment?

5. This chapter suggests connections between attachment style, mentalization, and critical thinking. Can you think of a clinical example when your ability to mentalize (i.e., understand that the mental states of yourself and another person are different and use this knowledge to understand the other's behavior) affected your ability to think critically (i.e., examine a problem or situation from different perspectives, evaluate competing evidence, and arrive at a professional judgment)?

References

Ainsworth, M. D. S. (1989). Attachments beyond infancy. *American Psychologist, 44*(4), 709–716.
Ainsworth, M. D. S., Blehar, M. C., Waters, E., & Wall, S. (1978). *Patterns of attachment: A psychological study of the Strange Situation*. Hillsdale, NJ: Erlbaum.
Belenky, M. F., Clinchy, B. M., Goldberger, N. R., & Tarule, J. M. (1986). *Women's ways of knowing: The development of self, voice, and mind*. New York: Basic Books.
Benack, S. (1988). Relativistic thought: A cognitive basis for empathy in counseling. *Counselor Education and Supervision, 27*(3), 216–232.
Bennett, S., & Deal, K. (2009). Beginnings and endings in social work supervision: The interaction between attachment and developmental processes. *Journal of Teaching in Social Work, 29*(1), 101–117.
Bennett, S., Mohr, J., BrintzenhofeSzoc, K., & Saks, L. (2008). General and supervision-specific attachment styles: Relations to student perceptions of social work field supervisors. *Journal of Social Work Education, 42*(2), 75–94.
Bennett, S., & Saks, L. (2006). A conceptual application of attachment theory and research to the social work student–field instructor supervisory relationship. *Journal of Social Work Education, 42*(3), 157–169.
Bordin, E. (1983). A working alliance based model of supervision. *The Counseling Psychologist, 11*, 35–42.
Bowlby, J. (1969/1982). *Attachment and loss: Vol. 1. Attachment* (2nd ed.). New York: Basic Books.
Clark, H. G. (2002). A comparison of the critical thinking skills of BSW and MSW students. *The Journal of Baccalaureate Social Work, 7*(2), 63–75.
Costa, P. T., Jr., & McCrae, R. R. (1992). *NEO-PI-R professional manual*. Lutz, FL: Psychological Assessment Resources.
Council on Social Work Education. (2008) *Educational Policy and Accreditation Standards*. Retrieved from http://www.cswe.org/NR/rdonlyres/2A81732E-1776-4175-AC42 65974E96B E66/0/2008EducationalPolicyandAccreditationStandards.pdf.
Cozzarelli, C., Hoekstra, S., & Bylsma, W. (2000). General versus specific mental models of attachment: Are they associated with different outcomes? *Personality and Social Psychology Bulletin, 26*, 605–618.
Creasey, G., & Ladd, A. (2005). Generalized and specific attachment representations: Unique and interactive roles in predicting conflict behaviors in close relationships. *Personality and Social Psychology Bulletin, 31*, 1026–1038.
Davidovitz, R., Mikulincer, M., Shaver, P., Izsak, R., & Popper, M. (2007). Leaders as attachment figures: Leaders' attachment orientations predict leadership-related mental representations and followers' performance and mental health. *Journal of Personality and Social Psychology, 93*(4), 632–650.
Deal, K. H., & Bennett, S. (2009). *Developmental-relational approach to field supervision: An empirically based training model*. San Antonio, TX: Council of Social Work Education Annual Program Meeting.

Deal, K. H., & Pittman, J. (2009). Examining predictors of social work students' critical thinking skills. *Advances in Social Work, 10*(1), 87–102.

Elliot, A. J., & Reis, H. T. (2003). Attachment and exploration in adulthood. *Journal of Personality and Social Psychology, 85*, 317–331.

Fonagy, P. (2003). The development of psychopathology from infancy to adulthood: The mysterious unfolding of disturbance in time. *Infant Mental Health Journal, 24*(3), 212–239.

Fonagy, P., & Target, M. (2002). Early intervention and the development of self-regulation. *Psychological Inquiry, 22*, 307–335.

Forguson, L., & Gopnik, A. (1988). The ontogeny of common sense. In J. W. Astington, P. L. Harris, & D. R. Olson (Eds.), *Developing theories of mind* (pp. 226–243). New York: Cambridge University Press.

Foster, J. T., Lichtenberg, J. W., & Peyton, V. (2007). The supervisory attachment relationship as a predictor of the professional development of the supervisee. *Psychotherapy Research, 17*(3), 343–350.

Geddes, H. (2003). Attachment and the child in school. Part 1: Attachment theory and the "dependent" child. *Emotional and Behavioral Difficulties, 8*(3), 231–242.

Geddes, H. (2005). Attachment and learning. Part II: The learning profile of the avoidant and disorganized patterns. *Emotional and Behavioral Difficulties, 10*(2), 79–93.

Gendrop, S. C., & Eisenhauer, L. A. (1996). A transactional perspective on critical thinking. *Scholarly Inquiry for Nursing Practice: An International Journal, 10*(4), 329–345.

Goldberg, A. D. (1974). Conceptual system as a predisposition toward therapeutic communication. *Journal of Counseling Psychology, 21*(5), 364–368.

Grossmann, K. E., Grossmann, K., & Zimmermann, P. (1999). A wider view of attachment and exploration: Stability and change during the years of immaturity. In J. Cassidy & P. R. Shaver (Eds.), *Handbook of attachment: Theory, research and clinical applications* (pp. 760–786). New York: Guilford Press.

Hazan, C., & Shaver, P. (1990). Love and work: An attachment – theoretical perspective. *Journal of Personality and Social Psychology, 59*, 511–524.

Hesse, E. (2008). The adult attachment interview: Protocol, method of analysis, and empirical studies. In J. Cassidy & P. Shaver (Eds.), *Handbook of attachment: Theory, research, and clinical applications* (2nd ed., pp. 552–598). New York: Guilford Press.

Humfress, H., O'Connor, T., Slaughter, J., Target, M., & Fonagy, P. (2002). General and relationship-specific models of social cognition: Explaining the overlap and discrepancies. *Journal of Child Psychology and Psychiatry, 43*(7), 873–883.

Kadushin, A., & Harkness, D. (2002). *Supervision in social work* (4th ed.). New York: Columbia University Press.

Keller, T. (2003). Parental images as a guide to leadership sensemaking: An attachment perspective on implicit leadership theories. *Leadership Quarterly, 14*, 141–160.

Kersting, R. C., & Mumm, A. M. (2001). Are we teaching critical thinking in the classroom. *The Journal of Baccalaureate Social Work, 7*(1), 53–67.

Kirkpatrick, L. (2005). *Attachment, evolution, and the psychology of religion*. New York: Guilford Press.

Klohnen, E. C., Weller, J. A., Luo, S., & Choe, M. (2005). Organization and predictive power of general and relationship-specific attachment models: One for all, and all for one? *Personality and Social Psychology Bulletin, 31*, 1665–1682.

Kurfiss, J. G. (1988). *Critical thinking: Theory, research, practice, and possibilities*. Washington, DC: Association for the Study of Higher Education.

Larose, S., Bernier, A., & Tarabulsy, G. M. (2005). Attachment state of mind, learning dispositions, and academic performance during the college transition. *Developmental Psychology, 41*(1), 281–289.

Mayseless, O., & Popper, M. (2007). Reliance on leaders and social institutions: An attachment perspective. *Attachment & Human Development, 9*(1), 73–93.

Mikulincer, M., & Shaver, P. (2007). *Attachment in adulthood: Structure, dynamics, and change*. New York: Guilford Press.

Mohr, J., Bennett, S., & Deal, K. (2009, August). Effects of a supervision training workshop on the supervisory relationship. In Theodore R. Burnes (Chair), *Reaching for the stars with counseling supervision: Training the new generation*. Symposium conducted at the Annual Meeting of the American Psychological Association, Toronto, Ontario, Canada.

Moss, E., & St-Laurent, D. (2001). Attachment at school age and academic performance. *Developmental Psychology, 37*, 107–119.

Munson, C. (2002). *Handbook of clinical social work supervision* (3rd ed.). New York: Haworth Press.

Neswald-McCalip, R. (1995). Development of the secure counselor: Case examples supporting Pistole & Watkins's (1995) discussion of attachment theory in counseling supervision. *Counselor Education and Supervision, 41*, 18–27.

Padykula, N. F. (2008). Baccalaureate social work curriculum: A study examining student attachment styles, capacity to mentalize, and reflective learning style (Doctoral dissertation, Smith College School for Social Work, 2008). *Dissertation Abstracts International* 69, 11A.

Paul, R. W. (1992). *Critical thinking: What every person needs to survive in a rapidly changing world*. Santa Rosa, CA: The Foundation for Critical Thinking.

Pierce, T., & Lydon, J. (2001). Global and specific relational models in the experience of social interactions. *Journal of Personality and Social Psychology, 80*, 613–631.

Pistole, C., & Watkins, E. (1995). Attachment theory, counseling process, and supervision. *The Counseling Psychologist, 23*, 457–478.

Plath, D., English, B., Connors, L., & Beveridge, A. (1999). Evaluating outcomes of intensive critical thinking instruction for social work students. *Social Work Education, 18*(2), 207–217.

Reio, T. G., Marcus, R. F., & Sanders-Reio, J. (2009). Contribution of student and instructor relationships and attachment style to school completion. *The Journal of Genetic Psychology, 170*(1), 53–71.

Riggs, S., & Bretz, K. (2006). Attachment processes in the supervisory relationship: An exploratory investigation. *Professional Psychology: Research and Practice, 37*, 558–566.

Rom, E., & Mikulincer, M. (2003). Attachment theory and group processes: The association between attachment style and group-related representations, goals, memoires, and functioning. *Journal of Personality and Social Psychology, 84*(6), 1220–1235.

Watkins, E. (1995). Pathological attachment styles in psychotherapy supervision. *Psychotherapy, 32*, 333–340.

White, V., & Queener, J. (2003). Supervisor and supervisee attachments and social provisions related to the supervisory working alliance. *Counselor Education & Supervision, 42*, 203–218.

Index

A

Adoption, second parent adoption, 199
Adult Attachment Interview (AAI)
    attentional flexibility and inflexibility, 34, 35
    cannot classify, 34, 36
    dismissing, 32, 34–38, 45, 88, 131
    earned secure, 50
    Grice, H. P., 35
    preoccupied, 32, 34–38, 44, 130, 131
    secure autonomous, 34, 35, 45, 261
    state-of-mind, 40
    unresolved disorganized, 32, 34, 38, 50
Adult children, 11, 84, 91, 93, 118, 127, 130,
    133, 136, 142, 208, 209, 211
Adult protective service (APS), 210
Affect regulation, 2, 25, 44–45, 48, 59, 60,
    62–64, 67–71, 83, 87, 99, 108, 113,
    115, 120, 148–150, 153, 161, 162, 166,
    168, 179, 223
African-American elders, 127–143
Ainsworth, M., 4, 17, 19–23, 26, 31–33, 36,
    49, 173, 206–208, 253, 261
Alcoholics Anonymous, 123, 178
Attachment Based Family Therapy (ABFT),
    164–166
Attachment patterns. *See* Attachment styles
Attachment processes (in/and)
    adoption, 11, 12, 60, 148, 160–162, 196–199
    batterers, 232, 240
    child abuse, 151, 158
    classrooms, 12, 167, 253, 255, 256, 259,
        260, 262
    domestic violence, 151, 169, 232, 240
    education (professional education),
        253, 262
    elders, 11, 12, 127–143, 196, 208–213
    families, 11–13, 18, 23–25, 41, 90,
        127–143, 147–169, 174, 180–183,
        195–213, 218, 222, 232, 241–245

    foster care, 11, 138, 152, 153, 159–162,
        166, 196, 198, 199, 217, 218, 222, 245
    graduate education, 12, 254, 255
    groups, 11, 36, 47–48, 51, 79, 88, 91, 99,
        130–132, 134, 143, 153, 168, 173–189,
        218, 222, 229, 241, 244, 254–258
    hard-to-reach clients, 113–125
    homeless military veterans, 240
    incarcerated mothers, 202–204, 213
    military service, 12, 176, 196, 206–208, 210
    organizations and institutions, 124, 166,
        175, 177–180, 189
    pair bonds (couples), 5, 11, 22, 24, 41,
        173, 174, 253
    parent-adolescent relationships, 228
    pets, 24
    post traumatic stress disorder (PTSD),
        38, 39, 87, 108, 178, 201, 241
    pregnancy, 181, 244
    religion and spirituality, 11, 135, 136, 140
    same-sex parents, 200, 204, 205
    sexual offenders, 241
    substance abuse, 11, 148, 158–160, 163,
        185, 196, 240
    supervision, 2, 12, 40, 49, 50, 253,
        256–258, 262
    trauma, 10, 13, 24, 41, 42, 63, 69, 71, 79,
        89, 90, 92, 115, 117–119, 140, 148,
        150–152, 160, 164, 167, 168, 178, 179,
        202, 241
    wilderness therapy, 228
    work place, 255–256
Attachment styles (or patterns;
    categories)–Adults
    ambivalent, 44–48, 134, 135, 210, 211
    anxious, 23, 32, 44–48, 87, 88, 130, 131,
        178, 210, 211
    autonomous (secure-autonomous),
        32, 34–37, 45, 149, 259, 261

Attachment styles (or patterns;
    categories)–Adults (*cont.*)
    avoidant, 4, 32, 37, 44–47, 88, 91, 130,
        131, 134–136, 175, 176, 210, 211, 223
    cannot classify, 34, 36
    dismissing, 34–37, 45, 88, 91, 130–132,
        140, 149, 241
    disorganized, 32, 34–38, 50, 88–89, 151
    earned security, 39
    fearful, 21, 32, 44, 45, 152
    general attachment, 41, 49, 131
    global interpersonal style, 49
    preoccupied, 32, 34–38, 87, 88, 92, 130,
        131, 142, 149, 151, 152, 256
    relationship-specific attachment, 12, 50
    secure, 4, 22, 24, 31–37, 39, 42, 44–47, 50,
        87, 90–91, 118, 130–136, 139, 141,
        142, 149, 150, 152, 163, 173–188, 210,
        211, 222, 229, 244
    unresolved (unresolved-disorganized),
        32, 34, 36, 38, 50, 151
Attachment styles (or patterns,
    categories)–Children
    insecure-avoidant, 4, 21, 22, 184, 201
    insecure-disorganized, 22, 63, 185
    insecure-resistant (insecure-ambivalent),
        4, 22, 105
    secure, 3, 4, 21, 32, 34, 36, 37, 44, 61, 115,
        116, 118, 120, 129, 133, 149, 151, 154,
        183, 185, 186, 201, 206, 222, 223, 259
Attachment system
    activation of attachment system, 23, 42, 80,
        81, 165, 187
    deactivation of attachment system,
        41, 86–88, 91, 92, 149
    hyperactivation of attachment system,
        41, 86, 87, 91, 165
Attention Deficit Hyperactivity Disorder
    (ADHD), 223

B

Beebe, B., 100, 105, 106, 108, 116
Bio-psychosocial, 10, 57–59, 61, 70, 97, 150, 153
Boston Change Process Study Group, 99
Bowlby, J.
    attachment, 1–4, 9–12, 17–21, 23, 25, 26,
        31, 32, 36, 37, 49, 57, 58, 64, 70, 71, 79,
        80, 83, 85, 87, 93, 127–129, 132, 147,
        149, 162, 174, 178, 195, 213, 254, 261
    loss, 18, 20, 23, 26, 79, 80, 83, 85, 86, 93,
        94, 127
    separation, 4, 10, 12, 17–21, 26, 79, 80, 83
Bowlby, R., 19

C

Caregiving, 1, 4, 11, 17, 18, 20, 22, 24, 36,
    41–43, 46, 47, 80–82, 84, 85, 89–92,
    94, 127–143, 149, 150, 155, 156, 158,
    160, 162, 165, 195–213, 232, 257
Caregiving system, 80, 81, 90, 129, 130
Cassidy, J., 32, 36, 224
Child abuse and neglect, sexual abuse,
    149, 168, 244
Child care, 19, 195, 196
Child custody policies/rulings
    approximation rule, 200, 201
    best interest standard, 199–201, 203
    least detrimental interest, 203
    nexus approach, 205
    per se approach, 205
    psychological parent, 199, 200, 203
Child protective service (CPS), 196
Circle of Security (CoS), 11, 183–188, 257
Compulsive self-reliance, 23, 92
Control theory, 19
Coping strategies, 9, 42, 45, 60, 69, 127, 134,
    140, 224
Council of Social Work Education
    (CSWE), 260
Couples. *See* Pair-bonds
Critical thinking, 9, 12, 253, 260–262
Culture
    African American elders, 11, 127–143
    African American mothers, 228, 241, 244
    Asian American adolescents, 224
    homosexual couples (gay and lesbian),
        13, 47, 196, 198, 205, 210

D

Darwin, C., 26
Depression, 26, 43, 48, 80, 86, 87, 97, 128,
    131, 135, 148, 155–158, 166, 167, 176,
    178–182, 201, 241
Dissociation, 22, 50, 69, 88, 89, 92, 100, 124
Diversity, 72, 139, 224
Divorce, 22, 79, 81, 84, 86, 90–92, 98, 122,
    152, 200, 218, 241, 245
Domestic violence (spousal violence), 151,
    169, 232, 240
Dysregulation, 60, 64, 71, 99, 152,
    153, 159, 165

E

Early Head Start Program, 184
Early intervention, 72, 98
Eating disorders, 2, 163, 176, 178, 229

Elders
    African American elders, 11, 127–143
    elder abuse, 209, 210
Ethology, 3, 19, 20, 26
Evolution, 1, 20, 25, 26, 62, 71, 81, 83,
    129, 174
Exploration. *See* Exploratory system
Exploratory system, 3, 4, 21, 22, 32,
    39, 44, 47, 101, 124, 129, 149–152,
    154, 157, 158, 162, 163, 165, 166,
    175, 176, 183, 184, 222, 228,
    240, 245, 256, 259–262

F

Family and Medical Leave Act, 208
Fathers, 36, 83, 93, 102, 106, 122, 123,
    136, 140, 143, 161, 166, 167, 177,
    182, 185, 198, 203, 205, 223, 228,
    229, 232, 241
Fonagy, P., 40, 115, 117–119, 260
Foster care, permanency planning, 199
Freud, A., 19, 57, 58, 63, 199
Freud, S., 19, 57, 58, 63, 70

G

Gender, 36, 46, 240
General attachment and specific attachment,
    50, 257, 258
Grandmothers, 102, 138, 155, 161, 162,
    202, 244
Grief (stages of)
    despair, 10, 23, 79, 80, 82, 84–86,
      90–92, 101
    detachment, 10, 19, 80, 82, 92
    protest, 10, 19, 22, 26, 80, 82–85, 87,
      90–92, 185
    reorganization, 23, 80, 82, 84–87,
      90–92, 141
Groups
    cognitive-behavioral group, 176,
      178, 180
    group alliance, 176, 177
    group attachment, 47, 177
    group cohesion, 254, 255
    group dynamics, 174, 175
    group interventions, 11, 173–189
    group processes, 174–177, 179, 185
    group therapy, 179, 183
    group work, 173
    inpatient group, 178
    therapeutic group process, 174, 176

H

Hazan, C., 1, 23, 32, 210, 256
Homecare and hospice care, 142, 143

I

Implicit communication, 10, 24, 61–68,
    99–101, 110
Implicit relational knowing, 10, 64, 65, 82, 83,
    94, 99, 100
Implicit self, 59, 61, 63, 70, 71
Intergenerational transmission of attachment,
    5, 11, 115, 147, 150, 153, 166–168,
    218, 232, 245
Internal working models, 1, 3, 4, 20, 21, 24,
    31, 33, 41, 44, 60, 62–64, 66, 69, 92,
    98, 149, 150, 164, 165, 177, 183, 197,
    206, 240
Intersubjectivity (or intersubjective), 58, 60,
    62, 64–71, 80, 82, 100, 101
Intimacy, 45, 50, 130, 167, 173, 177, 179–180,
    184, 185, 210, 255

K

Karen, R., 18

L

Lachmann, F., 100, 105, 108
London Child Guidance Clinic, 18
Lorenz, K., 19
Lyons-Ruth, K., 65, 89

M

Main, M., 1, 22, 23, 32
Mastery/exploration, 129, 149, 151, 152,
    162, 165
Mentalization (or mentalizing), 10, 12, 40, 69,
    113–125, 151, 260–263
Mentalization-based treatment (MBT), 10, 40,
    113, 114, 120–121, 124
Mental states, 10, 40, 64, 68, 101, 114, 116–118,
    120, 121, 124, 150, 151, 260, 263
Metacognitive monitoring, 40, 45, 114, 253,
    260, 261
Mikulincer, M., 5, 31–33, 36, 41, 43, 44, 46,
    47, 86–88, 129, 176, 255, 256
Military service, 12, 176, 196,
    206–208, 210
Mindful Parenting, 183
Minnesota Longitudinal Study, 181

N

Neurobiology (or neurobiological),
2, 9, 10, 23, 25, 44, 57–72,
98–101, 153, 162
Nonverbal communication, 10, 24, 46, 58,
61–68, 71, 72, 88, 100, 103, 106, 108,
114, 116, 117

P

Pair-bonds
heterosexual couples, 199, 205, 224
homosexual couples (gay and lesbian;
same-sex), 13, 47, 199, 204–206,
223, 224
romantic pair-bonds, 1, 5, 24, 41
sexual pair-bonds, 173, 174
Parents, 1, 18, 33, 65, 80, 98, 114, 127, 147,
173, 195, 217, 254
Personality disorders, 38, 40, 48, 60, 63, 64,
69, 71, 114, 119, 120, 125, 178
Person-in-environment, 2, 5, 24, 58
Post traumatic stress disorder (PTSD), 39, 87,
108, 178, 241
Prementalizing stages
pretend mode, 118, 119, 121,
123, 124
psychic equivalence (actual mode),
118, 119, 121–125
teleological mode, 118, 119
Prevention of insecure disorganized
attachment (PIDA), 183
Primary caregivers, 3, 33, 36, 59, 61–63, 79,
89, 116, 128, 130, 155, 206
Prosody, 66, 67
Protest, 10, 19, 22, 26, 32, 49, 80, 82–87,
90–92, 185, 255
Psychiatric symptom, 11, 174, 178, 179
Psychoanalysis, 19, 26, 40, 57–59, 66, 68, 70,
118, 120

R

Racism, prejudice, discrimination, 132
Reactive Attachment Disorder (RAD)
emotionally withdrawn/inhibited, 161
indiscriminate/inhibited, 161
Reflective functioning, 40, 114, 115, 118, 150,
151, 156, 158
Reflective-verbal communication, 99, 100
Regulation theory, 9, 10, 57–72
Religion and spirituality, 11, 135, 136
Research instruments

Adult Attachment Interview (AAI), 1, 5,
9, 23, 31–40, 43, 45–47, 50,
51, 89, 131
Adult Attachment Questionnaire
(AAQ), 43
Adult Attachment Scale, 175, 180
Attachment History Questionnaire
(AHQ), 41, 42
Attachment Story Completion Task
Revised, 223
Attachment Styles Questionnaire (ASQ),
43, 175, 178
Current Relationships Interview (CRI), 37
Experiences in Close Relationships Scale
(ECR, ECR-Revised), 43, 47, 175
Inventory of Parent and Peer Attachment
(IPPA), 42
Measure of Attachment Quality (MAQ), 134
Parental Bonding Instrument, 174
Relationship Structures (RS), 49
Relationship Style Questionnaire
(RSQ), 43
Strange situation, 1, 5, 21, 23, 32, 36, 37,
184, 185, 187, 222
Research methodologies
longitudinal research, 9, 23, 33, 37, 49, 50,
127, 132, 147, 149, 222
narrative research, 9, 32, 33, 40, 43, 50, 97,
122, 141, 142, 223, 228
self-report research, 1, 5, 9, 23, 31–33,
39–51, 131, 174, 175, 180, 228, 240, 241
Residential treatment, 12, 228
Right brain, 10, 24, 58–72, 101, 108
Right from the start (RFTS), 182
Risk and resiliency, 147, 153, 244
Robertson, J., 11, 19, 195

S

Safe haven, 3, 4, 44, 47, 49, 91, 129, 130, 150,
168, 186, 188, 254, 255, 257
Schore, A., 58, 59, 62, 65, 67, 101
Secure base, 3, 4, 22, 24, 42, 44, 47, 49, 71,
91, 93, 129, 149, 150, 152, 163, 167,
168, 173–189, 206, 228, 254, 256,
257, 262
Security/proximity seeking, 4, 162
Self-disclosure, 121, 175
Separation, loss, bereavement, 10, 20,
79–94
Shaver, P., 1, 5, 31–33, 36, 41–44, 46, 47,
86–88, 129, 210, 255, 256
Social ecology, 164, 174

Social welfare policies
    Adoption and Safe Families Act (ASFA),
        198, 203
    Adoption Assistance and
        Child Welfare, 198
    Older American Act, 209
    Uniform Marriage and Divorce Act, 200
Social work education (graduate education)
    academic learning, 253, 255
    field work internship, 12, 253–258
    supervision, 2, 12, 256–258, 262
Sroufe, A., 20, 23, 24, 37
Steele, H., 40
Steele, M., 40
Steps toward effective and enjoyable parenting
    (STEEP), 181
Stern, D., 99
Strange Situation, 1, 5, 21, 23, 32, 36, 37, 184,
    185, 187, 222
Suicide, 89, 92, 163, 165, 167, 240
Supervision and supervisory relationship
    supervision-specific attachment, 49, 50, 257
    supervisory working alliance,
        257, 258

T
Telephone treatment, 99–105
Tone, 10, 46, 65–67, 97–110, 116
Transference and countertransference,
    67–70

U
Unconscious and nonconscious, 10, 32, 33, 51,
    57–60, 62–71, 82, 83, 97, 99–101, 103,
    107, 108, 120, 175, 223

V
van IJzendoorn, M. H., 36, 38, 48
Vocal congruence, 100
Vocal rhythms, 97, 100, 105, 106

W
Winnicott, D., 19, 108, 188
Working alliance, 257, 258
World Health Organization
    (WHO), 19, 195